LIFE WRITING

EDITED BY

WINIFRED BRYAN HORNER
TEXAS CHRISTIAN UNIVERSITY

A BLAIR PRESS BOOK

PRENTICE HALL, UPPER SADDLE RIVER, NJ 07458

Library of Congress Cataloging-in-Publication Data

Life writing / [compiled by] Winifred Bryan Horner.
    p.   cm.
    Includes index.
    ISBN 0-13-079237-3 (pbk.)
    1. Readers—Autobiography.   2. Autobiography—Authorship—Problems, exercises, etc.
3. Biography—Authorship—Problems, exercises, etc.   4. English language—Rhetoric.   5. Readers—
Biography.   6. College readers.   I. Horner, Winifred Bryan.
PE1127.A9L54   1997
808'.0427—dc20

96–42302
CIP

Editorial Director: Charlyce Jones Owen
Publisher: Nancy Perry
Acquisitions Editor: Mary Jo Southern
Developmental Editor: Clare Payton
Director of Production and Manufacturing: Barbara Kittle
Managing Editor: Bonnie Biller
Project Manager: Karen Trost
Manufacturing Manager: Nick Sklitsis
Prepress and Manufacturing Buyer: Bob Anderson
Cover Design: Kiwi Design
Cover Art: Picasso, Pablo. *Girl Before a Mirror.* Boisgeloup, March 1932. Oil on canvas, 64 x 51¼". The
    Museum of Modern Art, New York. Gift of Mrs. Simon Guggenheim. Photograph © 1996 The Mu-
    seum of Modern Art, New York
Marketing Manager: Rob Mejia

This book was set in 11/12 Adobe Garamond by NK Graphics
and printed and bound by Courier Westford.
The cover was printed by Phoenix.

Acknowledgments appear on pages 341–342, which constitute a continuation of the copyright page.

A Blair Press Book

© 1997 by Prentice-Hall, Inc.
Simon & Schuster/A Viacom Company
Upper Saddle River, NJ 07458

Printed in the United States of America
10 9 8 7 6 5 4 3 2 1

ISBN 0-13-079237-3

PRENTICE-HALL INTERNATIONAL (UK) LIMITED, *London*
PRENTICE-HALL OF AUSTRALIA PTY. LIMITED, *Sydney*
PRENTICE-HALL CANADA INC., *Toronto*
PRENTICE-HALL HISPANOAMERICANA, S.A., *Mexico*
PRENTICE-HALL OF INDIA PRIVATE LIMITED, *New Delhi*
PRENTICE-HALL OF JAPAN, INC., *Tokyo*
SIMON & SCHUSTER ASIAN PTE. LTD., *Singapore*
EDITORA PRENTICE-HALL DO BRASIL, LTDA., *Rio de Janeiro*

PREFACE

For years we instructors have been advising students to write about what they know. For years students have ignored our words. Most are quite sure that what they know is not worth writing about. What can possibly be interesting about their lives? *Life Writing* aims to help students gain insight into their own lives, to see the importance of their experiences, and to gain the skills to write about them.

To help students recognize the value of their own experiences, this book offers a collection of forty-eight readings that chronicle lives both greatly important and not so. The readings also provide students with examples of the use of many different strategies in discussing topics from the eternal to the mundane. Life experiences are expressed from myriad angles: from microscopic details to global perspectives, from inner contemplation of the self to outer scrutiny of the motivations and actions of others, and from examining a known history from both the outside and the inside. All in all, these reading selections serve as clear yet creative models for the student's own writing.

As students follow these models, they become aware of how writers shift from the subjective internal to the objective external viewpoint. They learn to recognize the degree to which all writing is influenced by an intended readership, and which details should be retained or omitted for each audience. For example, diaries record daily happenings, sometimes merely recounting events, sometimes speculating on them, and are generally written only to the self. Letters serve much the same purpose, but the writer has a specific reader or readers in mind. In autobiography, biography, and essay, the concept of audience shifts and broadens; the writing becomes public. Autobiography is the recounting and interpreting of personal events for a public audience. In biography writers reach beyond themselves and search out fact far beyond their own experience. They read and research their subjects thoroughly and come to some conclusions about the person's life and work. In the personal essay, writers reach both into themselves and beyond themselves for meaning.

Features of *Life Writing*

The forty-eight selections in *Life Writing* include a wide range of voices and writing styles so that students can recognize the range of possibilities of the various forms and adapt them to their own writing. The writers represent a wide variety of cultural backgrounds and perspectives; the readings in each chapter have been organized in chronological order to show students the historical development of each genre.

This text has been organized so that students move from the subjective writing of diaries, letters, and autobiography to the more objective writing of biography and essays. Thus the student moves from writing about him/herself (journals and diaries) to writing for a limited audience (letters), then on to public writing based on personal experience (autobiographies) and that based on research (biographies). The final genre included is the essay, in which personal experience and accumulated knowledge are shared with a public readership.

The pedagogical material in this book has been kept to a minimum, because it has been my experience that you shape your own courses and assignments far better than anyone else could. The makeup of each class is different, and it is important when teaching life writing to select the material most interesting and useful to your particular students.

Following a general student introduction, each of the five chapters begins with an introduction to the genre, providing students with the necessary context for reading and writing. Preceding each selection is a biographical headnote, outlining the important facts about the author's life and positioning the work within its genre. Some attempt has also been made to comment on the significance of the topic (Why is he/she writing about this?) or its message (What does he/she want to say?). After each of the reading selections are "Musings," purposely unstructured questions designed as launching pads for class discussion or writing. In addition, suggestions for writing activities are included in many of the Musings. With these options you have the flexibility to explore any type of writing activity unhindered by rigid preconceived assignments.

In the front of the text a section called "Connections" offers links among selections in topic or style to be explored in class discussions or in writing. For example, a single author such as bell hooks has two selections, one she classifies as autobiography and one as essay. Why? Who determines such categories? The author? The audience? The public? Or consider the many perspectives included in the selections on war. What can we learn about the authors, about humanity, and about history by studying these selections in tandem? "Connections" has been presented separately so that you can use it at any point in the semester—or not.

In the end it is you instructors, knowing more than I about who your students are, who will decide what you want to accomplish in your course, which selections you will use, and how you will shape writing assignments.

Acknowledgments

No book is ever written without the help and inspiration of many people. Those foremost in my mind are the writers gathered in this volume. Some of our most skilled authors and their work lie at the heart of this book, and to fail to acknowledge their importance would be a serious omission.

Let me thank those instructors across the country who took the time to share their ideas on teaching life writing and who offered many wonderful suggestions for improving this book: Chris Anderson, Oregon State University; Lynn Bloom, University of Connecticut; Xin Liu Gale, University of Arkansas, Little Rock; Keith Gilyard, Syracuse University; Sharon Hamilton, Indiana University, Indianapolis; Jan Schmidt, State University of New York, New Paltz; and Mary Wood, University of Oregon.

I should also like to acknowledge my two editors, Nancy Perry, and especially Clare Payton, who knows her work so well that she suggested writers for inclusion and helped in additional untold ways. This book is partly hers. I also thank the Prentice Hall staff who guided this project from manuscript to bound book and out into the world: Bonnie Biller, Senior Managing Editor; Karen Trost, Production Editor; and Gina Sluss, Director of Marketing.

This book could not have happened without the devoted support of my research assistants, Maria Elena Madrigal Rodriguez, Debra Galliher, Lisa Higgins, and Denise Stodola. I must also thank Texas Christian University for supporting my work all these years through financial help for research and travel and time to accomplish it all. No scholar can ask for more.

Every writer needs a safe and ample haven in which to work. In closing, let me thank my husband, who always has to suffer alongside me through the writing of any book, and who recognizes that as with a birthing, his role is to hold my hand, to offer solace and help when needed, and to let me alone to work when I must. Certainly my grown children, although busy with their own families, have been understanding when I have had to be a writer rather than a mother, mother-in-law, or grandmother. To all of these people I offer my heartfelt gratitude.

Winifred Bryan Horner

Contents

INTRODUCTION

L ife writing involves an in-depth investigation into the nature of self and others that grows out of self-awareness and identification with others. As writers, we must always begin with what we know best—our own experience of the world—and attempt through words to make that experience meaningful for others.

All of the selections included in *Life Writing* draw their subject matter from the lives of real people. Each reading in this text, which includes selections from diaries, letters, autobiographies, biographies, and essays based on personal experience, is followed by suggested ways of writing about real life experiences. Life writing moves from the limited audience and highly personal subject matter of the diary to the public audience and expanded life experience of the essay.

As we work from the diary to the personal essay there is a subtle shift in subject matter. Writing about ourselves in the *diary,* the *letter,* and the *autobiography* is the easiest place to start, since we do not have to reach beyond ourselves for subject matter. In journals we keep a daily record, in autobiography we sort through our lives and see our experiences in retrospect, but in one way or another the subject remains the same—our own selves. In *biography* the subject matter shifts beyond the self to an exploration of the life and times of another. We move from personal subjective experience to a more objective view of the experience of another person. In the *essay* we move further from the experiences of ourselves and others to make meaning for the reader.

All writers compose with an audience in mind. It is impossible to write in a vacuum. As the subject matter expands from the diary to the essay, the audience shifts from the largely limited audience of the journal to the enlarged public audience of the essay. Even the *diary* has a real or imagined audience, but it can be assumed that such an audience needs little or no explanation of the context surrounding the event being recorded. The audience of the *letter* is usually limited to a single reader or a very small well-known audience. In *autobiography* we move on to one that is greatly enlarged, yet largely unknown. Audience becomes a more difficult concept than the well-known, intimate one of the diary and the letter. In the autobiography, the biography, and the essay, the accommodation the author must make to this new type of audience inevitably shapes and informs the writing. We may never have sat down over coffee or shaken hands with our readers, but we still must have them in mind during the writing process.

As subject matter and audience are altered, purposes for writing change; purpose, like subject and audience, shapes the form of our compositions. *Diaries* are usually highly introspective journeys. It is sometimes difficult to delve into our own psyches, but such writing can often serve as therapy or catharsis. More important, putting it in writing can shed new light on experiences and bring about new insight. We write *letters* in order to share our experiences with others. *Autobiography* gives our experiences shape and meaning, and is often written to justify, illuminate, or explain our actions. The purpose of *biography* varies but, like all life writing it is an attempt to interpret experience.

A commonly-held assumption is that all types of life writing are based on "true" experiences and thus fall into the category of nonfiction. But life writing, like all writing, can come close to fiction. Libraries and bookstores sometimes find it difficult to separate fiction from nonfiction. Tim O'Brien's chronicle of life in Vietnam is modeled closely on his own experience but he insists on calling it fiction, asserting that what he is after is "truth," not fact. Maxine Hong Kingston obviously mixes myth, fiction, and fact to represent "truth" in her tales of Chinese life. In all life writing, the selection of incidents and details represents the writer's perspective on the subject, not a chronological, or objective picture.

Just as the line between fact and fiction is blurred in life writing, the borders of the categories of diary, letter, autobiography, biography, and essay are indistinct. Seldom does a single selection fall neatly into a category. The best diarists interpret their experiences and, except for the carefully dated heading, a diary might just as well be classified as an essay. The letter that presents an in-depth description of another person might well serve as a biography, and the letter that is written for publication is shaped by a public readership in the same way as autobiography and biography. To complicate matters further, each category has sub-genres to distinguish different types of writing. For example, oral histories are types of biographies or autobiographies similar to family histories recorded on tape.

In life writing, we shape our own experiences and those of others according to our own perspectives on subject, audience, and purpose. By mixing fact and fiction, we search for "truth." Such in-depth investigation into the nature of the human condition is an ongoing voyage of discovery shared by readers and writers alike.

CONNECTIONS

The selections in this book, all examples of life writing, may be read individually or studied together according to similarities. This section of the book suggests ways in which you might read or analyze certain selections together. Some writers are grouped on the basis of their different points of view on a single subject, such as war. Others, such as "Prisoners," display different reactions to similar experiences. Finally, in some cases more than one selection by a particular author is included, but the readings occur in different categories, raising the question of how the writer chose among genres to shape ideas on different subjects.

The selections may also be read sequentially, moving from the journal to letters, to autobiography, to biography, and finally to the essay, emphasizing the dynamic and changing interrelationships among the author, the subject, and the reader, as well as the shift in audience, and the change in subject from the author's own personal life to experiences outside the realm of the writer. In the final chapter, the essay demonstrates the way in which life writing moves beyond the personal and individual to a broader meaning common to a culture or a community.

Travels

These are quite different voyages, described in journal and letter forms, and written to diverse audiences for various reasons. Columbus and Forster both encounter cultures that are unlike their own, but their intended audiences shape their writing. Evans and Stewart are women engaged in adventures—one a solitary trip, the other a group endeavor.

War

Wars of different periods and from different perspectives are included here: the Civil War from the viewpoint of a Confederate colonel, the Second World War from the viewpoints of a victim of the London bombings and of a young Jewish girl living in Germany, and the Vietnam War from the memoirs of a foot soldier. Three are diaries written during wartime, and one is a memoir.

Prisoners

Malcolm X, Frank, and King were all imprisoned against their wills in quite different situations. All of them used their time in distinct ways, and their writings—one a diary, one an autobiography, and one a letter—chronicle their responses to their incarceration.

Writers' Notebooks

Didion describes how and why she keeps a notebook, and Anderson's journal demonstrates another kind of notebook.

Abraham Lincoln

Lincoln writes in the mode of a statesman, while Vidal sees Lincoln not so much as a statesman but as a talented writer and a major literary figure.

One Writer, Different Subjects

Hooks, Didion, and White are the authors of two selections, writing in two different genres and in two different modes.

One Subject, Different Writers

Hurston writes about her own life in her autobiography; Walker also writes about Hurston's life and criticizes her autobiography. Abbey holds an imaginary conversation with Thoreau, whereas White writes a letter to the long-deceased philosopher. Lincoln writes a letter to his supporters in his role as president, whereas Vidal gives us a personal view of Lincoln and his other extraordinary talents.

Voyages of Discovery

Columbus describes a voyage of exploration within the real world of oceans and continents, while Frank and Sarton narrate searches within themselves.

Living with Nature

Three writers discuss their relationship with their environments, approaching it in different ways, but the message of all is basically similar—that we must learn to look at our world and live in harmony within that world.

Returning Home

These writers treat the homing instinct common to all animals. Eiseley chronicles the return of the brown wasps and his own search for his early home. Didion writes about her visit to her parents' home where she grew up. White describes his return with his son to a childhood vacation spot.

The African-American Experience

These selections present four different views of the world as seen by African-Americans, but they all demonstrate the inherent racism evident in the American culture.

Women's Experiences

The following selections speak of the authors' experiences as women. Coming from different cultures and different periods in history, all of them tell stories that are different but in many ways similar.

Character Sketches

The following professional writers skillfully describe the personalities they encounter in the following selections.

The Native-American Experience

The following Native Americans describe their life and attitudes toward their own people and the European-Americans that they encounter. Columbus reports on the first encounter between Europeans and "Indians," demonstrating his own ignorance and Eurocentrism.

Professional Women

Owens-Adair chronicles her difficulty in pursuing a profession. Heilbrun writes of Steinem's resolve to take control of her own life.

Epidemics: AIDS and Smallpox

Ashe and Selzer speak of their experience with AIDS—Ashe from the personal point of view, Selzer from a doctor's perspective. Voltaire writes of a cure for smallpox long before such knowledge was widely known in the medical community.

Capital Punishment

Orwell and Capote present two views of a hanging—one in essay form, the other as the conclusion to a biography of two murderers.

Public and Private Language

Rodriguez and Tan both write of the languages used in their homes, and the public English used both in the workplace and by the second-generation children of foreign-born Americans.

Family Influences

When writing about lives, it is impossible not to consider the overwhelming influence of the family. Personalities, histories, and beliefs of family members all affect how we think and act in the world. Lord Chesterfield and Joan Peyser can be compared to see how discussions of the family have changed. Stodola and Rubinstein's E-mail exchanges can be compared to and contrasted with Chesterfield's letters.

1

JOURNALS
AND
DIARIES

KEEPING A
DAILY RECORD

I remember receiving a small diary when I was eight years old. The most fascinating things about it were the lock on the leather binding that held it shut and the tiny key that came with it. In the five lines provided, I seldom went beyond the daily activities of getting up, eating, and going to school. As my entries became more and more repetitive I became increasingly bored—in spite of the thrill of locking my diary each night and carefully hiding the key in my underwear drawer, the most private space I had. Although there was little in it that anyone would care to read, I was afraid that someone would. In the beginning I never missed a day, but as my interest waned, I was less faithful. Many diaries have an element of secrecy about them and others are clearly written with publication in mind, but all are distinguished by their "daily-ness."

The words "diary" and "journal" are related to Latin and French words meaning "day"; it is that element that distinguishes them from other types of personal narrative. Diarists chronicle the day's events or their thoughts about those events. They are embedded in the present without the long view that characterizes memoir or autobiography. They lack the perspective that later experiences may give to an event. Losing a job might at the time seem a disaster, but if a person is later offered a better job the firing might be seen as a happy circumstance in retrospect.

The purpose of keeping a diary varies from person to person. Public figures often keep diaries to record their roles in world events. Politicians such as Richard Nixon and Robert Packwood both incriminated themselves because of their assiduously kept diaries. Diaries can also be used as a coping mechanism. Therapists often suggest keeping a diary as a way of working through problems. The many diaries of frontier women that are being recovered and published today were ways for those women to reach out to something beyond themselves, to build a world beyond the constricted and lonely reality in which they lived. For many women, like Stewart in her trip west, it was a way of ensuring that their experiences would be remembered.

Most of us keep diaries or journals when we take trips in order to record events and places of interest that we might wish to recall later. Such diaries are common, and probably the most enduring kind. Columbus, Abbey, Evans, and Anderson fall roughly into this category, but their journals are all strikingly different. Columbus's journal was a report to the Spanish monarch who sponsored his voyage. Evans wrote about a newly experienced strange and brutal land, and Abbey clearly wrote for publication.

Anderson's is a true travel diary that recorded his thoughts as he observed the passing scene in Paris.

Some diaries are pilgrimages of another sort—inward journeys of discovery. Those by Sarton and Thoreau clearly fall into this category. Thoreau explains his journal as "that of me which would else spill over and run to waste, gleanings from the field which in action I reap." Such chronicles not only record daily events but, more importantly, the significance of the events to the writers. Anne Frank's diary is certainly the prime example of this type of inner exploration as she writes, with touching insight, about her confused feelings of growing into womanhood. Her last entry reads "I twist my heart round again . . . and keep on trying to find a way of becoming what I would so like to be, and what I could be."

Many diarists do not write just for themselves. They usually imagine an audience or at least hope that there will be an audience someday. By the time May Sarton wrote *The House by the Sea,* she was well aware that she was writing for a large audience who had read her other published journals. When Edward Abbey wrote "Down the River with Thoreau" he was already a published writer and was obviously composing for others besides himself. Not all of the diaries excerpted here were written for large public audiences or wide distribution, although all of them, except that of Colonel Winans, eventually found their way into print, often long after they were written.

The writers of the works included in the chapter vary widely, yet the diaries reveal much about the sensitive and verbal nature that they share. Some of the writers, such as Thoreau, Sarton, and Abbey, were well-known long before they published their diaries—Thoreau as a philosopher and abolitionist, Sarton as a poet and writer, and Abbey as a widely published writer. Others, such as Anne Frank, gained fame because of their diaries. Winans is known only to a circle of friends and family who cherish his diary as a part of their family history.

Until fairly recently, women chose to record their lives in the form of diaries, letters, or private memoirs, since their stories were not considered important by mainstream publishers. Recently there has been an explosion in the recovery and publication of such records, furnishing new insights into all aspects of eighteenth- and nineteenth-century life.

The easiest place to start writing is with a daily journal, recording incidents from your own life and searching out their significance. You might wish to keep a log of books you have read, or television shows and films that you have watched. Record the words of songs that you like, quotations that you remember, and jokes that make you laugh, complete with sources. Joan Didion's essay, "On Keeping a Journal," which introduces this chapter, contains her reasons for keeping a journal and might provide an idea of how to begin. In addition to jogging your memory regarding events you want to remember, such jottings might serve as a source for future compositions. Finally, such a journal helps you to establish the habit of writing on a daily basis in a form that will not be judged as a formal composition.

Whether you keep a journal for your personal enrichment or your instructor suggests that you keep one for this course, there are many ways to keep such a record and many writing activities that can be included, such as the following:

- Write down events, facts, and feelings daily to create a written record of your life.
- Reflect on your daily experiences—how you think, feel, and grow each day.
- Experiment with different styles of writing as means of self-expression.
- Brainstorm about topics for an academic paper.
- Draft passages of a paper, letter, or other significant document.

Joan Didion (1934–)

Joan Didion's view of the world is always "unabashedly subjective" because "she takes things personally," as one reviewer notes. Didion uses intimate detail but always hones her writing to make sure that each word and sentence matter. A sophisticated and painstaking prose stylist, she assiduously reworks and revises each paragraph.

The following piece appropriately introduces the first section of this book. In it Didion describes why she keeps a notebook. Diaries, journals, and notebooks are kept for as many reasons as there are diarists. Many writers keep notebooks very much like what Didion describes in order to help them remember ideas otherwise lost in the dustbin of memory. Such notebooks often make little sense to an outside reader but can recall and refresh past happenings for the writer. Didion sees her notebook as helping her to "keep in touch," remember "what it was to be me."

Diaries usually incorporate the writer as subject. Rather than merely recording an event, they register the writer's perspective of an incident, person, or scene. Didion describes her notebook as "something private . . . bits of the mind's string too short to use, an indiscriminate and erratic assemblage with meaning only for its maker."

Didion comes from a family that settled in California in the first half of the nineteenth century. She has lived most of her life in California, writing novels and essays and collaborating with her husband, John Gregory Dunne, on a column for the Saturday Evening Post *and on a number of screenplays. She has received numerous awards for her work, including the Breadloaf Fellowship in Fiction in 1963 at age twenty-nine and the National Book Award Nomination in fiction in 1971. Her articles have appeared in a wide variety of magazines, including* Mademoiselle *and* The American Scholar. *Her works include an early novel,* Run River *(1963), and later publications* The White Album *(1979),* Salvador *(1983), and* Democracy *(1984). The idea of an uncertain society at risk runs through her works.*

The following selection is taken from her first collection of essays, Slouching Toward Bethlehem *(1968), published soon after the Vietnam War when Americans lost faith in their government and began to lock their doors. She chose as the epigraph for the book a quotation from William Butler Yeats: "Things fall apart; the centre cannot hold."*

On Keeping a Notebook

So the point of my keeping a notebook has never been, nor is it now, to have an accurate factual record of what I have been doing or thinking. That would be a different impulse entirely, an instinct for reality which I sometimes envy but do not possess. At no point have I ever been able successfully to keep a diary; my approach to daily life ranges from the grossly negligent to the merely absent, and on those few occasions when I have

1

tried dutifully to record a day's events, boredom has so overcome me that the results are mysterious at best. What is this business about "shopping, typing piece, dinner with E, depressed"? Shopping for what? Typing what piece? Who is E? Was this "E" depressed, or was I depressed? Who cares?

In fact I have abandoned altogether that kind of pointless entry; instead I tell what some would call lies. "That's simply not true," the members of my family frequently tell me when they come up against my memory of a shared event. "The party was *not* for you, the spider was *not* a black widow, *it wasn't that way at all.*" Very likely they are right, for not only have I always had trouble distinguishing between what happened and what merely might have happened, but I remain unconvinced that the distinction, for my purposes, matters. The cracked crab that I recall having for lunch the day my father came home from Detroit in 1945 must certainly be embroidery, worked into the day's pattern to lend verisimilitude; I was ten years old and would not now remember the cracked crab. The day's events did not turn on cracked crab. And yet it is precisely that fictitious crab that makes me see the afternoon all over again, a home movie run all too often, the father bearing gifts, the child weeping, an exercise in family love and guilt. Or that is what it was to me. Similarly, perhaps it never did snow that August in Vermont; perhaps there never were flurries in the night wind, and maybe no one else felt the ground hardening and summer already dead even as we pretended to bask in it, but that was how it felt to me, and it might as well have snowed, could have snowed, did snow.

How it felt to me: that is getting closer to the truth about a notebook. I sometimes delude myself about why I keep a notebook, imagine that some thrifty virtue derives from preserving everything observed. See enough and write it down, I tell myself, and then some morning when the world seems drained of wonder, some day when I am only going through the motions of doing what I am supposed to do, which is write—on that bankrupt morning I will simply open my notebook and there it will all be, a forgotten account with accumulated interest, paid passage back to the world out there: dialogue overheard in hotels and elevators and at the hatcheck counter in Pavillon (one middle-aged man shows his hat check to another and says, "That's my old football number"); impressions of Bettina Aptheker and Benjamin Sonnenberg and Teddy ("Mr. Acapulco") Stauffer; careful *aperçus* about tennis bums and failed fashion models and Greek shipping heiresses, one of whom taught me a significant lesson (a lesson I could have learned from F. Scott Fitzgerald, but perhaps we all must meet the very rich for ourselves) by asking, when I arrived to interview her in her orchid-filled sitting room on the second day of a paralyzing New York blizzard, whether it was snowing outside.

I imagine, in other words, that the notebook is about other people. But of course it is not. I have no real business with what one stranger said to another at the hatcheck counter in Pavillon; in fact I suspect that the line "That's my old football number" touched not my own imagination at all, but merely some memory of something once read, probably "The Eighty-Yard Run." Nor is my concern with a woman in a dirty crepe-de-Chine wrapper in a Wilmington bar. My stake is always, of course, in the unmentioned girl in the plaid silk dress. *Remember what it was to be me:* that is always the point.

It is a difficult point to admit. We are brought up in the ethic that oth-   5
ers, any others, all others, are by definition more interesting than ourselves; taught to be diffident, just this side of self-effacing. ("You're the least important person in the room and don't forget it," Jessica Mitford's governess would hiss in her ear on the advent of any social occasion; I copied that into my notebook because it is only recently that I have been able to enter a room without hearing some such phrase in my inner ear.) Only the very young and the very old may recount their dreams at breakfast, dwell upon self, interrupt with memories of beach picnics and favorite Liberty lawn dresses and the rainbow trout in a creek near Colorado Springs. The rest of us are expected, rightly, to affect absorption in other people's favorite dresses, other people's trout.

And so we do. But our notebooks give us away, for however dutifully   6
we record what we see around us, the common denominator of all we see is always, transparently, shamelessly, the implacable "I." We are not talking here about the kind of notebook that is patently for public consumption, a structural conceit for binding together a series of graceful *pensées* [thoughts]; we are talking about something private, about bits of the mind's string too short to use, an indiscriminate and erratic assemblage with meaning only for its maker.

And sometimes even the maker has difficulty with the meaning. There   7
does not seem to be, for example, any point in my knowing for the rest of my life that, during 1964, 720 tons of soot fell on every square mile of New York City, yet there it is in my notebook, labeled "FACT." Nor do I really need to remember that Ambrose Bierce liked to spell Leland Stanford's name "£eland $tanford" or that "smart women almost always wear black in Cuba," a fashion hint without much potential for practical application. And does not the relevance of these notes seem marginal at best?:

In the basement museum of the Inyo County Courthouse in Independence, California, sign pinned to a mandarin coat: "This MANDARIN COAT was often worn by Mrs. Minnie S. Brooks when giving lectures on her TEAPOT COLLECTION."

Redhead getting out of car in front of Beverly Wilshire Hotel, chinchilla stole, Vuitton bags with tags reading:

MRS. LOU FOX

HOTEL SAHARA

VEGAS

Well, perhaps not entirely marginal. As a matter of fact, Mrs. Minnie S.   8
Brooks and her MANDARIN COAT pull me back into my own childhood, for
although I never knew Mrs. Brooks and did not visit Inyo County until I
was thirty, I grew up in just such a world, in houses cluttered with Indian
relics and bits of gold ore and ambergris and the souvenirs my Aunt Mercy
Farnsworth brought back from the Orient. It is a long way from that
world to Mrs. Lou Fox's world, where we all live now, and is it not just as
well to remember that? Might not Mrs. Minnie S. Brooks help me to remember what I am? Might not Mrs. Lou Fox help me to remember what
I am not?

But sometimes the point is harder to discern. What exactly did I have   9
in mind when I noted down that it cost the father of someone I know
$650 a month to light the place on the Hudson in which he lived before
the Crash? What use was I planning to make of this line by Jimmy Hoffa:
"I may have my faults, but being wrong ain't one of them"? And although
I think it interesting to know where the girls who travel with the Syndicate
have their hair done when they find themselves on the West Coast, will I
ever make suitable use of it? Might I not be better off just passing it on to
John O'Hara? What is a recipe for sauerkraut doing in my notebook?
What kind of magpie keeps this notebook? *"He was born the night the Titanic went down."* That seems a nice enough line, and I even recall who
said it, but is it not really a better line in life than it could ever be in fiction?

But of course that is exactly it: not that I should ever use the line, but   10
that I should remember the woman who said it and the afternoon I heard
it. We were on her terrace by the sea, and we were finishing the wine left
from lunch, trying to get what sun there was, a California winter sun. The
woman whose husband was born the night the *Titanic* went down wanted
to rent her house, wanted to go back to her children in Paris. I remember
wishing that I could afford the house, which cost $1,000 a month. "Some-
day you will," she said lazily. "Someday it all comes." There in the sun on
her terrace it seemed easy to believe in someday, but later I had a low-
grade afternoon hangover and ran over a black snake on the way to the su-
permarket and was flooded with inexplicable fear when I heard the
checkout clerk explaining to the man ahead of me why she was finally di-
vorcing her husband. "He left me no choice," she said over and over as she
punched the register. "He has a little seven-month-old baby by her, he left
me no choice." I would like to believe that my dread then was for the
human condition, but of course it was for me, because I wanted a baby
and did not then have one and because I wanted to own the house that
cost $1,000 a month to rent and because I had a hangover.

It all comes back. Perhaps it is difficult to see the value in having one's   11
self back in that kind of mood, but I do see it; I think we are well advised

to keep on nodding terms with the people we used to be whether we find them attractive company or not. Otherwise they turn up unannounced and surprise us, come hammering on the mind's door at 4 A.M. of a bad night and demand to know who deserted them, who betrayed them, who is going to make amends. We forget all too soon the things we thought we could never forget. We forget the loves and the betrayals alike, forget what we whispered and what we screamed, forget who we were. I have already lost touch with a couple of people I used to be; one of them, a seventeen-year-old, presents little threat, although it would be of some interest to me to know again what it feels like to sit on a river levee drinking vodka-and-orange-juice and listening to Les Paul and Mary Ford and their echoes sing "How High the Moon" on the car radio. (You see I still have the scenes, but I no longer perceive myself among those present, no longer could even improvise the dialogue.) The other one, a twenty-three-year-old, bothers me more. She was always a good deal of trouble, and I suspect she will reappear when I least want to see her, skirts too long, shy to the point of aggravation, always the injured party, full of recriminations and little hurts and stories I do not want to hear again, at once saddening me and angering me with her vulnerability and ignorance, an apparition all the more insistent for being so long banished.

It is a good idea, then, to keep in touch, and I suppose that keeping in touch is what notebooks are all about. And we are all on our own when it comes to keeping those lines open to ourselves: your notebook will never help me, nor mine you. *So what's new in the whiskey business?* What could that possibly mean to you? To me it means a blonde in a Pucci bathing suit sitting with a couple of fat men by the pool at the Beverly Hills Hotel. Another man approaches, and they all regard one another in silence for a while. "So what's new in the whiskey business?" one of the fat men finally says by way of welcome, and the blonde stands up, arches one foot and dips it in the pool, looking all the while at the cabaña where Baby Pignatari is talking on the telephone. That is all there is to that, except that several years later I saw the blonde coming out of Saks Fifth Avenue in New York with her California complexion and a voluminous mink coat. In the harsh wind that day she looked old and irrevocably tired to me, and even the skins in the mink coat were not worked the way they were doing them that year, not the way she would have wanted them done, and there is the point of the story. For a while after that I did not like to look in the mirror, and my eyes would skim the newspapers and pick out only the deaths, the cancer victims, the premature coronaries, the suicides, and I stopped riding the Lexington Avenue IRT because I noticed for the first time that all the strangers I had seen for years—the man with the seeing-eye dog, the spinster who read the classified pages every day, the fat girl

12

who always got off with me at Grand Central—looked older than they once had.

It all comes back. Even that recipe for sauerkraut: even that brings it   13
back. I was on Fire Island when I first made that sauerkraut, and it was raining, and we drank a lot of bourbon and ate the sauerkraut and went to bed at ten, and I listened to the rain in the Atlantic and felt safe. I made the sauerkraut again last night and it did not make me feel any safer, but that is, as they say, another story.

MUSINGS

Most writers keep a journal very much like the one that Didion describes. Try carrying a notebook with you and jotting down overheard bits of conversation, lines from a favorite poem, words to a song, and other snippets of information that intrigue you. Also, record your reactions to a person, scene, or event. Write just enough to allow you to remember so that you can draw on your notebook for future writing.

CHRISTOPHER COLUMBUS (1451–1506)

Christopher Columbus, known as the discoverer of the Americas, was born in Genoa, Italy, an important port and trading center. He had little formal education but mastered Latin, Portugese, and Spanish through his travels. When he was in his late twenties, he conceived a plan to sail west from Europe in order to reach the East, an ever-growing source of trade then accessible only by long, arduous, and expensive overland trips. Portugal's Maritime Committee, to whom he applied first for funding to support his venture, rejected his proposal, but in 1492 Isabelle and Ferdinand, the Spanish sovereigns, agreed to finance his voyage. Setting sail with his three ships, the Niña, Pinta, and Santa Maria, he quelled a near mutiny of his crew, who feared that they would never have the proper winds to return to Spain because the wind was always at their backs as they sailed west. As signs of land began to appear the crew rallied, and after months at sea Columbus and his men welcomed the first sight of land.

Columbus landed on an island in what is now the Bahamas, believing that he was on an island off Asia. He pressed on to the present-day Cuba and, thinking that he was on the coast of China, sent emissaries to the emperor. They reported seeing "many people who carried a firebrand to light certain herbs the smoke of which they inhale." It was the Europeans' first sight of tobacco. Encountering violent storms on the homeward voyage, Columbus and his crew arrived in Spain eight months later to great acclaim, accompanied by six Indians outfitted in their native ceremonial garb.

In the following entry Columbus describes his first encounter with the natives. He and his crew were surprised to be greeted by a people who "do not bear arms or know them" and "became so entirely our friends that it was a wonder to see."

A Voyage of Discovery

Thursday, October 11th He navigated to the west-south-west; they had a rougher sea than they had experienced during the whole voyage. They saw petrels [seabirds] and a green reed near the ship. Those in the caravel *Pinta* saw a cane and a stick, and they secured another small stick, carved, as it appeared, with iron, and a piece of cane, and other vegetation which grows on land, and a small board. Those in the caravel *Niña* also saw other indications of land and a stick loaded with barnacles. At these signs, all breathed again and rejoiced. On this day, to sunset, they went twenty-seven leagues [approximately 81 miles]. After sunset, he steered his former course to the west; they made twelve miles an hour, and up to two hours before midnight they had made ninety miles, which are twenty-two leagues and a half. And since the caravel *Pinta* was swifter and went ahead of the admiral, she found land and made the signals which the admiral had commanded. This land was first sighted by a sailor called Rodrigo de Triana, although the admiral, at ten o'clock in the night, being on the sterncastle, saw a light. It was, however, so obscured that he would not affirm that it was land, but called Pero Gutierrez, butler of the King's dias, and told him that there seemed to be a light, and that he should watch for it. He did so, and saw it. He said the same also to Rodrigo Sanchez de Segovia, whom the King and Queen had sent in the fleet as *veedor* [comptroller], and he saw nothing since he was not in a position from which it could be seen. After the admiral had so spoken, it was seen once or twice, and it was like a small wax candle, which was raised and lowered. Few thought that this was an indication of land, but the admiral was certain that they were near land. Accordingly, when they said the *Salve*, which all sailors are accustomed to say and chant in their manner, and when they had all been gathered together, the admiral asked and urged them to keep a good look out from the forecastle and to watch carefully for land, and to him who should say first that he saw land, he would give at once a silk doublet apart from the other rewards which the Sovereigns had promised, which were ten thousand maravedis annually to him who first sighted it. Two hours after midnight land appeared, at a distance of about two leagues from them. They took in all sail, remaining with the mainsail, which is the great sail without bonnets, and kept jogging, waiting for day, a Friday, on which they reached a small island of the Lucayos, which is called in the language of the Indians "Guanahaní." Immediately they saw naked people, and the admiral went ashore in the armed boat, and Martin Alonso Pinzón and Vicente Yañez, his brother, who was captain of the *Niña*. The admiral brought out the royal standard, and the captains went with two banners of the Green Cross, which the admiral flew on all the ships as a flag, with an F and a Y, and over each letter their crown, one being on one side of the ✠ and the other on the other. When they had landed, they saw very green trees and much water and fruit of various kinds. The admiral called the two captains and the others who had landed, and Rodrigo de Escobedo, secretary of the whole fleet, and Rodrigo Sanchez de Segovia, and said that they should bear witness and testimony how he, before them all, took possession of the island, as in fact he did, for the King and Queen, his Sovereigns, making the declarations which are required, as is contained more at length in the testimonies which were there made in writing. Soon many people of the island gathered there. What follows are the actual words of the admiral, in his book of his first voyage and discovery of these Indies.

"I," he says, "in order that they might feel great amity towards us, because I knew that they were a people to be delivered and converted to our

2

holy faith rather by love than by force, gave to some among them some red caps and some glass beads, which they hung round their necks, and many other things of little value. At this they were greatly pleased and became so entirely our friends that it was a wonder to see. Afterwards they came swimming to the ships' boats, where we were, and brought us parrots and cotton thread in balls, and spears and many other things, and we exchanged for them other things, such as small glass beads and hawks' bells, which we gave to them. In fact, they took all and gave all, such as they had, with good will, but it seemed to me that they were a people very deficient in everything. They all go naked as their mothers bore them, and the women also, although I saw only one very young girl. And all those whom I did see were youths, so that I did not see one who was over thirty years of age; they were very well built, with handsome bodies and very good faces. Their hair is coarse almost like the hairs of a horse's tail and short; they wear their hair down over their eyebrows, except for a few strands behind, which they wear long and never cut. Some of them are painted black, and they are the colour of the people of the Canaries, neither black nor white, and some of them are painted white and some red and some in any colour that they find. Some of them paint their faces, some their whole bodies, some only the eyes, and some only the nose. They do not bear arms or know them, for I showed to them swords and they took them by the blade and cut themselves through ignorance. They have no iron. Their spears are certain reeds, without iron, and some of these have a fish tooth at the end, while others are pointed in various ways. They are all generally fairly tall, good looking and well proportioned. I saw some who bore marks of wounds on their bodies, and I made signs to them to ask how this came about, and they indicated to me that people came from other islands, which are near, and wished to capture them, and they defended themselves. And I believed and still believe that they come here from the mainland to take them for slaves. They should be good servants and of quick intelligence, since I see that they very soon say all that is said to them, and I believe that they would easily be made Christians, for it appeared to me that they had no creed. Our Lord willing, at the time of my departure I will bring back six of them to Your Highnesses, that they may learn to talk. I saw no beast of any kind in this island, except parrots." All these are the words of the admiral.

Saturday, October 13th As soon as day broke, there came to the shore many of these men, all youths, as I have said, and all of a good height, very handsome people. Their hair is not curly, but loose and coarse as the hair of a horse; all have very broad foreheads and heads, more so than has any people that I have seen up to now. Their eyes are very lovely and not small. They are not at all black, but the colour of Canarians, and nothing else could be expected, since this is in one line from east to west

3

with the island of Hierro in the Canaries. Their legs are very straight, all alike; they have no bellies but very good figures. They came to the ship in boats, which are made of a treetrunk like a long boat and all of one piece. They are very wonderfully carved, considering the country, and large, so that in some forty or forty-five men came. Others are smaller, so that in some only a solitary man came. They row them with a paddle, like a baker's peel [a long-handled tool to remove bread from ovens], and they travel wonderfully fast. If one capsizes, all at once begin to swim and right it, baling it out with gourds which they carry with them. They brought balls of spun cotton and parrots and spears and other trifles, which it would be tedious to write down, and they gave all for anything that was given to them. And I was attentive and laboured to know if they had gold, and I saw that some of them wore a small piece hanging from a hole which they have in the nose, and from signs I was able to understand that, going to the south or going round the island to the south, there was a king who had large vessels of it and possessed much gold. I endeavoured to make them go there, and afterwards saw that they were not inclined for the journey. I resolved to wait until the afternoon of the following day, and after that to leave for the south-west, for, as many of them indicated to me, they said that there was land to the south and to the south-west and to the north-west, and that those of the north-west often came to attack them. So I resolved to go to the south-west, to seek the gold and precious stones. This island is fairly large and very flat; the trees are very green and there is much water. In the centre of it, there is a very large lake; there is no mountain, and all is so green that it is a pleasure to gaze upon it. The people also are very gentle and, since they long to possess something of ours and fear that nothing will be given to them unless they give something, when they have nothing, they take what they can and immediately throw themselves into the water and swim. But all that they do possess, they give for anything which is given to them, so that they exchange things even for pieces of broken dishes and bits of broken glass cups. I even saw one give sixteen balls of cotton for three *ceotis* of Portugal, which are a Castilian *blanca* [copper coins], and in these balls there was more than an *arroba* [approximately 25 lbs.] of spun cotton. I should forbid this and should not allow anything to be taken, unless it be that I command all, if there be a quantity, to be taken for Your Highnesses. It grows here in this island, but owing to lack of time, I can give no definite account; and here is also produced that gold which they wear hanging from the nose. But, in order not to lose time, I wish to go and see if I can make the island of Cipangu. Now, as it was night, they all went to land in their boats.

As soon as I arrived in the Indies, in the first island which I found, I took some of the natives by force, in order that they might learn and might give me information of whatever there is in these parts. And so it

4

was that they soon understood us, and we them, either by speech or signs, and they have been very serviceable. At present, those I bring with me are still of the opinion that I come from Heaven, for all the intercourse which they have had with me. They were the first to announce this wherever I went, and the others went running from house to house, and to the neighbouring towns, with loud cries of, "Come! Come! See the men from Heaven!" So all came, men and women alike, when their minds were set at rest concerning us, not one, small or great, remaining behind, and they all brought something to eat and drink, which they gave with extraordinary affection.

In all the islands, they have very many canoes, which are like rowing   5
fustas, some larger and some smaller; some are greater than a fusta of eighteen benches. They are not so broad, because they are made of a single log of wood, but a fusta would not keep up with them in rowing, since their speed is an incredible thing. In these they navigate among all those islands, which are innumerable, and carry their goods. I have seen one of these canoes with seventy or eighty men in it, each one with his paddle.

In all these islands, I saw no great diversity in the appearance of the   6
people or in their manners and language. On the contrary, they all understand one another, which is a very curious thing, on account of which I hope that their Highnesses will determine upon their conversion to our holy faith, towards which they are very inclined.

I have already said how I went one hundred and seven leagues in a   7
straight line from west to east along the seashore of the island of Juana, and as a result of this voyage I can say that this island is larger than England and Scotland together, for, beyond these one hundred and seven leagues, there remain to the westward two provinces to which I have not gone. One of these provinces they call "Avan" [the northern part of Cuba], and there people are born with tails. These provinces cannot have a length of less than fifty or sixty leagues, as I could understand from those Indians whom I have and who know all the islands.

The other island, Española, has a circumference greater than all Spain   8
from Collioure by the seacoast to Fuenterabia in Vizcaya, for I voyaged along one side for one hundred and eighty-eight great leagues in a straight line from west to east. It is a land to be desired and, when seen, never to be left. I have taken possession of all for their Highnesses, and all are more richly endowed than I know how or am able to say, and I hold all for their Highnesses, so that they may dispose of them as they do of the kingdoms of Castile and as absolutely. But especially, in this Española, in the situation most convenient and in the best position for the mines of gold and for all trade as well with the mainland here as with that there, belonging to the Grand Khan, where will be great trade and profit, I have taken possession of a large town, to which I gave the name "Villa de Navidad," and in

it I have made fortifications and a fort, which will now by this time be entirely completed. In it I have left enough men for such a purpose with arms and artillery and provisions for more than a year, and a fusta, and one, a master of all seacraft, to build others, and I have established great friendship with the king of that land, so much so, that he was proud to call me "brother" and to treat me as such. And even were he to change his attitude to one of hostility towards these men, he and his do not know what arms are. They go naked, as I have already said, and they are the most timorous people in the world, so that the men whom I have left there alone would suffice to destroy all that land, and the island is without danger for their persons, if they know how to govern themselves.

In all these islands, it seems to me that all men are content with one woman, and to their chief or king they give as many as twenty. It appears to me that the women work more than do the men. I have not been able to learn if they hold private property; it seemed to me to be that all took a share in whatever any one had, especially of eatable things. 9

In these islands I have so far found no human monstrosities, as many expected, but on the contrary the whole population is very well formed, nor are they negroes as in Guinea, but their hair is flowing and they are not born where there is intense force in the rays of the sun. It is true that the sun there has great power, although it is distant from the equinoctial line twenty-six degrees. In these islands, where there are high mountains, the cold was severe this winter, but they endure it, being used to it and with the help of meats which they consume with many and extremely hot spices. Thus I have found no monsters, nor had a report of any, except in an island "Carib," which is the second at the coming into the Indies, and which is inhabited by a people who are regarded in all the islands as very fierce and who eat human flesh. They have many canoes with which they range through all the islands of India and pillage and take whatever they can. They are no more malformed than are the others, except that they have the custom of wearing their hair long like women, and they use bows and arrows of the same cane stems, with a small piece of wood at the end, owing to their lack of iron which they do not possess. They are ferocious among these other people who are cowardly to an excessive degree, but I make no more account of them than of the rest. These are they who have intercourse with the women of "Matinino," which is the first island met on the way from Spain to the Indies, in which there is not a man. These women engage in no feminine occupation, but use bows and arrows of cane, like those already mentioned, and they arm and protect themselves with plates of copper, of which they have much. 10

In another island, which they assure me is larger than Española, the people have no hair. In it there is incalculable gold, and from it and from the other islands I bring with me Indians as evidence. 11

MUSINGS

Voyages of discovery need not take place across oceans or vast tracts of land. New discoveries often occur in our everyday lives. Write about some experience that differed markedly from what you had expected—a party that you dreaded that turned out to be fun, an exam that you were sure you would fail but in fact did pass, a casual acquaintance who proved to be a real friend in a time of need—or some other experience that turned out to be a voyage of discovery for you.

HENRY DAVID THOREAU (1817–1862)

A consummate individualist and early naturalist, Henry David Thoreau built his own cabin in the woods near Walden Pond and spent almost two years, "living deep and sucking all the marrow out of life." Walden, from which this excerpt is taken, is his daily journal in which he extols the virtues of that life. After graduating from Harvard, he worked for several years in his father's pencil shop while teaching at a grammar school. He longed to lead a life free of material pursuits and subsequently decided to support his simple life-style by doing handyman jobs in Concord, Massachusetts, where he lived. At Walden Pond he spent his time writing, reading, and having philosophical discussions with his friends. He describes his cabin on Walden Pond and applauds the life of the simple woodcutter whom he has come to know.

Thoreau was an early environmentalist and an eloquent social critic. His essay "Civil Disobedience" was a powerful condemnation of the Mexican War, and in the 1960s his beliefs found root in the demonstrations against the Vietnam War. In the late twentieth century his ideas were incorporated in the passive resistance movements of Ghandi and Martin Luther King, Jr. His collected poems, letters, and journals were published in 1906. One critic asserts that Thoreau, in his journal from Walden Pond, became "a symbol of man's willed integrity, his inner freedom, and his ability to build his own life."

My House in the Woods

1 I think that I love society as much as most, and am ready enough to fasten myself like a bloodsucker for the time to any full-blooded man that comes in my way. I am naturally no hermit, but might possibly sit out the sturdiest frequenter of the bar-room, if my business called me thither.

2 I had three chairs in my house; one for solitude, two for friendship, three for society. When visitors came in larger and unexpected numbers there was but the third chair for them all, but they generally economized the room by standing up. It is surprising how many great men and women a small house will contain. I have had twenty-five or thirty souls, with their bodies, at once under my roof, and yet we often parted without being aware that we had come very near to one another. Many of our houses, both public and private, with their almost innumerable apartments, their huge halls and their cellars for the storage of wines and other munitions of peace, appear to me extravagantly large for their inhabitants. They are so vast and magnificent that the latter seem to be only vermin which infest them. I am surprised when the herald blows his summons before some Tremont or Astor or Middlesex House [hotels in Boston], to see

come creeping out over the piazza for all inhabitants a ridiculous mouse, which soon again slinks into some hole in the pavement.

One inconvenience I sometimes experienced in so small a house, the difficulty of getting to a sufficient distance from my guest when we began to utter the big thoughts in big words. You want room for your thoughts to get into sailing trim and run a course or two before they make their port. The bullet of your thought must have overcome its lateral and ricochet motion and fallen into its last and steady course before it reaches the ear of the hearer, else it may plough out again through the side of his head. Also, our sentences wanted room to unfold and form their columns in the interval. Individuals, like nations, must have suitable broad and natural boundaries, even a considerable neutral ground, between them. I have found it a singular luxury to talk across the pond to a companion on the opposite side. In my house we were so near that we could not begin to hear,—we could not speak low enough to be heard; as when you throw two stones into calm water so near that they break each other's undulations. If we are merely loquacious and loud talkers, then we can afford to stand very near together, cheek by jowl, and feel each other's breath; but if we speak reservedly and thoughtfully, we want to be farther apart, that all animal heat and moisture may have a chance to evaporate. If we would enjoy the most intimate society with that in each of us which is without, or above, being spoken to, we must not only be silent, but commonly so far apart bodily that we cannot possibly hear each other's voice in any case. Referred to this standard, speech is for the convenience of those who are hard of hearing; but there are many fine things which we cannot say if we have to shout. As the conversation began to assume a loftier and grander tone, we gradually shoved our chairs farther apart till they touched the wall in opposite corners, and then commonly there was not room enough.

My "best" room, however, my withdrawing room, always ready for company, on whose carpet the sun rarely fell, was the pine wood behind my house. Thither in summer days, when distinguished guests came, I took them, and a priceless domestic swept the floor and dusted the furniture and kept the things in order.

If one guest came he sometimes partook of my frugal meal, and it was no interruption to conversation to be stirring a hasty-pudding [cornmeal mush], or watching the rising and maturing of a loaf of bread in the ashes, in the mean while. But if twenty came and sat in my house there was nothing said about dinner, though there might be bread enough for two, more than if eating were a forsaken habit; but we naturally practised abstinence; and this was never felt to be an offence against hospitality, but the most proper and considerate course. The waste and decay of physical life, which so often needs repair, seemed miraculously retarded in such a case, and the vital vigor stood its ground. I could entertain thus a thousand as well as twenty; and if any ever went away disappointed or hungry from my house when they found me at home, they may depend upon it that I sympathized with them at least. So easy is it, though many housekeepers doubt it, to establish new and better customs in the place of the old. You need not rest your reputation on the dinners you give. For my own part, I was never so effectually deterred from frequenting a man's house, by any kind of Cerberus [the two-headed dog at the entrance to Hades, the mythical version of Hell] whatever, as by the parade one made about dining me, which I took to be a very polite and roundabout hint never to trouble him so again. I think I shall never revisit those scenes. I should be proud to have for the motto of my cabin those lines of Spenser which one of my visitors inscribed on a yellow walnut leaf for a card:—

> Arrived there, the little house they fill,
>> Ne looke for entertainment where none was;
> Rest is their feast, and all things at their will:
>> The noblest mind the best contentment has.

• • •

As for men, they will hardly fail one any where. I had more visitors   6 while I lived in the woods than at any other period of my life; I mean that I had some. I met several there under more favorable circumstances than I could any where else. But fewer came to see me upon trivial business. In this respect, my company was winnowed by my mere distance from town. I had withdrawn so far within the great ocean of solitude, into which the rivers of society empty, that for the most part, so far as my needs were concerned, only the finest sediment was deposited around me. Beside, there were wafted to me evidences of unexplored and uncultivated continents on the other side.

Who should come to my lodge this morning but a true Homeric   7 [Greek] or Paphlagonian [from a region on the North Sea] man,—he had so suitable and poetic a name that I am sorry I cannot print it here,—a Canadian, a wood-chopper and post-maker, who can hole fifty posts in a day, who made his last supper on a woodchuck which his dog caught. He, too, has heard of Homer, and, "if it were not for books," would "not know what to do rainy days," though perhaps he has not read one wholly through for many rainy seasons. Some priest who could pronounce the Greek itself taught him to read his verse in the testament in his native parish far away; and now I must translate to him, while he holds the book, Achilles' reproof to Patroclus for his sad countenance.—"Why are you in tears, Patroclus, like a young girl?"—

> Or have you alone heard some news from Phthia?
> They say that Menœtius lives yet, son of Actor,

And Peleus lives, son of Æacus, among the Myrmidons,
Either of whom having died, we should greatly grieve.

He says, "That's good." He has a great bundle of white-oak bark under his 8
arm for a sick man, gathered this Sunday morning. "I suppose there's no
harm in going after such a thing to-day," says he. To him Homer was a
great writer, though what his writing was about he did not know. A more
simple and natural man it would be hard to find. Vice and disease, which
cast such a sombre moral hue over the world, seemed to have hardly any
existence for him. He was about twenty-eight years old, and had left
Canada and his father's house a dozen years before to work in the States,
and earn money to buy a farm with at last, perhaps in his native country.
He was cast in the coarsest mould; a stout but sluggish body, yet gracefully
carried, with a thick sunburnt neck, dark bushy hair, and dull sleepy blue
eyes, which were occasionally lit up with expression. He wore a flat gray
cloth cap, a dingy wool-colored greatcoat, and cowhide boots. He was a
great consumer of meat, usually carrying his dinner to his work a couple of
miles past my house,—for he chopped all summer,—in a tin pail; cold
meats, often cold woodchucks, and coffee in a stone bottle which dangled
by a string from his belt; and sometimes he offered me a drink. He came
along early, crossing my beanfield, though without anxiety or haste to get
to his work, such as Yankees exhibit. He wasn't a-going to hurt himself. He
didn't care if he only earned his board. Frequently he would leave his dinner in the bushes, when his dog had caught a woodchuck by the way, and
go back a mile and a half to dress it and leave it in the cellar of the house
where he boarded, after deliberating first for half an hour whether he
could not sink it in the pond safely till nightfall,—loving to dwell long
upon these themes. He would say, as he went by in the morning, "How
thick the pigeons are! If working every day were not my trade, I could get
all the meat I should want by hunting,—pigeons, woodchucks, rabbits,
partridges,—by gosh! I could get all I should want for a week in one day."

He was a skilful chopper, and indulged in some flourishes and orna- 9
ments in his art. He cut his trees level and close to the ground, that the
sprouts which came up afterward might be more vigorous and a sled
might slide over the stumps; and instead of leaving a whole tree to support
his corded wood, he would pare it away to a slender stake or splinter
which you could break off with your hand at last.

He interested me because he was so quiet and solitary and so happy 10
withal; a well of good humor and contentment which overflowed at his
eyes. His mirth was without alloy. Sometimes I saw him at his work in the
woods, felling trees, and he would greet me with a laugh of inexpressible
satisfaction, and a salutation in Canadian French, though he spoke English as well. When I approached him he would suspend his work, and with

half-suppressed mirth lie along the trunk of a pine which he had felled, and, peeling off the inner bark, roll it up into a ball and chew it while he laughed and talked. Such an exuberance of animal spirits had he that he sometimes tumbled down and rolled on the ground with laughter at any thing which made him think and tickled him. Looking round upon the trees he would exclaim,—"By George! I can enjoy myself well enough here chopping; I want no better sport." Sometimes, when at leisure, he amused himself all day in the woods with a pocket pistol, firing salutes to himself at regular intervals as he walked. In the winter he had a fire by which at noon he warmed his coffee in a kettle; and as he sat on a log to eat his dinner the chicadees would sometimes come round and alight on his arm and peck at the potato in his fingers; and he said that he "liked to have the little *fellers* about him."

In him the animal man chiefly was developed. In physical endurance 11
and contentment he was cousin to the pine and the rock. I asked him once if he was not sometimes tired at night, after working all day; and he answered, with a sincere and serious look, "Gorrappit, I never was tired in my life." But the intellectual and what is called spiritual man in him were slumbering as in an infant. He had been instructed only in that innocent and ineffectual way in which the Catholic priests teach the aborigines, by which the pupil is never educated to the degree of consciousness, but only to the degree of trust and reverence, and a child is not made a man, but kept a child. When Nature made him, she gave him a strong body and contentment for his portion, and propped him on every side with reverence and reliance, that he might live out his threescore years and ten a child. He was so genuine and unsophisticated that no introduction would serve to introduce him, more than if you introduced a woodchuck to your neighbor. He had got to find him out as you did. He would not play any part. Men paid him wages for work, and so helped to feed and clothe him; but he never exchanged opinions with them. He was so simply and naturally humble—if he can be called humble who never aspires—that humility was no distinct quality in him, nor could he conceive of it. Wiser men were demigods to him. If you told him that such a one was coming, he did as if he thought that any thing so grand would expect nothing of himself, but take all the responsibility on itself, and let him be forgotten still. He never heard the sound of praise. He particularly reverenced the writer and the preacher. Their performances were miracles. When I told him that I wrote considerably, he thought for a long time that it was merely the handwriting which I meant, for he could write a remarkably good hand himself. I sometimes found the name of his native parish handsomely written in the snow by the highway, with the proper French accent, and knew that he had passed. I asked him if he ever wished to write his thoughts. He said that he had read and written letters for those who could

not, but he never tried to write thoughts,—no, he could not, he could not tell what to put first, it would kill him, and then there was spelling to be attended to at the same time!

I heard that a distinguished wise man and reformer asked him if he did 12 not want the world to be changed; but he answered with a chuckle of surprise in his Canadian accent, not knowing that the question had ever been entertained before, "No, I like it well enough." It would have suggested many things to a philosopher to have dealings with him. To a stranger he appeared to know nothing of things in general; yet I sometimes saw in him a man whom I had not seen before, and I did not know whether he was as wise as Shakespeare or as simply ignorant as a child, whether to suspect him of a fine poetic consciousness or of stupidity. A townsman told me that when he met him sauntering through the village in his small close-fitting cap, and whistling to himself, he reminded him of a prince in disguise.

His only books were an almanac and an arithmetic, in which last he was 13 considerably expert. The former was a sort of cyclopædia to him, which he supposed to contain an abstract of human knowledge, as indeed it does to a considerable extent. I loved to sound him on the various reforms of the day, and he never failed to look at them in the most simple and practical light. He had never heard of such things before. Could he do without factories? I asked. He had worn the homemade Vermont gray, he said, and that was good. Could he dispense with tea and coffee? Did this country afford any beverage beside water? He had soaked hemlock leaves in water and drank it, and thought that was better than water in warm weather. When I asked him if he could do without money, he showed the convenience of money in such a way as to suggest and coincide with the most philosophical accounts of the origin of this institution, and the very derivation of the word *pecunia* [Latin for wealth]. If an ox were his property, and he wished to get needles and thread at the store, he thought it would be inconvenient and impossible soon to go on mortgaging some portion of the creature each time to that amount. He could defend many institutions better than any philosopher, because, in describing them as they concerned him, he gave the true reason for their prevalence, and speculation had not suggested to him any other. At another time, hearing Plato's definition of a man,—a biped without feathers,—and that one exhibited a cock plucked and called it Plato's man, he thought it an important difference that the *knees* bent the wrong way. He would sometimes exclaim, "How I love to talk! By George, I could talk all day!" I asked him once, when I had not seen him for many months, if he had got a new idea this summer. "Good Lord," said he, "a man that has to work as I do, if he does not forget the ideas he has had, he will do well. May be the man you hoe with is inclined to race; then, by gorry, your mind must be there; you think of weeds." He would sometimes ask me first on such occasions, if I had made any improvement. One winter day I asked him if he was always satisfied with himself, wishing to suggest a substitute within him for the priest without, and some higher motive for living. "Satisfied!" said he; "some men are satisfied with one thing, and some with another. One man, perhaps, if he has got enough, will be satisfied to sit all day with his back to the fire and his belly to the table, by George!" Yet I never, by any manœuvring, could get him to take the spiritual view of things; the highest that he appeared to conceive of was a simple expediency, such as you might expect an animal to appreciate; and this, practically, is true of most men. If I suggested any improvement in his mode of life, he merely answered, without expressing any regret, that it was too late. Yet he thoroughly believed in honesty and the like virtues.

There was a certain positive originality, however slight, to be detected   14 in him, and I occasionally observed that he was thinking for himself and expressing his own opinion, a phenomenon so rare that I would any day walk ten miles to observe it, and it amounted to the re-origination of many of the institutions of society. Though he hesitated, and perhaps failed to express himself distinctly, he always had a presentable thought behind. Yet his thinking was so primitive and immersed in his animal life, that, though more promising than a merely learned man's, it rarely ripened to any thing which can be reported. He suggested that there might be men of genius in the lowest grades of life, however permanently humble and illiterate, who take their own view always, or do not pretend to see at all; who are as bottomless even as Walden Pond was thought to be, though they may be dark and muddy.

MUSINGS

Thoreau speaks eloquently of his simple cabin and his methods of "entertaining." Compare his cabin either with a house where you have celebrated a holiday dinner with family or with a place where you have ordered pizzas with friends.

Thoreau comments that physical distance is needed between persons in conversations. Such distances vary according to different cultures and different subjects. Try moving quite close to someone when you speak and describe his or her reactions.

In describing his friend Thoreau has little to say about his physical appearance but concentrates on the man's actions and words. Try describing a person by writing about what he or she does or says. You will need to use several different incidents and snatches of conversation to complete the picture as Thoreau does.

W. P. WINANS (1825–1863)

This record of the struggles of a colonel in charge of a group of Confederate soldiers touchingly depicts the daily life of a field commander who cared deeply for his men and their welfare. However, he lost patience with the ineptitude of the generals in charge as it became clear that the Southern forces were ill-equipped with supplies and men. His love for his family and his wife runs like an unbroken thread through his diary. He writes "partly to cheat ennui, but chiefly to gratify the best woman in the world—my wife."

Born in 1825, Colonel Winans was a lawyer in Shreveport, Louisiana, before the Civil War, and when he joined the army he left behind a wife and five children. One child died while he was gone, and after his death on the battlefield at the age of thirty-seven his diary was delivered to his wife by a passing soldier.

Diary of a Civil War Soldier

May 20th, 1862   Today I begin to keep some memoranda of daily events—not of emotions—partly to cheat ennui, but chiefly to gratify the best woman in the world—my wife. I have no hope of a letter reaching her by mail, now that the Mississippi river blockades the V. S. & T. R. Road by tearing up the road through the swamp and now the Mississippi itself is blockaded by the d--n Yankee's gunboats, for which last evil may posterity curse the stupid imbecility of Jeff Davis [general in charge of the Confederate Army], for I am not able to do the subject justice. Well, as I was going on to say, I record these daily events for *her* sake, so that if ever I find some one journeying to that far off "bourne from which no traveller returns" (Caddo) (none have lately), I will tear out these leaves and send them to that "word which sums up all bliss," my wife. 1

We have slept in the trenches (bivouacked) for more than a fortnight, occasionally in our tents, and occasionally interspersed with picket service. This is tic(k)lish business: Yankee bullets and Southern ticks both perforate our cuticles. 2

We have had warm work today with the pickets, especially at two positions—the sentinels are shooting at each other constantly. One of our men, a brave boy not more than 18 years old, imprudently got beyond our lines in trying to get a shot. His leg was broken and was amputated above the knee. His name was McDonald of Co. A., poor fellow. What a little hero he is! 3

May 21st Weather still delightful. Musketry still continues on both   4
our lines, and extends from the lower Farmington to the Purdy roads. Yesterday we had a little cannonading and Brother Surats (our Chaplain's
Brother) house was burned by the 42 Mississippi Regiment. It was used by
the Yankees as a refuge. Today the enemy killed Sergeant John Vickers in
[an] house on the extreme of my right. We were unable to recover his
body. This evening several regiments supported by artillery drove back my
pickets through this whole line. My men fell back splendidly—did not
withdraw their lines more than two hundred yards to the rear and kept up
their communications throughout. Beside driving back our picket, the
enemy shelled our Regiment and the Mississippi Regiment bivouacked on
the hill to the rear of the Bridge Creek for about an hour or more. I drew
up the two Regts. on both sides of the road so as to protect the pieces of
artillery sent to our support. The shells flew very close, several striking
very near us. Three in 30 yards. Our men behaved well except one of our
waggoners who, when I ordered all the ambulances and waggons to the
rear, didn't stop till he got to Camp.

May 22d We were relieved about sundown and men drawn up, ready   5
to march back to camp, when a Courier from Colonel Marks (our
Brigadier Commander) ordered me to report at once to him on the Upper
Farmington Road. At dark we reached the creek on the *upper* Farmington
Road, but no Colonel Marks there. Sent a Courier back to Corinth for instructions and to have our blankets (that the waggoner had run off with)
brought back to us. About midnight came Courier and blankets. Men all
asleep on the ground, worn out with fatigue after two days fighting and
loss of sleep. Courier reports Col. Marks on *Lower* Farmington Road. I
conclude to let the men sleep till just before day, when I would be able to
rejoin my brigade by light in time for the grand assault in today's great battle. I slept only cat-naps. Anxiety for the morrow's fierce battle and charge
upon the enemy's breastworks, apprehension for fear I would oversleep
and fail to get in in time, kept me awake. I reached Col. Marks and our
Brigade in ample time. We spent all day in idleness and suspense. Late in
the day we had some excitement. A battery and two Regiments drove
some of the enemy from a house they held near us. At dark we were ordered back to our camp, a command most joyfully obeyed. I had not been
in camp with the regiment more than 10 or 15 minutes, and had just un-
dressed preparatory to enjoying a good night's sleep, when an order came
to move with my command to the trenches. We fell in slowly and sadly,
when an order came countermanding. We joyfully obeyed the order to
stay.

This morning and yesterday deserters were shot very near me, but I   6
would not see the execution.

May 23d Last night as our column, part of Hindman's Division, 7
marched into Camp in the hazy twilight, the long line of troops winding
across the fields and through the woods, infantry and cavalry, presented
quite a Rembrandt picture. So much did it resemble a night scene as the
hand of some master might have sketched it, that there were few of the
Common Soldiers who did not notice the poetic value of the scene.

Today I heard that Howell, the husband of Isabel Whitworth had lately 8
arrived from Caddo. I went over to the 25th Regiment to see if he did not
bring a letter for me. But there was no letter from Wife. He came off without giving my Darling a chance to write. I dreamed two nights ago. Wife
approached me with a look so sad and so reproving, and handed me a
small scrap of paper, on which was written "get a coffin for my little boy."
Even in my dream I marked the singular number of the pronoun "my" instead of the accustomed, endearing one "our," as indicative of sorrowful
displeasure. This was on picket at Bridge Creek. But it is very weak to
think about and much more to record such idle fantasy. Yet I write for one
who will be interested in anything that gives a glimpse of her husband's
loving heart.

Today I applied for a flag of truce to get the body of Sergeant Vickers 9
and to get Dr. Cutliff appointed our surgeon. Nice Dr. Rochelle resigned.
I first applied to General Hindmans, then to Generals Brag and Beauregard Headquarters in succession. I was instructed to address Gen. Brag
through his Adjutant General and send written communications by or-
derly to my Brigade Commander and so through the "Circumlocution
Office" and my requests should meet favorable and immediate attention. I
returned to my quarters and did as instructed. No answer yet and it is
night and nearly bedtime. If granted, the flag of truce will come too late
for Vickers' body. The more I have to do with officials, the more I am convinced that insolence, ignorance and general incompetency, placed in office by favoritism or nepotism, is helping to "jeff davis" [president of the
Confederate States] us to the devil. And what a nice dodge and yankee
trick is this system of red tape, or as immortalized by the satyrist in the
"Circumlocution Office" of Bleak House. (Was it *Bleak House?*)

At night it is still raining—been raining since noon, and drizzled some 10
before.

May 27th Still on picket. Relieved guard at daylight. While at break- 11
fast, Genl. Hindman's Ast. Insp. Gen. Capt. Crockett called upon me to
go round my lines. He is an active efficient officer, a little too fond of
praising his own cleverness. He expressed himself pleased with my zeal,
etc. Today I stopped Capt. Avery from further communication with the
Yankees on the pass of Genl. Hardie: told him he must have authority

from Genl. Beauregard. All is quiet on our lines while the firing is fierce on both sides. The Yankees sent us a flag of truce and brought us seven surgeons from various Regts. taken at different battles and now returned to us, with two papers for the Genl. They required me to give receipt for Doctors and Dispatches as I would an invoice of goods. There was a striking contrast between the elegant soldierly appointment of the Yankee Col. and his escort, and myself and my gypsy looking crowd. The little Col. was as nice as a banbox, as sweet as a toilet table, and as saucy looking as any short legged Dutch Yankee need be. Quite a splendid cavalcade approached from our side in the evening with white flag and trumpet and demanded a parley. I refused to let them pass my sentinels unless they had a special permit from Beauregard when a fine, soldierly, striking looking man rode up to me and with a winning smile assured me he had the pass word from the Genl, and whispered to me a word that I did not know was right or wrong. I very politely told Col. "John Morgan" he could pass. I knew Beauregard's body guard that accompanied the renowned Kentuckyan, but I had not received the password. What the long conference he held with the enemy was, never was divulged to us. Col. Morgan looks the man rumor makes him, brave, dashing and generous, he was dressed as a civilian and escorted by a party of horse under command of a Major.

May 30 Left Corinth at nine o'clock, or were to have done so, but did   12
not pass the depot until midnight. Marched all night till just before day. Made only 6 miles, and bivouacked about one hour. Poor people, where an army passes. The breath of the siroc is not more fatal to prosperous vegetation than is war's hot breath. Curse on war and on our army that tramples on all private rights and family privacy. An army rolls over a flourishing plantation as lava desolates a green field. Fences and enclosures are swept away, and fields, gardens and orchards are ruthlessly trampled under foot and utterly destroyed. Marched all day and camped on shady creek. An old man pretending to ownership gave Lt. Bowman Wall a pig. I ask no questions for "Conscience Sake."

MUSINGS

Winans vows that he is recording "these daily events" for his wife's sake and that he will "tear out these leaves" and send them to her if "ever I find some one journeying" that way. There was no reliable mail during the Civil War, and of course no telephone or E-mail—forms of communication that we rely on so heavily today. This diary was his way of keeping in touch with his wife in his own mind. He does much more than record "daily events"; he also recounts his reactions—"anxiety for the morrow's fierce battle" and apprehension for "fear I would oversleep." He describes the line of troops "winding across the fields and through the woods" that resembled a "Rembrandt picture . . . a night scene as the hand of some master might have sketched it."

Record the events of a single day and then select one incident and describe your reaction to it—either your feelings about it or a personal connection.

PRISCILLA MERRIMAN EVANS (1835–?)

This is a harrowing account of a group of Mormons who walked 1330 miles from Iowa City to Salt Lake City suffering crippling injury to their legs and feet as well as hunger and disease. Priscilla Merriman Evans's husband had only one leg and walked twenty to twenty-five miles each day on a wooden stump. Each family was assigned a cart which carried their supplies and which they pulled across the rough terrain by hand. Wagons drawn by mule teams carried the tents and surplus flour.

No one rode in the wagons. Strong men would help the weaker ones, until they themselves were worn out, and some died from the struggle and want of food, and were buried along the wayside. It was heart rending for parents to move on and leave their loved ones. Children and young folks too, had to move on and leave father or mother or both.

Evans was born in Wales, where she later joined the Mormon Church. She and her husband migrated to the United States and joined Captain Edward Bunker's Third Handcart Party in the five-month trek which she describes here. She concludes her account with the motto of her life: "Not to look back—but forward" and "thanked the Lord for a contented mind, a home and something to eat." She and her husband had seven daughters and five sons. The date of her death is not known.

The Mormon Migration

We landed in Boston on May 23rd, then travelled in cattle cars three hundred miles to Iowa City. We remained in Iowa City three weeks, waiting for our carts to be made. We were offered many inducements to stay there. My husband was offered ten dollars a day to work at his trade of Iron Roller, but money was no inducement to us, for we were anxious to get to Zion [Salt Lake City]. We learned afterwards that many who stayed there apostatized or died of cholera. 1

When the carts were ready we started on a three-hundred-mile walk to Winterquarters on the Missouri River. There were a great many who made fun of us as we walked, pulling our carts, but the weather was fine and the roads were excellent and although I was sick and we were tired out at night, we still thought, "This is a glorious way to come to Zion." 2

We began our journey of one thousand miles on foot with a handcart for each family, some families consisting of man and wife, and some had quite large families. There were five mule teams to haul the tents and sur- 3

39

plus flour. Each handcart had one hundred pounds of flour, that was to be divided and [more got] from the wagons as required. At first we had a little coffee and bacon, but that was soon gone and we had no use for any cooking utensils but a frying pan. The flour was self-raising and we took water and baked a little cake; that was all we had to eat.

After months of travelling we were put on half rations and at one time, before help came, we were out of flour for two days. We washed out the flour sacks to make a little gravy. 4

Our company was three-hundred Welsh Saints. There were about a dozen in our tent, six of whom could not speak the Welsh language, myself among the number. Don't you think I had a pleasant journey traveling for months with three-hundred people of whose language I could not understand a word? My husband could talk Welsh, so he could join in their festivities when he felt like it. [Priscilla spoke no Welsh because English was the language she learned at home and Welsh was not taught in school.] 5

There were in our tent my husband with one leg, two blind men . . . a man with one arm, and a widow with five children. The widow, her children, and myself were the only ones who could not talk Welsh. My husband was commissary for our tent, and he cut his own rations short many times to help little children who had to walk and did not have enough to eat to keep up their strength. 6

The tent was our covering, and the overcoat spread on the bare ground with the shawl over us was our bed. My feather bed, and bedding, pillows, all our good clothing, my husband's church books, which he had collected through six years of missionary work, with some genealogy he had collected, all had to be left in a storehouse. We were promised that they would come to us with the next emigration in the spring, but we never did receive them. It was reported that the storehouse burned down, so that was a dreadful loss to us. 7

Edward Bunker was the Captain of our Company. His orders of the day were, "If any are sick among you, and are not able to walk, you must help them along, or pull them on your carts." No one rode in the wagons. Strong men would help the weaker ones, until they themselves were worn out, and some died from the struggle and want of food, and were buried along the wayside. It was heart rending for parents to move on and leave their loved ones to such a fate, as they were so helpless, and had no material for coffins. Children and young folks too, had to move on and leave father or mother or both. 8

Sometimes a bunch of buffaloes would come and the carts would stop until they passed. Had we been prepared with guns and ammunition, like people who came in wagons, we might have had meat, and would not have come to near starving. President Young ordered extra cattle sent 9 along to be killed to help the sick and weak, but they were never used for that purpose. One incident happened which came near being serious. Some Indians came to our camp and my husband told an Indian who admired me that he could have me for a pony. He was always getting off jokes. He thought no more about it, but in a day or two, here came the Indian with the pony, and wanted his pretty little squaw. It was no joke with him. I never was so frightened in all my life. There was no place to hide, and we did not know what to do. The Captain was called, and they had some difficulty in settling with the Indian without trouble.

In crossing rivers, the weak women and the children were carried over   10 the deep places, and they waded the others. We were much more fortunate than those who came later, as they had snow and freezing weather. Many lost limbs, and many froze to death. President Young advised them to start earlier, but they got started too late. My husband, in walking from twenty to twenty-five miles per day, [had pain] where the knee rested on the pad: the friction caused it to gather and break and was most painful. But he had to endure it, or remain behind, as he was never asked to ride in a wagon.

One incident shows how we were fixed for grease. My husband and   11 John Thayne, a butcher, in some way killed an old lame buffalo. They sat up all night and boiled it to get some grease to grease the carts, but he was so old and poor, there was not a drop of grease in him. We had no grease for the squeaking carts or to make gravy for the children and old people.

We reached Salt Lake City on October 2, 1856, tired, weary, with   12 bleeding feet, our clothing worn out and so weak we were nearly starved, but thankful to our Heavenly Father for bringing us to Zion. William R. Jones met us on the Public Square in Salt Lake City and brought us to his home in Spanish Fork. I think we were over three days coming from Salt Lake City to Spanish Fork by ox team, but what a change to ride in a wagon after walking 1330 miles from Iowa City to Salt Lake City!

We stayed in the home of an ex-bishop, Stephen Markham. His home   13 was a dugout. It was a very large room built half underground. His family consisted of three wives, and seven children. . . . There was a large fireplace in one end with bars, hooks, frying pans, and bake ovens, where they did the cooking for the large family, and boiled, fried, baked, and heated their water for washing.

There was a long table in one corner, and pole bedsteads fastened to the   14 walls in the three other corners. They were laced back and forth with rawhide cut in strips, and made a nice springy bed. There were three trundle beds, made like shallow boxes, with wooden wheels, which rolled under the mother's bed in the daytime to utilize space. There was a dirt roof, and the dirt floor was kept hard and smooth by sprinkling and sweeping. The bed ticks were filled with straw raised in Palmyra before the famine. [Palmyra, on the river between Spanish Fork and Utah Lake, suffered the famine to which Priscilla Evans alludes shortly before the Evanses' arrival. Fifty families moved to Spanish Fork and lived in the dugouts she describes.]

Aunt Mary [Markham] put her two children . . . in the foot of her bed 15 and gave us the trundle bed. . . . How delightful to sleep on a bed again, after sleeping on the ground for so many months with our clothes on. We had not slept in a bed since we left the ship *Sam Curling.*

MUSINGS

Evans's description of her incredible journey is heartbreakingly vivid. The trip itself is horrifying to the modern reader, and she makes see and feel the hardships by relating a number of memorable details. She describes their washing out the flour sacks "to make a little gravy," and sleeping on a bed made of an "overcoat spread on the bare ground with the shawl over us" within the tent which held her husband and herself, "two blind men, a man with one arm, and a widow with five children."

After they reached Salt Lake City, they stayed in a dugout which she describes in vivid detail. Describe any room—your bedroom, kitchen, dorm room, or classroom—using similar detail. Think first of the main impression you want to give, such as pleasant, messy, ugly, or cheerful. Then, select details that support your view, as Evans does to illustrate how difficult her journey was.

SHERWOOD ANDERSON (1876–1941)

This journal, taken from Sherwood Anderson's Paris Notebook *(1921), differs from the other diaries and journals included here in that it does not record daily events but is rather a random selection of thoughts. No attempt at continuity between the ideas is made. Each idea stands alone as an isolated description of a person or place, with a concluding thought that often startles with its perfect rightness. This notebook demonstrates Anderson's ability to draw meaning from isolated events.*

Anderson wrote about small-town America with an often uncanny sense of what such a life was like and an unwavering ability to make it known to a reader. Winesburg, Ohio: A Group of Tales of Ohio Small Town Life *(1919), which depicts an American small-town at the beginning of the twentieth century, established him as a well-known American writer. Although Anderson produced a number of later novels, none achieved the same success. He said in his* Memoirs *that "For all my egotism I know I am but a minor figure"—an opinion refuted by a number of critics. The following excerpt, unlike his other works, records anecdotes about his life abroad. Nevertheless, his essentially American point of view is always present.*

Passing Thoughts

Went to walk with K B who I knew years ago in America. He has no money but is living in a beautiful apartment overlooking the old fortification and the Cluny hills. Some friend has given him the apartment for the summer. Such things are always happening to him, always will be happening to him. He is the most delightful man I have ever known because he has no center of his own, no strong individual passion possesses him. For an hour, an evening, a day, a month he gives himself completely to the man or woman he is with. 1

I spoke of the American negro and my hope that some day an American artist would see the beauty of their caracters and persons and write or paint that beauty so that the negro should also see it. K B became at once inflamed with the idea—was all sympathy and understanding. Tomorrow he will have forgotten the negro of America forever. 2

The man has lived in almost every country in Europe and has become thoroughly European. He spoke with enthusiasm of the Russian caracter. "Paris and all western Europe is but the front door of America," he said. "Out there something new is growing up." 3

When we had talked for some time another man came in who at once began to condemn the Russian revolution and all social revolutions. 4

"When revolutions come art and the impulse toward beauty dies. All men think of improving their material welfare."

It was an interesting moment. K B wavered. In some way the revolutionary idea had taken hold of him. Then his passion for swinging off his own center and giving himself to the impulses of others took hold on him and his loyalty to the Russians and their social experiment became weak. 5

I have known K B for years. All men and most women who come into contact with him love him. It be perhaps that they love what of themselves they see reflected in him. 6

Walked with P in the garden of the Palais Royal. We talked of America, both agreeing that while American cities were all comparatively ugly nothing could tempt us to come away to live permanently in a European city. We agreed that it was in some way a man's part to play the hand fate had delt him in life. 7

I wondered if—were a man born over here—his note in life would be essentially different. P thought not. "There is something men are striving for now that is bigger than nationalities" he said. "The effort to go down into the hidden parts of ourselves and find out about people down there hasn't much to do with nationalities." 8

In a cafe a Parisian said to me, "It is as bad not to marry as to marry. Both plans in life are unsuccessful." 9

A night of love and love making. You go into the little park back of Notre Dame, you stand on many bridges, you go to see how that, when the moonlight falls on it, the Louvre looks a white frozen things. Everywhere lovers. Lips are being pressed to lips. Womens bodies are being pressed closely against the bodies of men. The lovers are in all the little dark places, on the bridges, on the stairway leading down to the dark river. A young girls body is held tightly against the trunk of a tree in the shadows of Notre Dame. A bearded man is holding it there. He presses his great body against it. The lovers are all silent. 10

Americans make a great mistake in being timid and in staying about hotels where other Americans live. Here, as everywhere it is the common people who receive you most generously, who are delighted to help you in your difficulties with the language, who take you into their everyday life. 11

A Frenchman and his wife who have lived in America have been entertaining some wealthy American friends. The American men wanted to see the night life of Paris and have spent huge sums doing it. What they have got is a specially prepared stage set for them. They and their wives who have been in the big shops throwing money about have been cheated glo- 12 riously. My friend the Frenchman and his wife are rather pleased at what has happened to these Americans and I sympathise with their feeling.

A French girl leaning out a window I saw in a village, two women 13 working in a field, their bodies bending and unbending slowly, the librare at the chateau at Fontainebleau, to sit in the far corner of the court late in the afternoon when everyone has gone away and look at Saint Chapelle, the spire of Saint Chapelle, seen at night from a bridge, Jacques in the early morning with women sewing in the little park and carts rattling past in the street, an old workman washing his shirt in the Seine, his bare back very strong, a beautifully dressed aristocrat among women who alighted from a motor, the Louve at night, in the late afternoon, in the morning, the rose window on the side of Notre Dame that faces the river—this seen at night with the three ghostly stone figures stepping down from above, an old woman with a pipe in her mouth at the tiller of a barge on the Seine, the upper chapel of S. C. in the early afternoon with the light flooding in, a garden on the hill in the old village of Provence, the lovely wood carving on doors in many old buildings, the singing of a nightingale at night in the city. To sit in a cafe drinking and reading, now and then to glance up at people passing. To accept France as you can accept America, thinking of it only as a place you dont understand—to drink beer with men and women you love, in a cafe, under a giant tree, in the forest of Fontaine-bleau.

•　•　•

There are places that must be seen alone. The exclamations of people 14 terrify, they are like whiplashes on tender flesh. Even intelligent comment is hurtful. One does not receive the caress of beauty thro the intellect. It creeps upon you or flashes down on you like a stroke of lightning. There is the necessity of readjustment, of rebuilding something within. Every new and beautiful thing seen destroys while it seals [heals?]. You are a tender hurt, shattered thing emerging from the womb of some great mother. Silence and solitude the sweet, the golden thing. Long after perhaps we shall speak to each other.

•　•　•

In a castle where kings, emperors, queens, the mistresses of kings have 15 lived. The guide escorts a troop of people into a room where one of these women has lived. He makes little oily jokes. The women in the party giggle. The men think thoughts of lying in beds with queens. There is a combined effort to invade the lives of these queen, mistresses of queen, kings, emperors. It is as though we all threw mud at them. There is a deep fear in all of us. We are afraid that the great may after all have been great.

A man, an artist, an American who has lived in Paris for 20 years. To   16
dine with him. Three times during the evening he said the same thing. "A
man is of no importance who hasn't his roots deep in his native soil." There
was something tragic in his insistence. "Can't you go back?" I asked. "Not
now. I have blown about too long. I'm an empty thing."

There was in his face something shrewd, yankee but his accent was   17
English. All evening I kept remembering certain, dry, shrewd horse owners
I knew long ago. He was like a man who has taken horses from track to
track, all over the world, but has never won a race.

MUSINGS

The last sentence in each of the above sections neatly sums up Anderson's
thoughts on the subject. In his description of K B he comments, "All men
and most women who come into contact with him love him. It be perhaps
that they love what of themselves they see reflected in him." Or, "There is
a deep fear in all of us. We are afraid that the great may after all have been
great."

Try starting with a truism or some well-known proverb and describe an
incident that illustrates the idea.

VIRGINIA WOOLF (1882–1941)

Considered one of the most influential writers of the twentieth century, Virginia Woolf was born to a distinguished family who actively appreciated the arts. Unable to attend school because of frequent illness, she was exposed at an early age to her father's extensive library and a rich cultural world within her own home; art, literature, and politics were discussed daily by her family and their friends. In many ways her life was tragic. Her half sister's mental illness and her cousin's madness from an accidental head injury clouded her childhood and youth. Quentin Bell in his 1972 biography alleged that Woolf was sexually abused by her half brother. Whether from genetic or environmental causes, she suffered from depression and mental illness most of her life.

In 1912 she married Leonard Woolf, who sustained and nurtured her until her death. Calling herself "a confirmed melancholic," Woolf finally committed suicide in 1941 after several failed attempts by weighting her pockets down with rocks and walking into the Ouse River. She left a note for her husband declaring: "I am doing what seems the best thing to do . . . if anybody could have saved me it would have been you."

Woolf's early novels, Mrs. Dalloway *(1925) and* To the Lighthouse *(1927), established her place in the literary world. She was far ahead of her own time and argued with force and eloquence for the rights of women;* A Room of One's Own *has become a canonical feminist text. Woolf was recognized a half century after her death as a leading contributor to the development of the modern English novel. As John Lehman comments, "one can truly say that she enlarged the sensibility of her time, and changed English literature."*

In this day-by-day account of the bombing of London in World War II, Woolf contemplates her daily activities and ponders her death. She reacts to the loss of her home: "Exhilaration at losing possessions—save at times I want my books and chairs and carpets and beds—how I worked to buy them—one by one—And the pictures. . . . But its odd—the relief at losing possessions." It was not long after she wrote these entries, however, that she succumbed to despair and committed suicide. Woolf was a prolific diarist, and her entries were collected by her husband after her death and published in 1953.

The Bombing of London

Thursday 5 September 1941   Hot, hot, hot. Record heat wave,   1
record summer if we kept records this summer. At 2.30 a plane zooms; ten
minutes later air raid sounds; twenty later, all clear. Hot, I repeat; and
doubt if I'm a poet. An idea. All writers are unhappy. The picture of the
world in books is thus too dark. The wordless are the happy; women in
cottage gardens. Now, in my nightgown, to walk on the marshes.

Saturday 7 September 1941 An air raid in progress. Planes zooming. 2
No, that one's gone over very quick and loud. Couldn't see if it were English. More planes over the house, going I suppose to London, which is
raided every night.

Tuesday 10 September 1941 Back from half a day in London—per- 3
haps our strangest visit. Mecklenburgh Square roped off. Wardens there,
not allowed in. The house about thirty yards from ours struck at one this
morning by a bomb. Completely ruined. Another bomb in the Square still
unexploded. We walked round the back. The house was still smouldering.
That is a great pile of bricks. Underneath all the people who had gone
down to their shelter. Scraps of cloth hanging to the bare walls at the side
still standing. A looking glass I think swinging. Like a tooth knocked
out—a clean cut. Our house undamaged. The garage man at the back—
blear eyed and jerky—told us he had been blown out of his bed by the explosion; made to take shelter in a church. He said the Jerrys had been over
for three nights trying to bomb King's Cross. So we went on to Gray's Inn.
Left the car and saw Holborn. A vast gap at the top of Chancery Lane.
Smoking still. Some great shop entirely destroyed: the hotel opposite like
a shell. Heaps of blue green glass in the road at Chancery Lane. Men
breaking off fragments left in the frames. Then to the *New Statesman* office: windows broken, but house untouched. We went over it. Deserted.
Wet passages. Glass on stairs. Doors locked. So back to the car. A great
block of traffic. The cinema behind Mme Tussaud's torn open: the stage
visible; some decoration swinging. All the Regent's Park houses with broken windows, but undamaged. And then miles and miles of ordinary
streets—all Bayswater—as usual. Streets empty. Faces set and eyes bleared.
Then at Wimbledon a siren—people began running. We drove, through
almost empty streets, as fast as possible. Horses taken out of the shafts.
Cars pulled up. The people I think of now are the very grimy [Blooms-
bury] lodging house keepers; with another night to face: old wretched
women standing at their doors; dirty, miserable. Well—as Nessa said on
the phone, its coming very near.

Wednesday 11 September 1941 Churchill has just spoken. A clear, 4
measured, robust speech. Says the invasion is being prepared. Its for the
next two weeks apparently if at all. Ships and barges massing at French
ports. The bombing of London of course preparation to invasion. Our
majestic city—&c, which touches me, for I feel London majestic. Another
raid last night on London. Time bomb struck the Palace. John rang up.
Wants the Press moved at once. L. is to go up on Friday. Our windows are
broken John says. Mecklenburgh Square evacuated.

We count now on an air raid about 8.30. Anyhow, whether or not, we 5 hear the sinister sawing noise about then, which loudens and fades; then a pause; then another comes. "They're at it again" we say as we sit, I doing my work, L. making cigarettes. Now and then there's a thud. The windows shake. So we know London is raided again.

Thursday 12 September 1941   A gale has risen. Weather broken. Ter-   6
rific air traffic last night. But the raid beaten off by new London barrage. This is cheering. If we can hold out this week—next week—week after— if the weather's turned—if the force of the raids on London is broken— We go up tomorrow to see John about moving Press; to patch the windows, rescue valuables, and get letters—if that is we're allowed in the Square.

Friday 13 September 1941   Just back from half day in London. Raid,   7
unheard by us, started outside Wimbledon. Saw a pink brick shelter. Twice we left. More guns. Came back. At last started, keeping an eye on shelters and people's behaviour. Reached Russell Hotel. Loud gunfire. We sheltered. Started for Mecklenburgh Square: met John, who said the Square still closed; so lunched in the hotel. Decided the Press emergency—to employ Garden City Press [Letchworth]—in twenty minutes. Raid still on. Walked to Mecklenburgh Square. Refused admittance. John told us the story of Monday night. He rather white and shaky. Left him with distant guns firing. Started back. All clear in Marylebone High Street.

Saturday 14 September 1941   A sense of invasion—that is lorries of   8
soldiers and machines—like cranes—walloping along to Newhaven. An air raid is on. A little pop rattle which I take to be machine guns, just gone off. Planes soaring and roaring. Mabel comes out and looks. Asks if we want fish fried or boiled. As the result of a friendly cool talk it's settled, I think, that she leaves here. A great relief. I like being alone in our little boat. I like provisioning and seeing all's shipshape and not having dependents.

The great advantage of this page is that it gives me a fidget ground. Fid-   9
gets: caused by losing at bowls and invasion; caused by another howling banshee, by having no book I must read; and so on. I think I will begin my new book by reading Ifor Evans' sixpenny Penguin [*A Short History of English Literature*]. And whatever happens I will settle and sun on the moment. Fifty-eight—not so many more. I sometimes think about violent death. Who's whistling in the churchyard? Keep out the war from this page, now and then.

Sunday 15 September 1941   No invasion yet. Rumours that it was   10
attempted, but barges sunk with great loss. Raids over Brighton this after-

noon. Mabel goes tomorrow; so pray God the Church Bells don't ring tonight. Now we go to our last Cook cooked dinner for I don't know how long. Could it be the end of resident servants for ever? This I pray this lovely fitful evening, as well as the usual Damn Hitler prayer.

Monday 16 September 1941   Well, we're alone in our ship. Mabel stumped off, with her bunions, carrying her bags, at 10. Thank you for all your kindness, she said the same to us both. "I hope we shall meet again" I said. She said Oh no doubt—thinking I referred to death. So that five years' uneasy mute but very passive and calm relation is over.

To Charleston this afternoon, after provisioning for our siege in Lewes. Great air traffic all night—some loud explosions. I listened for Church Bells, thinking largely I admit, of finding ourselves prisoned here with Mabel. She thought the same. Said that if one is to be killed one will be killed. Prefers death in a Holloway shelter playing cards—naturally—to death here.

Tuesday 17 September 1941   No invasion. High wind. Yesterday in the Public Library I took down a book of Peter Lucas's criticism. This turned me against writing my book. Turned me against all Lit. crit.; these so clever, so airless, so fleshless ingenuities and attempts to prove—that T. S. Eliot for example is a worse critic than F. L. Lucas. I dipped for five minutes and put the book back depressed. The man asked What do you want Mrs Woolf? I said a history of English Literature. But was sickened, I couldn't look. There were so many.

Wednesday 18 September 1941   "We have need of all our courage" are the words that come to the surface this morning; on hearing that all our windows are broken, ceilings down, and most of our china smashed at Mecklenburgh Square. The bomb exploded. Why did we ever leave Tavistock?—what's the good of thinking that? The Press—what remains—is to be moved to Letchworth. A grim morning. But I did forge ahead with *Pointz Hall* all the same.

Thursday 19 September 1941   Another loud night. Another bad raid. Oxford Street now smashed. John Lewis, Selfridge, Bourne & Hollingsworth, all my old haunts. Also British Museum forecourt. A gale and rain here.

Saturday 21 September 1941   We've just bottled our honey. Very still and warm today. So invasion becomes possible. The river high; all softly blue and milky; autumn quiet—twelve planes in perfect order, back from the fight, pass overhead.

Wednesday 25 September 1941 All day—Monday—in London, in 17
the flat; dark; carpets nailed to windows; ceilings down in patches; heaps
of grey dust and china under kitchen table; back rooms untouched. A
lovely September day—tender—three days of tender weather. John came.
We are moved to Letchworth. *Roger* surprisingly sells. Invasion again with-
draws.

Thursday 26 September 1941 A talk on the phone with Nessa. [She] 18
held the trump card. "Both our studios have been destroyed. The roofs
fallen in. Still burning. Pictures burnt." So I had to pipe low. My fallen
ceilings a trifle. Gathering apples all the afternoon. German raider comes
over. Shots fired at Asheham. Bombs towards Seaford. Writing I remain
unmoved. Only a German bomber? Oh that's all—No I didn't look out—
Consider this remark last year—still more, ten years, still more fifty years
ago. In flush with *Pointz Hall* thank God.

Saturday 29 September 1941 A bomb dropped so close I cursed L. 19
for slamming the window. I was writing to Hugh, and the pen jumped
from my fingers. I was thinking (among other things): that this is a lazy
life. Breakfast in bed. Read in bed. Bath. Order dinner. Out to Lodge.
After rearranging my room (turning table to get the sun: Church on right;
window left; a new very lovely view) tune up, with cigarette: write till 12;
stop; visit L.; look at papers; return; type till 1. Listen in. Lunch. Read papers. Walk to Southease. Back 3. Gather and arrange apples. Tea. Write a
letter. Bowls. Type again. Read Michelet and write here. Cook dinner.
Music. Embroidery. 9.30 read (or sleep) till 11.30. Bed. Compare with the
old London day. Three afternoons someone coming. One night, dinner
party. Saturday a walk. Thursday shopping. Tuesday going to tea with
Nessa. One City walk. Telephone ringing. L. to meetings. Kingsley Martin
or Robson bothering—that was an average week; with Friday to Monday
here.
 I think, now we're marooned, I ought to cram in a little more reading. 20
Yet why? A happy, a very free, and disengaged—a life that rings from one
simple melody to another. Yes; why not enjoy this after all those years of
the other?
 Nessa rang up. A statue and frigidaire alone salved. 21

Thursday 10 October 1941 Rather flush of ideas, because I have had 22
an idle day, a non-writing day—what a relief once in a way—a Vita talking day. About what? Oh the war; bombs; which house hit, which not;
then our books—all very ample easy and satisfying. She has a hold on life,
knows plants and their minds and bodies; [is] large and tolerant and mod-
est, with her hands loosely upon so many reins: sons; Harold; garden;

farm. Humorous too, and deeply, I mean awkwardly, dumbly affectionate. I'm glad that our love has weathered so well.

Saturday 12 October 1941   If it were not treasonable to say so, a day   23
like this is almost too—I won't say happy: but amenable. I can't stop looking: October blooms; brown plough; and the fading and freshening of the marsh. Now the mist comes up. And one thing's "pleasant" after another: breakfast, writing, walking, tea, bowls, reading, sweets, bed. But I was thinking I must intensify. In London, now, or two years ago, I'd be owling through the streets. More pack and thrill than here. So I must supply that—how? I think book inventing. Scraps of memoirs come so coolingly to my mind. Wound up by those three little articles (one sent today) I unwound a page about Thoby.

But I want to look back on these war years as years of positive some-   24
thing or other. Queer the contraction of life to the village radius. All our friends are isolated over winter fires. No cars. No petrol. Trains uncertain. And we on our lovely free autumn island. But I will read Dante.

MUSINGS

Woolf's diary records the days' events during the traumatic blitzkrieg of London which destroyed and scarred so much of the city during World War II. She pictures the devastation left by the bombings through the generous use of metaphors and similes: "A looking glass I think swinging. Like a tooth knocked out—a clean cut." But, "whatever happens I will settle and sun on the moment."

Describe some scene of devastation, such as a vacant corner lot, an abandoned building, or a trash heap. Look for details—individual objects—and try to use appropriate metaphors and similes.

MAY SARTON (1912–1995)

May Sarton is best known for her poetry and the journals that chronicle her daily life. She was a popular lecturer and taught creative writing at a number of universities, including Harvard. Widely honored during her career, Sarton received many awards for her writing and more than a dozen honorary degrees. She was also greatly respected for the dignity of her life as chronicled in her poetry and journals. In her journals Sarton writes eloquently of her love for her home by the sea, where she is surrounded by the books and plants that she treasures.

In Journal of Solitude *Sarton writes of her loneliness after the death of Judy, her longtime companion. Four years later at age 61, she writes* The House by the Sea, *from which the following is taken. Sarton writes of "growing into solitude" as "one way of growing to the end." She also speaks of being "nourished" by visits from "new friends, old friends who are passing by, for everyone comes to Maine sooner or later." The following selection describes such a visit from a young admirer who "breaks down the wall" of her solitude.*

A Visit with Jody

Thursday, January 8th   My hope that I would have a whole series of empty days, days without interruption, days in which to think and laze, (for creation depends as much on laziness as on hard work), was, of course, impossible. Three days ago in the morning a young woman called Jody who had written me in November to say she might turn up, hitchhiking from Ohio, phoned from Portland and asked to come over. I'm afraid I was not exactly welcoming . . . I felt dismay at the prospect, and never got back to work that morning.

She came yesterday, in workman's boots, overalls, a thin short coat (how not freeze to death at below zero yesterday here?), and a tam-o'-shanter, carrying the usual canvas tote over her shoulder. And I was suddenly delighted!

I met her at Foster's and drove her in over what is now a nearly impassable road on foot, and very slippery even in a car, every rut glare ice. I was delighted because Jody, unlike anyone I have ever met, perhaps represents a new breed. She is not, I feel sure, unique in her thirst for rootless wandering from place to place—Berkeley for a time, then New Orleans, now perhaps Boston. In her knapsack three of my books and a slim blue notebook in which she jots down poems. I liked her face at once, the quirky

1

2

3

mouth and keen blue eyes behind huge gold-rimmed glasses, mousy hair all over the place.

Setting her down here in front of the big fireplace in the library, I felt disgustingly rich and safe. But after all I am over sixty and she is twenty-three. When I was twenty-three I too wandered (though in those days only real bums hitchhiked) and had many love affairs and worried about them. But there are differences. Jody takes LSD now and then. I think she takes it when she gets scared, scared of herself and where she is going, and realizes that time is running out. Soon she will be twenty-five, then thirty.

When I asked her why she thought my work attracted the young now (as it had not before), she answered, "Because it's so trippy" (that was about the poems, many of which she could quote from memory, especially the Santa Fe one "Meditation in Sunlight," which she had read when on LSD). And when I asked what she meant by that, she said, "Cosmic, relating." I suppose that intensity of feeling plus detachment (the detachment of the craftsman) is a little like LSD in its effect. I explained that I couldn't take drugs because I had to keep my mind clear and to tamper with it would be too frightening.

She spoke warmly about her father (a mechanic) and mother, but feels stifled in the small college town where she grew up—and that I understand perfectly. That orange has been sucked dry. Her brother is "brilliant, but close to becoming an alcoholic." What does he want out of life? "To be loved."

She is religious, was tempted to join a Christian commune in Columbus, and may still do so. Under the anarchic life rooted nowhere there is, of course, a tremendous hunger for roots and for community. I suggested that, since she takes odd jobs just to keep alive, why not take a meaningful job such as working in a nursing home or insane asylum?

As we talked, I came to a fresh understanding about dedication and responsibility. How hope to find roots without taking the far greater risk of commitment? Far greater even than the risks attendant upon an unrooted, floating-free life that may, at first glance, appear "adventurous" and/or "dangerous"? The leap into commitment, in love, or in work, or in religion, demands far greater courage. It is just from that that Jody draws back, because she isn't sure enough of anything. What one fears for such a person is an accidental taking root simply because of circumstances . . . at the moment Jody is staying with a friend in Portland and next door lives a man alone with his two small children. Perhaps in the five days Jody has been there, he has fallen in love with her. He is a mechanic and she is drawn to this kind of nonintellectual. What if she "floats" into a permanent relationship there? Finds herself caught (because, after all, why *not* settle down?) bringing up another woman's children, almost by accident, no real commitment having been made at first?

Jody has not even begun to realize what being dedicated (I prefer that 9
word to the overused "committed") to an art means. She jots down poem
ideas, but never revises, never breaks it down, uses it as she uses everything
else for a moment's interest or kick. The writing of poems is the best way I
know to understand what is really going on inside the psyche, but to do it
you have to use your mind and you have to look at it as a craft not a self-
indulgence. There is a huge gulf here between Jody and myself at her age.
For I was writing poems and I knew that in doing that I was serving something greater than myself, or at least other than myself. One does not "find
oneself" by pursuing one's self, but on the contrary by pursuing something else and learning through some discipline or routine (even the routine of making beds) who one is and wants to be.

At four I drove Jody back to Route I and left her there, by the snowy 10
barrier left by the ploughs. I felt like a mother who has to let her daughter
go, even into danger, must not hold her back, but I left her there with an
awful pang. I had slipped some chocolates into her knapsack and gave her
a warm mohair scarf. But what else had I given? Not good advice—that
comes a dime a dozen. But perhaps (I hope) the sign that one may be
rooted and surrounded by plants and beautiful objects and still not be a
square, still be alive and open.

And what did I learn? That it's all very well to shut myself up to write 11
poems, but life is going to break down the wall—and it had better!

MUSINGS

Sarton describes Jody and touches briefly on what she learns of Jody's behavior. However, she provides only those details that lead her to speculate
on the encounter. More important than the visit itself, Sarton writes of her
own reactions and outlines what she has learned.

How often do you ask yourself the question "What did I learn?" as Sarton
does? It is a useful habit for a writer. Ask yourself that question about a recent encounter with another person and write your answers. Select details
carefully and include only those that are pertinent to your speculations.

EDWARD ABBEY (1927–1989)

"Henry, I say, what the devil do you mean?" In his book Down the River *(1982) Edward Abbey questions Henry David Thoreau, his imaginary companion. Abbey's question follows a long quotation from Thoreau, an environmentalist who lived nearly a century earlier in a simpler, less populated world. Abbey's rejoinders are biting, often severe, but his work rings with his passion for the preservation of the wilderness.*

Abbey worked as a ranger for the National Park Service; out of this experience came his love of the open desert spaces of the Southwest. His first successful book, Desert Solitaire, *helped to initiate the early environmentalist movement of the 1960s. One critic stated that Abbey's work as a park ranger predated the era of "the parked trailers, their windows blue tinged at night while the inmates, instead of watching the desert stars, watch TV and listen to the canned laughter of Hollywood." That same critic hailed Abbey as a "voice crying in the wilderness,* for *the wilderness." Abbey was a prolific writer and the author of a number of novels and works of nonfiction, none of which attained the success of* Desert Solitaire. *He was both a Fulbright and Guggenheim Fellow and received the Western Heritage Award for Best Novel in 1963.*

Down the River with Thoreau

November 5, 1980   We did not go far yesterday. We rowed and drifted   1
two miles down the river and then made camp for the night on a silt bank at
the water's edge. There had been nobody but ourselves at Mineral Bottom
but the purpose, nonetheless, was to "get away from the crowd," as Rennie
Russell explained. We understood. We cooked our supper by firelight and
flashlight, ate beneath the stars. Somebody uncorked a bottle of wine. Rennie played his guitar, his friend Ted Seeley played the fiddle, and Dusty Teale
played the mandolin. We all sang. Our music ascended to the sky, echoing
softly from the cliffs. The river poured quietly seaward, making no sound
but here and there, now and then, a gurgle of bubbles, a trilling of ripples off
the hulls of our half-beached boats.

Sometime during the night a deer stalks nervously past our camp. I   2
hear the noise and, when I get up before daybreak, I see the dainty heart-
shaped tracks. I kindle the fire and build the morning's first pot of black,
rich, cowboy coffee, and drink in solitude the first cupful, warming my
hands around the hot cup. The last stars fade, the sky becomes brighter,
passing through the green glow of dawn into the fiery splendor of sunrise.

The others straggle up, one by one, and join me around the fire. We stare   3 at the shining sky, the shining river, the high canyon walls, mostly in silence, until one among us volunteers to begin breakfast. Yes, indeed, we are a lucky little group. Privileged, no doubt. At ease out here on the edge of nowhere, loafing into the day, enjoying the very best of the luckiest of nations, while around the world billions of other humans are sweating, fighting, striving, procreating, starving. As always, I try hard to feel guilty. Once again I fail.

"If I knew for a certainty that some man was coming to my house with   4
the conscious intention of doing me good," writes our Henry [Thoreau], "I would run for my life."

We Americans cannot save the world. Even Christ failed at that. We   5
Americans have our hands full in trying to save ourselves. And we've barely tried. The Peace Corps was a lovely idea—for idle and idealistic young Americans. Gave them a chance to see a bit of the world, learn something. But as an effort to "improve" the lives of other peoples, the inhabitants of the so-called underdeveloped nations (our nation is overdeveloped), it was an act of cultural arrogance. A piece of insolence. The one thing we could do for a country like Mexico, for example, is to stop every illegal immigrant at the border, give him a good rifle and a case of ammunition, and send him home. Let the Mexicans solve their customary problems in their customary manner.

If this seems a cruel and sneering suggestion, consider the current   6
working alternative: leaving our borders open to unlimited immigration until—and it won't take long—the social, political, economic life of the United States is reduced to the level of life in Juarez. Guadalajara. Mexico City. San Salvador. Haiti. India. To a common peneplain of overcrowding, squalor, misery, oppression, torture, and hate.

What could Henry have said to this supposition? He lived in a relatively   7
spacious America of only 24 million people, of whom one-sixth were slaves. A mere 140 years later we have grown to a population ten times larger, and we are nearly all slaves. We are slaves in the sense that we depend for our daily survival upon an expand-or-expire agro-industrial empire—a crackpot machine—that the specialists cannot comprehend and the managers cannot manage. Which is, furthermore, devouring world resources at an exponential rate. We are, most of us, dependent employees.

What would Henry have said? He said, "In wildness is the preservation   8
of the world." He said, somewhere deep in his thirty-nine-volume *Journal*, "I go to my solitary woodland walks as the homesick return to their homes." He said, "It would be better if there were but one inhabitant to a square mile, as where I live." Perhaps he did sense what was coming. His last words, whispered from the deathbed, are reported to us as being "moose . . . Indians . . ."

Looking upriver toward Tidwell Bottom, a half mile away, I see a lone   9
horse grazing on the bunch grass, the Indian rice grass, the saltbush, and

sand sage of the river's old floodplain. One horse, unhobbled and untended, thirty miles from the nearest ranch or human habitation, it forages on its own. That horse, I'm thinking, may be the one that got away from me years ago, in another desert place, far from here. Leave it alone. That particular horse has found at least a temporary solution to the question of survival. Survival with honor, I mean, for what other form of survival is worth the trouble? That horse has chosen, or stumbled into, solitude and independence. Let it be. Thoreau defined happiness as "simplicity, independence, magnanimity and trust."

But solitude? Horses are gregarious beasts, like us. This lone horse on   10
Tidwell Bottom may be paying a high price for its freedom, perhaps in some form of equine madness. A desolation of the soul corresponding to the grand desolation of the landscape that lies beyond these canyon walls.

"I never found the companion that was so companionable as solitude,"   11
writes Henry. "To be in company, even with the best, is soon wearisome and dissipating."

Perhaps his ghost will forgive us if we suspect an element of *extrava-*   12
gance in the above statement. Thoreau had a merry time in the writing of *Walden;* it is an exuberant book, crackling with humor, good humor, gaiety, with joy in the power of words and phrases, in ideas and emotions so powerful they tend constantly toward the outermost limit of communicable thought.

"The sun is but a morning star." Ah yes, but what exactly does that   13
mean? Maybe the sun is also an evening star. Maybe the phrase had no exact meaning even in Thoreau's mind. He was, at times, what we today might call a put-on artist. He loved to shock and exasperate; Emerson complains of Henry's "contrariness." The power of Thoreau's assertion lies not in its meaning but in its exhilarating suggestiveness. Like poetry and music, the words imply more than words can make explicit.

Henry was no hermit. Hardly even a recluse. His celebrated cabin at   14
Walden Pond—some of his neighbors called it a "shanty"—was two miles from Concord Common. A half-hour walk from pond to post office. Henry lived in it for only two years and two months. He had frequent human visitors, sometimes too many, he complained, and admitted that his daily rambles took him almost every day into Concord. When he tired of his own cooking and his own companionship he was always welcome at the Emersons' for a free dinner. Although it seems that he earned his keep there. He worked on and off for years as Emerson's household handyman, repairing and maintaining things that the great Ralph Waldo was too busy or too incompetent to attend to himself. "Emerson," noted Thoreau in a letter, "is too much the gentleman to push a wheelbarrow." When Mrs. Emerson complained that the chickens were scratching up her flower beds, Henry attached little cloth booties to the chickens' feet. A witty fel-

low. Better and easier than keeping them fenced in. When Emerson was off on his European lecture tours, Thoreau would look after not only Emerson's house but also Emerson's children and wife.

We shall now discuss the sexual life of Henry David Thoreau.   15

November 6, 1980   Awaking as usual sometime before the dawn, frost   16 on my beard and sleeping bag, I see four powerful lights standing in a vertical row on the eastern sky. They are Saturn, Jupiter, Mars, and, pale crescent on a darkened disc, the old moon. The three great planets seem to be rising from the cusps of the moon. I stare for a long time at this strange, startling apparition, a spectacle I have never before seen in all my years on planet Earth. What does it mean? If ever I've seen a portent in the sky this must be it. Spirit both forms and informs the universe, thought the New England transcendentalists, of whom Thoreau was one; all Nature, they believed, is but symbolic of a greater spiritual reality beyond. And within.

Watching the planets, I stumble about last night's campfire, breaking   17 twigs, filling the coffeepot. I dip waterbuckets in the river; the water chills my hands. I stare long at the beautiful, dimming lights in the sky but can find there no meaning other than the lights' intrinsic beauty. As far as I can perceive, the planets signify nothing but themselves. "Such suchness," as my Zen friends say. And that is all. And that is enough. And that is more than we can make head or tail of.

"Reality is fabulous," said Henry; "be it life or death, we crave nothing   18 but reality." And goes on to describe in precise, accurate, glittering detail the most subtle and minute aspects of life in and about his Walden Pond; the "pulse" of water skaters, for instance, advancing from shore across the surface of the lake. Appearance *is* reality, Thoreau implies; or so it appears to me. I begin to think he outgrew transcendentalism rather early in his career, at about the same time that he was overcoming the influence of his onetime mentor Emerson; Thoreau and the transcendentalists had little in common—in the long run—but their long noses, as a friend of mine has pointed out.

Scrambled eggs, bacon, green chiles for breakfast, with hot *salsa*,   19 toasted tortillas, and leftover baked potatoes sliced and fried. A gallon or two of coffee, tea and—for me—the usual breakfast beer. Henry would not have approved of this gourmandising. To hell with him. I do not approve of his fastidious puritanism. For one who claims to crave nothing but reality, he frets too much about *purity.* Purity, purity, he preaches, in the most unctuous of his many sermons, a chapter of *Walden* called "Higher Laws."

"The wonder is how they, how you and I," he writes, "can live this   20 slimy, beastly life, eating and drinking. . . ." Like Dick Gregory, Thoreau recommends a diet of raw fruits and vegetables; like a Pythagorean, he finds even beans impure, since the flatulence that beans induce disturbs his more ethereal meditations. (He would not agree with most men that "farting is such sweet sorrow.") But confesses at one point to a sudden violent lust for wild woodchuck, devoured raw. No wonder; Henry was probably anemic.

He raised beans not to eat but to sell—his only cash crop. During his lifetime his beans sold better than his books. When a publisher shipped back to Thoreau 706 unsellable copies of his *A Week on the Concord and Merrimack Rivers* (the author had himself paid for the printing of the book), Henry noted in his *Journal,* "I now have a library of 900 volumes, over 700 of which I wrote myself." 21

Although professing disdain for do-gooders, Thoreau once lectured a poor Irish immigrant, a neighbor, on the advisability of changing his ways. "I tried to help him with my experience. . . ." but the Irishman, John Field, was only bewildered by Thoreau's earnest preaching. "Poor John Field!" Thoreau concludes; "I trust he does not read this, unless he will improve by it. . . ." 22

Nathaniel Hawthorne, who lived in Concord for a time and knew Thoreau, called him "an intolerable bore." 23

On the subject of sex, as we would expect, Henry betrays a considerable nervous agitation. "The generative energy, which, when we are loose, dissipates and makes us unclean, when we are continent invigorates and inspires us. Chastity is the flowering of man. . . ." (But not of flowers?) "We are conscious of an animal in us, which awakens in proportion as our higher nature slumbers. It is reptile and sensual. . . ." "He is blessed who is assured that the animal is dying out in him day by day. . . ." In a letter to his friend Harrison Blake, Henry writes: "What the essential difference between man and woman is, that they should be thus attracted to one another, no one has satisfactorily answered." 24

Poor Henry. We are reminded of that line in Whitman (another great American oddball), in which our good gray poet said of women, "They attract with a fierce, undeniable attraction," while the context of the poem makes it clear that Whitman himself found young men and boys much more undeniable. 25

Poor Thoreau. But he could also write, in the late essay "Walking," "The wildness of the savage is but a faint symbol of the awful ferity with which good men and lovers meet." Ferity—now there's a word. What could it have meant to Thoreau? Our greatest nature lover did not have a loving nature. A woman acquaintance of Henry's said she'd sooner take the arm of an elm tree than that of Thoreau. 26

Poor Henry David Thoreau. His short (forty-five years), quiet, passionate life apparently held little passion for the opposite sex. His relationship with Emerson's wife Lidian was no more than a long brother-sisterly 27 friendship. Thoreau never married. There is no evidence that he ever enjoyed a mutual love affair with any human, female or otherwise. He once fell in love with and proposed marriage to a young woman by the name of Ellen Sewall; she rejected him, bluntly and coldly. He tried once more with a girl named Mary Russell; she turned him down. For a young man of Thoreau's hypersensitive character, these must have been cruel, perhaps disabling blows to what little male ego and confidence he possessed to begin with. It left him shattered, we may assume, on that side of life; he never again approached a woman with romantic intentions on his mind. He became a professional bachelor, scornful of wives and marriage. He lived and probably died a virgin, pure as shriven snow. Except for those sensual reptiles coiling and uncoiling down in the root cellar of his being. Ah, purity!

But we make too much of this kind of thing nowadays. Modern men   28
and women are obsessed with the sexual; it is the only realm of primordial adventure still left to most of us. Like apes in a zoo, we spend our energies on the one field of play remaining; human lives otherwise are pretty well caged in by the walls, bars, chains, and locked gates of our industrial culture. In the relatively wild, free America of Henry's time there was plenty of opportunity for every kind of adventure, although Henry himself did not, it seems to me, take advantage of those opportunities. (He could have toured the Western plains with George Catlin!) He led an unnecessarily constrained existence, and not only in the "generative" region.

Thoreau the spinster-poet. In the year 1850, when Henry reached the   29
age of thirty-three, Emily Dickinson in nearby Amherst became twenty. Somebody should have brought the two together. They might have hit it off.

November 7, 1980

•   •   •

For an example of science in the whole and wholesome sense read   30
Thoreau's description of an owl's behavior in "Winter Visitors." Thoreau observes the living animal in its native habitat, and watches it for weeks. For an example of science in its debased sense take this: According to the L.A. *Times*, a psychologist in Los Angeles defends laboratory experimentation on captive dogs with the assertion that "little is known about the psychology of dogs." Anyone who has ever kept a dog knows more about dogs than that psychologist—who doubtless considers himself a legitimate scientist—will learn in a year of Sundays.

Or this: Researchers in San Francisco have confined chimpanzees in air-   31
tight glass cubicles (gas chambers) in order to study the effect of various dosages of chemically polluted air on these "manlike organisms." As if

there were not already available five million human inhabitants of the Los Angeles basin, and a hundred other places, ready, willing, and eager to supply personally informed testimony on the subject under scrutiny. Leaving aside any consideration of ethics, morality, and justice, there are more intelligent ways to study living creatures. Or nonliving creations: rocks have rights too.

That which today calls itself science gives us more and more informa- 32 tion, an indigestible glut of information, and less and less understanding. Thoreau was well aware of this tendency and foresaw its fatal consequences. He could see the tendency in himself, even as he partially succumbed to it. Many of the later *Journals* are filled with little but the enumeration of statistical data concerning such local Concord phenomena as the rise and fall of lake levels, or the thickness of the ice on Flint's Pond on a January morning. Tedious reading—pages and pages of "factoids," as Norman Mailer would call them—attached to no coherent theory, illuminated by neither insight nor outlook nor speculation.

Henry may have had a long-range purpose in mind but he did not live 33 long enough to fulfill it. Kneeling in the snow on a winter's day to count the tree rings in a stump, he caught the cold that led to his death on May 6, 1862. He succumbed not partially but finally to facticity.

Why'd you do it, Henry? I ask him through the flames. 34

The bearded face with the large, soft, dark eyes, mournful and thought- 35 ful as the face of Lincoln, smiles back at me but offers no answer. He evades the question by suggesting other questions in his better-known, "mystical" vein:

"There was a dead horse in the hollow by the path to my house, which 36 compelled me sometimes to go out of my way, especially in the night when the air was heavy, but the assurance it gave me of the strong appetite and inviolable health of Nature was my compensation for this. I love to see that Nature is so rife with life that myriads can be afforded to be sacrificed and suffered to prey on one another. . . . The impression made on a wise man is that of universal innocence. Compassion is a very untenable ground. It must be expeditious. Its pleadings will not bear to be stereotyped."

Henry, I say, what the devil do you mean? 37

He smiles again and says, "I observed a very small and graceful hawk, 38 like a nighthawk, alternately soaring like a ripple and tumbling a rod or two over and over, showing the underside of its wings, which gleamed like a satin ribbon in the sun. . . . The merlin it seemed to me it might be called; but I care not for its name. It was the most ethereal flight I have ever witnessed. It did not simply flutter like a butterfly, nor soar like the larger hawks, but it sported with proud reliance in the fields of the air. . . . It appeared to have no companion in the universe . . . and to need none but the morning and the ether with which it played. It was not lonely, but made all the earth lonely beneath it."

Very pretty, Henry. Are you speaking for yourself? I watch his lined, 39 gentle face, the face of his middle age (though he had no later) as recorded in photographs, and cannot help but read there the expression, engraved, of a patient, melancholy resignation. All babies look identical; boys and adolescents resemble one another, in their bewildered hopefulness, more than they differ. But eventually the inner nature of the man appears on his outer surface. Character begins to shine through. Year by year a man reveals himself, while those with nothing to show, show it. Differentiation becomes individuation. By the age of forty, if not before, a man is responsible for his face. The same is true of women too, certainly, although women, obeying the biological imperative, strive harder than men to preserve an appearance of youthfulness—the reproductive look—and lose it sooner. Appearance *is* reality.

Henry replies not to my question but, as befits a ghostly seer, to my 40 thought: "Nothing can rightly compel a simple and brave man to a vulgar sadness."

We'll go along with that, Henry; you've been accused of many things 41 but no one, to my knowledge, has yet accused you of vulgarity. Though Emerson, reacting to your night in jail for refusing to pay the poll tax, called the gesture "mean and skulking and in bad taste." In bad taste! How typically Emersonian. Robert Louis Stevenson too called you a "skulker" on the grounds that you preached more strongly than you practiced, later recanting when he learned of your activity in the antislavery movement. The contemporary author Alan Harrington, in his book *The Immortalist,* accuses you of writing, at times, like "an accountant of the spirit." That charge he bases on your vague remarks concerning immorality, and on such lines as "Goodness is the only investment that never fails."

Still other current critics, taking their cue from those whom Nabokov 42 specified as "the Viennese quacks," would deflect the force of your attacks on custom, organized religion, and the state by suggesting that you suffered from a complex of complexes, naturally including the castration complex and the Oedipus complex. Your defiance of authority, they maintain, was in reality no more than the rebelliousness of an adolescent rejecting his father—in this case the meek and mousy John Thoreau.

Whatever grain of truth may be in this diagnosis, such criticism betrays 43 the paternalistic condescension of these critics toward human beings in general. The good citizen, they seem to be saying, is like the obedient child; the rebellious man is a bad boy. "The people are like children," said our own beloved, gone but not forgotten, Richard Nixon. The psychiatric approach to dissidence has been most logically applied in the Soviet Union, where opposition to the state is regarded and treated as a form of mental illness.

In any case, Henry cannot be compelled to confess to a vulgar sadness.   44
The vulgarity resides in the tactics of literary Freudianism. Of the opposition. Psychoanalysis is the neurosis of the psychoanalyst—and of the psy-
choanalytic critic. Why should we bother any more with this garbage? I
thought we stopped talking about Freud back in 1952. Sometime near the
end of the Studebaker era.

Fading beyond the last flames of the fire, Henry lulls me to sleep with   45
one of his more soporific homilies:

"The light which puts out our eyes is darkness to us. Only that day   46
dawns to which we are awake. There is more day to dawn. The sun . . ."

Yes, yes, Henry, we know. How true. Whatever it means. How late it is.   47
Whatever the hour.

I rise from my log, heap the coals of the fire together, and by their glim-   48
mering light and the cold light of the stars fumble my way back and into
the luxury of my goosedown nest. Staring up at mighty Orion, trying to
count six of the seven Pleiades, a solemn thought comes to me: We Are
Not Alone.

I nuzzle my companion's cold nose, the only part of her not burrowed   49
deep in her sleeping bag. She stirs but does not wake. We're not alone, I
whisper in her ear. I know, she says; shut up and go to sleep. Smiling, I face
the black sky and the sapphire stars. Mark Twain was right. Better the savage wasteland with Eve than Paradise without her. Where she is, there is
Paradise.

Poor Henry.   50

And then I hear that voice again, far off but clear: "All Nature is my   51
bride."

MUSINGS

All through this selection Abbey chats with Thoreau, chastising him for
his insincerity and lack of understanding of true environmentalism. He
speaks with humor and a touch of bitterness at Thoreau's posturing and
hypocrisy, and "takes him to task" on his stand on sex and chastity.

Select a book, an article from a magazine, or a newspaper editorial with
which you disagree and present your point of view by writing a dialogue
between yourself and the author.

ANNE FRANK (1929–1945)

Anne Frank, a young Jewish girl living in what was then Holland, kept her diary from June 12, 1942 to August 1, 1944 while hiding from the Nazis, who were rounding up all Jews and sending them to concentration camps. The family had moved from Germany because of Nazi persecution, but as Nazi oppression increased in Holland the Frank family began preparing for their escape to a secret annex in a warehouse by carrying clothes and furniture piece by piece in order not to be suspected. When Anne's 16-year-old sister received a "call-up," which induced "visions of concentration camps and lonely cells," the family went into hiding, where they remained for two years.

Anne kept her diary faithfully, at first only for herself, but inspired by a broadcast in 1944 by Gerrit Bolkestein, a member of the Dutch government in exile, she decided to write a book based on her diary that would document the Nazi mistreatment of the Dutch people. Consequently, she began revising and editing her diary entries. Tragically, Ann never lived to see her dream come true. On August 4, 1944 all members of her family were arrested and sent to concentration camps, and Anne died a year later, either by starvation, illness, or gassing.

Two secretaries who worked in the warehouse found her diary scattered on the floor of the secret annex and later gave it to Anne's father, Otto Frank. In 1947, after long deliberation, he fulfilled Anne's wish and published the diary. He carefully expurgated sections that he felt might embarrass others or damage Anne's memory. When Otto Frank died he willed the manuscripts to the Netherlands State Institute for War Documentation in Amsterdam. A definitive edition of the full diary was published in 1991, edited by Otto H. Frank and Mirjam Pressler and translated into English by Susan Massotty. The following entries are taken from Otto Frank's original edition.

The Diary of a Young Girl

Hence, this diary. In order to enhance in my mind's eye the picture of the friend for whom I have waited so long, I don't want to set down a series of bald facts in a diary like most people do, but I want this diary itself to be my friend, and I shall call my friend Kitty. No one will grasp what I'm talking about if I begin my letters to Kitty just out of the blue, so, albeit unwillingly, I will start by sketching in brief the story of my life.

• • •

Tuesday, 7 March, 1944

Dear Kitty,

If I think now of my life in 1942, it all seems so unreal. It was quite a [2] different Anne who enjoyed that heavenly existence from the Anne who has grown wise within these walls. Yes, it was a heavenly life. Boy friends at every turn, about twenty friends and acquaintances of my own age, the darling of nearly all the teachers, spoiled from top to toe by Mummy and Daddy, lots of sweets, enough pocket money, what more could one want?

You will certainly wonder by what means I got around all these people. [3] Peter's word "attractiveness" is not altogether true. All the teachers were entertained by my cute answers, my amusing remarks, my smiling face, and my questioning looks. That is all I was—a terrible flirt, coquettish and amusing. I had one or two advantages, which kept me rather in favor. I was industrious, honest, and frank. I would never have dreamed of cribbing from anyone else. I shared my sweets generously, and I wasn't conceited.

Wouldn't I have become rather forward with so much admiration? It [4] was a good thing that in the midst of, at the height of, all this gaiety, I suddenly had to face reality, and it took me at least a year to get used to the fact that there was no more admiration forthcoming.

How did I appear at school? The one who thought of new jokes and [5] pranks, always "king of the castle," never in a bad mood, never a crybaby. No wonder everyone liked to cycle with me, and I got their attentions.

Now I look back at that Anne as an amusing, but very superficial girl, [6] who has nothing to do with the Anne of today. Peter said quite rightly about me: "If ever I saw you, you were always surrounded by two or more boys and a whole troupe of girls. You were always laughing and always the center of everything!"

What is left of this girl? Oh, don't worry, I haven't forgotten how to [7] laugh or to answer back readily. I'm just as good, if not better, at criticizing people, and I can still flirt if . . . I wish. That's not it though, I'd like that sort of life again for an evening, a few days, or even a week; the life which seems so carefree and gay. But at the end of that week, I should be dead beat and would be only too thankful to listen to anyone who began to talk about something sensible. I don't want followers, but friends, admirers who fall not for a flattering smile but for what one does and for one's character.

I know quite well that the circle around me would be much smaller. [8] But what does that matter, as long as one still keeps a few sincere friends?

Yet I wasn't entirely happy in 1942 in spite of everything; I often felt [9] deserted, but because I was on the go the whole day long, I didn't think about it and enjoyed myself as much as I could. Consciously or unconsciously, I tried to drive away the emptiness I felt with jokes and pranks.

Now I think seriously about life and what I have to do. One period of my life is over forever. The carefree schooldays are gone, never to return.

I don't even long for them any more; I have outgrown them, I can't just   10
only enjoy myself as my serious side is always there.

I look upon my life up till the New Year, as it were, through a powerful   11
magnifying glass. The sunny life at home, then coming here in 1942, the sudden change, the quarrels, the bickerings. I couldn't understand it, I was taken by surprise, and the only way I could keep up some bearing was by being impertinent.

The first half of 1943: my fits of crying, the loneliness, how I slowly   12
began to see all my faults and shortcomings, which are so great and which seemed much greater then. During the day I deliberately talked about anything and everything that was farthest from my thoughts, tried to draw Pim to me; but couldn't. Alone I had to face the difficult task of changing myself, to stop the everlasting reproaches, which were so oppressive and which reduced me to such terrible despondency.

Things improved slightly in the second half of the year, I became a   13
young woman and was treated more like a grownup. I started to think, and write stories, and came to the conclusion that the others no longer had the right to throw me about like an india-rubber ball. I wanted to change in accordance with my own desires. But *one* thing that struck me even more was when I realized that even Daddy would never become my confidant over everything. I didn't want to trust anyone but myself any more.

At the beginning of the New Year: the second great change, my   14
dream. . . . And with it I discovered my longing, not for a girl friend, but for a boy friend. I also discovered my inward happiness and my defensive armor of superficiality and gaiety. In due time I quieted down and discovered my boundless desire for all that is beautiful and good.

And in the evening, when I lie in bed and end my prayers with the   15
words, "I thank you, God, for all that is good and dear and beautiful," I am filled with joy. Then I think about "the good" of going into hiding, of my health and with my whole being of the "dearness" of Peter, of that which is still embryonic and impressionable and which we neither of us dare to name or touch, of that which will come sometime; love, the future, happiness and of "the beauty" which exists in the world; the world, nature, beauty and all, all that is exquisite and fine.

I don't think then of all the misery, but of the beauty that still remains.   16
This is one of the things that Mummy and I are so entirely different about. Her counsel when one feels melancholy is: "Think of all the misery in the world and be thankful that you are not sharing in it!" My advice is: "Go outside, to the fields, enjoy nature and the sunshine, go out and try to re-

capture happiness in yourself and in God. Think of all the beauty that's still left in and around you and be happy!"

I don't see how Mummy's idea can be right, because then how are you   17
supposed to behave if you go through the misery yourself? Then you are lost. On the contrary, I've found that there is always some beauty left—in nature, sunshine, freedom, in yourself; these can all help you. Look at these things, then you find yourself again, and God, and then you regain your balance.

And whoever is happy will make others happy too. He who has courage   18
and faith will never perish in misery!

Yours, Anne

Sunday, 12 March, 1944

Dear Kitty,

I can't seem to sit still lately; I run upstairs and down and then back   19
again. I love talking to Peter, but I'm always afraid of being a nuisance. He has told me a bit about the past, about his parents and about himself. It's not half enough though and I ask myself why it is that I always long for more. He used to think I was unbearable; and I returned the compliment; now I have changed my opinion, has he changed his too?

I think so; still it doesn't necessarily mean that we shall become great   20
friends, although as far as I am concerned it would make the time here much more bearable. But still, I won't get myself upset about it—I see quite a lot of him and there's no need to make you unhappy about it too, Kitty, just because I feel so miserable.

On Saturday afternoon I felt in such a whirl, after hearing a whole lot   21
of sad news, that I went and lay on my divan for a sleep. I only wanted to sleep to stop myself thinking. I slept till four o'clock, then I had to go into the living room. I found it difficult to answer all Mummy's questions and think of some little excuse to tell Daddy, as an explanation for my long sleep. I resorted to a "headache," which wasn't a lie, as I had one . . . but inside!

Ordinary people, ordinary girls, teen-agers like myself, will think I'm a   22
bit cracked with all my self-pity. Yes, that's what it is, but I pour out my heart to you, then for the rest of the day I'm as impudent, gay, and self-confident as I can be, in order to avoid questions and getting on my own nerves.

Margot is very sweet and would like me to trust her, but still, I can't tell   23
her everything. She is a darling, she's good and pretty, but she lacks the nonchalance for conducting deep discussions; she takes me so seriously, much too seriously, and then thinks about her queer little sister for a long time afterwards, looks searchingly at me, at every word I say, and keeps

on thinking: "Is this just a joke or does she really mean it?" I think that's because we are together the whole day long, and that if I trusted someone completely, then I shouldn't want them hanging around me all the time.

When shall I finally untangle my thoughts, when shall I find peace and rest within myself again?   24

Yours, Anne

Tuesday, 14 March, 1944

Dear Kitty,

Perhaps it would be entertaining for you—though not in the least for me—to hear what we are going to eat today. As the charwoman is at work downstairs, I'm sitting on the Van Daans' table at the moment. I have a handkerchief soaked in some good scent (bought before we came here) over my mouth and held against my nose. You won't gather much from this, so let's "begin at the beginning."   25

The people from whom we obtained food coupons have been caught, so we just have our five ration cards and no extra coupons, and no fats. As both Miep and Koophuis are ill, Elli hasn't time to do any shopping, so the atmosphere is dreary and dejected, and so is the food. From tomorrow we shall not have a scrap of fat, butter, or margarine left. We can't have fried potatoes (to save bread) for breakfast any longer, so we have porridge instead, and as Mrs. Van Daan thinks we're starving, we have bought some full cream milk "under the counter." Our supper today consists of a hash made from kale which has been preserved in a barrel. Hence the precautionary measure with the handkerchief! It's incredible how kale can stink when it's a year old! The smell in the room is a mixture of bad plums, strong preservatives, and rotten eggs. Ugh! the mere thought of eating that muck makes me feel sick.   26

Added to this, our potatoes are suffering from such peculiar diseases that out of two buckets of *pommes de terre,* one whole one ends up on the stove. We amuse ourselves by searching for all the different kinds of diseases, and have come to the conclusion that they range from cancer and smallpox to measles! Oh, no, it's no joke to be in hiding during the fourth year of the war. If only the whole rotten business was over!   27

Quite honestly, I wouldn't care so much about the food, if only it were more pleasant here in other ways. There's the rub: this tedious existence is beginning to make us all touchy.   28

The following are the views of the five grownups on the present situation: 29

Mrs. Van Daan: "The job as queen of the kitchen lost its attraction a long time ago. It's dull to sit and do nothing, so I go back to my cooking again. Still, I have to complain that it's impossible to cook without any fats,   30 and all these nasty smells make me feel sick. Nothing but ingratitude and rude remarks do I get in return for my services. I am always the black sheep, always the guilty one. Moreover, according to me, very little progress is being made in the war; in the end the Germans will still win. I'm afraid we're going to starve, and if I'm in a bad mood I scold everyone."

Mr. Van Daan: "I must smoke and smoke and smoke, and then the food, the political situation, and Kerli's moods don't seem so bad. Kerli is a darling wife." 31

But if he hasn't anything to smoke, then nothing is right, and this is what one hears: "I'm getting ill, we don't live well enough, I must have meat. Frightfully stupid person, my Kerli!" After this a terrific quarrel is sure to follow. 32

Mrs. Frank: "Food is not very important, but I would love a slice of rye bread now, I feel so terribly hungry. If I were Mrs. Van Daan I would have put a stop to Mr. Van Daan's everlasting smoking a long time ago. But now I must definitely have a cigarette, because my nerves are getting the better of me. The English make a lot of mistakes, but still the war is progressing. I must have a chat and be thankful I'm not in Poland." 33

Mr. Frank: "Everything's all right, I don't require anything. Take it easy, we've ample time. Give me my potatoes and then I will keep my mouth shut. Put some of my rations on one side for Elli. The political situation is very promising, I'm extremely optimistic!" 34

Mr. Dussel: "I must get my task for today, everything must be finished on time. Political situation 'outschtänding' and it is 'eempossible' that we'll be caught. 35

"I, I, I . . . !" 36

Yours, Anne

MUSINGS

In her diary Anne explores her feelings, doubts, and fears as she stands on the brink of womanhood. She explores her awakening feelings for Peter and compares her former life to her present one. In her loneliness and isolation she speaks to her diary as to her one true friend, evidencing great self-awareness about her stirring emotions. Through it all comes her loneliness and wish for a confidante. Her diary fills that need. The outstanding quality of this writing is its shining honesty.

Describe your feelings about someone you know well and whom you either like or dislike. Try to make your writing as honest as Anne's.

2

LETTERS

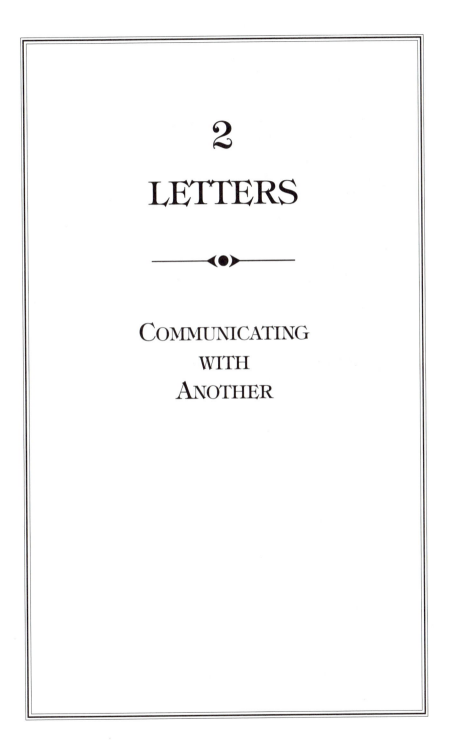

COMMUNICATING
WITH
ANOTHER

Letters are a testimony to the enduring attempts of human beings to bridge the communication gap between themselves and others. In contrast to the inward journeys taken by diary or journal writers, letter writers reach out, often across time and space, to other human beings.

In most cases, a letter is addressed to a single person, who is usually well-known to the writer. The reader is separated from the writer, sometimes only temporarily, but has shared many experiences with the writer. Because of this, letter writers need to supply little background information, although obviously more is needed than for entries in a diary. For example, the recipient of Lord Chesterfield's letters knew the writer well. A letter originally intended for a small audience may later be published and so acquire a larger, public audience. Lord Chesterfield considered his letters personal and addressed them only to his son. Years after his death his family continued to respect his wishes. Today, widely published and reprinted, they have become public in a way he never expected nor desired. In other cases, letters are written to a group, such as Lincoln's letter to his supporters, or Martin Luther King's letter from the Birmingham jail, and thus require that the writer supply more background information. Lincoln probably expected that his letter would be read aloud to his supporters and therefore presented his case as a series of well-considered and well-reasoned arguments, appropriate for such an occasion. No president is allowed the privilege of private correspondence, so he probably wrote it with the expectation that it might be published at some time. Martin Luther King was writing as a public figure to a group of fellow clergymen to answer their objections to his presence in Birmingham. He may or may not have expected it to find print, but certainly never visualized the wide circulation that it has attained today, as a model of a carefully crafted argument presented in a persuasive and disarming manner. In still other cases, documents intended from the start for the general public can be written purposely in letter form, such as Voltaire's letter concerning smallpox.

The subject matter of the letter, like the diary, is usually drawn from the writer's daily experience; alternatively, it can be cast in a more thoughtful vein, as an attempt to make the writer's reasoning process clear to another person or group of persons, as evidenced by the Lincoln and King selections. Writing often helps people work through problems; in making ideas clear to their readers, letter writers are able to clarify their own positions.

Letters are composed for a number of purposes. One of the most common is to record travel experiences through narration and description. The letters of Stewart and Forster are good examples of this type. Letters that chronicle a journey are often written to set the experiences in the writer's mind and are preserved as reminders of the trip.

The common purpose of Lincoln and King's letters was to explain a response to a certain situation—for Lincoln the Emancipation Proclamation and for King the march into Birmingham—to a group that, although supportive, questioned the writer's participation in a particular event.

Some women write in order to make connections, often reaching out from isolation. We see this in the letters of both Dinesen and Stewart: Dinesen had been brought to Africa by her first husband, a large-game hunter, and Stewart, like thousands of women on the American frontier, had moved west with her husband to find land and a better life for her family. Stewart's letters are examples of skilled and artfully crafted language. They were actually personal letters written to friends "back home," but, for Stewart and many other women, letters also served as an outlet for their creativity. Women's letters from the past form a special category, for, as Elizabeth Goldsmith asserts, "to be virtuous was to be modest, self-effacing, above all not talked about, and most certainly not published." Consequently, letters afforded women a way out of anonymity—the difference between being totally forgotten and perhaps remembered—for those to whom the regular avenues of publication were closed.

Letters can also serve as fictional narrative. In the eighteenth century, the genre of the epistolary novel was established by Samuel Richardson in *Clarissa,* his highly moralistic tale told through an exchange of letters. The selection by E.B. White included in this chapter is an example of such a fictional letter, dictated to his imagined secretary and addressed to the long-dead American writer Henry David Thoreau on the subject of Walden Pond and the ideal life described in Thoreau's famous journal (p. 117).

Today, the telephone and E-mail have taken the place of letters as a way of communicating. The exchanges between Denise Stodola and Sandy Rubinstein are examples of the immediacy and intimacy possible on the Internet. Although such missives have little chance of survival in a world that is always ready with the delete key, they are testimony to enduring attempts of human beings to bridge the communication gap between themselves and others. There is an immediacy that the telephone and E-mail provide that is lacking in a letter that may take days or weeks to arrive, but letters can be read and reread, and can act as permanent reminders of the past in a way that telephone conversations and remembered E-mail cannot.

Letters often endure through time and out of context. Without some background, however, letters can seem to float in limbo and can be grossly misunderstood. Lincoln's letter is much more easily understood if it is studied in conjunction with the Emancipation Proclamation and knowledge of his intended audience. Editors who compile collections of letters have the responsibility to make the context and all references clear to the reader; with the power to select and omit letters, they shape the overall intention and significance of the correspondence. Such work is dauntingly difficult and requires that the editor know a great deal about the writer and the period in which the letters were written. The letters included in this book are all from edited collections, and the headnotes that accompany them, often extrapolated from the editors' notes, attempt to provide context and are crucial for your understanding.

In writing letters, you must be acutely aware of your audience. Ask yourself the following questions when you write your next letter:

- What is your relationship to your reader?
- How familiar is your reader with your context?
- How much information must you include? How much does the reader already know?
- How much can you leave out?
- Do you make an attempt to gain the goodwill of your reader in the introduction and in the conclusion?

VOLTAIRE (1694–1778)

Francois Marie Arouet de Voltaire was a leading figure in eighteenth-century thought; his ideas endure to this day. His letters on smallpox, which take the form of missives written to a friend, were first published in London in 1733. After their publication in France, Voltaire was imprisoned in the bastille and banished to England as his works were deemed "likely to inspire a license of thought most dangerous to religion and civil order." In June 1734 the French Parliament condemned the collection to be burned and shredded by the hangman. Ernest Dilworth, a modern translator, comments, it was at this point that "the true work of Voltaire had begun, and our lives are different because of it."

Voltaire was as interested in practical matters as he was in government policy or philosophy. He was a popularizer who scorned specialization and viewed science as based on common sense. The following letter demonstrates that attitude. Voltaire advocated a method of preventing smallpox ten years before Edward Jenner, the commonly acknowledged discoverer of the smallpox vaccination, was born and nearly fifty years before Jenner began his experiments. Voltaire's letters are an interesting demonstration of scientific inquiry based on observation and common sense.

On Inoculation with Smallpox

In Christian Europe people gently aver that the English are fools and madmen: fools because they give their children smallpox to keep them from having it; madmen because they lightheartedly communicate to these children a disease that is certain and frightful, with a view to preventing an evil that may never befall them. The English, on their side, say, "The other Europeans are cowardly and unnatural: they are cowardly in fearing to hurt their children a little; unnatural in exposing them to the danger of dying some day of smallpox." To help decide who is right on this question, here is the story of that famous practice of inoculation, which outside England people speak of with such horror. 1

The women of Circassia have from time immemorial had the custom of giving smallpox to their children, when as little as six months old, by making an incision on the arm and inserting in that incision a pustule that they have carefully removed from the body of another child. That pustule has, in the arm into which it has been slipped, the effect of yeast in dough; it ferments there and spreads through the mass of the blood the characteristics with which it is marked. The pustules of the child who has been 2

76

given this artificial smallpox are used to carry the same disease to others. The circulation of the disease goes on in Circassia almost without pause; and when unfortunately there is no smallpox at all in the country, people are as much troubled as they are in a bad year elsewhere.

What caused the rise in Circassia of a custom that appears so strange to other peoples was nevertheless something that the whole earth shares with them, and that is mother-love and self-interest.   3

The Circassians are poor and their daughters are beautiful, so most of their trade is in them; they furnish with beauties the harems of the Sultan, the Sophy of Persia, and such others as are rich enough to buy and maintain this precious merchandise. With the most honest and virtuous intentions, they bring up these girls to take the initiative with the male sex by caressing them, to improvise dances fraught with lust and voluptuousness, and, by all the most sensual artifices, to revive the appetite of the disdainful masters whom they are destined to serve. Every day these poor creatures rehearse their lessons with their mother, as our little girls recite their catechism, without understanding any of it.   4

Now it often happened that a father and a mother, after having taken great pains to give their children a good education, suddenly found themselves frustrated in their hopes. Smallpox broke out in the family; one daughter died of it, another lost an eye, a third recovered with a big nose; and the poor parents were ruined, all their resources gone. Often, what is more, when there was an actual epidemic of smallpox, commerce was interrupted for several years, causing a notable diminution in the seraglios [harems] of Persia and of Turkey.   5

A commercial nation is always quick to see its interest, and neglects no branch of learning that may prove useful to its trade. The Circassians observed that, out of a thousand persons, hardly one could be found who had had a complete case of smallpox twice; that in fact some people have undergone three or four light attacks, but never two unequivocal and dangerous ones; that, in a word, no one really gets this disease twice in a lifetime. They noticed also that when smallpox is very benign, and when the eruptions have only a fine and delicate skin to break through, no mark is left on the face. From these natural observations they concluded that if an infant of six months or a year old had a mild case of smallpox, it would not die of it, would not be marked, and would be done with that disease for the rest of its life.   6

And so, to preserve the life and the beauty of their children, what they had to do was give them smallpox early. That is what they did, inserting in the body of a child a pustule from as completely developed and yet mild a case of smallpox as could be found. The experiment could not fail. The Turks, who are sensible people, immediately adopted the custom, and today there is not a Pasha [military or civil officer] in Constantinople who   7 doesn't give smallpox to his son and his daughter when they are being weaned.

There are some people who maintain that in ancient times the Circassians learned this custom from the Arabs; but we will leave this historical point to be cleared up by some learned Benedictine, who will not fail to compose on the subject several folio volumes along with the documents. All I have to say on the matter is that at the beginning of the reign of George I, Lady Mary Wortley Montagu, one of the wittiest and most strong-minded women in England, being with her husband on his embassy to Constantinople, took the step, without hesitation, of giving smallpox to a child she had borne in that country. It was no use her chaplain telling her that the experiment was not Christian and could only succeed among infidels: Lady Mary's son recovered splendidly. The lady herself, on her return to London, told her story to the Princess of Wales, who is now queen. It must be acknowledged that, apart from titles and crowns, this princess was born to encourage all the arts and to do good to mankind; she is a gracious philosopher on a throne. She has never lost either a chance to learn or a chance to put her generosity to work. It is she who, having learned that a daughter of Milton was still living, and living in poverty, sent her at once the present of a considerable sum; it is she who is the protector of that poor Father Courayer; it is she who condescended to mediate between Dr. Clarke and Mr. Leibniz. As soon as she had heard of the inoculation or insertion of smallpox, she had it tested on four criminals who had been condemned to death. Their lives she doubly saved, for not only did she deliver them from the gallows, but, by means of this artificial smallpox she prevented the natural kind, which they would probably otherwise have caught, and perhaps died of, at a more advanced age.

The princess, assured of the usefulness of her test, had her own children inoculated. England followed her example, and since that time at least ten thousand children of good family owe their lives, in the same way, to the Queen and to Lady Mary Wortley Montagu, and as many girls are indebted to them for their beauty.

Out of every hundred persons in the world, at least sixty get smallpox; of these sixty, twenty die of it in the most favorable years, and twenty keep unhappy traces of it with them for ever. That makes a fifth of mankind for certain, killed or disfigured by this disease. Of all those who are inoculated in Turkey or in England, not a one dies, unless he is infirm and condemned to death in other respects; no one is marked with it; no one gets smallpox a second time, so long as the inoculation was perfect.

Thus it is certain that if some French ambassadress had brought this secret from Constantinople to Paris, she would have rendered a service of everlasting benefit to the nation. The Duc de Villequier, father of the present Duc d'Aumont, the best set up and healthiest man in France, would not have died in the flower of his age; the Prince de Soubise, who enjoyed the most radiant health, would not have been carried off at the age of twenty-five; Monseigneur, the grandfather of Louis XV, would not have been buried in his fiftieth year; twenty thousand persons who died in Paris of smallpox in 1723 would still be alive. Well, then, have the French no liking for life? Don't their women care about their beauty? Really, we are odd people! Perhaps ten years from now we may adopt this English custom, if the curates and the doctors allow us; or who knows but that within three months the French will take up inoculation for a whim, if the English lose their taste for it through fickleness.

I find that the Chinese have practiced this custom for a hundred years; that is a great recommendation, the example of a country that passes for being the wisest and most civilized in the universe. It is true that the Chinese go about it in a different fashion; they make no incision but give smallpox through the nose, like snuff. This way is pleasanter, but it comes to the same thing, and serves equally to confirm the fact that if inoculation had been practiced in France, the lives of thousands would have been saved. 12

MUSINGS

In this treatise Voltaire demonstrates his ability to listen to the opinions of others, to make his own observations, and to form a judgment. He recounts these observations and his conclusion in a manner that is convincing to his reader.

Write to a reader who might be a friend of yours, giving some judgment that you have formed on the basis of your observations and the opinions of others. Keeping that reader in mind, make your judgment convincing.

PHILIP DORMER STANHOPE, EARL OF CHESTERFIELD (1694–1773)

In 1773, the year of Chesterfield's death, Edward Gibbon characterized him as "sought and feared, liked and not loved, by most of his acquaintances." When Letters to His Son *was published over his family's objections, many critics castigated Chesterfield, while others praised his wit and elegance. Henry Lord Brougham expressed the concern of many when he accused Chesterfield of "strenuously inculcating in his son the duties of seduction and intrigue." The advice that Chesterfield gives to his son is at best worldly advice and at worst often morally reprehensible. Robert Southey in 1831 said that he read the letters "with more disgust than pleasure, and more pity than disgust." Southey asserted that the letters "must have defeated their own main purpose, and made the poor youth awkward, by impressing him with a continual dread of appearing so."*

Chesterfield continued his letters until his son's death in 1768. In 1761 he also began a series of letters to his godson. Chesterfield served in the House of Commons and as ambassador to the Hague. In 1746 he was offered a dukedom and was appointed Secretary of State; he resigned from the latter position in opposition to the War of the Austrian Succession. Chesterfield was deaf during the last part of his life, and upon his death in 1771 his godson succeeded him in his earldom.

Letters to His Son

London, March 27, O.S. 1747

Pleasure is the rock which most young people split upon; they launch out with crowded sails in quest of it, but without a compass to direct their course, or reason sufficient to steer the vessel; for want of which, pain and shame, instead of Pleasure, are the returns of their voyage. Do not think that I mean to snarl at Pleasure, like a Stoic, or to preach against it, like a parson; no, I mean to point it out, and recommend it to you, like an Epicurean: I wish you a great deal; and my only view is to hinder you from mistaking it.

The character which most young men first aim at is, that of a Man of Pleasure; but they generally take it upon trust; and, instead of consulting their own taste and inclinations, they blindly adopt whatever those, with whom they chiefly converse, are pleased to call by the name of Pleasure; and a *Man of Pleasure,* in the vulgar acceptation of that phrase, means only a beastly drunkard, an abandoned whoremaster, and a profligate swearer and curser. As it may be of use to you, I am not unwilling, though at the same time ashamed, to own, that the vices of my youth proceeded much more from my silly resolution of being what I heard called a Man of Pleasure, than from my own inclinations. I always naturally hated drinking; and yet I have often drunk, with disgust at the time, attended by great sickness the next day, only because I then considered drinking as a necessary qualification for a fine gentleman, and a Man of Pleasure.

The same as to gaming. I did not want money, and consequently had no occasion to play for it; but I thought Play another necessary ingredient in the composition of a Man of Pleasure, and accordingly I plunged into it without desire, at first; sacrificed a thousand real pleasures to it; and made myself solidly uneasy by it, for thirty of the best years of my life.   3

I was even absurd enough, for a little while, to swear, by way of adorning and completing the shining character which I affected; but this folly I soon laid aside, upon finding both the guilt and the indecency of it.   4

Thus seduced by fashion, and blindly adopting nominal pleasures, I lost real ones; and my fortune impaired, and my constitution shattered, are, I must confess, the just punishment of my errors.   5

Take warning then by them; choose your pleasures for yourself, and do not let them be imposed upon you. Follow nature, and not fashion: weigh the present enjoyment of your pleasures against the necessary consequences of them, and then follow your common sense.   6

Were I to begin the world again, with the experience which I now have of it, I would lead a life of real, not of imaginary, pleasure. I would enjoy the pleasures of the table, and of wine; but stop short of the pains inseparably annexed to an excess in either. I would not, at twenty years, be a preaching missionary of abstemiousness and sobriety; and I should let other people do as they would, without formally and sententiously rebuking them for it: but I would be most firmly resolved not to destroy my own faculties and constitution, in compliance to those who have no regard to their own. I would play to give me pleasure, but not to give me pain; that is, I would play for trifles, in mixed companies, to amuse myself, and conform to custom: but I would take care not to venture for sums, which, if I won, I should not be the better for; but, if I lost, should be under a difficulty to pay; and, when paid, would oblige me to retrench in several other articles. Not to mention the quarrels which deep play commonly occasions.   7

I would pass some of my time in reading and the rest in the company of people of sense and learning, and chiefly those above me; and I would frequent the mixed companies of men and women of fashion, which, though often frivolous, yet they unbend and refresh the mind, not uselessly, because they certainly polish and soften the manners.   8

These would be my pleasures and amusements, if I were to live the last   9 thirty years over again: they are rational ones; and moreover, I will tell you, they are really the fashionable ones: for the others are not, in truth, the pleasures of what I call people of fashion, but of those who only call themselves so. Does good company care to have a man reeling drunk among them? Or to see another tearing his hair, and blaspheming, for having lost, at play, more than he is able to pay? Or a whoremaster, with half a nose, and crippled by coarse and infamous debauchery? No; these practices, and, much more, those who brag of them, make no part of good company, and are most unwillingly, if ever admitted into it. A real man of fashion and pleasure observes decency; at least, neither borrows nor affects vices; and, if he unfortunately has any, he gratifies them with choice, delicacy, and secrecy.

I have not mentioned the pleasures of the mind (which are the 10 solid and permanent ones), because they do not come under the head of what people commonly call pleasures, which they seem to confine to the senses. The pleasure of virtue, of charity, and of learning, is true and lasting pleasure; which I hope you will be well and long acquainted with. Adieu!

London, October 9, O.S. 1747

People of your age have, commonly, an unguarded frankness about 11 them; which makes them the easy prey and bubbles of the artful and the inexperienced: they look upon every knave or fool, who tells them that he is their friend, to be really so; and pay that profession of simulated friendship, with an indiscreet and unbounded confidence, always to their loss, often to their ruin. Beware, therefore, now that you are coming into the world, of these proffered friendships. Receive them with great civility, but with great incredulity too; and pay them with compliments, but not with confidence. Do not let your vanity, and self-love, make you suppose that people become your friends at first sight, or even upon a short acquaintance. Real friendship is a slow grower; and never thrives, unless ingrafted upon a stock of known and reciprocal merit.

There is another kind of nominal friendship, among young people, 12 which is warm for the time, but, by good luck, of short duration. This friendship is hastily produced, by their being accidentally thrown together, and pursuing the same course of riot and debauchery. A fine friendship, truly! and well cemented by drunkenness and lewdness. It should rather be called a conspiracy against morals and good manners, and be punished as such by the civil magistrate. However, they have the impudence, and the folly, to call their confederacy a friendship. They lend one another money for bad purposes; they engage in quarrels, offensive and defensive, for their accomplices; they tell one another all they know, and often more too; when, of a sudden, some accident disperses them, and they think no more of each other, unless it be to betray and laugh at their imprudent confidence. Remember to make a great difference between companions and friends; for a very complaisant and agreeable companion may, and often does, prove a very improper and dangerous friend.

People will, in a great degree, and not without reason, form their opinion of you, upon that which they have of your friends; and there is a Spanish proverb, which says very justly, *Tell me whom you live with, and I will tell you who you are.* One may fairly suppose, that a man who makes a knave or a fool his friend, has something very bad to do or to conceal. But, at the same time that you carefully decline the friendship of knaves and fools, if it can be called friendship, there is no occasion to make either of them your enemies, wantonly, and unprovoked; for they are numerous bodies; and I would rather choose a secure neutrality, than alliance, or war, with either of them. You may be a declared enemy to their vices and follies, without being marked out by them as a personal one. Their enmity is the next dangerous thing to their friendship. Have a real reserve with almost everybody, and have a seeming reserve with almost nobody; for it is very disagreeable to seem reserved, and very dangerous not to be so. Few people find the true medium; many are ridiculously mysterious and reserved upon trifles; and many imprudently communicative of all they know. 13

The next thing to the choice of your friends, is the choice of your company. Endeavour, as much as you can, to keep company with people above you. There you rise, as much as you sink with people below you; for you are, whatever the company you keep is. Do not mistake, when I say company above you, and think that I mean with regard to their birth; that is the least consideration: but I mean with regard to their merit, and the light in which the world considers them. 14

There are two sorts of good company; one, which is called the *beau monde,* and consists of those people who have had the lead in Courts, and the gay part of life; the other consists of those who are distinguished by some peculiar merit, or who excel in some particular and valuable art or science. For my own part, I used to think myself in company as much above me, when I was with Mr. Addison and Mr. Pope, as if I had been with all the Princes in Europe. What I mean by low company which should by all means be avoided, is the company of those, who, absolutely insignificant and contemptible in themselves, think they are honoured by being in your company, and who flatter every vice and every folly you have, in order to engage you to converse with them. The pride of being the first of the company, is but too common; but it is very silly, and very prejudicial. Nothing in the world lets down a character more, than that wrong turn. 15

You may possibly ask me, whether a man has it always in his power to get into the best company? and how? I say, Yes, he has, by deserving it; provided he is but in circumstances which enable him to appear upon the 16 footing of a gentleman. Merit and good-breeding will make their way everywhere. Knowledge will introduce him, and good breeding will endear him to the best companies; for, as I have often told you, politeness and good-breeding are absolutely necessary to adorn any, or all other good qualities or talents. Without them, no knowledge, no perfection whatsoever, is seen in its best light. The scholar, without good-breeding, is a pedant; the philosopher, a cynic; the soldier, a brute; and every man disagreeable.

I long to hear, from my several correspondents at Leipsig, of your arrival there, and what impression you make on them at first; for I have Arguses, with a hundred eyes each, who will watch you narrowly, and relate to me faithfully. My accounts will certainly be true; it depends on you, entirely, of what kind they shall be. Adieu! 17

London, October 16, O.S. 1747

The art of pleasing is a very necessary one to possess; but a very difficult one to acquire. It can hardly be reduced to rules; and your own good sense and observation will teach you more of it than I can. "Do as you would be done by," is the surest method that I know of pleasing. Observe carefully what pleases you in others, and probably the same things in you will please others. If you are pleased with the complaisance and attention of others to your humours, your tastes, or your weaknesses, depend upon it, the same complaisance and attention on your part, to theirs, will equally please them. Take the tone of the company that you are in, and do not pretend to give it; be serious, gay, or even trifling, as you find the present humour of the company; this is an attention due from every individual to the majority. Do not tell stories in company; there is nothing more tedious and disagreeable: if by chance you know a very short story, and exceedingly applicable to the present subject of conversation, tell it in as few words as possible; and even then, throw out that you do not love to tell stories; but that the shortness of it tempted you. 18

Of all things, banish the egotism out of your conversation, and never think of entertaining people with your own personal concerns or private affairs; though they are interesting to you, they are tedious and impertinent to everybody else: besides that, one cannot keep one's own private affairs too secret. Whatever you think your own excellencies may be, do not affectedly display them in company; nor labour, as many people do, to give that turn to the conversation, which may supply you with an opportunity of exhibiting them. If they are real, they will infallibly be discovered, without your pointing them out yourself, and with much more advantage. Never maintain an argument with heat and clamour, though you think or know yourself to be in the right; but give your opinions modestly and coolly, which is the only way to convince; and, if that does not 19 do, try to change the conversation, by saying, with good-humour, "We shall hardly convince one another; nor is it necessary that we should, so let us talk of something else."

Remember that there is a local propriety to be observed in all compa-   20
nies; and that what is extremely proper in one company, may be, and often is, highly improper in another.

The jokes, the *bon-mots,* the little adventures, which may do very well   21
in one company, will seem flat and tedious when related in another. The particular characters, the habits, the cant of one company may give merit to a word, or a gesture, which would have none at all if divested of those accidental circumstances. Here people very commonly err; and fond of something that has entertained them in one company, and in certain circumstances, repeat it with emphasis in another, where it is either insipid, or, it may be, offensive, by being ill-timed or misplaced.

Nay, they often do it with this silly preamble, "I will tell you an excel-   22
lent thing," or, "I will tell you the best thing in the world." This raises expectations, which when absolutely disappointed, make the relator of this excellent thing look, very deservedly, like a fool.

If you would particularly gain the affection and friendship of particular   23
people, whether men or women, endeavour to find out their predominant excellency, if they have one, and their prevailing weakness, which everybody has; and do justice to the one, and something more than justice to the other. Men have various objects in which they may excel, or at least would be thought to excel; and though they love to hear justice done to them, where they know that they excel, yet they are most and best flattered upon those points where they wish to excel, and yet are doubtful whether they do or not. As for example: Cardinal Richelieu, who was undoubtedly the ablest statesman of his time, or perhaps of any other, had the idle vanity of being thought the best poet too: he envied the great Corneille his reputation, and ordered a criticism to be written upon the *Cid.* Those, therefore, who flattered skilfully, said little to him of his abilities in state affairs, or at least but *en passant,* as it might naturally occur. But the incense which they gave him—the smoke of which they knew would turn his head in their favour—was as a *bel esprit* and a poet. Why?—Because he was sure of one excellency, and distrustful as to the other.

You will easily discover every man's prevailing vanity by observing his   24
favourite topic of conversation; for every man talks most of what he has most a mind to be thought to excel in. Touch him but there, and you touch him to the quick. The late Sir Robert Walpole (who was certainly an able man) was open to flattery upon that head, for he was in no doubt himself about it; but his prevailing weakness was, to be thought to have a polite and happy turn to gallantry—of which he had undoubtedly less

than any man living. It was his favourite and frequent subject of conversation, which proved to those who had any penetration that it was his prevailing weakness, and they applied to it with success.

Women have, in general, but one object, which is their beauty; upon   25
which, scarce any flattery is too gross for them to follow. Nature has hardly formed a woman ugly enough to be insensible to flattery upon her person; if her face is so shocking that she must, in some degree, be conscious of it, her figure and air, she trusts, make ample amends for it. If her figure is deformed, her face, she thinks, counterbalances it. If they are both bad, she comforts herself that she has graces; a certain manner; a *je ne sais quoi* still more engaging than beauty. This truth is evident, from the studied and elaborate dress of the ugliest woman in the world. An undoubted, uncontested, conscious beauty is, of all women, the least sensible of flattery upon that head; she knows it is her due, and therefore obliged to nobody for giving it her. She must be flattered upon her understanding, which, though she may possibly not doubt of herself, yet she suspects that men may distrust.

Do not mistake me, and think that I mean to recommend to you abject   26
and criminal flattery: no; flatter nobody's vices or crimes: on the contrary, abhor and discourage them. But there is no living in the world without a complaisant indulgence for people's weaknesses, and innocent, though ridiculous vanities. If a man has a mind to be thought wiser, and a woman handsomer, than they really are, their error is a comfortable one to themselves, and an innocent one with regard to other people; and I would rather make them my friends by indulging them in it, than my enemies by endeavouring (and that to no purpose) to undeceive them.

These are some of the *arcana* necessary for your initiation in the great   27
society of the world. I wish I had known them better at your age; I have paid the price of three-and-fifty years for them, and shall not grudge it if you reap the advantage. Adieu!

Bath, March 9, O.S. 1748

I must from time to time, remind you of what I have often recom-   28
mended to you and of what you cannot attend to too much; *sacrifice to the Graces*. The different effects of the same things, said or done, when accompanied or abandoned by them, is almost inconceivable. They prepare the way to the heart; and the heart has such an influence over the understanding, that it is worth while to engage it in our interest. It is the whole of women, who are guided by nothing else: and it has so much to say, even with men, and the ablest men too, that it commonly triumphs in every struggle with the understanding. Monsieur de Rochefoucault, in his *Maxims,* says, that *l'esprit est souvent la dupe du coeur.* If he had said, instead of *souvent, presque toujours,* I fear he would have been nearer the truth. This being the case, aim at the heart. Intrinsic merit alone will not do; it will

gain you the general esteem of all; but not the particular affection, that is, the heart of any. To engage the affection of any particular person, you must, over and above your general merit, have some particular merit to that person, by services done or offered; by expressions of regard and esteem; by complaisance, attentions, etc., for him: and the graceful manner of doing all these things opens the way to the heart, and facilitates, or rather insures, their effects.

From your own observation, reflect what a disagreeable impression an awkward address, a slovenly figure, an ungraceful manner of speaking whether stuttering, muttering, monotony, or drawling, an unattentive behaviour, etc., make upon you, at first sight, in a stranger, and how they prejudice you against him, though, for aught you know, he may have great intrinsic sense and merit. And reflect, on the other hand, how much the opposites of all these things prepossess you, at first sight, in favour of those who enjoy them. You wish to find all good qualities in them, and are in some degree disappointed if you do not. A thousand little things, not separately to be defined, conspire to form these Graces, this *je ne sais quoi*, that always pleases. A pretty person, genteel motions, a proper degree of dress, an harmonious voice, something open and cheerful in the countenance, but without laughing; a distinct and properly varied manner of speaking: all these things, and many others, are necessary ingredients in the composition of the *je ne sais quoi*, which everybody feels, though nobody can describe.

Having mentioned laughing, I must particularly warn you against it: and I could heartily wish that you may often be seen to smile, but never heard to laugh while you live. Frequent and loud laughter is the characteristic of folly and ill manners: it is the manner in which the mob express their silly joy at silly things; and they call it being merry. In my mind there is nothing so illiberal, and so ill-bred, as audible laughter. True wit, or sense, never yet made anybody laugh; they are above it: they please the mind, and give a cheerfulness to the countenance. But it is low buffoonery, or silly accidents, that always excite laughter; and that is what people of sense and breeding should show themselves above. A man's going to sit down, in the supposition that he had a chair behind him, and falling down upon his breech for want of one, sets a whole company a laughing, when all the wit in the world would not do it; a plain proof, in my mind, how low and unbecoming a thing laughter is. Not to mention the disagreeable noise that it makes, and the shocking distortion of the face that it occasions. Laughter is easily restrained by a very little reflection; but, as it is generally connected with the idea of gaiety, people do not enough attend to its absurdity. I am neither of a melancholy, nor a cynical disposition; and am as willing, and as apt, to be pleased as anybody; but I am sure that, since I have had the full use of my reason, nobody has ever heard me laugh. Many people, at first from awkwardness and *mauvaise bonte,* have

29

30

got a very disagreeable and silly trick of laughing whenever they speak: and I know a man of very good parts, Mr. Waller, who cannot say the commonest thing without laughing; which makes those, who do not know him, take him at first for a natural fool.

Some put their fingers in their nose, others scratch their head, others 31 twirl their hats; in short, every awkward, ill-bred body has his trick. But the frequency does not justify the thing; and all these vulgar habits and awkwardness, though not criminal indeed, are most carefully to be guarded against, as they are great bars in the way of the art of pleasing. Remember, that to please, is almost to prevail, or at least a necessary previous step to it. You, who have your fortune to make, should more particularly study this art. You had not, I must tell you, when you left England, *les manières prévenantes;* and I must confess they are not very common in England: but I hope that your good sense will make you acquire them abroad. If you desire to make yourself considerable in the world (as, if you have any spirit, you do), it must be entirely your own doing; for I may very possibly be out of the world at the time you come into it. Your own rank and fortune will not assist you; your merit and your manners can alone raise you to figure and fortune. I have laid the foundations of them; but you must build the superstructure yourself.

MUSINGS

Imagine that these letters were written to you by your father, another older member of your family, or a friend. How would you react? In the letter dated March 27, 1747, Chesterfield speaks of his own mistakes and uses himself as an example of what his son should *not* do. Ordinarily this is an effective tactic, but the other letters selected here fail to follow that approach.

Try writing a letter to a younger relative or friend who is planning to attend college. Offer advice on how to manage one aspect of college life during the first year.

ABRAHAM LINCOLN (1809–1865)

Abraham Lincoln, the sixteenth president of the United States, is credited with preserving the Union at a time when the North and the South angrily disagreed about a number of issues, including slavery. He was born the son of Nancy Hanks and Thomas Lincoln, poor pioneer farmers in Kentucky. He had little formal education but was an avid reader, often forced to read by firelight as his family was too poor to buy lamp oil. Lincoln worked on a flatboat, built rail fences, and clerked in a store. He became a lawyer's apprentice in 1833 (then the only method of entering the profession) while also working as a postmaster and a surveyor to pay off debts incurred in a failed shopkeeping venture. He married in 1842, and he and his wife had four children, three of whom died in childhood.

Lincoln was elected to the state legislature, and in 1837 he and two other members formally issued a protest against slavery. His political career continued until he was nominated for president in 1860 on a platform of slavery restriction and tax reform. When Lincoln was elected president in 1861, he was faced with a bitter confederacy, which seceded from the Union. In 1863 he issued the Emancipation Proclamation, which is partially reprinted here, announcing that all slaves would be free "then, thenceforward, and forever." Lincoln was assassinated on April 14, 1865 at Ford's Theatre in Washington, D.C., and was deeply mourned by his countrymen. A brilliant statesman and a consummate orator, Lincoln ranks as one of the greatest U.S. presidents.

Lincoln was able to preserve the Union after the war by careful and studied negotiations between the angry factions. He sought to restore peace and heal deep wounds "with malice toward none; with charity for all." The ensuing letter, written the August following the proclamation, is addressed to the leader of a group that believed strongly in the preservation of the Union, a group that Lincoln knew to be his supporters. Nevertheless, not all were in favor of the emancipation of slaves. Lincoln attempts to explain his rationale in a series of well-reasoned arguments, more pragmatic than ideological.

The Emancipation Proclamation

January 1, 1863

By the President of the United States of America

A PROCLAMATION

Whereas, on the twenty-second day of September, in the year of our   1
Lord one thousand eight hundred and sixty-two, a proclamation was issued by the President of the United States, containing, among other
things, the following, to wit:

That on the first day of January, in the year of our Lord one thousand   2
eight hundred and sixty-three, all persons held as slaves within any state or
designated part of a state, the people whereof shall then be in rebellion
against the United States, shall be then, thenceforward, and forever free;
and the executive government of the United States, including the military
and naval authority thereof, will recognize and maintain the freedom of
such persons, and will do no act or acts to repress such persons, or any of
them, in any efforts they may make for their actual freedom.

• • •

And by virtue of the power, and for the purpose aforesaid, I do order   3
and declare that all persons held as slaves within said designated states, and
parts of states, are, and henceforward shall be free; and that the executive
government of the United States, including the military and naval authorities thereof, will recognize and maintain the freedom of said persons.

And I hereby enjoin upon the people so declared to be free to abstain   4
from all violence, unless in necessary self-defense; and I recommend to
them that, in all cases when allowed, they labor faithfully for reasonable
wages.

And I further declare and make known, that such persons of suitable   5
condition, will be received into the armed service of the United States to
garrison forts, positions, stations, and other places, and to man vessels of
all sorts in said service.

And upon this act, sincerely believed to be an act of justice, warranted   6
by the Constitution, upon military necessity, I invoke the considerate
judgment of mankind, and the gracious favor of Almighty God.

IN WITNESS WHEREOF, I have hereunto set my hand and caused the seal of the United States to be affixed.   7

Done at the City of Washington, this first day of January, in the year of our Lord one thousand eight hundred and sixty-three, and of the independence of the United States of America the eighty-seventh.

By the President, Abraham Lincoln

•   •   •

Executive Mansion,
Washington, August 26, 1863

Hon. James C. Conkling

My Dear Sir:

Your letter inviting me to attend a mass meeting of unconditional   8
Union men to be held at the capital of Illinois, on the 3d day of September, has been received.

It would be very agreeable to me, to thus meet my old friends, at my   9
own home; but I cannot, just now, be absent from here, so long as a visit there, would require.

The meeting is to be of all those who maintain unconditional devotion   10
to the Union; and I am sure my old political friends will thank me for tendering, as I do, the nation's gratitude to those other noble men, whom no partisan malice, or partisan hope, can make false to the nation's life.

There are those who are dissatisfied with me. To such I would say: You   11
desire peace; and you blame me that we do not have it. But how can we attain it? There are but three conceivable ways. First, to suppress the rebellion by force of arms. This, I am trying to do. Are you for it? If you are, so far we are agreed. If you are not for it, a second way is, to give up the Union. I am against this. Are you for it? If you are, you should say so plainly. If you are not for *force*, nor yet for *dissolution*, there only remains some imaginable *compromise*. I do not believe any compromise, embracing the maintenance of the Union, is now possible. All I learn, leads to a directly opposite belief. The strength of the rebellion, is its military—its army. That army dominates all the country, and all the people, within its range. Any offer of terms made by any man or men within that range, in opposition to that army, is simply nothing for the present; because such man or men, have no power whatever to enforce their side of a compromise, if one were made with them. To illustrate—Suppose refugees from

the South, and peace men of the North, get together in convention, and frame and proclaim a compromise embracing a restoration of the Union; in what way can that compromise be used to keep Lee's army out of Pennsylvania? Meade's army can keep Lee's army out of Pennsylvania; and, I think, can ultimately drive it out of existence. But no paper compromise, to which the controllers of Lee's army are not agreed, can, at all, affect that army. In an effort at such compromise we should waste time, which the enemy would improve to our disadvantage; and that would be all. A compromise, to be effective, must be made either with those who control the rebel army, or with the people first liberated from the domination of that army, by the success of our own army. Now allow me to assure you, that no word or intimation, from that rebel army, or from any of the men controlling it, in relation to any peace compromise, has ever come to my knowledge or belief. All charges and insinuations to the contrary, are deceptive and groundless. And I promise you, that if any such proposition shall hereafter come, it shall not be rejected, and kept a secret from you. I freely acknowledge myself the servant of the people, according to the bond of service—the United States Constitution; and that, as such, I am responsible to them.

But, to be plain, you are dissatisfied with me about the negro. Quite 12 likely there is a difference of opinion between you and myself upon that subject. I certainly wish that all men could be free, while I suppose you do not. Yet I have neither adopted, nor proposed any measure, which is not consistent with even your view, provided you are for the Union. I suggested compensated emancipation; to which you replied you wished not to be taxed to buy negroes. But I had not asked you to be taxed to buy negroes, except in such way, as to save you from greater taxation to save the Union exclusively by other means.

You dislike the emancipation proclamation; and, perhaps, would have 13 it retracted. You say it is unconstitutional—I think differently. I think the constitution invests its commander-in-chief, with the law of war, in time of war. The most that can be said, if so much, is, that slaves are property. Is there—has there ever been—any question that by the law of war, property, both of enemies and friends, may be taken when needed? And is it not needed whenever taking it, helps us, or hurts the enemy? Armies, the world over, destroy enemies' property when they cannot use it; and even destroy their own to keep it from the enemy. Civilized belligerents do all in their power to help themselves, or hurt the enemy, except a few things regarded as barbarous or cruel. Among the exceptions are the massacre of vanquished foes, and noncombatants, male and female.

But the proclamation, as law, either is valid, or is not valid. If it is not 14 valid, it needs no retraction. If it is valid, it cannot be retracted, any more than the dead can be brought to life. Some of you profess to think its retraction would operate favorably for the Union. Why better *after* the retraction, than *before* the issue? There was more than a year and a half of trial to suppress the rebellion before the proclamation issued, the last one hundred days of which passed under an explicit notice that it was coming, unless averted by those in revolt, returning to their allegiance. The war has certainly progressed as favorably for us, since the issue of the proclamation as before. I know as fully as one can know the opinions of others, that some of the commanders of our armies in the field who have given us our most important successes, believe the emancipation policy, and the use of colored troops, constitute the heaviest blow yet dealt to the rebellion; and that, at least one of those important successes, could not have been achieved when it was, but for the aid of black soldiers. Among the commanders holding these views are some who have never had any affinity with what is called abolitionism, or with Republican party politics; but who hold them purely as military opinions. I submit these opinions as being entitled to some weight against the objections, often urged, that emancipation, and arming the blacks, are unwise as military measures, and were not adopted, as such, in good faith.

You say you will not fight to free negroes. Some of them seem willing to 15 fight for you; but, no matter. Fight you, then, exclusively to save the Union. I issued the proclamation on purpose to aid you in saving the Union. Whenever you shall have conquered all resistance to the Union, if I shall urge you to continue fighting, it will be an apt time, then, for you to declare you will not fight to free negroes.

I thought that in your struggles for the Union, to whatever extent the 16 negroes should cease helping the enemy, to that extent it weakened the enemy in his resistance to you. Do you think differently? I thought that whatever negroes can be got to do as soldiers, leaves just so much less for white soldiers to do, in saving the Union. Does it appear otherwise to you? But negroes, like other people, act upon motives. Why should they do anything for us, if we will do nothing for them? If they stake their lives for us, they must be prompted by the strongest motive—even the promise of freedom. And the promise being made, must be kept.

Thanks to all. For the great republic—for the principle it lives by, and 17 keeps alive—for man's vast future—thanks to all.

Peace does not appear so distant as it did. I hope it will come soon, and 18 come to stay; and so come as to be worth the keeping in all future time. It will then have been proved that, among free men, there can be no successful appeal from the ballot to the bullet; and that they who take such appeal are sure to lose their case, and pay the cost. And then, there will be some black men who can remember that, with silent tongue, and clenched teeth, and steady eye, and well-poised bayonet, they have helped mankind on to this great consummation; while, I fear, there will be some white ones, unable to forget that, with malignant heart, and deceitful speech, they have strove to hinder it.

Still let us not be oversanguine of a speedy final triumph. Let us be quite sober. Let us diligently apply the means, never doubting that a just God, in His own good time, will give us the rightful result. 19

Yours very truly, A. Lincoln

MUSINGS

In a series of carefully constructed arguments Lincoln explains his reasons for the emancipation of the slaves. Can you trace his contentions and analyze the support he offers for his views? Lincoln's letter, although addressed only to the leader of "unconditional Union men," was obviously meant for the whole group, possibly to be read in part or in whole at a mass meeting. Would his reasons be convincing to this group?

Select a controversial issue and argue your viewpoint in a letter to a group that opposes you. Start with an introduction like Lincoln's, which gains the goodwill of his audience by reinforcing their friendship and expressing the "nation's gratitude" for their support of the Union.

ELINORE RUPERT STEWART (1876–1933)

Elinore Rupert Stewart was one of nine children born into a poor family in Fort Smith, Arkansas. Her parents died when she was fourteen; she quit school to support her brothers and sisters. Stewart was an avid reader, however, and managed to educate herself. She married, bore a child, Jerrine, and began writing short articles for the Kansas City Star, *which she continued to do after her husband's untimely death in a railroad accident four years later.*

The employment opportunities for women were limited at that time, so Stewart supported herself and her child with cleaning and laundry. Later, she cooked and stoked the furnace for Mrs. Coney, who became a lifelong friend and with whom she continued to correspond after she moved to Wyoming. At age thirty-three, she answered an ad for a housekeeper placed by a Wyoming sheep ranger and six weeks later the two were married.

In the following letters she signs herself Elinore Rupert as she wrote them under her first husband's name. Her voluminous correspondence with Mrs. Coney is collected in two volumes, Letters of a Woman Homesteader *and* Letters on an Elk Hunt. *The following selection is an eloquent example of remarkable use of language by a person who has read widely and well.*

———◀●▶———

A Trip on Horseback

May 24, 1909

Dear, Dear Mrs. Coney,

Well, I have filed on my land and am now a bloated landowner. I   1
waited a long time to even *see* land in the reserve, and the snow is yet too
deep, so I thought that as they have but three months of summer and
spring together and as I wanted the land for a ranch anyway, perhaps I had
better stay in the valley. So I have filed adjoining Mr. Stewart and I am
well pleased. I have a grove of twelve swamp pines on my place, and I am
going to build my house there. I thought it would be very romantic to live
on the peaks amid the whispering pines, but I reckon it would be powerfully uncomfortable also, and I guess my twelve can whisper enough for
me; and a dandy thing is, I have all the nice snow-water I want; a small
stream runs right through the center of my land and I am quite near
wood.

A neighbor and his daughter were going to Green River, the county-   2

95

seat, and said I might go along, so I did, as I could file there as well as at the land office; and oh, that trip! I had more fun to the square inch than Mark Twain or Samantha Allen *ever* provoked. It took us a whole week to go and come. We camped out, of course, for in the whole sixty miles there was but one house, and going in that direction there is not a tree to be seen, nothing but sage, sand, and sheep. About noon the first day out we came near a sheepwagon, and stalking along ahead of us was a lanky fellow, a herder, going home for dinner. Suddenly it seemed to me I should starve if I had to wait until we got where we had planned to stop for dinner, so I called out to the man, "Little Bo-Peep, have you anything to eat? If you have, we'd like to find it." And he answered, "As soon as I am able it shall be on the table, if you'll but trouble to get behind it." Shades of Shakespeare! Songs of David, the Shepherd Poet! What do you think of us? Well, we got behind it, and a more delicious "it" I never tasted. Such coffee! And out of *such* a pot! I promised Bo-Peep that I would send him a crook with pink ribbons on it, but I suspect he thinks I am a crook without the ribbons.

The sagebrush is so short in some places that it is not large enough to   3
make a fire, so we had to drive until quite late before we camped that night. After driving all day over what seemed a level desert of sand, we came about sundown to a beautiful cañon, down which we had to drive for a couple of miles before we could cross. In the cañon the shadows had already fallen, but when we looked up we could see the last shafts of sunlight on the tops of the great bare buttes. Suddenly a great wolf started from somewhere and galloped along the edge of the cañon, outlined black and clear by the setting sun. His curiosity overcame him at last, so he sat down and waited to see what manner of beast we were. I reckon he was disappointed for he howled most dismally. I thought of Jack London's "The Wolf."

After we quitted the cañon I saw the most beautiful sight. It seemed as   4
if we were driving through a golden haze. The violet shadows were creeping up between the hills, while away back of us the snow-capped peaks were catching the sun's last rays. On every side of us stretched the poor, hopeless desert, the sage, grim and determined to live in spite of starvation, and the great, bare, desolate buttes. The beautiful colors turned to amber and rose, and then to the general tone, dull gray.

Then we stopped to camp, and such a scurrying around to gather brush   5
for the fire and to get supper! Everything tasted so good! Jerrine ate like a man. Then we raised the wagon tongue and spread the wagon sheet over it and made a bedroom for us women. We made our beds on the warm, soft sand and went to bed.

It was too beautiful a night to sleep, so I put my head out to look and   6
to think. I saw the moon come up and hang for a while over the moun-

tains as if it were discouraged with the prospect, and the big white stars flirted shamelessly with the hills.

At length a cloud came up and I went to sleep, and next morning was covered several inches with snow. It didn't hurt us a bit, but while I was struggling with stubborn corsets and shoes I communed with myself after the manner of prodigals, and said; "How much better that I were down in Denver, even at Mrs. Coney's, digging with a skewer into the corners seeking dirt which *might* be there, yea, even eating codfish, than that I should perish on this desert—of imagination." So I turned the current of my imagination and fancied that I was at home before the fireplace, and that the backlog was about to roll down. My fancy was in such good working trim that before I knew it I kicked the wagon wheel, and I certainly got as warm as the most "sot" Scientist that ever read Mrs. Eddy could possibly wish. [7]

After two more such days I "arrived." When I went up to the office where I was to file, the door was open and the most taciturn old man sat before a desk. I hesitated at the door, but he never let on. I coughed, yet no sign but a deeper scowl. I stepped in and modestly kicked over a chair. He whirled around like I had shot him. "Well?" he interrogated. I said, "I am powerful glad of it. I was afraid you were sick, you looked in such pain." He looked at me a minute, then grinned and said he thought I was a bookagent. Fancy me, a fat, comfortable widow, trying to sell books! [8]

Well, I filed and came home. If you will believe me, the Scot was glad to see me and didn't herald the Campbells for two hours after I got home. I'll tell you, it is mighty seldom any one's so much appreciated. [9]

No, we have no rural delivery. It is two miles to the office, but I go whenever I like. It is really the jolliest kind of fun to gallop down. We are sixty miles from the railroad, but when we want anything we send by the mail-carrier for it, only there is nothing to get. [10]

I know this is an inexcusably long letter, but it is snowing so hard and you know how I like to talk. [11]

Baby has the rabbit you gave her last Easter a year ago. In Denver I was afraid my baby would grow up devoid of imagination. Like all the kindergartners, she depended upon others to amuse her. I was very sorry about it, for my castles in Spain have been real homes to me. But there is no fear. She has a block of wood she found in the blacksmith shop which she calls her "dear baby." A spoke out of a wagon wheel is "little Margaret," and a barrel stave is "bad little Johnny." [12]

Well, I must quit writing before you vote me a nuisance. With lots of love to you, [13]

Your sincere friend,
Elinore Rupert

September 28, 1909

Dear Mrs. Coney,

Your second card just reached me and I am plumb glad because, al- 14
though I answered your other, I was wishing I could write you, for have
had the most charming adventure.

It is the custom here for as many women as care to, to go in a party over 15
into Utah to Ashland (which is over a hundred miles away) after fruit.
They usually go in September, and it takes a week to make the trip. They
take wagons and camp out and of course have a good time, but, the
greater part of the way, there isn't even the semblance of a road and it is
merely a semblance anywhere. They came over to invite me to join them.
I was of two minds—I wanted to go, but it seemed a little risky and a big
chance for discomfort, since we would have to cross the Unita Mountains,
and a snowstorm likely any time. But I didn't like to refuse outright, so we
left it to Mr. Stewart. His "Ye're nae gang" sounded powerful final, so the
ladies departed in awed silence and I assumed a martyr-like air and acted
like a very much abused woman, although he did only what I wanted him
to do. At last, in sheer desperation he told me the "bairn canna make the
treep," and that was why he was so determined.

I knew why, of course, but I continued to look abused lest he get it into 16
his head that he can boss me. After he had been reduced to the proper
plane of humility and had explained and begged my pardon and had told
me to consult only my own pleasure about going and coming and using
his horses, not only to "expoose" the bairn, why, I forgave him and we
were friends once more.

Next day all the men left for the round-up, to be gone a week. I knew I 17
never could stand myself a whole week. In a little while the ladies came
past on their way to Ashland. They were all laughing and were so happy
that I really began to wish I was one of the number, but they went their
way and I kept wanting to go somewhere. I got reckless and determined to
do something real bad. So I went down to the barn and saddled Robin
Adair, placed a pack on "Jeems McGregor," then Jerrine and I left for a
camping-out expedition.

It was nine o'clock when we started and we rode hard until about four, 18
when I turned Robin loose, saddle and all, for I knew he would go home
and some one would see him and put him into the pasture. We had gotten
to where we couldn't ride anyway, so I put Jerrine on the pack and led
"Jeems" for about two hours longer; then, as I had come to a good place to
camp, we stopped.

While we had at least two good hours of daylight, it gets so cold here in 19
the evening that fire is very necessary. We had been climbing higher into
the mountains all day and had reached a level tableland where the grass

was luxuriant and there was plenty of wood and water. I unpacked "Jeems" and staked him out, built a roaring fire, and made our bed in an angle of a sheer wall of rock where we would be protected against the wind. Then I put some potatoes into the embers, as Baby and I are both fond of roasted potatoes. I started to a little spring to get water for my coffee when I saw a couple of jack rabbits playing, so I went back for my little shotgun. I shot one of the rabbits, so I felt very like Leatherstocking because I had killed but one when I might have gotten two. It was fat and young, and it was but the work of a moment to dress it and hang it up on a tree.

Then I fried some slices of bacon, made myself a cup of coffee, and Jer-   20
rine and I sat on the ground and ate. Everything smelled and tasted so good! This air is so tonic that one gets delightfully hungry. Afterward we watered and restaked "Jeems," I rolled some logs on to the fire, and then we sat and enjoyed the prospect.

The moon was so new that its light was very dim, but the stars were   21
bright. Presently a long, quivering wail arose and was answered from a dozen hills. It seemed just the sound one ought to hear in such a place. When the howls ceased for a moment we could hear the subdued roar of the creek and the crooning of the wind in the pines. So we rather enjoyed the coyote chorus and were not afraid, because they don't attack people. Presently we crept under our Navajos and, being tired, were soon asleep.

I was awakened by a pebble striking my cheek. Something prowling on   22
the bluff above us had dislodged it and it struck me. By my Waterbury it was four o'clock, so I arose and spitted my rabbit. The logs had left a big bed of coals, but some ends were still burning and had burned in such a manner that the heat would go both under and over my rabbit. So I put plenty of bacon grease over him and hung him up to roast. Then I went back to bed. I didn't want to start early because the air is too keen for com-fort early in the morning.

The sun was just gilding the hilltops when we arose. Everything, even   23
the barrenness, was beautiful. We have had frosts, and the quaking aspens were a trembling field of gold as far up the stream as we could see. We were 'way up above them and could look far across the valley. We could see the silvery gold of the willows, the russet and bronze of the currants, and patches of cheerful green showed where the pines were. The splendor was relieved by a background of sober gray green hills, but even on them gay streaks and patches of yellow showed where rabbit brush grew. We washed our faces at the spring—the grasses that grew around the edge and dipped into the water were loaded with ice. Our rabbit was done to a burn, so I made some delicious coffee. Jerrine got herself a can of water, and we breakfasted. Shortly afterwards we started again. We didn't know where we were going, but we were on our way.

That day was more toilsome than the last, but a very happy one. The   24 meadowlarks kept singing like they were glad to see us. But we were still climbing and soon got beyond the larks and sage chickens and up into the timber, where there are lots of grouse. We stopped to noon by a little lake, where I got two small squirrels and a string of trout. We had some trout for dinner and salted the rest with the squirrels in an empty can for future use. I was anxious to get a grouse and kept close watch, but was never quick enough.

Our progress was now slower and more difficult, because in places we could scarcely get through the forest. Fallen trees were everywhere and we had to avoid the branches, which was powerful hard to do. Besides, it was quite dusky among the trees long before night, but it was all so grand and awe-inspiring. Occasionally there was an opening through which we could see the snowy peaks, seemingly just beyond us, toward which we were headed. But when you get among such grandeur you get to feel how little you are and how foolish is human endeavor, except that which reunites us with the mighty force called God. I was plumb uncomfortable, because all my own efforts have always been just to make the best of everything and to take things as they come.   25

At last we came to an open side of the mountain where the trees were scattered. We were facing south and east, and the mountain we were on sheered away in a dangerous slant. Beyond us still greater wooded mountains blocked the way, and in the cañon between night had already fallen. I began to get scary. I could only think of bears and catamounts, so, as it was five o'clock, we decided to camp. The trees were immense. The lower branches came clear to the ground and grew so dense that any tree afforded a splendid shelter from the weather, but I was nervous and wanted one that would protect us against any possible attack. At last we found one growing in a crevice of what seemed to be a sheer wall of rock. Nothing could reach us on two sides, and in front two large trees had fallen so that I could make a log heap which would give us warmth and make us safe. So with rising spirits I unpacked and prepared for the night.   26

I soon had a roaring fire up against the logs and, cutting away a few branches, let the heat into as snug a bedroom as any one could wish. The pine needles made as soft a carpet as the wealthiest could afford. Springs abound in the mountains, so water was plenty. I staked "Jeems" quite near so that the firelight would frighten away any wild thing that tried to harm him. Grass was very plentiful, so when he was made "comfy" I made our bed and fried our trout. The branches had torn off the bag in which I had my bread, so it was lost in the forest, but who needs bread when they have good, mealy potatoes? In a short time we were eating like Lent was just over. We lost all the glory of the sunset except what we got by reflection, being on the side of the mountain we were, with the dense woods be-   27 tween. Big sullen clouds kept drifting over and a wind got lost in the trees that kept them rocking and groaning in a horrid way. But we were just as cozy as we could be and rest was as good as anything.

I wish you could once sleep on the kind of bed we enjoyed that night. 28 It was both soft and firm, with the clean, spicy smell of the pine. The heat from our big fire came in and we were warm as toast. It was so good to stretch out and rest. I kept thinking how superior I was since I dared to take such an outing when so many poor women down in Denver were bent on making their twenty cents per hour in order that they could spare a quarter to go to the "show." I went to sleep with a powerfully self-satisfied feeling, but I awoke to realize that pride goeth before a fall.

I could hardly remember where I was when I awoke, and I could almost 29 hear the silence. Not a tree moaned, not a branch seemed to stir. I arose and my head came in violent contact with a snag that was not there when I went to bed. I thought either I must have grown taller or the tree shorter during the night. As soon as I peered out, the mystery was explained.

Such a snowstorm I never saw! The snow had pressed the branches 30 down lower, hence my bumped head. Our fire was burning merrily and the heat kept the snow from in front. I scrambled out and poked up the fire; then, as it was only five o'clock, I went back to bed. And then I began to think how many kinds of idiot I was. Here I was thirty or forty miles from home, in the mountains where no one goes in the winter and where I knew the snow got to be ten or fifteen feet deep. But I could never see the good of moping, so I got up and got breakfast while Baby put her shoes on. We had our squirrels and more baked potatoes and I had delicious black coffee.

After I had eaten I felt more hopeful. I knew Mr. Stewart would hunt 31 for me if he knew I was lost. It was true, he wouldn't know which way to start, but I determined to rig up "Jeems" and turn him loose, for I knew he would go home and that he would leave a trail so that I could be found. I hated to do so, for I knew I should always be powerfully humble afterwards.

Anyway, it was still snowing, great, heavy flakes; they looked as large as 32 dollars. I didn't want to start "Jeems" until the snow stopped because I wanted him to leave a clear trail. I had sixteen loads for my gun and I reasoned that I could likely kill enough food to last twice that many days by being careful what I shot at. It just kept snowing, so at last I decided to take a little hunt and provide for the day. I left Jerrine happy with the towel rolled into a baby, and went along the brow of the mountain for almost a mile, but the snow fell so thickly that I couldn't see far. Then I happened to look down into the cañon that lay east of us and saw smoke. I looked toward it a long time, but could make out nothing but smoke, but presently I heard a dog bark and I knew I was near a camp of some kind. I resolved to join them, so went back to break my own camp.

At last everything was ready and Jerrine and I both mounted. Of all the times! If you think there is much comfort, or even security, in riding a pack horse in a snow storm over mountains where there is no road, you are plumb wrong. Every once in a while a tree would unload its snow down our backs. "Jeems" kept stumbling and threatening to break our necks. At last we got down the mountain-side, where new danger confronted us—we might lose sight of the smoke or ride into a bog. But at last, after what seemed hours, we came into a "clearing" with a small log house and, what is rare in Wyoming, a fireplace. Three or four hounds set up their deep baying, and I knew by the chimney and the hounds that it was the home of a Southerner. A little old man came bustling out, chewing his tobacco so fast, and almost frantic about his suspenders, which it seemed he couldn't get adjusted. 33

As I rode up, he said, "Wither, friend?" I said "Hither." Then he asked, "Are you spying around for one of them dinged game wardens after that deer I killed yisteddy?" I told him I had never even seen a game warden and that I didn't know he had killed a deer. "Wall," he said, "Are you spying around arter that gold mine I diskivered over on the west side of Baldy?" But after a while I convinced him that I was no more nor less than a foolish woman lost in the snow. Then he said, "Light, stranger, and look at your saddle." So I "lit" and looked, and then I asked him what part of the South he was from. He answered, "Yell County, by gum! The best place in the United States, or in the world, either." This was my introduction to Zebulon Pike Parker. 34

Only two "Johnny Rebs" could have enjoyed each other's company as Zebulon Pike and myself did. He was so small and so old, but so cheerful and so sprightly, and a real Southerner! He had a big, open fireplace with backlogs and andirons. How I enjoyed it all! How we feasted on some of the deer killed "yestiddy," and real corn-pone baked in a skillet down on the hearth. He was so full of happy recollections and had a few that were not so happy! He is, in some way, a kinsman of Pike of Pike's Peak fame, and he came west "jist after the wah" on some expedition and "jist stayed." He told me all about his home life back in Yell County . . . 35

I got home at twelve and found, to my joy, that none of the men had returned, so I am safe from their superiority for a while, at least. 36

With many apologies for this outrageous letter, I am,
Your ex-Washlady,
Elinore Rupert

MUSINGS

Stewart includes vivid descriptions of her environment as she continues on her trip. Her writing is marked by two qualities that distinguish all good writers: inclusion of all five senses in her descriptions and use of figures of speech. She speaks of her bed "which was both soft and firm, with the clean, spicy smell of pine," appealing to both the sense of touch and smell. She describes her food, which she obviously savored, in great detail, appealing to both the sense of smell and the sense of taste. She enables us to hear the coyotes' "long, quivering wail" and the "subdued roar of the creek and the crooning of the wind in the pines." Her writing appeals to senses other than sight.

Stewart uses figures of speech artfully, particularly personification. She writes that "a wind got lost in the trees that kept them rocking and groaning in a horrid way." Stewart also makes good use of informal words, such as when she tells Mrs. Coney that "she is plumb wrong" or speaks of something being "powerful hard to do." Such language never detracts from her writing, and the meaning is always clear.

Try writing a description of an outdoor scene, appealing to all five senses and using some personification.

E. M. FORSTER (1879–1970)

In his many letters to his mother in England, E. M. Forster faithfully documents his first trip to India, the country that was to play such an important role in his future writings. In the following letter he describes his initial visit with the maharaja. Forster evidences his love for the country and his personal admiration for the Indian ruler. India was then a colony of the British Empire, whose response to growing Indian nationalism was an increasingly repressive regime. A special criminal code was adopted that provided trial without jury for treason and deportation or imprisonment for Indian agitators. A strict class system isolated Indian nationals from British rulers and members of the East India Company. These early letters reveal Forster's love for the country and its people, but little of the ongoing internal strife of India.

When Forster returned a decade later, however, to work as the maharaja's secretary, he gained insight into imperialism from both the Indian and the British viewpoints. The British finally recognized Indian nationalism and granted India independence on August 15, 1947. A government based on Western concepts of democracy was established, although the country suffered for many years from internal strife arising from antagonism between the Muslims and the Sikhs.

Forster is best known for his novels A Room with a View, Howard's End, *and his later and most highly critically acclaimed novel,* A Passage to India, *which grew out of his Indian experiences and his heightened sensitivity to the plight of the natives. When his letters, edited by Mary Lago and P. N. Furbank, were published in 1980, they revealed much about his character and, as one critic noted, "greater insight into the relationship between Forster's life and his art." Forster thought highly of his own works and read them often, going "gently over the bits I think are bad." He maintained that he "always found writing pleasant" and did not understand what people meant by the "throes of creation."*

Chhatarpur, Central India

Guest House, Chhatarpur, Bundelkhand,
Central India, 1 December 1912

Dearest Mother

Letters reach this paradise slowly, and I may have to post this before I receive your (third) letter from Florence. I seem to keep on saying 'this *is* the best of all', but really Chhatarpur *is*. The scenery, of which I have often complained, is here most lovely. The Guest House stands on a ridge, and from its broad Verandah we look down on the temples of the city, rising

1

104

out of trees, and over a green plain out of which rise other ridges, and hills like the Dartmoor Tors. The whole country is Jungle. Tigers—(but far too well mannered to eat men)—reside quite near, and monkeys of the sweetest sort come & sit in the trees half a dozen yards away. The ladies sit with their babies clinging to them; the gentlemen swing about in search of tropical fruit. Half a mile off is the Palace, where we go daily, and between us and it is a tank in which the population bathes. The nearest Englishman is 15 miles off, and the nearest Ry Station 35. So we have gone & done it.

We arrived at the station 4 days ago, in the evening, and the Maharaja's motor met us—the servants came on with the luggage afterwards. It was a wonderful moonlight drive. Bob's hat flew off. At the Guest House we were welcomed by many officials but no supper. It came at last, but oh so slowly, and we got to bed very late. The bedrooms are large & airy, and we also have three sitting rooms. The food is not up to sample, and whether owing to it or to something at Gwalior, Dickinson has had a bad digestive upset. The Doctor (Indian of course) is an able man, and I think he has had every comfort, but it is very unlucky for him and even unluckier for the Maharaja who is thirsting for philosophic talk with him: they have only met once. I think he is better tonight, but remains in bed. Bob and I are very well. Finding the place so pleasant and the Maharaja so hospitable and charming, I had at once determined to stop on when D. and T. left, as it will fill up my gap between this and Xmas; and now they too are stopping on owing to D's illness, and will also stop after his recovery to see the Khujraho temples. Bob has quite changed—no hurry—plenty of time. So the atmosphere is restful.

Well, I will describe a typical day, for we are already settling into a routine. Baldeo brings tea at 7.0—I often have it on the verandah and see the sunrise: a new experience for me. Breakfast about 9.0, and then the Doctor and Private Secretary drive up—the first a Hindu, very fat, but charming and kind, the second a Hindu-ised Mahommedan who was educated at Aligarh. He is an able and entertaining man, and, being Chief Magistrate as well, is very important in the state. We drive away with him after a time, and come back to lunch. Then the Maharaja's carriage comes for us—perhaps at 2.0. perhaps at 4.—so crowded with menials to do us honour that the horses can scarcely draw it—coachman, coachman's companion, footman, messenger, most of them in rags, and the carriage itself—(a landau going to seed)—smells of grease most terrible. As we go through the town, every one bows. The Palace is white washed; a very beautiful entrance hall in native architecture. We are set down here while the messenger goes to the Maharaja and returns with the message 'He sends his salaams.' We go down the hall into a courtyard, where the ugliest little man you can imagine greets us under an enormous umbrella. It is more like a tent without sides than an umbrella, and when the conversation is above my head, as often, I raise my eyes to it—most gorgeous: tigers elephants deer &ᶜᵗ interlaced by foliage: it must be a priceless piece of work. We sit on chairs: His Highness squats on a cane lounge-chair: the Private Secretary sits like Buddha on a rug at his feet. The interview is very queer and sometimes lasts three hours. The chief subjects are philosophy and religious speculation, in which I do not shine; in fact I haven't made as good an impression as the other two. I gathered from the Morisons that the Maharaja is absurd, but this is quite wrong. He has certainly read bad books as well as good and—(like many would-be[']s nearer home)—can't distinguish between them; but he is so sensible and shrewd, and so full of fun, that listening & talking to him are both delightful. He would be a remarkable man in any country, and out here is very strange indeed. He hates ruling, and I think rules badly, and here he is in a wild jungle with no one to talk to on subjects he cares about. He is pleased with us, for he has let us see his Mystery Players—scarcely any Englishmen have done this, the Private Secretary tells me. His dress is a frock coat of dark buff, buttoned to the throat, knickers of thin white stuff embroidered, and socks. He wears little earrings, and at the base of his snub nose yellow paint is smeared, in honour of Krishna. He cannot eat with us, receive us inside the palace, or offer us his own cigarettes; but he can discuss why he does not do these things, and his mind is more fresh and tolerant than the average European's. His kindness is tremendous—but this, I believe, is usual in India. We are driven everywhere and offered everything, and he is now wanting to wire for an English Doctor, but this won't be necessary, for I'm glad to say that (since I began this letter) D. is much better. To conclude our day. When he has had enough he dismisses us with 'But I will not tire you longer' or something of the sort, and we drive up to the Guest House again. If the sun hasn't set, we then go a little walk; the colours are wonderful.

The Khajraho expedition is waiting for D's recovery. Tents are already there, officials too, and we have given everyone, the Private Secretary in particular, much trouble: I am glad that I had a separate introduction to him through his brother at Aligarh. Khajraho (8ᵗʰ cent. Temples) is 20 miles off—a motor road—and we were to spend the night there. I do hope we shall bring it off soon. I am so afraid of making the State Bankrupt for it is very poor and would show a deficit if it hadn't dug up an enormous treasure of gold coins in a deserted building two or three years ago. It exports betel nut and bones, but gets nothing for the bones for no Hindu will touch them, and outcasts from other states come & pick them off the fields &ᶜᵗ for nothing.—On the other hand it is a very healthy place— plague & cholera are almost unknown among the people, however poor, and even malaria is uncommon. There is no religious bitterness, such as I found at Lahore, and (as far as I can see) no irritation against the English. The climate is charming—sun and a gentle breeze.

The Mystery Play was at night on a terrace at the top of the Palace. Poor D. couldn't go, and Bob and I saw it alone with the Private Secretary. It was very impressive. The musicians salaamed when we entered, but the actors sat on their thrones—Krishna, Rad[h]a his wife, and four attendant women. As soon as we arrived they began by dances, at the same time singing—not words, but sounds. The musicians also sang, and the performance worked up to a real crisis, like the Russian Ballet, after which they returned to their thrones. After two such displays, the play came—a Nativity Story, reminding one of the Magi. A blue shawl edged with gold was held up by the attendants at the other end of the stage. This symbolised the wall of a house, behind which was Krishna as a baby in the arms of his mother. We could see their heads, but they were not supposed to be seen by the other actor—an old Hermit who comes to see the child: in his hand is a cobra (papier maché of course). The mother calls from the house 'No, you cannot see him—you are a demon with snakes about you & will harm him.' He explains that he has only disguised himself for the journey, but she still refuses. Then he cries 'I want to see him, for he is my god.' (K. is one of the incarnations of Vishnu.) 'Your child is a god and you do not know it, but I do.' She answers 'Hush—go away—you will frighten the baby—he is too young.' He answers 'He is not too young, for he is divine.' Then they drive him away, and he goes saying 'He is my god and will come after me', and as soon as he is out of sight the baby begins to cry! They can't stop him and have to call the hermit back, and the blue shawl is dropped to the ground. The mother carries Krishna out and the Hermit adores him. She then begs him to stop there for ever. He answers 'I cannot do that, but I will come whenever the Baby cries.'!—It was more of an opera than a drama: there was a running accompaniment on the orchestra, and the Hermit all through danced,—not in the Western fashion, but he moved with elaborate and dignified little steps. It was a beautiful little play, and the music was seldom uncouth—it is 'male music'—the actors being boys and different to the 'female' nautch music, which is all that I have heard in India so far. Much of this was in our own major & minor keys, whereas Heaven only knows what the 'female' was in.—I have written rather a long account because I seem to have seen something very uncommon and I wished to write it down. Missionaries often censure Krishna, but his conduct was impeccable on this occasion. When the Maharaja is there, he takes the performance very seriously, sitting on the floor out of respect to the actors and garlanding with marygolds at the end. I think that is why he would not witness the performance with us. We asked the Private Secretary to compliment the Actors for us, but he addressed not them but their teacher, who sat among the musicians. They remained expressionless on their thrones.—Then we went down winding stairs through the Library where Herbert Spencer & Huxley mixed with Indian Bedclothes, lay in piles on the floor. The only conclusion I come to is that His Highness has really first class taste. The whole performance was very good, and whatever ornaments &ct I have caught sight of in the palace are beautiful. The next day he showed us some pictures of Krishna. These too were good. It is a relief after the hideous big palace at Gwalior.

Yesterday morning we went on an Elephant into the Jungle, the Private Secretary with us. Elephant was a dear, and walked quicker & more easily than the lady of Gwalior. When he came to rocks, he hated it, and felt everything with his trunk. He also made a queer vibrating noise—rather like the rumbling at the beginning of Reinhardt's Oedipus—which I thought might be a distant tiger and the P.S. did too for he asked the Mahout, who replied No, it came from Elephant's own inside, and he made it when he hoped he was getting to the end of his journey. We stopped at the bottom of the shrine to the Goddess of Rain, which stands on a crag in the wildest part of the jungle, and climbed up to it. There was a splendid view. Bob wanted to bring out his poetry there. The Brahman who should have been in attendance was away gathering wild fruits, so we had a good view of the Goddess—an elementary person, painted vermilion. The shrine was between enormous boulders, over which were twisted the roots of a tree. Returning, we found Elephant up to his knees in a marsh, lunching off reeds and very happy. More splendid trees by its edge and many water birds; there was even a tank in which Bob was allowed to bathe.—This is the place where an annual fair is held during the Rains. The people all make merry with rain falling gently on them, which they like, the Raja comes out of Chhatarpur to look at them, and the Brahman gets rich with tips.

I must stop, though there is heaps to tell: e.g. I have inspected the Hospital & the Jail—the latter a most cheerful place: the people in India live so simply and eat so little that it is impossible to punish them. They sat about in the sun, talking as much as they liked, and working gently at carpets. I bought a 'durry' or light rug—it is quite cheap and washes: not a bad design, though too mattress-like in parts. Measure, about 7 feet by 4. I don't know what will be its fate, but it will have pleasant memories.

Oh I forgot! At Simla I met William Archer—he who censured Howards End—and he turned up again at Agra, where we saw a good deal of him. I liked him very much. I don't know whether he remembered he had written about me. We shared carriages with him several times, and on leaving he gave me some introductions for Hardwar that will be very useful to me—to the Arya Somaj College, but it's too late to explain what that is.

Well—since beginning this letter, I have had yours, to my great delight—the one in which you say that you have just heard from me. How long it all takes! A pertikly interesting & amusing letter. We were thrilled by your romantic adventure near the Carmine and wonder whose the house was. Miss Breton sounds trying. You must be a mistress of languages now—Italian as well as French. I think I could have got on with Urdu if I had had decent grammar, but there seems none. I have to learn by asking people the words. I'm anxious for your next letter, as it may tell me whether you will risk Venice. I hope not, as you know. It too may reach me here, as I have only Bhopal and Indore to 'put in' before Xmas, and my other luggage has been sent for from the station.

Good night, dearest mummy, from your loving Poppy.

Chhatarpur, 16 December 1912

Dearest Mother

We are still here—no difficulty in stopping but much in getting away.   10
Dickinson's poor inside is as well as it can ever expect to be so far East, and we should have left today—Monday. "No, no, I cannot have it, I will not speak of it. Journeys begun on Monday always end disastrously." Then Bob flew into a passion—fortunately when we left the Maharaja's presence. "I simply *will* go on Monday. I don't care what he says—we've given in too much already and he thinks he can behave as he likes. You & Dickinson can stop, but I shall just go on alone." So it was agreed to stand firm, and then when we went to the Mystery Play again last night, the Private Secretary stopped me at the Palace Door with "Oh Mr Forster, His Highness is so unhappy, and though I have warned him not to persist, he will. Do, do, intercede with your friends to grant him this little favour." I said "I'm afraid they must go." However they haven't. They gave in, and Bob is now quite happy again. Well, well. I am very glad to stop on myself, being very fond indeed of the Maharaja, and the two chief officials of the State—the Private Secretary and the Prime Minister—are also ~~very~~ nice, though fortunately more practical than His Highness, who is the Prince of Muddlers, even of Indian muddlers. Nothing ever happens here either when or as it is planned. Khujraho has at last been accomplished, but with endless bungling, Bob and I going to sleep there in tents one day, and D[ickinson] being sent alone in a motor the other. The temples are very wonderful but nightmares—all exactly alike and covered with sculptures from top to toe. There are about 30 in all, mostly deserted. The tents were ~~quite~~ comfortable, though Bob had rats and birds and a dripping lamp in his, and slept badly. I did very well.

We see the Maharaja every day, and he usually takes us a motor drive. A   11
'poor cousin' comes too, and carries his opera glasses, cigarettes, betel nut, umbrella, stick, and State sword, together with a bundle which I suppose contains food, but he always eats in solitude. Poor cousin sits in front with

the chauffeur: we and the Maharaja are squeezed behind. Here and there about the roads we come on State carriages, who would pick us up if the car broke—very necessary, for there are no garages. The roads are very good and the country in parts superb. Bears, tigers, leopards, are said to 'rebound', but it is difficult to believe, and as they never attack man, one is perfectly safe. The only surprises are the monkeys, who go about in flocks. There are two kinds—the grey apes with black faces are dears, but they are not as sacred as the others, because they ran away from a battle in which they had promised to help Rama, and their faces turned black as a punishment. The brave monkeys, who did not run away, have red faces, and are horrible. There are also the most wonderful birds. When we were sitting on the roof of a deserted palace upon the side of a hill, one perched on a tree close against us. It was like a swallow in shape, but twice as large, and crimson. The Maharaja exclaimed 'It flashes like a jewel—it must be a Robin Redbreast.' He loves scenery and architecture and all that is beautiful in a way that is very rare for an Indian.

I go on after an explosion of wrath with the Munshi (head servant at the Guest House), who has, for the second night running, left some of the lamps without wicks and the rest without oil. Smell and darkness all over the house. They have not treated us well here, and, being guests of State, one naturally did not complain; but we have been urged to do so not only by other passing guests but by the Private Secretary himself, who says that the State will be charged for all sorts of things that we have not had ('This is inevitable') and that we are to insist on everything being right. So my few words of Urdu are useful, and I wish they were more. The Munshi is a venerable and very tiresome old man. When I complained of the lamps yesterday he said the Prime Minister would not let him have any oil!

Another disappointment is that my mail has not reached me here, so that I write without receiving your 4th letter from Florence; it will wander after me to Bhopal. I do hope it won't go astray. I am so anxious to hear whether you kept to your plan of Venice. The journey to Bhopal will be horrid. I have to sleep in the waiting room at Jhansi, and then either travel in a '3rd Class only' at 5.0. next morning, or else hang about Jhansi station till 4.0. in the afternoon. Sad dilemma. Howsomenever. One can't get off the beaten track without these difficulties, and I have had a lovely time here.

Your loving Poppy

MUSINGS

Forster seems to be unaware of the tensions in India, although his British imperial attitude is patently evident. However, his letter also reflects his love for the country and his respect and liking for the Indian ruler. Nevertheless, the message is mixed, and his impatience with the country's customs often comes through. Forster seldom mentions his emotions, but his detailed descriptions and his choice of incidents make his feelings clear.

Forster initially describes only one day, but he carefully selects the details to present a coherent, overall picture of his surroundings and the people. Write a letter to a family member describing a day when you found yourself in an environment that was foreign to you—visiting a friend, neighborhood, church, or school where the practices differ from yours. Select one or two particular incidents or persons that will best reflect the character of the new environment.

Isak Dinesen (1885–1962)

Isak Dinesen is the pseudonym of Baroness Karen Blixen, who was born in Denmark; she wrote eloquently in both English and her native Danish. As David Lehman notes in Newsweek, *"Isak Dinesen led a life as wildly improbable and flamboyantly romantic as her exotic and spellbinding tales." Her childhood was interrupted by the unhappy suicide of her father, who hanged himself. Theirs had been a close relationship, and she maintained that his death caused her the kind of pain that only children experience. She was "suddenly pushed into the foremost row of life, bereft of the joy and irresponsibility of childhood." Her brother later surmised that their father had suffered from syphilis, a disease that Dinesen later contracted from her husband.*

As a child Dinesen was tutored at home and showed great artistic talent, which she believed influenced her ability to visualize a scene and write descriptions. Dinesen entered the Royal Academy in Copenhagen but, because of an unrequited love affair with her cousin, she left Denmark in 1910 to study art in Paris. She returned to the family estate later that year and began writing. She subsequently married Baron Bror Blixen, and together they moved to Africa to start a coffee plantation outside of Nairobi. Divorced in 1921, he became a full-time big-game hunter while she stayed on the farm and remained greatly attached to the native helpers.

Dinesen lived most of her life in an upper-class atmosphere, and she reflects those attitudes and the prevailing outlook of colonialism so prevalent in the Africa of her time. These perspectives come across in her condescending and patronizing attitude toward her helpers, despite her genuine love and concern for them.

In the following letter written to her family in Denmark, Dinesen describes in gory and heartrending detail an accident that occurred with her workers' children when one of them inadvertently gets hold of a handgun. One child dies in her arms, and she faithfully visits another as he recovers in the hospital. She also worries about the fate of the child who accidentally shot the gun and wonders what his future will be within the native culture.

The following selection is taken from her collected letters edited by Frans Lasson, translated by Anne Born, and published in 1978.

Letter From Africa

In the hope of attracting workers to the farm I am going to start a
school here in the new year; I have wanted to do this for a very long time,
but Dickens was very opposed to it, but now has come to think better of
it. We will use rooms in "Charlie's House," Thomas knows where that is,

and I think it will be a great pleasure. It will only be in the evening so as not to <u>interfere</u> with work on the farm. Unfortunately the Wakambas in particular are very much against the Catholics,—I don't know why; they have a theory that they do not teach them enough,—so that I shall have to upset my friends at the French Mission against my will, but it is no good opposing the wishes of the natives in such matters when one particularly wants to attract them to come here. I think that every large farm ought to have a school; there is no point in saying that natives are more happy in their primitive state; besides that being very questionable in itself, it is impossible to keep them there and by making no attempt to educate them all that results is that they get hold of all the worst aspects of civilization, like the frightful type of "Nairobi boys" that has developed since I first came out here, which is on a par with those at home, with "their hair over their eyes," that Uncle Rentz thought should be taken out to Nørrefælled and shot. After all, it is an honest ambition in the natives to be eager to learn. As I say, I am very glad to be getting this going.

Major Taylor came out this week to look at the farm, and it was really a great joy to hear his opinion of it. He has not been out since February and so can see the changes in it better than I and Dickens, who go around staring at it every day. I expect he will be sending a report home. On the same day that he had been here something terrible and sad happened. I was in my bath before dinner when I heard a shot,—which I always hate to hear, especially at night, but I thought it was one of the white people shooting at a hyena. A little later Thaxton came tearing up here on his motorcycle and said there had been an accident; while his cook was out, his kitchen toto had got some other small boys together in his hut, and one of them had got hold of a shotgun that Thaxton was keeping on his verandah with which to frighten birds of prey away from his poultry, and had fired it into the midst of them. Thaxton was completely beside himself and did not know how many had been wounded, and asked me to go down with him. I put on some clothes and ran down to his house,—the one Thomas had during the last part of his stay here,—with him. I heard later that three other children had been slightly wounded, they had run off—when we got there there were only two. One of them, Maturri, whom Thomas may perhaps remember, such a sweet happy little toto, had been shot in the neck and chest,—he was lying unconscious in a great pool of blood; the other was sitting up with blood streaming out of his mouth, or what was left of his mouth,—the lower part of his jaw was completely shot away.

I bandaged him up as well as I could, but it was difficult with only the light of a wretched lantern, and then fetched my car to drive them in to the hospital. My lights were not working, that is to say, I have no lights, and the car would not start; it seemed an eternity before we got started,—it was not at all easy to get them settled in the car, and then you feel every bump in the road so frightfully in such a situation,—but we got there. Thaxton, and Kamante, whom Thomas knows, were with me; Farah happened to be away that night. When we lifted Maturri out of the car the poor child died. The other one had lost a great deal of blood, the whole car was covered with it, and was in a pitiable state, but is still alive. I went in to see him the next day. I think it would have been better for him if he had died, and he would certainly have died if we had not taken him in, but one *cannot* think like that. I do not think he suffered, the shock had no doubt been too great; when I was running down through the wood I could hear him screaming and sobbing, but when I got down there and took his head in my hands and said to him: calm down, I have come to help you,—he did not make another sound, not once all the way in, when he was jolted about a lot. Maturri cannot have felt anything at all; he had the whole charge, with No. 4 shot, in the chest,—he was moaning but was unconscious.

We drove down to the police station at once to report it, and they kept   4 us there for hours; we did not get back until three in the morning,—the accident had probably happened about half past seven. Of course the police cannot say anything; it was obviously an accident, or caused by children playing. But Thaxton will probably get a fine for leaving his gun out loaded. The poor child who shot it off has disappeared; naturally he must be absolutely terrified. It happened last Wednesday and we have been searching for him ever since, and of course so have his family, he is Kanino's son. I think he may perhaps have run over to the Masai and is hiding there; Farah has a theory that he will stay there until "he has married six or five wife," and as he is only eight it will no doubt be some time before I get to see him again. If only I knew that he was being safely looked after somewhere. One can never rely on natives' nerves. Three other children were slightly wounded, but nothing to worry about.

I had to go into Nairobi again the next morning as I had an appointment   5 with Hunter in order to get some money for my white people before Christmas, which they naturally wanted and deserved, as they have waited for their money so patiently. I had lunch with the McMillans and then went to the hospital to see Wanjangiri. It is a really excellent native hospital and a good doctor. He had drunk some milk, and he knew me and understood what I said to him, and now they are going to try to sew him up; but they would not be able to see how things would go with him until later on, and I do not know what they can do, as his teeth and jawbone have been shot away. They said he had been well bandaged up and that had stopped the bleeding; that was pure luck, as I could hardly see anything. Since then his brother has been in to see him, and he was about the same. I caught such a cold from being out driving at night; I had hardly any clothes on, only a skirt and a coat and shoes, and next day I completely lost my voice, perhaps that was something to do with nerves; I was so tired when I got back that night from the expedition, as if I had walked for five miles, so I have been in bed for a day or two. Old Mr. Bulpett drove out to see me, that was nice of him.

Little Maturri who died was such a fine little toto; he was with me for a time but then went to work at sorting coffee at the factory, and he always waved and laughed when I went down there; I had seen him there the same afternoon, when I was there with Charles Taylor, and it seems so strange that he should have died in my arms a few hours later. . . . 6

• • •

I went into Nairobi again yesterday. . . . I had the joy of finding my child in hospital much better; they were tidying up the wards, and he was lying on a stretcher outside and waved to me when I arrived. I took Kamante, whom Thomas knew, with me, so that he could comfort him by telling him how ill he had once been, and now is so big and strong and plays football; so he sat on his bed and gave him a lecture, but as the conversation was in Kikuyu I could not take much part in it. . . . 7

I feel so sorry for the little toto who shot the other two; he has completely vanished. His family have been out searching for him all over the area; we have had people from Nairobi hunting too, but we cannot find the slightest trace of him. His own people think that he was so terrified that he has taken his own life; natives are so inclined to do this as soon as life becomes difficult, even about things one can see would be overcome in the course of a few days, but they find it impossible to look ahead. And then a little child like that, if he runs into the jungle to hide, can easily be caught by leopards or lions. But another possibility is that he has run away to the Masai,—that strange dying race is eager to grasp any of the children of other tribes that they can lay hands on, and they will not give them back; they accept them into the tribe and bequeath all their earthly goods to them, and they can be of great value, so that would be a kind of promotion for Kabiro; but of course they are lost to their own tribe. Something of this kind happened just recently to one of Kamante's brothers, who ran away from his family fifteen years ago because he had lost a sheep and was frightened of his father, and who recently, when he saw Kamante and his other brothers walking on the other side of the river, came down and called across to them and told them like another Joseph that he had been adopted by a chief's family, owned great herds and was married to two Masai wives, but that he had promised never to go back to Kikuyu. This is a comedown for the Masai who used to despise the Kikuyu in the old days, but now no children are born to them. I hope this is what has happened to Kanino's son, but it is not possible to find out . . . 8

MUSINGS

Although this incident occurred some time ago in Africa, it still holds meaning in today's American society. We think of those who are injured as the only victims, but as this incident makes clear the boy who held the gun is no less a victim than those he shot.

Dinesen demonstrates her care and concern through physical actions and many small details. Write a letter to a friend describing an accident or the illness of a person with whom you were concerned. Rather than telling of your concern, show it through the details of small things that you and others did to care for the person.

E. B. WHITE (1899–1985)

After E. B. White graduated from Cornell University, he worked for several years as a roving reporter, driving cross-country with one of his friends. When they ran out of money they performed for food and gasoline on an instrument that White had constructed out of wire and tin cans. He later began writing for The New Yorker, *composing the well-known "Talk of the Town" section. White's urbane style set the distinctive tone of that publication, and his talents extended to all areas; he wrote some advertisements and fillers, and even painted a cover for the magazine. His mastery of style is evidenced in his essays, many of which were published in* The New Yorker. *White encouraged his good friend James Thurber to publish his line drawings, originally composed for the amusement of the office staff, by retrieving them from the wastebasket and turning them in himself.*

A gentle humor and wisdom underlie all of E. B. White's work. Although White is recognized as one of the finest essayists of the twentieth century, he is probably best known for his popular children's classics, Stuart Little *(1945) and* Charlotte's Web *(1952).* Stuart Little *is the story of a two-inch-tall mouse that goes through a number of misadventures, such as being rolled up in a window shade and dropped into a bathtub drain. White was criticized for the ending that finds Stuart Little still searching for his lover, but he defends his conclusion by saying that "Stuart's journey symbolizes the continuing journey that everybody takes—in search of what is perfect and unattainable"; as one critic comments, "such a quest is never completed." In* Charlotte's Web, *the themes of death and birth are intermingled in the sad demise of the beloved arachnid savior of Wilbur the pig and the simultaneous birth of her hundreds of children.*

In the following letter, probably part fiction and part fact, White demonstrates his concern for the environment and, with underlying humor and basic goodwill, laments the devastation that now surrounds the cabin that Thoreau described so eloquently in the excerpt from his diary included in the first section of this book (p. 27). White also contrasts the complications of modern life with the simplicity of Thoreau's life on Walden Pond. Choosing to cast his ideas in the form of a letter to Thoreau, White begins the essay by asking his fictional secretary to "take a letter."

Walden

Miss Nims, take a letter to Henry David Thoreau. Dear Henry: I 1
thought of you the other afternoon as I was approaching Concord doing

fifty on Route 62. That is a high speed at which to hold a philosopher in one's mind, but in this century we are a nimble bunch.

On one of the lawns in the outskirts of the village a woman was cutting the grass with a motorized lawn mower. What made me think of you was that the machine had rather got away from her, although she was game enough, and in the brief glimpse I had of the scene it appeared to me that the lawn was mowing the lady. She kept a tight grip on the handles, which throbbed violently with every explosion of the one-cylinder motor, and as she sheered around bushes and lurched along at a reluctant trot behind her impetuous servant, she looked like a puppy who had grabbed something that was too much for him. Concord hasn't changed much, Henry; the farm implements and the animals still have the upper hand. 2

I may as well admit that I was journeying to Concord with the deliber- ate intention of visiting your woods; for although I have never knelt at the grave of a philosopher nor placed wreaths on moldy poets, and have often gone a mile out of my way to avoid some place of historical interest, I have always wanted to see Walden Pond. The account which you left of your sojourn there is, you will be amused to learn, a document of increasing pertinence; each year it seems to gain a little headway, as the world loses ground. We may all be transcendental yet, whether we like it or not. As our common complexities increase, any tale of individual simplicity (and yours is the best written and the cockiest) acquires a new fascination; as our goods accumulate, but not our well-being, your report of an existence without material adornment takes on a certain awkward credibility. 3

My purpose in going to Walden Pond, like yours, was not to live cheaply or to live dearly there, but to transact some private business with the fewest obstacles. Approaching Concord, doing forty, doing forty-five, doing fifty, the steering wheel held snug in my palms, the highway held grimly in my vision, the crown of the road now serving me (on the right- hand curves), now defeating me (on the lefthand curves), I began to rouse myself from the stupefaction which a day's motor journey induces. It was a delicious evening, Henry, when the whole body is one sense, and im- bibes delight through every pore, if I may coin a phrase. Fields were richly brown where the harrow, drawn by the stripped Ford, had lately sunk its teeth; pastures were green; and overhead the sky had that same everlasting great look which you will find on Page 144 of the Oxford pocket edition. I could feel the road entering me, through tire, wheel, spring, and cush- ion; shall I not have intelligence with earth too? Am I not partly leaves and vegetable mold myself?—a man of infinite horsepower, yet partly leaves. 4

Stay with me on 62 and it will take you into Concord. As I say, it was a delicious evening. The snake had come forth to die in a bloody S on the highway, the wheel upon its head, its bowels flat now and exposed. The turtle had come up too to cross the road and die in the attempt, its hard 5 shell smashed under the rubber blow, its intestinal yearning (for the other side of the road) forever squashed. There was a sign by the wayside which announced that the road had a "cotton surface." You wouldn't know what that is, but neither, for that matter, did I. There is a cryptic ingredient in many of our modern improvements—we are awed and pleased without knowing quite what we are enjoying. It is something to be traveling on a road with a cotton surface.

The civilization round Concord today is an odd distillation of city, village, farm, and manor. The houses, yards, fields look not quite suburban, not quite rural. Under the bronze beech and the blue spruce of the departed baron grazes the milch goat of the heirs. Under the porte-cochère stands the reconditioned station wagon; under the grape arbor sit the puppies for sale. (But why do men degenerate ever? What makes families run out?)

It was June and everywhere June was publishing her immemorial stanza; in the lilacs, in the syringa, in the freshly edged paths and the sweetness of moist beloved gardens, and the little wire wickets that preserve the tulips' front. Farmers were already moving the fruits of their toil into their yards, arranging the rhubarb, the asparagus, the strictly fresh eggs on the painted stands under the little shed roofs with the patent shingles. And though it was almost a hundred years since you had taken your ax and started cutting out your home on Walden Pond, I was interested to observe that the philosophical spirit was still alive in Massachusetts: in the center of a vacant lot some boys were assembling the framework of the rude shelter, their whole mind and skill concentrated in the rather inauspicious helter-skeleton of studs and rafters. They too were escaping from town, to live naturally, in a rich blend of savagery and philosophy.

That evening, after supper at the inn, I strolled out into the twilight to dream my shapeless transcendental dreams and see that the car was locked up for the night (first open the right front door, then reach over, straining, and pull up the handles of the left rear and the left front till you hear the click, then the handle of the right rear, then shut the right front but open it again, remembering that the key is still in the ignition switch, remove the key, shut the right front again with a bang, push the tiny keyhole cover to one side, insert key, turn, and withdraw). It is what we all do, Henry. It is called locking the car. It is said to confuse thieves and keep them from making off with the laprobe. Four doors to lock behind one robe. The driver himself never uses a laprobe, the free movement of his legs being vital to the operation of the vehicle; so that when he locks the car it is a pure and unselfish act. I have in my life gained very little essential heat from laprobes, yet I have ever been at pains to lock them up.

The evening was full of sounds, some of which would have stirred your memory. The robins still love the elms of New England villages at sun-

6

7

8

9

down. There is enough of the thrush in them to make song inevitable at the end of day, and enough of the tramp to make them hang round the dwellings of men. A robin, like many another American, dearly loves a white house with green blinds. Concord is still full of them.

Your fellow-townsmen were stirring abroad—not many afoot, most of them in their cars; and the sound which they made in Concord at evening was a rustling and a whispering. The sound lacks steadfastness and is wholly unlike that of a train. A train, as you know who lived so near the Fitchburg line, whistles once or twice sadly and is gone, trailing a memory in smoke, soothing to ear and mind. Automobiles, skirting a village green, are like flies that have gained the inner ear—they buzz, cease, pause, start, shift, stop, halt, brake, and the whole effect is a nervous polytone curiously disturbing.

As I wandered along, the toc toc of ping pong balls drifted from an attic window. In front of the Reuben Brown house a Buick was drawn up. At the wheel, motionless, his hat upon his head, a man sat, listening to Amos and Andy on the radio (it is a drama of many scenes and without an end). The deep voice of Andrew Brown, emerging from the car, although it originated more than two hundred miles away, was unstrained by distance. When you used to sit on the shore of your pond on Sunday morning, listening to the church bells of Acton and Concord, you were aware of the excellent filter of the intervening atmosphere. Science has attended to that, and sound now maintains its intensity without regard for distance. Properly sponsored, it goes on forever.

A fire engine, out for a trial spin, roared past Emerson's house, hot with readiness for public duty. Over the barn roofs the martins dipped and chittered. A swarthy daughter of an asparagus grower, in culottes, shirt, and bandanna, pedalled past on her bicycle. It was indeed a delicious evening, and I returned to the inn (I believe it was your house once) to rock with the old ladies on the concrete veranda.

Next morning early I started afoot for Walden, out Main Street and down Thoreau, past the depot and the Minuteman Chevrolet Company. The morning was fresh, and in a bean field along the way I flushed an agriculturalist, quietly studying his beans. Thoreau Street soon joined Number 126, an artery of the State. We number our highways nowadays, our speed being so great we can remember little of their quality or character and are lucky to remember their number. (Men have an indistinct notion that if they keep up this activity long enough all will at length ride somewhere, in next to no time.) Your pond is on 126.

I knew I must be nearing your woodland retreat when the Golden Pheasant lunchroom came into view—Sealtest ice cream, toasted sandwiches, hot frankfurters, waffles, tonics, and lunches. Were I the proprietor, I should add rice, Indian meal, and molasses—just for old time's sake. The Pheasant, incidentally, is for sale: a chance for some nature lover who wishes to set himself up beside a pond in the Concord atmosphere and live deliberately, fronting only the essential facts of life on Number 126. Beyond the Pheasant was a place called Walden Breezes, an oasis whose porch pillars were made of old green shutters sawed into lengths. On the porch was a distorting mirror, to give the traveler a comical image of himself, who had miraculously learned to gaze in an ordinary glass without smiling. Behind the Breezes, in a sun-parched clearing, dwelt your philosophical descendants in their trailers, each trailer the size of your hut, but all grouped together for the sake of congeniality. Trailer people leave the city, as you did, to discover solitude and in any weather, at any hour of the day or night, to improve the nick of time; but they soon collect in villages and get bogged deeper in the mud than ever. The camp behind Walden Breezes was just rousing itself to the morning. The ground was packed hard under the heel, and the sun came through the clearing to bake the soil and enlarge the wry smell of cramped housekeeping. Cushman's bakery truck had stopped to deliver an early basket of rolls. A camp dog, seeing me in the road, barked petulantly. A man emerged from one of the trailers and set forth with a bucket to draw water from some forest tap.

Leaving the highway I turned off into the woods toward the pond, which was apparent through the foliage. The floor of the forest was strewn with dried old oak leaves and *Transcripts.* From beneath the flattened popcorn wrapper (*granum explosum*) peeped the frail violet. I followed a footpath and descended to the water's edge. The pond lay clear and blue in the morning light, as you have seen it so many times. In the shallows a man's waterlogged shirt undulated gently. A few flies came out to greet me and convoy me to your cove, past the No Bathing signs on which the fellows and the girls had scrawled their names. I felt strangely excited suddenly to be snooping around your premises, tiptoeing along watchfully, as though not to tread by mistake upon the intervening century. Before I got to the cove I heard something which seemed to me quite wonderful: I heard your frog, a full, clear *troonk,* guiding me, still hoarse and solemn, bridging the years as the robins had bridged them in the sweetness of the village evening. But he soon quit, and I came on a couple of young boys throwing stones at him.

Your front yard is marked by a bronze tablet set in a stone. Four small granite posts, a few feet away, show where the house was. On top of the tablet was a pair of faded blue bathing trunks with a white stripe. Back of it is a pile of stones, a sort of cairn, left by your visitors as a tribute I suppose. It is a rather ugly little heap of stones, Henry. In fact the hillside itself seems faded, browbeaten; a few tall skinny pines, bare of lower limbs, a smattering of young maples in suitable green, some birches and oaks, and a number of trees felled by the last big wind. It was from the bole of

15

16

one of these fallen pines, torn up by the roots, that I extracted the stone which I added to the cairn—a sentimental act in which I was interrupted by a small terrier from a nearby picnic group, who confronted me and wanted to know about the stone.

I sat down for a while on one of the posts of your house to listen to the bluebottles and the dragonflies. The invaded glade sprawled shabby and mean at my feet, but the flies were tuned to the old vibration. There were the remains of a fire in your ruins, but I doubt that it was yours; also two beer bottles trodden into the soil and become part of earth. A young oak had taken root in your house, and two or three ferns, unrolling like the ticklers at a banquet. The only other furnishings were a DuBarry pattern sheet, a page torn from a picture magazine, and some crusts in wax paper. 17

Before I quit I walked clear round the pond and found the place where you used to sit on the northeast side to get the sun in the fall, and the beach where you got sand for scrubbing your floor. On the eastern side of the pond, where the highway borders it, the State has built dressing rooms for swimmers, a float with diving towers, drinking fountains of porcelain, and rowboats for hire. The pond is in fact a State Preserve, and carries a twenty-dollar fine for picking wild flowers, a decree signed in all solemnity by your fellow-citizens Walter C. Wardwell, Erson B. Barlow, and Nathaniel I. Bowditch. There was a smell of creosote where they had been building a wide wooden stairway to the road and the parking area. Swimmers and boaters were arriving; bodies plunged vigorously into the water and emerged wet and beautiful in the bright air. As I left, a boatload of town boys were splashing about in mid-pond, kidding and fooling, the young fellows singing at the tops of their lungs in a wild chorus: 18

Amer-ica, Amer-ica, God shed his grace on thee,
And crown thy good with brotherhood
From sea to shi-ning sea!

I walked back to town along the railroad, following your custom. The rails were expanding noisily in the hot sun, and on the slope of the roadbed the wild grape and the blackberry sent up their creepers to the track. 19

The expense of my brief sojourn in Concord was: 20

Canvas shoes	$1.95	
Baseball bat	.25 ⎫	gifts to take back
Left-handed fielder's glove	1.25 ⎭	to a boy
Hotel and meals	4.25	
In all	$7.70	

As you see, this amount was almost what you spent for food for eight months. I cannot defend the shoes or the expenditure for shelter and food: they reveal a meanness and grossness in my nature which you would find contemptible. The baseball equipment, however, is the kind of impediment with which you were never on even terms. You must remember that the house where you practiced the sort of economy which I respect was haunted only by mice and squirrels. You never had to cope with a short-stop.

MUSINGS

It is interesting that White chooses to cast an essay in the form of a letter addressed to Thoreau. What does he gain by addressing Thoreau directly? Edward Abbey (p. 56) also addresses Thoreau directly as he writes in his diary, although these two authors' attitudes toward Thoreau and their subjects are quite different. Note that although the letter is obviously a fiction since he certainly never sent it, you feel from his vivid descriptions and his copious use of detail that his trip to Walden Pond was real. Does White's use of a secretary lend credence to the letter form?

Write a fictional letter or e-mail message on some subject of special interest to you. Consider carefully the person whom you choose to address, since that will shape your message.

MARTIN LUTHER KING, JR. (1929–1968)

Martin Luther King, Jr., an early spokesman for the U.S. civil rights movement, was an eloquent preacher; he was also a skilled writer, as exemplified by the following letter. King was selected as one of ten outstanding personalities of 1956 by Time *magazine relatively early in his career; in 1963 he was selected as its Man of the Year. He was awarded the Nobel Prize for Peace in 1964 and the Presidential Medal of Freedom in 1977, nine years after he was downed by an assassin's bullet.*

In 1959 King visited India to learn about Gandhi's philosophy of nonviolence. This view influenced much of King's thinking and future actions. In preparing for the Birmingham campaign, he initiated training sessions for the protesters, teaching them how "to resist without bitterness; to be cursed and not reply; to be beaten and not hit back." Teenagers and children were involved in the protest, and to the horror of people worldwide the police beat them back with jets of water and finally released dogs on them. The world was shocked by the news photographs. President Kennedy intervened and King's campaign was finally successful, although he was initially jailed for his efforts.

The following letter, written in King's jail cell in answer to criticisms from eight fellow clergymen, has been called "a classic in protest literature, the most elegant and learned expression of the goals and philosophy of the nonviolent movement ever written." It was later incorporated into his book Why We Can't Wait *(1964). King's words ring true today: "Injustice anywhere is a threat to justice everywhere. We are caught in an inescapable network of mutuality, tied in a single garment of destiny."*

Letter from Birmingham Jail

April 16, 1963

My Dear Fellow Clergymen:

 While confined here in the Birmingham city jail, I came across your recent statement calling my present activities "unwise and untimely." Seldom do I pause to answer criticism of my work and ideas. If I sought to answer all the criticisms that cross my desk, my secretaries would have little time for anything other than such correspondence in the course of the day, and I would have no time for constructive work. But since I feel that you are men of genuine good will and that your criticisms are sincerely set forth, I want to try to answer your statement in what I hope will be patient and reasonable terms. 1

 I think I should indicate why I am here in Birmingham, since you have 2 been influenced by the view which argues against "outsiders coming in." I have the honor of serving as president of the Southern Christian Leadership Conference, an organization operating in every southern state, with headquarters in Atlanta, Georgia. We have some eighty-five affiliated organizations across the South, and one of them is the Alabama Christian Movement for Human Rights. Frequently we share staff, educational, and financial resources with our affiliates. Several months ago the affiliate here in Birmingham asked us to be on call to engage in a nonviolent direct-action program if such were deemed necessary. We readily consented, and when the hour came we lived up to our promise. So I, along with several members of my staff, am here because I was invited here. I am here because I have organizational ties here.

But more basically, I am in Birmingham because injustice is here. Just as the prophets of the eighth century B.C. left their villages and carried their "thus saith the Lord" far beyond the boundaries of their home towns, and just as the Apostle Paul left his village of Tarsus and carried the gospel of Jesus Christ to the far corners of the Greco-Roman world, so am I compelled to carry the gospel of freedom beyond my own home town. Like Paul, I must constantly respond to the Macedonian call for aid. 3

Moreover, I am cognizant of the interrelatedness of all communities and states. I cannot sit idly by in Atlanta and not be concerned about what happens in Birmingham. Injustice anywhere is a threat to justice everywhere. We are caught in an inescapable network of mutuality, tied in a single garment of destiny. Whatever affects one directly, affects all indirectly. Never again can we afford to live with the narrow, provincial "outside agitator" idea. Anyone who lives inside the United States can never be considered an outsider anywhere within its bounds. 4

You deplore the demonstrations taking place in Birmingham. But your statement, I am sorry to say, fails to express a similar concern for the conditions that brought about the demonstrations. I am sure that none of you would want to rest content with the superficial kind of social analysis that deals merely with effects and does not grapple with underlying causes. It is unfortunate that demonstrations are taking place in Birmingham, but it is even more unfortunate that the city's white power structure left the Negro community with no alternative. 5

In any nonviolent campaign there are four basic steps: collection of the facts to determine whether injustices exist; negotiation; self-purification; and direct action. We have gone through all these steps in Birmingham. There can be no gainsaying the fact that racial injustice engulfs this community. Birmingham is probably the most thoroughly segregated city in the United States. Its ugly record of brutality is widely known. Negroes have experienced grossly unjust treatment in the courts. There have been more unsolved bombings of Negro homes and churches in Birmingham 6 than in any other city in the nation. These are the hard, brutal facts of the case. On the basis of these conditions, Negro leaders sought to negotiate with the city fathers. But the latter consistently refused to engage in good-faith negotiation.

Then, last September, came the opportunity to talk with leaders of Birmingham's economic community. In the course of the negotiations, certain promises were made by the merchants—for example, to remove the stores' humiliating racial signs. On the basis of these promises, the Reverend Fred Shuttlesworth and the leaders of the Alabama Christian Movement for Human Rights agreed to a moratorium on all demonstrations. As the weeks and months went by, we realized that we were the victims of a broken promise. A few signs, briefly removed, returned; the others remained. 7

As in so many past experiences, our hopes had been blasted, and the shadow of deep disappointment settled upon us. We had no alternative except to prepare for direct action, whereby we would present our very bodies as a means of laying our case before the conscience of the local and the national community. Mindful of the difficulties involved, we decided to undertake a process of self-purification. We began a series of workshops on nonviolence, and we repeatedly asked ourselves: "Are you able to accept blows without retaliating?" "Are you able to endure the ordeal of jail?" We decided to schedule our direct-action program for the Easter season, realizing that except for Christmas, this is the main shopping period of the year. Knowing that a strong economic-withdrawal program would be the by-product of direct action, we felt that this would be the best time to bring pressure to bear on the merchants for the needed change. 8

Then it occurred to us that Birmingham's mayoral election was coming up in March, and we speedily decided to postpone action until after election day. When we discovered that the Commissioner of Public Safety, Eugene "Bull" Connor, had piled up enough votes to be in the runoff, we decided again to postpone action until the day after the run-off so that the demonstrations could not be used to cloud the issues. Like many others, we waited to see Mr. Connor defeated, and to this end we endured postponement after postponement. Having aided in this community need, we felt that our direct-action program could be delayed no longer. 9

You may well ask: "Why direct action? Why sit-ins, marches, and so forth? Isn't negotiation a better path?" You are quite right in calling for negotiation. Indeed, this is the very purpose of direct action. Nonviolent direct action seeks to create such a crisis and foster such a tension that a community which has constantly refused to negotiate is forced to confront the issue. It seeks so to dramatize the issue that it can no longer be ignored. My citing the creation of tension as part of the work of the nonviolent-resister may sound rather shocking. But I must confess that I am not afraid 10 of the word "tension." I have earnestly opposed violent tension, but there is a type of constructive, nonviolent tension which is necessary for growth. Just as Socrates felt that it was necessary to create a tension in the mind so that individuals could rise from the bondage of myths and half-truths to the unfettered realm of creative analysis and objective appraisal, so must we see the need for nonviolent gadflies to create the kind of tension in society that will help men rise from the dark depths of prejudice and racism to the majestic heights of understanding and brotherhood.

The purpose of our direct-action program is to create a situation so crisis-packed that it will inevitably open the door to negotiation. I therefore concur with you in your call for negotiation. Too long has our beloved Southland been bogged down in a tragic effort to live in monologue rather than dialogue. 11

One of the basic points in your statement is that the action that I and my associates have taken in Birmingham is untimely. Some have asked: "Why didn't you give the new city administration time to act?" The only answer that I can give to this query is that the new Birmingham administration must be prodded about as much as the outgoing one, before it will act. We are sadly mistaken if we feel that the election of Albert Boutwell as mayor will bring the millennium to Birmingham. While Mr. Boutwell is a much more gentle person than Mr. Connor, they are both segregationists, dedicated to maintenance of the status quo. I have hope that Mr. Boutwell will be reasonable enough to see the futility of massive resistance to desegregation. But he will not see this without pressure from devotees of civil rights. My friends, I must say to you that we have not made a single gain in civil rights without determined legal and nonviolent pressure. Lamentably, it is an historical fact that privileged groups seldom give up their privileges voluntarily. Individuals may see the moral light and voluntarily give up their unjust posture; but, as Reinhold Niebuhr has reminded us, groups tend to be more immoral than individuals. 12

We know through painful experience that freedom is never voluntarily given by the oppressor; it must be demanded by the oppressed. Frankly, I have yet to engage in a direct-action campaign that was "well timed" in the view of those who have not suffered unduly from the disease of segregation. For years now I have heard the word "Wait!" It rings in the ear of every Negro with piercing familiarity. This "Wait" has almost always meant "Never." We must come to see, with one of our distinguished jurists, that "justice too long delayed is justice denied." 13

We have waited for more than 340 years for our constitutional and God-given rights. The nations of Asia and Africa are moving with jetlike speed toward gaining political independence, but we still creep at horse-and-buggy pace toward gaining a cup of coffee at a lunch counter. Perhaps it is easy for those who have never felt the stinging darts of segregation to 14 say, "Wait." But when you have seen vicious mobs lynch your mothers and fathers at will and drown your sisters and brothers at whim; when you have seen hate-filled policemen curse, kick, and even kill your black brothers and sisters; when you see the vast majority of your twenty million Negro brothers smothering in an airtight cage of poverty in the midst of an affluent society; when you suddenly find your tongue twisted and your speech stammering as you seek to explain to your six-year-old daughter why she can't go to the public amusement park that has just been advertised on television, and see tears welling up in her eyes when she is told that Funtown is closed to colored children, and see ominous clouds of inferiority beginning to form in her little mental sky, and see her beginning to distort her personality by developing an unconscious bitterness toward white people; when you have to concoct an answer for a five-year-old son who is asking: "Daddy, why do white people treat colored people so mean?"; when you take a cross-country drive and find it necessary to sleep night after night in the uncomfortable corners of your automobile because no motel will accept you; when you are humiliated day in and day out by nagging signs reading "white" and "colored"; when your first name becomes "nigger," your middle name becomes "boy" (however old you are) and your last name becomes "John," and your wife and mother are never given the respected title "Mrs."; when you are harried by day and haunted by night by the fact that you are a Negro, living constantly at tiptoe stance, never quite knowing what to expect next, and are plagued with inner fears and outer resentments; when you are forever fighting a degenerating sense of "nobodiness"—then you will understand why we find it difficult to wait. There comes a time when the cup of endurance runs over, and men are no longer willing to be plunged into the abyss of despair. I hope, sirs, you can understand our legitimate and unavoidable impatience.

You express a great deal of anxiety over our willingness to break laws. 15 This is certainly a legitimate concern. Since we so diligently urge people to obey the Supreme Court's decision of 1954 outlawing segregation in the public schools, at first glance it may seem rather paradoxical for us consciously to break laws. One may well ask: "How can you advocate breaking some laws and obeying others?" The answer lies in the fact that there are two types of laws: just and unjust. I would be the first to advocate obeying just laws. One has not only a legal but a moral responsibility to obey just laws. Conversely, one has a moral responsibility to disobey unjust laws. I would agree with St. Augustine that "an unjust law is no law at all."

Now, what is the difference between the two? How does one determine 16 whether a law is just or unjust? A just law is a manmade code that squares with the moral law or the law of God. An unjust law is a code that is out of harmony with the moral law. To put it in the terms of St. Thomas Aquinas: An unjust law is a human law that is not rooted in eternal law and natural law. Any law that uplifts human personality is just. Any law that degrades human personality is unjust. All segregation statutes are unjust because segregation distorts the soul and damages the personality. It gives the segregator a false sense of superiority and the segregated a false sense of inferiority. Segregation, to use the terminology of the Jewish philosopher Martin Buber, substitutes an "I–it" relationship for an "I–thou" relationship and ends up relegating persons to the status of things. Hence segregation is not only politically, economically, and sociologically unsound, it is morally wrong and sinful. Paul Tillich has said that sin is separation. Is not segregation an existential expression of man's tragic separation, his awful estrangement, his terrible sinfulness? Thus it is that I can urge men to obey the 1954 decision of the Supreme Court, for it is morally right; and I can urge them to disobey segregation ordinances, for they are morally wrong.

17 Let us consider a more concrete example of just and unjust laws. An unjust law is a code that a numerical or power majority group compels a minority group to obey but does not make binding on itself. This is *difference* made legal. By the same token, a just law is a code that a majority compels a minority to follow and that it is willing to follow itself. This is *sameness* made legal.

18 Let me give another explanation. A law is unjust if it is inflicted on a minority that, as a result of being denied the right to vote, had no part in enacting or devising the law. Who can say that the legislature of Alabama which set up that state's segregation laws was democratically elected? Throughout Alabama all sorts of devious methods are used to prevent Negroes from becoming registered voters, and there are some counties in which, even though Negroes constitute a majority of the population, not a single Negro is registered. Can any law enacted under such circumstances be considered democratically structured?

19 Sometimes a law is just on its face and unjust in its application. For instance, I have been arrested on a charge of parading without a permit. Now, there is nothing wrong in having an ordinance which requires a permit for a parade. But such an ordinance becomes unjust when it is used to maintain segregation and to deny citizens the First-Amendment privilege of peaceful assembly and protest.

20 I hope you are able to see the distinction I am trying to point out. In no sense do I advocate evading or defying the law, as would the rabid segregationist. That would lead to anarchy. One who breaks an unjust law must do so openly, lovingly, and with a willingness to accept the penalty. I submit that an individual who breaks a law that conscience tells him is unjust,

and who willingly accepts the penalty of imprisonment in order to arouse the conscience of the community over its injustice, is in reality expressing the highest respect for law.

Of course, there is nothing new about this kind of civil disobedience. It was evidenced sublimely in the refusal of Shadrach, Meshach, and Abednego to obey the laws of Nebuchadnezzar [Biblical story], on the ground that a higher moral law was at stake. It was practiced superbly by the early Christians, who were willing to face hungry lions and the excruciating pain of chopping blocks rather than submit to certain unjust laws of the Roman Empire. To a degree, academic freedom is a reality today because Socrates practiced civil disobedience. In our own nation, the Boston Tea Party represented a massive act of civil disobedience. 21

We should never forget that everything Adolf Hitler did in Germany was "legal" and everything the Hungarian freedom fighters did in Hungary was "illegal." It was "illegal" to aid and comfort a Jew in Hitler's Germany. Even so, I am sure that, had I lived in Germany at the time, I would have aided and comforted my Jewish brothers. If today I lived in a Communist country where certain principles dear to the Christian faith are suppressed, I would openly advocate disobeying that country's antireligious laws. 22

I must make two honest confessions to you, my Christian and Jewish brothers. First, I must confess that over the past few years I have been gravely disappointed with the white moderate. I have almost reached the regrettable conclusion that the Negro's great stumbling block in his stride toward freedom is not the White Citizen's Counciler or the Ku Klux Klanner, but the white moderate, who is more devoted to "order" than to justice: who prefers a negative peace which is the absence of tension to a positive peace which is the presence of justice; who constantly says: "I agree with you in the goal you seek, but I cannot agree with your methods of direct action"; who paternalistically believes he can set the timetable for another man's freedom; who lives by a mythical concept of time and who constantly advises the Negro to wait for a "more convenient season." Shallow understanding from people of good will is more frustrating than absolute misunderstanding from people of ill will. Lukewarm acceptance is much more bewildering than outright rejection. 23

I had hoped that the white moderate would understand that law and order exist for the purpose of establishing justice and that when they fail in this purpose they become the dangerously structured dams that block the flow of social progress. I had hoped that the white moderate would understand that the present tension in the South is a necessary phase of the transition from an obnoxious negative peace, in which the Negro passively accepted his unjust plight, to a substantive and positive peace, in which all men will respect the dignity and worth of human personality. Actually, we 24 who engage in nonviolent direct action are not the creators of tension. We merely bring to the surface the hidden tension that is already alive. We bring it out in the open, where it can be seen and dealt with. Like a boil that can never be cured so long as it is covered up but must be opened with all its ugliness to the natural medicines of air and light, injustice must be exposed, with all the tension its exposure creates, to the light of human conscience and the air of national opinion before it can be cured.

In your statement you assert that our actions, even though peaceful,   25 must be condemned because they precipitate violence. But is this a logical assertion? Isn't this like condemning a robbed man because his possession of money precipitated the evil act of robbery? Isn't this like condemning Socrates because his unswerving commitment to truth and his philosophical inquiries precipitated the act by the misguided populace in which they made him drink hemlock? Isn't this like condemning Jesus because his unique God-consciousness and never-ceasing devotion to God's will precipitated the evil act of crucifixion? We must come to see that, as the federal courts have consistently affirmed, it is wrong to urge an individual to cease his efforts to gain his basic constitutional rights because the quest may precipitate violence. Society must protect the robbed and punish the robber.

I had also hoped that the white moderate would reject the myth con-   26 cerning time in relation to the struggle for freedom. I have just received a letter from a white brother in Texas. He writes: "All Christians know that the colored people will receive equal rights eventually, but it is possible that you are in too great a religious hurry. It has taken Christianity almost two thousand years to accomplish what it has. The teachings of Christ take time to come to earth." Such an attitude stems from a tragic misconception of time, from the strangely irrational notion that there is something in the very flow of time that will inevitably cure all ills. Actually, time itself is neutral; it can be used either destructively or constructively. More and more I feel that the people of ill will have used time much more effectively than have the people of good will. We will have to repent in this generation not merely for the hateful words and actions of the bad people but for the appalling silence of the good people. Human progress never rolls in on wheels of inevitability; it comes through the tireless efforts of men willing to be co-workers with God, and without this hard work, time itself becomes an ally of the forces of social stagnation. We must use time creatively, in the knowledge that the time is always ripe to do right. Now is the time to make real the promise of democracy and transform our pending national elegy into a creative psalm of brotherhood. Now is the time to lift our national policy from the quicksand of racial injustice to the solid rock of human dignity.

You speak of our activity in Birmingham as extreme. At first I was   27 rather disappointed that fellow clergymen would see my nonviolent efforts as those of an extremist. I began thinking about the fact that I stand in the middle of two opposing forces in the Negro community. One is a force of complacency, made up in part of Negroes who, as a result of long years of oppression, are so drained of self-respect and a sense of "somebodiness" that they have adjusted to segregation; and in part of a few middle-class Negroes who, because of a degree of academic and economic security and because in some ways they profit by segregation, have become insensitive to the problems of the masses. The other force is one of bitterness and hatred, and it comes perilously close to advocating violence. It is expressed in the various black nationalist groups that are springing up across the nation, the largest and best-known being Elijah Muhammad's Muslim movement. Nourished by the Negro's frustration over the continued existence of racial discrimination, this movement is made up of people who have lost faith in America, who have absolutely repudiated Christianity, and who have concluded that the white man is an incorrigible "devil."

I have tried to stand between these two forces, saying that we need emulate neither the "do-nothingism" of the complacent nor the hatred and despair of the black nationalist. For there is the more excellent way of love and nonviolent protest. I am grateful to God that, through the influence of the Negro church, the way of nonviolence became an integral part of our struggle. 28

If this philosophy had not emerged, by now many streets of the South would, I am convinced, be flowing with blood. And I am further convinced that if our white brothers dismiss as "rabblerousers" and "outside agitators" those of us who employ nonviolent direct action, and if they refuse to support our nonviolent efforts, millions of Negroes will, out of frustration and despair, seek solace and security in black-nationalist ideologies—a development that would inevitably lead to a frightening racial nightmare. 29

Oppressed people cannot remain oppressed forever. The yearning for freedom eventually manifests itself, and that is what has happened to the American Negro. Something within has reminded him of his birthright of freedom, and something without has reminded him that it can be gained. Consciously or unconsciously, he has been caught up by the *Zeitgeist* [spirit of the age], and with his black brothers of Africa and his brown and yellow brothers of Asia, South America and the Caribbean, the United States Negro is moving with a sense of great urgency toward the promised land of racial justice. If one recognizes this vital urge that has engulfed the Negro community, one should readily understand why public demonstrations are taking place. The Negro has many pent-up resentments and latent frustrations, and he must release them. So let him march; let him make prayer pilgrimages to the city hall; let him go on freedom rides— 30 and try to understand why he must do so. If his repressed emotions are not released in nonviolent ways, they will seek expression through violence; this is not a threat but a fact of history. So I have not said to my people: "Get rid of your discontent." Rather, I have tried to say that this normal and healthy discontent can be channeled into the creative outlet of nonviolent direct action. And now this approach is being termed extremist.

But though I was initially disappointed at being categorized as an extremist, as I continued to think about the matter I gradually gained a measure of satisfaction from the label. Was not Jesus an extremist for love: "Love your enemies, bless them that curse you, do good to them that hate you, and pray for them which despitefully use you, and persecute you." Was not Amos an extremist for justice: "Let justice roll down like waters and righteousness like an ever-flowing stream." Was not Paul an extremist for the Christian gospel: "I bear in my body the marks of the Lord Jesus." Was not Martin Luther an extremist: "Here I stand; I cannot do otherwise, so help me God." And John Bunyan: "I will stay in jail to the end of my days before I make a butchery of my conscience." And Abraham Lincoln: "This nation cannot survive half slave and half free." And Thomas Jefferson: "We hold these truths to be self-evident, that all men are created equal . . ." So the question is not whether we will be extremists, but what kind of extremists we will be. Will we be extremists for hate or for love? Will we be extremists for the preservation of injustice or for the extension of justice? In that dramatic scene on Calvary's hill three men were crucified. We must never forget that all three were crucified for the same crime—the crime of extremism. Two were extremists for immorality, and thus fell below their environment. The other, Jesus Christ, was an extremist for love, truth, and goodness, and thereby rose above his environment. Perhaps the South, the nation, and the world are in dire need of creative extremists.

I had hoped that the white moderate would see this need. Perhaps I was too optimistic; perhaps I expected too much. I suppose I should have realized that few members of the oppressor race can understand the deep groans and passionate yearnings of the oppressed race, and still fewer have the vision to see that injustice must be rooted out by strong, persistent, and determined action. I am thankful, however, that some of our white brothers in the South have grasped the meaning of this social revolution and committed themselves to it. They are still all too few in quantity, but they are big in quality. Some—such as Ralph McGill, Lillian Smith, Harry Golden, James McBride Dabbs, Ann Braden, and Sarah Patton Boyle— have written about our struggle in eloquent and prophetic terms. Others have marched with us down nameless streets of the South. They have languished in filthy, roach-infested jails, suffering the abuse and brutality of policemen who view them as "dirty nigger-lovers." Unlike so many of their moderate brothers and sisters, they have recognized the urgency of the moment and sensed the need for powerful "action" antidotes to combat the disease of segregation.

Let me take note of my other major disappointment. I have been so greatly disappointed with the white church and its leadership. Of course, there are some notable exceptions. I am not unmindful of the fact that each of you has taken some significant stands on this issue. I commend you, Reverend Stallings, for your Christian stand on this past Sunday, in welcoming Negroes to your worship service on a nonsegregated basis. I commend the Catholic leaders of this state for integrating Spring Hill College several years ago. 33

But despite these notable exceptions, I must honestly reiterate that I have been disappointed with the church. I do not say this as one of those negative critics who can always find something wrong with the church. I say this as a minister of the gospel, who loves the church; who was nurtured in its bosom; who has been sustained by its spiritual blessings and who will remain true to it as long as the cord of life shall lengthen. 34

When I was suddenly catapulted into the leadership of the bus protest in Montgomery, Alabama, a few years ago, I felt we would be supported by the white church. I felt that the white ministers, priests, and rabbis of the South would be among our strongest allies. Instead, some have been outright opponents, refusing to understand the freedom movement and misrepresenting its leaders; all too many others have been more cautious than courageous and have remained silent behind the anesthetizing security of stained-glass windows. 35

In spite of my shattered dreams, I came to Birmingham with the hope that the white religious leadership of this community would see the justice of our cause and, with deep moral concern, would serve as the channel through which our just grievances could reach the power structure. I had hoped that each of you would understand. But again I have been disappointed. 36

I have heard numerous southern religious leaders admonish their worshipers to comply with a desegregation decision because it is the law, but I have longed to hear white ministers declare: "Follow this decree because integration is morally right and because the Negro is your brother." In the midst of blatant injustices inflicted upon the Negro, I have watched white churchmen stand on the sideline and mouth pious irrelevancies and sanctimonious trivialities. In the midst of a mighty struggle to rid our nation of racial and economic injustice, I have heard many ministers say: "Those are social issues, with which the gospel has no real concern." And I have watched many churches commit themselves to a completely otherworldly religion which makes a strange, un-Biblical distinction between body and soul, between the sacred and the secular. 37

I have traveled the length and breadth of Alabama, Mississippi, and all 38
the other southern states. On sweltering summer days and crisp autumn
mornings I have looked at the South's beautiful churches with their lofty
spires pointing heavenward. I have beheld the impressive outlines of her
massive religious-education buildings. Over and over I have found myself
asking: "What kind of people worship here? Who is their God? Where
were their voices when the lips of Governor Barnett [of Mississippi]
dripped with words of interposition and nullification? Where were they
when Governor Wallace [of Alabama] gave a clarion call for defiance and
hatred? Where were their voices of support when bruised and weary Negro
men and women decided to rise from the dark dungeons of complacency
to the bright hills of creative protest?"

Yes, these questions are still in my mind. In deep disappointment I have 39
wept over the laxity of the church. But be assured that my tears have been
tears of love. There can be no deep disappointment where there is not
deep love. Yes, I love the church. How could I do otherwise? I am in the
rather unique position of being the son, the grandson and the great-grand-
son of preachers. Yes, I see the church as the body of Christ. But, oh! How
we have blemished and scarred that body through social neglect and
through fear of being nonconformists.

There was a time when the church was very powerful—in the time when 40
the early Christians rejoiced at being deemed worthy to suffer for what they
believed. In those days the church was not merely a thermometer that
recorded the ideas and principles of popular opinion; it was a thermostat
that transformed the mores of society. Whenever the early Christians entered a town, the people in power became disturbed and immediately
sought to convict the Christians for being "disturbers of the peace" and
"outside agitators." But the Christians pressed on, in the conviction that
they were "a colony of heaven," called to obey God rather than man. Small
in number, they were big in commitment. They were too God-intoxicated
to be "astronomically intimidated." By their effort and example they
brought an end to such ancient evils as infanticide and gladiatorial contests.

Things are different now. So often the contemporary church is a weak, 41
ineffectual voice with an uncertain sound. So often it is an archdefender of
the status quo. Far from being disturbed by the presence of the church, the
power structure of the average community is consoled by the church's
silent—and often even vocal—sanction of things as they are.

But the judgment of God is upon the church as never before. If today's 42
church does not recapture the sacrificial spirit of the early church, it will
lose its authenticity, forfeit the loyalty of millions, and be dismissed as an
irrelevant social club with no meaning for the twentieth century. Every
day I meet young people whose disappointment with the church has
turned into outright disgust.

Perhaps I have once again been too optimistic. Is organized religion too   43
inextricably bound to the status quo to save our nation and the world?
Perhaps I must turn my faith to the inner spiritual church, the church
within the church, as the true *ekklesia* [assembly of the people] and the
hope of the world. But again I am thankful to God that some noble souls
from the ranks of organized religion have broken loose from the paralyzing chains of conformity and joined us as active partners in the struggle
for freedom. They have left their secure congregations and walked the
streets of Albany, Georgia, with us. They have gone down the highways of
the South on tortuous rides for freedom. Yes, they have gone to jail with
us. Some have been dismissed from their churches, have lost the support
of their bishops and fellow ministers. But they have acted in the faith that
right defeated is stronger than evil triumphant. Their witness has been the
spiritual salt that has preserved the true meaning of the gospel in these
troubled times. They have carved a tunnel of hope through the dark
mountain of disappointment.

I hope the church as a whole will meet the challenge of this decisive   44
hour. But even if the church does not come to the aid of justice, I have no
despair about the future. I have no fear about the outcome of our struggle
in Birmingham, even if our motives are at present misunderstood. We will
reach the goal of freedom in Birmingham and all over the nation, because
the goal of America is freedom. Abused and scorned though we may be,
our destiny is tied up with America's destiny. Before the pilgrims landed at
Plymouth, we were here. Before the pen of Jefferson etched the majestic
words of the Declaration of Independence across the pages of history, we
were here. For more than two centuries our forebears labored in this country without wages; they made cotton king; they built the homes of their
masters while suffering gross injustice and shameful humiliation—and yet
out of a bottomless vitality they continued to thrive and develop. If the inexpressible cruelties of slavery could not stop us, the opposition we now
face will surely fail. We will win our freedom because the sacred heritage of
our nation and the eternal will of God are embodied in our echoing demands.

Before closing I feel impelled to mention one other point in your state-   45
ment that has troubled me profoundly. You warmly commended the
Birmingham police force for keeping "order" and "preventing violence." I
doubt that you would have so warmly commended the police force if you
had seen its dogs sinking their teeth into unarmed, nonviolent Negroes. I
doubt that you would so quickly commend the policemen if you were to
observe their ugly and inhumane treatment of Negroes here in the city jail;
if you were to watch them push and curse old Negro women and young
Negro girls; if you were to see them slap and kick old Negro men and
young boys; if you were to observe them, as they did on two occasions,

refuse to give us food because we wanted to sing our grace together. I cannot join you in your praise of the Birmingham police department.

It is true that the police have exercised a degree of discipline in handling   46
the demonstrators. In this sense they have conducted themselves rather "nonviolently" in public. But for what purpose? To preserve the evil system of segregation. Over the past few years I have consistently preached that nonviolence demands that the means we use must be as pure as the ends we seek. I have tried to make clear that it is wrong to use immoral means to attain moral ends. But now I must affirm that it is just as wrong, or perhaps even more so, to use moral means to preserve immoral ends. Perhaps Mr. Connor and his policemen have been rather nonviolent in public, as was Chief Pritchett in Albany, Georgia, but they have used the moral means of nonviolence to maintain the immoral end of racial injustice. As T. S. Eliot has said: "The last temptation is the greatest treason: To do the right deed for the wrong reason."

I wish you had commended the Negro sit-inners and demonstrators of   47
Birmingham for their sublime courage, their willingness to suffer, and their amazing discipline in the midst of great provocation. One day the South will recognize its real heroes. They will be the James Merediths, with the noble sense of purpose that enables them to face jeering and hostile mobs, and with the agonizing loneliness that characterizes the life of the pioneer. They will be old, oppressed, battered Negro women, symbolized in a seventy-two-year-old woman in Montgomery, Alabama, who rose up with a sense of dignity and with her people decided not to ride segregated buses, and who responded with ungrammatical profundity to one who inquired about her weariness: "My feets is tired, but my soul is at rest." They will be the young high school and college students, the young ministers of the gospel and a host of their elders, courageously and nonviolently sitting in at lunch counters and willingly going to jail for conscience' sake. One day the South will know that when these disinherited children of God sat down at lunch counters, they were in reality standing up for what is best in the American dream and for the most sacred values in our Judaeo-Christian heritage, thereby bringing our nation back to those great wells of democracy which were dug deep by the founding fathers in their formulation of the Constitution and the Declaration of Independence.

Never before have I written so long a letter. I'm afraid it is much too   48
long to take your precious time. I can assure you that it would have been much shorter if I had been writing from a comfortable desk, but what else can one do when he is alone in a narrow jail cell, other than write long letters, think long thoughts, and pray long prayers?

If I have said anything in this letter that overstates the truth and indi-   49
cates an unreasonable impatience, I beg you to forgive me. If I have said

anything that understates the truth and indicates my having a patience that allows me to settle for anything less than brotherhood, I beg God to forgive me.

I hope this letter finds you strong in the faith. I also hope that circumstances will soon make it possible for me to meet each of you, not as an integrationist or a civil-rights leader but as a fellow clergyman and a Christian brother. Let us all hope that the dark clouds of racial prejudice will soon pass away and the deep fog of misunderstanding will be lifted from our fear-drenched communities, and in some not too distant tomorrow the radiant stars of love and brotherhood will shine over our great nation with all their scintillating beauty. 50

Yours for the cause of Peace and Brotherhood,
Martin Luther King, Jr.

MUSINGS

King obviously wrote and rewrote this letter during his imprisonment. The letter is carefully crafted, and the language is elegant as well as eloquent. Not only does King establish his goodwill by recognizing that his readers are "men of goodwill" whose "criticisms are sincerely set forth," but he also confirms his own credibility by his concern for constructive rather than destructive activities and his hope that his answer will be in "patient and reasonable terms."

Write a letter to a group with whom you disagree, setting forth in "patient and reasonable terms" the grounds for your viewpoint. Establish your credibility at the outset and gain the goodwill of your audience by recognizing their viewpoint. Your credibility must rest on the reasonableness of your arguments, as King's does.

DENISE STODOLA (1962–)
AND SANDY RUBINSTEIN (1971–)

The following is an E-mail exchange between two sisters. Denise, in her early thirties, is a single mother of two boys, Nathan and Matthew, ages twelve and nine. She is working on a Ph.D. in English at the University of Missouri, Columbia. Sandy, in her mid-twenties, lives in San Antonio, Texas, works at the Center for the Study of Women and Gender, and is completing a master's degree in history at the University of Texas at San Antonio. Already close, Denise and Sandy were drawn even closer, exploring together their shock and grief over the sudden death of their mother three months earlier. They yearn for the days when calling "I want my Mommy" meant she'd come; they wonder about their father, nicknamed "Barn"; and they revel in their affection for Nathan and Matthew, "the little munchkins." Amidst the sprinkling of nicknames (Deker, Sandinka) and coinages ("Later!," "I suck"), a keen intelligence emerges, along with a fierce desire to move on and to live honestly and well.

E-mail represents a new kind of communication vastly different from traditional letter correspondence. Its ability to provide an instantaneous exchange stands in sharp contrast to many of the earlier missives that may have taken weeks or months to reach their destination. Several exchanges occurred on the same night or within twenty-four hours. The reader looking over the shoulders of these two sisters as they "talk" is struck by the intimacy and immediacy achieved by E-mail. These messages draw on shared experiences and allusions such as the significance of Tuesday, the day of their mother's death, that sometimes only the two sisters fully understand. Although their references to family members such as Fanny and events such as the "October stuff" are something of a mystery to us, most families share such myths.

Note also the quotation from Anne Hebert, a contemporary French poet, that appears in what is known as a signature file, a field that is automatically inserted at the end of every message.

E-mail is rapidly developing its own distinctive style of communication through use of the keyboard to abbreviate words or emphasize them. "BTW" (by the way) is one of a number of handy and universally understood abbreviations for the e-mail writer who is looking for shortcuts. "IRL" (in real life) is an abbreviation for the real world, outside of the surreal world of the Internet. To designate emphasis the sisters use the established symbols "* . . . *" and "> . . . <" on each end of a word: >you<. Punctuation marks are also used to show emotion by forming symbols called "emoticons": for example, a sideways smiley face is formed by a colon, hyphen, and parentheses :-) and crying is represented by ;-(. Denise and Sandy often wink ;-) at each other to elicit smiles.

E-mail correspondence is seldom re-read or saved but goes the way of so much computer writing—deleted at the stroke of a key to make space for more. In replacing the telephone, E-mail, through its own distinctive style, has brought about a revival of written communication, as more and more people reach out to one another without the barriers of space or time.

Between Sisters: An E-Mail Exchange

Date: Fri, 30 Aug 1996 07:01:33 -0500 (CDT)
From: denise stodola
To: Sandy Rubinstein
Subject: hey hon

Sandina--

I know what you mean about the "I want my mommy" days. Me too.   1
I had a dream the other night that I dreamed (yes, a dream within a
dream) that mom was a ghost that I could see, but that she couldn't
recognize me. She didn't "know" me ;-(. I'm amazed at how incredibly painful this seems to remain--plus the fact that I am, more or
less, functioning "normally."

Anyway, I tried to call you last night to check on ya, but no answer.   2
Talk to you tonight--

Deker (Wuv!)

****

Que celui qui a recu fonction del la parole vous prenne en charge   3
comme un coeur tenebreux de surcroit, et n'ait de cesse que soient
justifies les vivants et les morts en un seul chant parmi l'aube et les
herbes.*

--Anne Hebert

*Translation: Let he who has the power of the word function like an extra
dark heart and don't let him stop until he justifies the living and the dead
in a single song among the dawn and the grasses.

• • •

Date: Mon, 9 Sep 1996 00:30:20 -0500 (CDT)
From: sandy
To: Denise Stodola
Subject: ERG!

Well, I'm apparently turning into you--I'm having a real self-depre-   4
cation fest. I've killed just about every plant in the house, and I finally got organized enough to realize that I'm so far behind on my
work that I'll never, ever catch up. WAAAAAAAHHHHHHHH! :(

Anyway, I hope >you< are feeling better. I won't have any more of   5
this talk of failure, got it? Aren't you supposed to set a good example for me or something? Especially now that I'm thinking of "following in your footsteps."

I promised I'd tell you about that, didn't I? Well, when I told my He-   6
brew teacher that you were getting a Ph.D. in English and our
brother was a musician, she said, "Your father must be hysterical."
Well, that's probably true. Actually, he seemed very receptive when I
suggested that I wanted to apply to Ph.D. programs. He's pretty cool
sometimes, that Barn.

Anyway, after about an hour-and-a-half of talking to me, my Hebrew   7
teacher suggested that I do more research and gather more information before making any rash career decisions. Of course, one thing
she said really stuck with me. She said that all jobs have positives
and negatives, so you pick one where you can tolerate the negatives
for the sake of the benefits. Yup, that sounds like a Ph.D. to me. I've
got a list of all the major Ph.D. programs in Religion, and now I'll
have to start sending off for applications. Man, I am terrified. Help
me, I'm flailing . . .

Speaking of flailing, have you calmed down? Are the kids still mak-   8
ing you a little on the nutty side? Well, you'd better be sweet to my
little monsters. And no, they can't come stay with me! ;)

Well, I guess I should get back to work. I just wanted to write you a   9
nice, long message. I have so much in my head these days, and it just
rattles around in there.

Anyway, I'll write again tomorrow, if I get the chance. You have a   10
good day, sweetie.

sand

p.s. I really like your quote. I don't know how to set up a sig [signa-   11
ture] file on our system, but I have a quote that I got in Hebrew class
today. I can't remember the Yiddish, but the translation is "Men
plan, and God laughs." For my own purposes, however, I think I'll
change it to "Mortals plan, and God laughs."

Haw, haw, haw . . .   12

• • •

Date: Mon, 9 Sep 1996 06:08:05 -0500 (CDT)
from denise stodola
To: Sandy Rubinstein
Subject: organization, Hebrew, and little monsters . . .

Sandina,

Okay, okay: so I do a fine job of slamming myself, BUT *my* plant is still alive, and I don't feel all that organized. Besides, you're the one who makes lists of things to do that include "writing a list of things to do"! ;-)   13

Did I tell you about my plant? The Student Association sent it to me just shortly after mom died. I have to keep that plant alive--it'd be too terrible for it to die too. . . Sorry for the maudlin thing, but the bad dreams still stay with me. I suppose it's normal for one's sub-conscious to work these things out so we don't go *entirely* insane, but I still can't figure out why mom's ghost would be able to see me but not recognize me (and that I would somehow understand that). Enough of that, I suppose.   14

So this week it's a PhD. in Religion? ;-) Actually, you seem to be more comfortable with this decision than any of the previous ones. Sometimes I think that higher education becomes a religion of a sort anyway. You have to be dedicated to some "greater purpose" if you actually stick with it. Oh, and your Hebrew teacher sounds way cool: I wish someone had been able to sit down with me for a while to figure out my life, but I imagine (knowing myself as I do) that I wouldn't have listened anyway ;-).   15

That reminds me; you may hear me explode (even 1000 miles away) if one more guy tries to "rescue" the poor, pitiful single mom by "fix-ing" something around the apartment. I know they mean well, but, as you know, I have my own set of tools, and I can fix things with the best of 'em! (Thanks again for the tool set--it still looks ever-so-lovely in the cosmetics case we picked out for it. ;-))   16

Hon, I hope you have a good day, and that nothing frustrates you at work today.   17

Wuv!
Deker

• • •

Date: Tue, 10 Sep 1996 08:13:01 -0500 (CDT)
From: sandy
To: Denise Stodola
Subject: GRRRRRR!

Hi, Deker!

Any more weird dreams? I'm having trouble from worrying about   18
one of the dogs cutting out on us. Foxy and Dolly are getting so old
and tired, and I get sick when I think of them dying. I had a dream
that I washed Foxy in the washing machine, and I was really upset
when she wouldn't breathe. Of course, I got her to breathe, and the
dream ended O.K. Pretty strange, huh?

I hope you're holding up well. I've got so very much just rattling   19
around in my head these days, and so many emotions moving
through me at an unbelievably rapid pace. Of course, the usual
worry--am I nuts?--is present. I guess I just have to learn to surf
that psychological sea, if you know what I mean.

I have lots more to tell you, but I've got to get to work. I'll post again   20
later, hon.

Lovey-love-love,
sand

p.s. Man, I really wish you were here. And the boys, too. Kisses all   21
around.

• • •

Date: Tue, 10 Sep 1996 16:54:11 -0500 (CDT)
From: sandy
To: Denise Stodola
Subject: hey, baby, que paso?

Denita--

Speaking of making it through, I really miss Ma today. I don't guess   22
I miss her any more than I did yesterday, but I'm maybe more aware
of it today than usual. Oh, wait, it's Tuesday. Doggone it! I can't believe that my subconscious is more aware of the day of the week
than the rest of my mind is. I really am sick, aren't I? <heehn,
heehn, heehn>

So have you written to Aunt Lindy yet? I haven't talked to her yet   23
this week, but I imagine I'll call her soon. I did talk to our cousin
over the weekend, and she asked how everyone is doing. She'll be in
for a whirlwind weekend during High Holy Days. Are you & my
sweet little boys going to services for it? Can I show your cool poem
to my Hebrew teacher? I think she'd really like it. We talked about
the Book of Life, the closing gates, etc. during class. I think I'm re-

ally looking forward to it this year. I hope maybe I'll understand a little more of what's going on.

Well, enough of my chatter. I've got about a hundred pages to skim.   24
I'll talk to you later.

Help me, I'm melting!!!!!!
sand

•   •   •

Date: Mon, 23 Sep 1996 17:25:58 -0500 (CDT)
From: sandy
To: Denise Stodola
Subject: very superstitious

Do you hear that funky keyboard? I'm feelin' a little Stevie Wonder-   25
ish.

Anyway, it's funny you should bring it up, because I was thinking   26
this morning that I should have replied to that part of the message.
There was a little girl at Temple with a red ribbon in her hair, and I
remembered that I completely failed to respond to that.

So, well, you know, the red ribbon comes from a different part of the   27
family than the October stuff. The red ribbon to keep the canaries--
the kana hari--away from Fannie. Most of our other superstitions
are from Mama's side, especially the October stuff.

I still think Fannie must have been a gypsy. Did you know that she   28
read cards? At least, that's what the cousins say. They also said she
used to dance around in the back yard, trailing a scarf behind her.

As for Mama's family, they were a lot more Old World than one   29
would think after so much time here. I don't know how they kept
their traditions. For that matter, I don't know which traditions are
which. A lot of the stuff is Irish, but some of it seems American Indian, and still other stuff matches the Gypsy stuff I've read.

BTW, did you know that it used to be the practice to ritually kill a   30
chicken for Yom Kippur? You would circle it around everyone's
heads and recite a prayer that made it clear that the chicken was to
act as your proxy, your redemptive sacrifice. That's just what I read
somewhere, but it doesn't sound like anything I've ever heard before. Strange, huh?

Also, speaking of strange, I went into a bookstore today to look at   31
their cards and stones and things. I had a couple of things I wanted
to buy, until I saw the case with the "dark stuff" in it. A lot of it
looked suspect, and then I saw the knives. Yes, knives. They were
wavy and made of something black. It was way too creepy, and I
didn't stick around long enough to buy anything. I was out of there
so fast. . . .

Well, there was more stuff I wanted to tell you about, but I can't re- 32
member it all right now, so I'll write again later. I'll probably be at
the computer most of the evening, trying to finish up all of this
work. Waaaaaaaaah!

Have a groovy evening, and try to get to feeling better. 33

Love you
sand

• • •

Date: Mon, 23 Sep 1996 21:26:20 -0500 (CDT)
From: denise stodola
To: sandy
Subject: Re: very superstitious

Hon,

About the October thing--is that an old superstition or is it one that 34
mom created when she lost the two babies in October? What Native
American superstitions do you know of? Just curious.

As for Fannie being a gypsy, that makes sense . . . she did used to 35
love scarves . . . in fact, I think in her later klepto years she probably lifted a few ;-). I never heard that she danced around in the back
yard, though. I wonder if she danced for her sisters at the kitchen
sink until they wanted to run screaming into the sunset. Boy, do I
miss doing dishes in your and Teenie's presence. (It just isn't the
same, dancin' all by myself . . .)

What still bugs me is how she met up with Doc? Wish I could've seen 36
that one. Now his original name was D'Arto? Did you and pop ever
figure out the trail his family must've taken? I recall you guys doing
that when we visited dad last, but I think I was otherwise occupied
with settling some sort of fraternal dispute between the boys.

The sacrifice thing--funny you should mention that, 'cause I was read- 37
ing the Isaac and Abraham story in an Old English version. I wonder
if they used creepy dark, wavy ritualistic knives back then? ;-)

Some people are just *too* freaky. (Unfortunately, it seems that they 38
are the same people who want to date us . . . ;-))

Talk to you later, wuvvie! (Hey, I'd better save you some of this cold 39
medicine!)

Deke

• • •

Date: Mon, 23 Sep 1996 22:40:55 -0500 (CDT)
From: sandy
To: denise stodola
Subject: Re: Eek!

I didn't know that Ma lost the babies in October! That's pretty weird. 40
Actually, the October thing is an old family thing. It's kinda funny
that opals (which are bad news) are the birthstone for October. Now,
get this: Opals were once thought to offer special protection for
blondes. In Ireland, if a blonde person is the first person to enter
your home, it's considered a bad omen (that started when the only
blondes around that part of the world were the Viking invaders). So,
have I lost you yet? As for American Indian stuff, it's mostly the fact
that a screech owl is a harbinger of death. There are probably other
things, but I don't remember them right now.

I miss our little dance fests in the kitchen too. 41

Well, we never really figured out the scoop about Doc, but it seems 42
pretty likely that the story about impersonating a priest during the
Inquisition is true. They did probably come through Spain, and may
very well have headed to England from there. As for how Doc &
Fanny met, I can't remember, but it seems that they met while he
was doing business in Dallas. Probably some kind of underworld
thing. What kind of genetic time bombs are we, anyway?

So, hon, feel better. I miss you. BTW, I talked to Aunt Lindy tonight. She 43
would probably love to hear from you. Don't let me forget to make
sure that you have the right phone number and address for her. It
doesn't sound like her part of the family is holding up any better than
ours. In fact, I wonder why we almost seem to be handling it >too<
well. Of course, I can't listen to the radio because too many songs
make me cry, and I keep expecting Ma to call, and I heard someone's
voice today that reminded me of hers, and I still get angry and sick
and scared sometimes. Hmmm . . . Pass the cold medicine . . . ;-)

Later, Denita!
sand

MUSINGS

Compare this form of letter with other letters in this chapter, and note any
differences. Can you explain the reasons for those differences? What features of spoken language do you recognize in these messages? Review a recent E-mail message that you or a friend has sent or received. Does it have
other E-mail features not evident in this selection?

Send an E-mail message to someone in the class and account for any
differences from the E-mail exchange here.

3
AUTOBIOGRAPHY

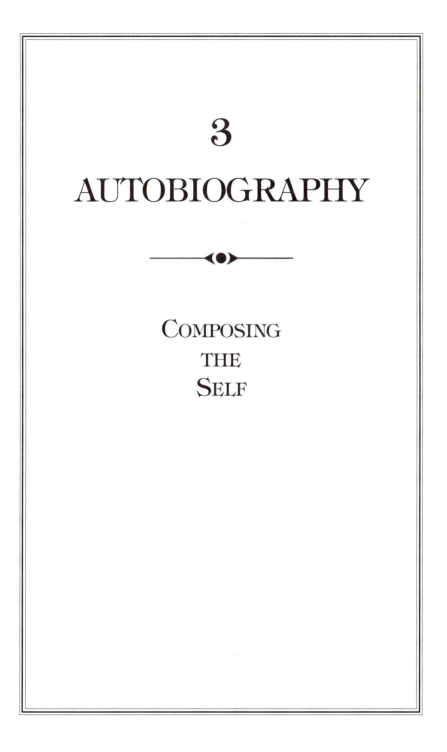

Composing
the
Self

Autobiography is the story of the writer's own life as recollected in memory, sometimes with the help of personal writing, such as journals and letters. It is not merely a record of events in perfect chronological order. Rather, the author selects and perhaps alters events in order to get at what Tim O'Brien calls "the essence of things." O'Brien's selection, included in this chapter, is drawn from his book-length autobiography, which he labeled "a semi-fictionalized account of his own experiences." He explains that "one does not invent merely for the sake of inventing," but "to arrive at some kind of spiritual truth that one can't discover simply by recording the world-as-it-is." Like all life writing, autobiography, by its very nature, mediates between fact and fiction.

Whereas diaries and journals record events immediately after they happen, in order to get at the "essence of things" autobiographies rely on memory and examine experiences with the perspective of passing time. The present alters and shapes our view of the past just as events of the past affect the future. An event such as losing a job that may have seemed disastrous at the time might in the long run have the positive effect of leading to a far better position.

As many different accounts of a single life can be written as there are reasons for writing an autobiography, among them egotism, a longing for distinction, or, at the very least, a wish not to be forgotten. Autobiography serves to put life in perspective for the writer as well as the reader; any writer attempting to write autobiography soon learns that writing about the past causes long-forgotten memories to surface. Finally, autobiography can serve as a way of learning from the past in order to enlighten the present, a way for the writer to consider the deeper meaning of his or her life.

Although writers of autobiography, like those of journals and letters, still draw their subject matter out of their own experiences, the audience has grown from the personal and private one of the diary or the limited audience of the letter to a large public readership. Whereas diarists and letter writers are aware of the identities of their readers, autobiographers compose for a large, anonymous audience. The writer does not know their gender, their religion, or their politics. Consequently, the writer must supply background information that is unnecessary in the diary or letter.

Annie Dillard, whose essay appears later in this book, writes that autobiography is "about waking up," what it feels like to "notice that you have been set down in a going world," as you enter into the intimate life of the author. The "going world" of the autobiography may be quite different from the audience's world. Readers may learn not only about another life, but also about another culture and the way in which one individual sees herself or himself within that culture. Although the kind of addiction that he describes was frowned on even in his day, De Quincey discusses his drug addiction within an age that accepted the casual use of opium; in his culture it was considered little different from an aspirin or a cup of coffee in today's world. The authors represented in this chapter each come from a particular culture with its own history, but are also deeply entangled with pressing issues in the present.

Some of the writers included here were well-known when they wrote, such as Arthur Ashe, a public figure much admired for the conduct of his personal life as well as for his athletic ability. Many were already established authors to whom such an undertaking came easily. On the other hand, some of the writers were unknown when they wrote, and remain virtually unknown today. Their stories are included to provide glimpses into lives and times with which the reader may be unfamiliar.

As stated above, in writing autobiography you may arrange your material in any number of ways, not necessarily in the order that events happened or as you remember them. For example, you may start with the description of an important event and then explore the circumstances that led up to it and its effect on your life. What is most important is that you make clear to your reader the interpretation of your experience. In writing autobiography you might ask yourself the following questions:

- What is the truth about my experience that I am trying to get across to my readers?
- How much do I need to tell my readers about myself, my culture, my colleagues, and my physical surroundings? How much can I leave out?
- What details do I need to include in order to arrive at the essence of things? What details are unnecessary?

THOMAS DE QUINCEY (1785–1859)

Thomas De Quincey ran away from school as a young man and spent several years as a homeless drifter, an experience that he brings to life vividly in Confessions. *He finally returned to attend Oxford University, where he became friends with Samuel Taylor Coleridge and William Wordsworth, both of whom went on to become well-known literary figures. Settling in the English lake country in order to be near his friends in a cottage once owned by the Wordsworths, De Quincey married a local farmer's daughter with whom he had eight children. To support his opium habit, he exhausted his private fortune and spent the rest of his life struggling to make a living. One of his achievements was a psychological study of his dreams, in which he explored the symbols that represent childhood struggles and sufferings. It was written years before Freud's seminal work on the same subject.* Confessions, *first published in* London Magazine *in 1821, brought him instant fame. It was his only sustained work of any import; he spent the rest of his life writing articles and reviews, mainly for journals in Scotland, in an effort to earn money.*

De Quincey began taking opium while he was a student at Oxford and became permanently addicted in his late twenties. Opium taken in mild doses was considered comparatively harmless and was the aspirin of the day, according to one critic writing about De Quincey: "Even soothing syrups for babies contained opium. Addiction, however, was not considered socially acceptable." It was no secret from her friends and family that Elizabeth Barrett Browning took opium to help her sleep. De Quincey hid his addiction for many years, and in Confessions *he describes in vivid prose the original highs, the misery of addiction, and the excruciating pain in his struggle to break the habit.*

Confessions of an English Opium Eater

How unmeaning a sound was opium at that time! what solemn chords 1
does it now strike upon my heart! what heart-quaking vibrations of sad
and happy remembrances! Reverting for a moment to these, I feel a mystic
importance attached to the minutest circumstances connected with the
place, and the time, and the man (if man he was), that first laid open to
me the paradise of opium-eaters. It was a Sunday afternoon, wet and
cheerless; and a duller spectacle this earth of ours has not to show than a
rainy Sunday in London. My road homewards lay through Oxford Street;
and near 'the *stately* Pantheon' (as Mr. Wordsworth has obligingly called it)
I saw a druggist's shop. The druggist (unconscious minister of celestial

151

pleasures!), as if in sympathy with the rainy Sunday, looked dull and stupid, just as any mortal druggist might be expected to look on a rainy London Sunday; and when I asked for the tincture of opium, he gave it to me as any other man might do; and, furthermore, out of my shilling returned to me what seemed to be real copper halfpence, taken out of a real wooden drawer. Nevertheless, and notwithstanding all such indications of humanity, he has ever since figured in my mind as a beatific vision of an immortal druggist, sent down to earth on a special mission to myself. And it confirms me in this way of considering him that, when I next came up to London, I sought him near the stately Pantheon, and found him not; and thus to me, who knew not his name (if, indeed, he had one), he seemed rather to have vanished from Oxford Street than to have flitted into any other locality, or (which some abominable man suggested) to have absconded from the rent. The reader may choose to think of him as, possibly, no more than a sublunary druggist; it may be so, but my faith is better. I believe him to have evanesced [vanished]. So unwillingly would I connect any mortal remembrances with that hour, and place, and creature that first brought me acquainted with the celestial drug.

Arrived at my lodgings, it may be supposed that I lost not a moment in taking the quantity prescribed. I was necessarily ignorant of the whole art and mystery of opium-taking; and what I took I took under every disadvantage. But I took it; and in an hour, O heavens! what a revulsion! what a resurrection, from its lowest depths of the inner spirit! what an apocalypse of the world within me. That my pains had vanished was now a trifle in my eyes; this negative effect was swallowed up in the immensity of those positive effects which had opened before me, in the abyss of divine enjoyment thus suddenly revealed. Here was a panacea, a φάρμακον νηπενθές, for all human woes; here was the secret of happiness, about which philosophers had disputed for so many ages, at once discovered; happiness might now be bought for a penny, and carried in the waistcoatpocket; portable ecstasies might be had corked up in a pint-bottle; and peace of mind could be sent down by the mail.

• • •

This, then, let me repeat: I postulate that, at the time I began to take opium daily, I could not have done otherwise. Whether, indeed, afterwards I might not have succeeded in breaking off the habit, even when it seemed to me that all efforts would be unavailing, and whether many of the innumerable efforts which I *did* make might not have been carried much further, and my gradual re-conquests of lost ground might not have been followed up much more energetically—these are questions which I must decline. Perhaps I might make out a case of palliation. . . .

• • •

Desperate or not, however, the issue of the struggle in 1813 was what I have mentioned; and from this date the reader is to consider me as a regular and confirmed opium-eater, of whom to ask whether on any particular day he had or had not taken opium, would be to ask whether his lungs had performed respiration, or the heart fulfilled its functions. Now, then, reader, you understand what I am; and you are by this time aware, that no old gentleman, 'with a snow-white beard,' will have any chance of persuading me (like Anastasius) to surrender 'the little golden receptacle of the pernicious drug.' No; I give notice to all, whether moralists or surgeons, that, whatever be their pretensions and skill in their respective lines of practice, they must not hope for any countenance from me, if they think to begin by any savage proposition for a Lent or Ramadan of abstinence from opium. This being fully understood between us, we shall in future sail before the wind; now, then, reader, from the year 1813, where all this time we have been sitting down and loitering, rise up, if you please, walk forward about three years more; draw up the curtain, and you shall see me in a new character.

• • •

And now reader, we have run through all the ten categories of my condition, as it stood about 1816–17, up to the middle of which latter year I judge myself to have been a happy man; and the elements of that happiness I have endeavoured to place before you, in the above sketch of the interior of a scholar's library, in a cottage among the mountains, on a stormy winter evening, rain driving vindictively and with malice aforethought against the windows, and darkness such that you cannot see your own hand when held up against the sky.

But now farewell, a long farewell, to happiness, winter or summer! farewell to smiles and laughter! farewell to peace of mind, to tranquil dreams, and to the blessed consolations of sleep! For more than three years and a-half I am summoned away from these. Here opens upon me an Iliad of woes: for I now enter upon

The Pains of Opium

• • •

In thus describing and illustrating my intellectual torpor, I use terms that apply, more or less, to every part of the years during which I was under the Circean spells of opium. But for misery and suffering, I might, indeed, be said to have existed in a dormant state. I seldom could prevail on myself to write a letter; an answer of a few words, to any that I received, was the utmost that I could accomplish; and often *that* not until the letter had lain for weeks, or even months, on my writing-table. Without the aid of M——, my whole domestic economy, whatever became of political economy, must have gone into irretrievable confusion. I shall not afterwards allude to this part of the case; it is one, however, which the opium-eater will find, in the end, most oppressive and tormenting, from the sense of incapacity and feebleness, from the direct embarrassments incident to the neglect or procrastination of each day's appropriate labours, and from the remorse which must often exasperate the stings of these evils to a conscientious mind. The opium-eater loses none of his moral sensibilities or aspirations; he wishes and longs as earnestly as ever to realise what he believes possible, and feels to be exacted by duty; but his intellectual apprehension of what is possible infinitely outruns his power, not of execution only, but even of proposing or willing. He lies under a world's weight of incubus and nightmare; he lies in sight of all that he would fain perform, just as a man forcibly confined to his bed by the mortal languor of paralysis, who is compelled to witness injury or outrage offered to some object of his tenderest love:—he would lay down his life if he might but rise and walk; but he is powerless as an infant, and cannot so much as make an effort to move.

· · ·

Now, at last, I had become awestruck at the approach of sleep, under the condition of visions so afflicting, and so intensely lifelike as those which persecuted my phantom-haunted brain. More and more also I felt violent palpitations in some internal region, such as are commonly, but erroneously, called palpitations of the heart—being, as I suppose, referable exclusively to derangements in the stomach. These were evidently increasing rapidly in frequency and in strength. Naturally, therefore, on considering how important my life had become to others besides myself, I became alarmed; and I paused seasonably; but with a difficulty that is past all description. Either way it seemed as though death had, in military language, 'thrown himself astride of my path.' Nothing short of mortal anguish, in a physical sense, it seemed, to wean myself from opium; yet, on the other hand, death through overwhelming nervous terrors—death by brain fever or by lunacy—seemed too certainly to besiege the alternative course. Fortunately I had still so much of firmness left as to face that choice, which, with most of instant suffering, showed in the far distance a possibility of final escape.

8

This possibility was realised: I *did* accomplish my escape. And the issue   9
of that particular stage in my opium experiences (for such it was—simply
a provisional stage, that paved the way subsequently for many milder
stages, to which gradually my constitutional system accommodated itself)
was, pretty nearly in the following words, communicated to my readers in
the earliest edition of these Confessions:—

I triumphed. But infer not, reader, from this word *'triumphed,'* a con-   10
dition of joy or exultation. Think of me as of one, even when four months
had passed, still agitated, writhing, throbbing, palpitating, shattered; and
much, perhaps, in the situation of him who has been racked, as I collect
the torments of that state from the affecting account of them left by a
most innocent sufferer [William Lithgow] (in the time of James I). Mean-
time, I derived no benefit from any medicine whatever, except ammoni-
ated tincture of valerian. The moral of the narrative is addressed to the
opium-eater; and therefore, of necessity, limited in its application. If he is
taught to fear and tremble, enough has been effected. But he may say that
the issue of my case is at least a proof that opium, after an eighteen years'
use, and an eight years' abuse of its powers, may still be renounced; and
that he may chance to bring to the task greater energy than I did, or that,
with a stronger constitution, he may obtain the same results with less. This
may be true; I would not presume to measure the efforts of other men by
my own. Heartily I wish him more resolution; heartily I wish him an equal
success. Nevertheless, I had motives external to myself which he may unfortunately want; and these supplied me with conscientious supports, such
as merely selfish interests might fail in supplying to a mind debilitated by
opium.

Lord Bacon conjectures that it may be as painful to be born as to die.   11
That seems probable; and, during the whole period of diminishing the
opium, I had the torments of a man passing out of one mode of existence
into another, and liable to the mixed or the alternate pains of birth and
death. The issue was not death, but a sort of physical regeneration; and I
may add, that ever since, at intervals, I have had a restoration of more than
youthful spirits.

One memorial of my former condition nevertheless remains: my   12
dreams are not calm; the dread swell and agitation of the storm have not
wholly subsided; the legions that encamped in them are drawing off, but
not departed; my sleep is still tumultuous; and, like the gates of Paradise
to our first parents when looking back from afar, it is still (in the tremendous line of Milton)—

'With dreadful faces thronged and fiery arms.

MUSINGS

De Quincey describes his addiction in vivid detail and colorful prose, and in the last paragraph he writes of the one remaining aftermath of his addiction—his dreams. He later studied the psychological significance of those dreams. Although De Quincey's prose is somewhat dated, it is still vibrant.

Try to describe a recent imagined nightmare, using metaphors similar to those of De Quincey: "the dread swell and agitation of the storm have not wholly subsided" or, "the legions that encamped in them are drawing off, but not departed." Try to write about the nightmare as though it is posing a threat to you.

BETHENIA OWENS-ADAIR (1840–1926)

Bethenia Owens-Adair was a woman of great courage, dedication, and intelligence who dared to defy many of the customs of the day that shackled and confined women. One of nine children of a family that emigrated to Oregon, she assumed a large part of the care of her younger siblings. Married at age fourteen, Owens-Adair soon realized that her husband was seriously lacking "in industry and perseverance." She wrote that "in one way and another he managed to idle away the summer, going to camp meetings, reading novels, and hunting." After losing their home for nonpayment on the mortgage, she petitioned for divorce, a rare event in those days. Forced to return to live with her parents, Owens-Adair was determined to become a doctor. She began her studies at a medical school in Philadelphia and maintained a rigid schedule, which included rising at 4 A.M. and taking a cold bath. The following year she moved to Oregon, where she practiced medicine. Continuing her studies at the University of Michigan, she graduated in 1880 when she was forty years old.

Owens-Adair was ahead of her time. She formulated a bill to raise the age of sexual consent from age fourteen to age sixteen and advocated exercise and shorter skirts for women. Fiercely independent in her own life, she consistently fought for the rights of all women. The following excerpt from her autobiography, published in 1906, begins with her discouragement after separation from her husband, and her subsequent determination to pursue her education.

An Early Woman Doctor

And now, at eighteen years of age, I found myself, broken in spirit and health, again in my father's house, from which, only four short years before, I had gone with such a happy heart, and such bright hopes for the future. . . .

It seemed to me now that I should never be happy or strong again. I was, indeed, surrounded with difficulties seemingly insurmountable; a husband for whom I had lost all love and respect; a divorce, the stigma of which would cling to me all my future life, and a sickly babe of two years in my arms, all rose darkly before me.

At this time I could scarcely read or write, and four years of trials and hardships and privations sufficient to crush a mature woman, had wrought a painful change in the fresh, blooming child who had so buoyantly taken the duties and burdens of wifehood and motherhood on her young shoulders. I realized my position fully, and resolved to meet it bravely, and do my very best.

My little George, too, felt the beneficial change fully as I did; for my mother's idea of raising children could not be improved upon; simply give them sufficient wholesome food, keep them clean and happy, and let them live out of doors as much as possible.

George was such a tiny creature, and so active in his movements that my young brothers and sisters felt him no burden, and always had him out of doors; so after pondering the matter for some time, I said one day:

"Mother do you think I might manage to go to school?"

"Why yes," she answered: "go right along. George is no trouble. The children will take care of him."

I joyfully accepted this opportunity, and from that day on, I was up early and out to the barn, assisting with the milking, and doing all the work possible in the house, until 8:30, when I went to school with the children, my younger brothers and sisters. Saturdays, with the aid of the children, I did the washing and ironing of the family, and kept up with my studies.

At the end of my first four months' term I had finished the third reader, and made good progress with my other studies of spelling, writing, geography, and arithmetic. . . .

Before going to Clatsop, in the fall of 1859, with my sister, I applied for a divorce, and the custody of my child and petitioned for the restoration of my maiden name of Owens. . . . The suit was strongly contested on account of the child. . . . My father employed Hon. Stephen F. Chadwick on my behalf, and he won my suit. . . . After the decree of the court was rendered giving me custody of my child, and my father's name, which I have never since discarded, and never will, I felt like a free woman.

• • •

Late in the fall of 1860, sister and I went over to Oysterville, Wash., to visit my old and much beloved girl friend, Mrs. S.S. Munson. . . . I told Mrs. Munson of my great anxiety for an education, and she immediately said:

"Why not, then, stay here with me, and go to school? We have a good school here, and I should like so much to have you with me, especially farther on."

To this generous offer I replied that I would gladly accept it if I could only find some way of earning my necessary expenses while attending school. Mrs. Munson replied:

"There are my brother and his hired man: I can get you their washing, which will bring you in from $1.00 to $1.50 per week, which will be all you will need."

To this I gratefully assented and I did their washing evenings. Work to me then was scarcely more than play.

Thus passed one of the pleasantest, and most profitable winters of my life, while, whetted by what it fed on, my desire for knowledge grew daily stronger. My sister, Mrs. Hobson, now urged me to come back to her, and I said to her: I am determined to get at least a common school education. I now know that I can support and educate myself and my boy, and I am resolved to do it: furthermore, I do not intend to do it over a washtub, either. Nor will I any longer work for my board and clothes alone. You need me, and I am willing to stay with you the next six months, if you will arrange for me to go to school in Astoria next winter. She agreed to this, and some time later I said to her: "Diane, don't you think I could teach a little summer school here on the plains? I can rise at four, and help with the milking, and get all the other work done by 8 a.m., and I can do the washing mornings and evenings, and on Saturdays."   16

She said: "You can try," so the following day I asked Mr. Hobson if he would not get up a little school for me.   17

He replied: "Take the horse and go around and among the neighbors and work it up yourself."   18

I lost no time in carrying out his suggestion, and succeeded in getting the promise of sixteen pupils, for which I was to receive $2 each for three months.   19

This was my first attempt to instruct others. I taught my school in the old Presbyterian church, the first Presbyterian church building ever erected in Oregon. Of my sixteen pupils, there were three who were more advanced than myself, but I took their books home with me nights, and, with the help of my brother-in-law, I managed to prepare the lessons beforehand, and they never suspected my incompetency.   20

From this school I received my first little fortune of $25; and I added to this by picking wild blackberries at odd times, which found a ready sale at fifty cents a gallon.   21

Fall found me settled at the old Boelling Hotel in Astoria, with my nephew, Frank Hobson, and my little son George. Our board was paid, I taking care of our small room, and our clothes, with the privilege of doing our washing and ironing on Saturdays. And now I encountered one of my sharpest trials, for, on entering school, and being examined in mental arithmetic, I was placed in the primary class!   22

Mr. Deardorff, the principal, kindly offered to assist me in that study after school, and, later, permitted me to enter both classes. Words can never express my humiliation at having to recite with children of from eight to fourteen years of age. This, however, was of brief duration, for in a few weeks, I had advanced to the next class above, and was soon allowed to enter the third (and highest) class in mental arithmetic.   23

At the end of the term of nine months, I had passed into most of the advanced classes; not that I was an apt scholar, for my knowledge has   24 always been acquired by the hardest labor, but by sheer determination, industry and perseverance. At 4 a.m. my lamp was always burning, and I was poring over my books, never allowing myself more than eight hours of sleep.

Nothing was permitted to come between me and this, the greatest opportunity of my life.   25

• • •

In due time, I announced that in two weeks I would leave for Philadelphia, to enter a medical school. As I have said, I expected disapproval from my friends and relatives, but I was not prepared for the storm of opposition that followed. My family felt they were disgraced, and even my own child was influenced and encouraged to think I was doing him an irreparable injury, by my course. People sneered and laughed derisively. Most of my friends seemed to consider it their Christian duty to advise against, and endeavor to prevent me from taking this "fatal" step. I was literally kept on the rack. But as all things must have an end, the day of my departure was at last at hand. . . .   26

I had taken the decisive step, and I would never turn back. . . . My decision was now irrevocably made, and I was comforted.   27

Stage travel was no hardship for me, for, like the sailor on his ship, I felt at home in the stage. For several years I had gone to San Francisco spring and fall by land, when the nearest railroad connection was at Marysville, California. . . .   28

On reaching Philadelphia, I matriculated in the Eclectic School of Medicine, and employed a private tutor. I also attended the lectures and clinics in the great Blockly Hospital twice a week, as did all the medical students of the city. In due time I received my degree, and returned to Roseburg to wind up my business, which I had left in charge of my sister. A few days after my return, an old man without friends died, and the six physicians who had all attended him at various times, decided to hold an autopsy. At their meeting, Dr. Palmer, who had not forgotten my former "impudence" in using his instrument, made a motion to invite the new "Philadelphia" doctor to be present. This was carried, and a messenger was dispatched to me with a written invitation. I knew this meant no honor for me, but I said: "Give the doctors my compliments, and say that I will be there in a few minutes." The messenger left, and I followed close behind him. I waited outside until he went in and closed the door. I heard him say, in excited tones: "She said to give you her compliments, and that she'd be here in a minute." Then came a roar of laughter, after which I quietly opened the door and walked in, went forward, and shook hands with Dr. Hoover, who advanced to meet me, saying: 29

"Do you know that the autopsy is on the genital organs?"   30

"No," I answered; "but one part of the human body should be as sacred 31
to the physician as another."

Dr. Palmer here stepped back, saying: "I object to a woman's being pre- 32
sent at a male autopsy, and if she is allowed to remain, I shall retire!"

"I came here by written invitation," I said; "and I will leave it to a vote 33
whether I go or stay: but first I would like to ask Dr. Palmer what is the
difference between the attendance of a woman at a male autopsy, and the
attendance of a man at a female autopsy?"

Dr. Hoover said: "Well, I voted for you to come, and I will stick to it." 34
Another said: "I voted yes, and I'll not go back on it. . . ."

One of the doctors opened an old medicine case, and offered it to me. 35

"You do not want me to do the work, do you?" I asked, in surprise. 36

"Oh, yes, yes, go ahead," he said. I took the case and complied. The 37
news of what was going on had spread to every house in town, and the excitement was at fever-heat.

When I had at last finished the dissection, the audience (not the doc- 38
tors) gave me three cheers. As I passed out and down on my way home,
the street was lined on both sides with men, women and children, all anxious to get a look at "the woman who dared," to see what sort of a strange,
anomalous being she was. The women were shocked and scandalized! The
men were disgusted, but amused, thinking it "such a good joke on the
doctors. . . ."

And now, as I look back, I believe that all that saved me was the fact 39
that my brothers, Flem and Josiah, lived there, and although they disap-
proved of my actions quite as much as the rest of the community did, yet
"blood is thicker than water," and they would have died in their tracks before they would have seen me subjected to indignities, or driven out of
town. And as everyone knew they would shoot at the drop of a hat, good
care was taken to lay no violent hands on me.

MUSINGS

It is hard to imagine in the present day how difficult it might have been for
a woman to perform an autopsy on a male cadaver. Owens-Adair describes
the scene effectively using dialogue to add to the impact. She comes across
as a courageous woman not by what she says, but by what she does.

Think of a time when you demonstrated spirit and determination in an
unfriendly or unfamiliar situation. Describe your actions and your words
under those circumstances, as well as the actions and words of the people
around you.

SARAH WINNEMUCCA (1844–1891)

Sarah Winnemucca's grandfather was Chief Truckee of the Paiutes, a nomadic tribe from the deserts of northern Nevada. Winnemucca saw the tragic deaths of nearly half her family, who were driven from reservation to reservation. She lived for some time with the family of an English trader, where she learned English, which then enabled her to become a translator. She supported her people all her life, even after she started working for the U.S. Army and became a popular lecturer on the East Coast; wherever she traveled, she always returned to the reservation. Before her grandfather died, he asked Winnemucca to promise that his grandchildren would attend a mission school. The children only remained in the school a few weeks, however, as other parents violently objected to admitting Native Americans to the all-white school.

The following is an account of a threatened attack, followed by a description of some of the Native American customs that initiate young girls into womanhood. It is taken from her autobiography, Life Among the Piutes *(as it was then spelled) edited by Winnemucca's good friend and supporter, Mrs. Horace Mann.*

An Indian Woman Looks Back

That same fall, very late, the emigrants kept coming. It was this time that our white brothers first came amongst us. They could not get over the mountains, so they had to live with us. It was on Carson River, where the great Carson City now stands. You call my people bloodseeking. My people did not seek to kill them, nor did they steal their horses—no, no, far from it. During the winter my people helped them. They gave them such as they had to eat. They did not hold out their hands and say: "You can't have anything to eat unless you pay me." No—no such word was used by us savages at that time. . . .

The following spring, before my grandfather returned home, there was a great excitement among my people on account of fearful news coming from different tribes . . . there was a fearful story they told us children. Our mothers told us that the whites were killing everybody and eating them. So we were all afraid of them. Every dust that we could see blowing in the valleys we would say it was the white people. In the late fall my father told his people to go to the rivers and fish, and we all went to Humboldt River, and the women went to work gathering wild seed, which they grind between the rocks. The stones are round, big enough to hold in the hands. The women did this when they got back, and when they had gathered all they could they put it in one place and covered it with grass, and then over the grass, mud. After it is covered it looks like an Indian wigwam.

What a fright we all got one morning to hear some white people were coming. Every one ran as best they could. . . . My aunt overtook us, and she said to my mother: "Let us bury our girls, or we shall all be killed and eaten up." So they went to work and buried us, and told us if we heard any noise not to cry out, for if we did they would surely kill us and eat us. So our mothers buried me and my cousin, planted sage bushes over our faces to keep the sun from burning them, and there we were left all day. 3

Can any one imagine my feelings buried alive, thinking every minute that I was to be unburied and eaten up by the people that my grandfather loved so much? With my heart throbbing, and not daring to breathe, we lay there all day. It seemed that the night would never come. . . . At last we heard some whispering. We did not dare to whisper to each other, so we lay still. I could hear their footsteps coming nearer and nearer. I thought my heart was coming right out of my mouth. Then I heard my mother say, "'T'is right here!" Oh, can any one in this world ever imagine what were my feelings when I was dug up by my poor mother and father . . . ? 4

Well, while we were in the mountains hiding, the people that my grandfather called our white brothers came along to where our winter supplies were. They set everything we had left on fire. It was a fearful sight. It was all we had for the winter, and it was all burnt during that night. My father took some of his men during the night to try and save some of it, but they could not; it had burnt down before they got there. 5

Those were the last white men that came along that fall. My people talked fearfully that winter about those they called our white brothers. . . . This whole band of white people [undoubtedly the Donner Party] perished in the mountains, for it was too late to cross them. We could have saved them, only my people were afraid of them. We never knew who they were, or where they came from. So, poor things, they must have suffered fearfully, for they all starved there. The snow was too deep. . . . 6

We remained there all winter; the next spring emigrants came as usual, and my father and grandfather and uncles, and many more went down the Humboldt River on fishing excursions. While they were thus fishing, their white brothers came upon them and fired on them, and killed one of my uncles, and wounded another. Nine more were wounded, and five died afterwards. My other uncle got well again, and is living yet. Oh, that was a fearful thing indeed. . . . The widow of my uncle who was killed, and my mother and father all had long hair. They cut off their hair, and also cut long gashes in their arms and legs, and they were all bleeding as if they would die with the loss of blood. This continued for several days, for this is the way we mourn for our dead. When the woman's husband dies, she is 7 first to cut off her hair, and then she braids it and puts it across her breast; then his mother and sisters, his fathers and brothers and all his kinfolk cut their hair. The widow is to remain unmarried until her hair is the same length as before, and her face is not to be washed all that time, and she is to use no kind of paint, nor to make any merriment with other women until the day is set for her to do so by her father-in-law and by her mother-in-law, and then she is at liberty to go where she pleases. The widower is at liberty when his wife dies; but he mourns for her in the same way, by cutting his hair off. . . .

Our children are very carefully taught to be good. Their parents tell 8 them stories, traditions of old times, even of the first mother of the human race; and love stories, stories of giants, and fables; and when they ask if these last stories are true, they answer, "Oh, it is only coyote," which means that they are make-believe stories. Coyote is the name of a mean, crafty little animal, half wolf, half dog, and stands for everything low. It is the greatest term of reproach one Indian has for another. Indians do not swear—they have no words for swearing till they learn them of white men. The worst they call each other is "bad" or "coyote," but they are very sincere with one another, and if they think each other in the wrong, they say so.

We are taught to love everybody. We don't need to be taught to love our 9 fathers and mothers. We love them without being told to. Our tenth cousin is as near to us as our first cousin, and we don't marry into our relations. Our young women are not allowed to talk to any young man that is not their cousin, except at the festive dances, when both are dressed in their best clothes, adorned with beads, feathers or shells, and stand alternately in the ring and take hold of hands. These are very pleasant occasions to all the young people. . . .

My people have been so unhappy for a long time they wish now to dis- 10 increase, instead of multiply. The mothers are afraid to have more children, for fear they shall have daughters, who are not safe even in their mother's presence.

The grandmothers have the special care of the daughters just before and 11 after they come to womanhood. The girls are not allowed to get married until they have come to womanhood; and that period is recognized as a very sacred thing, and is the subject of a festival, and has peculiar customs. The young woman is set apart under the care of two of her friends, somewhat older, and a little wigwam, called a teepee, just big enough for the three, is made for them, to which they retire. She goes through certain labors which are thought to be strengthening, and these last twenty-five days. Every day, three times a day, she must gather, and pile up as high as she can, five stacks of wood. This makes fifteen stacks a day. At the end of every five days the attendants take her to a river to bathe. She fasts from all flesh-meat during these twenty-five days, and continues to do this for five days in every month all her life. At the end of twenty-five days she returns to the family lodge, and gives all her clothing to her attendants in payment for their care. Sometimes the wardrobe is quite extensive.

It is thus publicly known that there is another marriageable woman, and any young man interested in her, or wishing to form an alliance, comes forward. But the courting is very different from the courting of the white people. He never speaks to her, or visits the family, but endeavors to attract her attention by showing his horsemanship, etc. As he knows that she sleeps next to her grandmother, in the lodge, he enters in full dress after the family has retired for the night, and seats himself at her feet. If she is not awake, the grandmother wakes her. He does not speak to either young woman or grandmother, but when the young woman wishes him to go away, she rises and goes and lies down by the side of her mother. He then leaves as silently as he came in.   12

This goes on sometimes for a year or longer, if the young woman has not made up her mind. She is never forced by her parents to marry against her wishes. When she knows her own mind, she makes a confidant of her grandmother, and then the young man is summoned by the father of the girl, who asks him in her presence, if he really loves his daughter, and reminds him, if he says he does, of all the duties of a husband. He then asks his daughter the same question, and sets before her minutely all her duties. And these duties are not slight.   13

She is to dress the game, prepare the food, clean the buckskins, make his moccasins, dress his hair, bring all the wood—in short, do all the household work. She promises to "be himself," and she fulfills her promise. . . . [This meant that the women promised their fathers to make their husbands "themselves."] They faithfully keep with them in all the dangers they can share. They not only take care of the children together, but they do everything together; and when they grow blind, which, I am sorry to say is very common, for the smoke they live in destroys their eyes at last, they take sweet care of one another. Marriage is a sweet thing when people love each other.   14

At the wedding feast, all the food is prepared in baskets. The young woman sits by the young man, and hands him the basket of food prepared for him with her own hands. He does not take it with his right hand; but seizes her wrist, and takes it with the left hand. This constitutes the marriage ceremony, and the father pronounces them man and wife. They go to a wigwam of their own, where they live till the first child is born. This event also is celebrated. Both father and mother fast from all flesh, and the father goes through the labor of piling the wood for twenty-five days, and assumes all his wife's household work during that time.   15

If he does not do his part in the care of the child, he is considered an outcast. Every five days his child's basket is changed for a new one, and the   16 five are all carefully put away at the end of the days, the last one containing the navel-string, carefully wrapped up, and all are put up into a tree, and the child put into a new and ornamented basket. All this respect shown to the mother and child makes the parents feel their responsibility, and makes the tie between parents and children very strong.

The young mothers often get together and exchange their experiences 17 about the attentions of their husbands; and inquire of each other if the fathers did their duty to their children, and were careful of their wives' health. When they are married they give away all the clothing they have . . . and dress themselves anew. . . .

My people teach their children never to make fun of anyone, no matter 18 how they look. If you see your brother or sister doing something wrong, look away, or go away from them. If you make fun of bad persons, you make yourself beneath them. Be kind to all, both poor and rich, and feed all that come to your wigwam, and your name can be spoken of by every one far and near. In this way you will make many friends for yourself. Be kind both to bad and good, for you don't know your own heart. This is the way my people teach their children. It was handed down from father to son for many generations. I never in my life saw our children rude as I have seen white children and grown people in the streets. . . .

MUSINGS

In her autobiography Winnemucca reveals her fear of whites and then patiently explains some of the customs and attitudes that she was taught by her family. She writes for an audience of whites, whom she knew to be largely hostile toward her people, attempting to justify Native American perspectives and beliefs.

Explore the customs surrounding the obligations of a husband or a wife in your family or circle of friends. Write for an audience that does not agree with your ideas and try to make one of those customs understandable to that audience.

Zora Neale Hurston (1903?–1960)

Zora Neale Hurston was encouraged by her mother to "jump at the sun." At age thirteen she was forced to leave school to care for her brother's children, but three years later she secured work with a woman who helped her to return and graduate from high school. She later attended Howard University, then Barnard College, and finally Columbia University where she studied anthropology. After graduation she returned to her hometown to study African-American folklore, and, because of her distaste for any kind of social or intellectual snobbery, she proved to be a talented folklore collector. Langston Hughes wrote of Hurston: "Almost nobody else could stop the average Harlemite on Lenox Avenue and measure his head with a strange-looking, anthropological device and not get bawled out for the attempt, except Zora, who used to stop anyone whose head looked interesting and measure it." Hurston herself maintained that she was born in the "crib of Negroism" and that black folklore fitted her like a "tight chemise" so that she could not really see it: "It was only when I was off at college that I could see myself like somebody else and stand off and see my garment."

Although sharply criticized for glossing over racial injustice, Hurston stoutly insisted, as she does in the following selection, that she did not consider it: "I do not belong to the sobbing school of Negrohood who hold that nature somehow has given them a lowdown dirty deal and whose feelings are all hurt about it. . . . No, I do not weep at the world—I am too busy sharpening my oyster knife." Associated with the Harlem Renaissance, she stoutly refused to spend her life constantly reacting to an omnipresent racism.

The author of four novels and two books of folklore, Hurston received a number of honors, including two Guggenheims. However, she died in relative obscurity and poverty, and only recently has interest in her work been revived. The following selection is taken from her autobiography, Dust Tracks on a Road.

Looking Things Over

Well, that is the way things stand up to now. I can look back and see 1
sharp shadows, high lights, and smudgy inbetweens. I have been in Sorrow's kitchen and licked out all the pots. Then I have stood on the peaky mountain wrappen in rainbows, with a harp and a sword in my hands.

What I had to swallow in the kitchen has not made me less glad to have 2
lived, nor made me want to low-rate the human race, nor any whole sections of it. I take no refuge from myself in bitterness. To me, bitterness is the under-arm odor of wishful weakness. It is the graceless acknowledg-

167

ment of defeat. I have no urge to make any concessions like that to the world as yet. I might be like that some day, but I doubt it. I am in the struggle with the sword in my hands, and I don't intend to run until you run me. So why give off the smell of something dead under the house while I am still in there tussling with my sword in my hand?

If tough breaks have not soured me, neither have my glory-moments caused me to build any altars to myself where I can burn incense before God's best job of work. My sense of humor will always stand in the way of my seeing myself, my family, my race or my nation as the whole intent of the universe. When I see what we really are like, I know that God is too great an artist for we folks on my side of the creek to be all of His best works. Some of His finest touches are among us, without doubt, but some more of His masterpieces are among those folks who live over the creek. 3

So looking back and forth in history and around the temporary scene, I do not visualize the moon dripping down in blood, nor the sun batting his fiery eyes and laying down in the cradle of eternity to rock himself into sleep and slumber at instances of human self-bias. I know that the sun and the moon must be used to sights like that by now. I too yearn for universal justice, but how to bring it about is another thing. It is such a complicated thing, for justice, like beauty, is in the eye of the beholder. There is universal agreement on the principle, but the application brings on the fight. Oh, for some disinterested party to pass on things! Somebody will hurry to tell me that we voted God to the bench for that. But the lawyers who interpret His opinions, make His decisions sound just like they made them up themselves. Being an idealist, I too wish that the world was better than I am. Like all the rest of my fellow men, I don't want to live around people with no more principles than I have. My inner fineness is continually outraged at finding that the world is a whole family of Hurstons. 4

Seeing these things, I have come to the point by trying to make the day at hand a positive thing, and realizing the uselessness of gloominess. 5

What do I want, then? I will tell you in a parable. A Negro deacon was down on his knees praying at a wake held for a sister who had died that day. He had his eyes closed and was going great guns, when he noticed that he was not getting any more "amens" from the rest. He opened his eyes and saw that everybody else was gone except himself and the dead woman. Then he saw the reason. The supposedly dead woman was trying to sit up. He bolted for the door himself, but it slammed shut so quickly that it caught his flying coat-tails and held him sort of static. "Oh, no Gabriel!" the deacon shouted, "dat aint no way for you to do. I can do my own running, but you got to 'low me the same chance as the rest." 6

I don't know any more about the future than you do. I hope that it will be full of work, because I have come to know by experience that work is 7 the nearest thing to happiness that I can find. No matter what else I have among the things that humans want, I go to pieces in a short while if I do not work. What all my work shall be, I don't know that either, every hour being a stranger to you until you live it. I want a busy life, a just mind and a timely death.

But if I should live to be very old, I have laid plans for that so that it will not be too tiresome. So far, I have never used coffee, liquor, nor any form of stimulant. When I get old, and my joints and bones tell me about it, I can sit around and write for myself, if for nobody else, and read slowly and carefully the mysticism of the East, and re-read Spinoza with love and care. All the while my days can be a succession of coffee cups. Then when the sleeplessness of old age attacks me, I can have a likker bottle snug in my pantry and sip away and sleep. Get mellow and think kindly of the world. I think I can be like that because I have known the joy and pain of deep friendship. I have served and been served. I have made some good enemies for which I am not a bit sorry. I have loved unselfishly, and I have fondled hatred with the red-hot tongs of Hell. That's living.

I have no race prejudice of any kind. My kinfolks, and my "skin-folks" are dearly loved. My own circumference of everyday life is there. But I see their same virtues and vices everywhere I look. So I give you all my right hand of fellowship and love, and hope for the same from you. In my eyesight, you lose nothing by not looking just like me. I will remember you all in my good thoughts, and I ask you kindly to do the same for me. Not only just me. You, who play the zig-zag lightning of power over the world, with the grumbling thunder in your wake, think kindly of those who walk in the dust. And you who walk in humble places, think kindly too, of others. There has been no proof in the world so far that you would be less arrogant if you held the lever of power in your hands. Let us all be kissing-friends. Consider that with tolerance and patience, we godly demons may breed a noble world in a few hundred generations or so. Maybe all of us who do not have the good fortune to meet, or meet again, in this world, will meet at a barbecue.

• • •

I do not say that my conclusions about anything are true for the Universe, but I have lived in many ways, sweet and bitter, and they feel right for me. I have seen and heard. I have sat in judgment upon the ways of others, and in the voiceless quiet of the night I have also called myself to judgment. I cannot have the joy of knowing that I found always a shining reflection of honor and wisdom in the mirror of my soul on those occasions. I have given myself more harrowing pain than anyone else has ever been capable of giving me. No one else can inflict the hurt of faith unkept.

I have had the corroding insight at times, of recognizing that I am a bundle of sham and tinsel, honest metal and sincerity that cannot be untangled. My dross has given my other parts great sorrow.

But, on the other hand, I have given myself the pleasure of sunrises   11
blooming out of oceans, and sunsets drenching heaped-up clouds. I have walked in storms with a crown of clouds about my head and the zigzag lightning playing through my fingers. The gods of the upper air have uncovered their faces to my eyes. I have found out that my real home is in the water, that the earth is only my stepmother. My old man, the Sun, sired me out of the sea.

Like all mortals, I have been shaped by the chisel in the hand of   12
Chance, bulged out here by a sense of victory, shrunken there by the press of failure and the knowledge of unworthiness. But it has been given to me to strive with life, and to conquer the fear of death. I have been correlated to the world so that I know the indifference of the sun to human emotions. I know that destruction and construction are but two faces of Dame Nature, and that it is nothing to her if I choose to make personal tragedy out of her unbreakable laws.

So I ask of her few things. May I never do good consciously nor evil un-   13
consciously [sic]. Let my evil be known to me in advance of my acts, and my good when Nature wills. May I be granted a just mind and a timely death.

While I am still far below the allotted span of time, notwithstanding, I   14
feel that I have lived. I have the joy and pain of strong friendships. I have served and been served. I have made enemies of which I am not ashamed. I have been faithless, and then I have been faithful and steadfast until the blood ran down into my shoes. I have loved unselfishly with all the ardor of a strong heart, and I have hated with all the power of my soul. What waits for me in the future? I do not know. I cannot even imagine, and I am glad for that. But already I have touched the four corners of the horizon, for from hard searching it seems to me that tears and laughter, love and hate, make up the sum of life.

MUSINGS

Her masterful use of words is what distinguishes Hurston's writing. Study her language carefully and notice her use of words that are not in the dictionary: "wrappen," "likker bottle," and "skin-folks." She also seems to think as well as write in startling and splendid metaphors: "I have been in Sorrow's kitchen and licked out all the pots," and her reference to the dead as "those folks who live over the creek." Try reading part of the selection out loud and notice the sound of the writing—her use of *onomatopoeia* (words whose sounds suggest their meanings), *alliteration* (repetition of words starting with the same sound), and rhyme.

In this selection Hurston looks "back and forth" in her history and outlines "what she wants." Look "back and forth" in your own history and outline what you want in the future. Pay close attention to the language you use; you may have to do considerable rewriting and polishing.

MALCOLM X (1925–1965)

Malcolm Little assumed his more familiar name, Malcolm X, the one under which he wrote his autobiography, when he joined the Black Muslims. While in prison serving seven years for robbery, Malcolm X educated himself, copying the dictionary page by laborious page and reading everything at hand, often by the corridor light at night. He also wrote long letters each day to Elijah Muhammad, the leader of the Black Muslims. Although he previously led a reckless and drug-dominated existence, he maintained that in prison he had never been "so truly free in his life."

After his release Malcolm X became what one critic described as "an articulate, mercurial spokesperson for the radical black perspective." He became increasingly critical of the Black Muslims and especially of Elijah Muhammad, who was inclined toward expensive clothes and flashy cars. In 1963 Malcolm traveled to Mecca, the Muslim shrine, after which he converted and broke with the Black Muslims. The following year he founded the worldwide Organization of Afro-American Unity for Blacks. In 1965, as he began a speech in Harlem, he was gunned down by an assassin thought to be associated with his former leader.

The following excerpt describes his life in prison and is taken from his autobiography, which he dictated to Alex Haley, a well-known novelist who later wrote Roots. *The autobiography was published in 1965 soon after his death. In this selection Malcolm X tells of his frustration at his inability to write down the language he is able to speak so fluently and describes how he learned to write while in prison.*

Books Are My Alma Mater

It was because of my letters that I happened to stumble upon starting to acquire some kind of a homemade education.   1

I became increasingly frustrated at not being able to express what I wanted to convey in letters that I wrote, especially those to Mr. Elijah Muhammad. In the street, I had been the most articulate hustler out there—I had commanded attention when I said something. But now, trying to write simple English, I not only wasn't articulate, I wasn't even functional. How would I sound writing in slang, the way I would *say* it, something such as "Look, daddy, let me pull your coat about a cat, Elijah Muhammad—"   2

Many who today hear me somewhere in person, or on television, or those who read something I've said, will think I went to school far beyond the eighth grade. This impression is due entirely to my prison studies.   3

It had really begun back in the Charlestown Prison, when Bimbi first   4
made me feel envy of his stock of knowledge. Bimbi had always taken
charge of any conversation he was in, and I had tried to emulate him. But
every book I picked up had few sentences which didn't contain anywhere
from one to nearly all of the words that might as well have been in Chinese. When I just skipped those words, of course, I really ended up with
little idea of what the book said. So I had come to the Norfolk Prison
Colony still going through only book-reading motions. Pretty soon, I
would have quit even these motions, unless I had received the motivation
that I did.

I saw that the best thing I could do was get hold of a dictionary—to   5
study, to learn some words. I was lucky enough to reason also that I should
try to improve my penmanship. It was sad. I couldn't even write in a straight
line. It was both ideas together that moved me to request a dictionary along
with some tablets and pencils from the Norfolk Prison Colony school.

I spent two days just riffling uncertainly through the dictionary's pages.   6
I'd never realized so many words existed! I didn't know *which* words I
needed to learn. Finally, just to start some kind of action, I began copying.

In my slow, painstaking, ragged handwriting, I copied into my tablet   7
everything printed on that first page, down to the punctuation marks.

I believe it took me a day. Then, aloud, I read back, to myself, every-   8
thing I'd written on the tablet. Over and over, aloud, to myself, I read my
own handwriting.

I woke up the next morning, thinking about those words—immensely   9
proud to realize that not only had I written so much at one time, but I'd
written words that I never knew were in the world. Moreover, with a little
effort, I also could remember what many of these words meant. I reviewed
the words whose meanings I didn't remember. Funny thing, from the dictionary first page right now, that "aardvark" springs to my mind. The dictionary had a picture of it, a long-tailed, long-eared, burrowing African
mammal, which lives off termites caught by sticking out its tongue as an
anteater does for ants.

I was so fascinated that I went on—I copied the dictionary's next page.   10
And the same experience came when I studied that. With every succeeding
page, I also learned of people and places and events from history. Actually
the dictionary is like a miniature encyclopedia. Finally the dictionary's A
section had filled a whole tablet—and I went on into the B's. That was the
way I started copying what eventually became the entire dictionary. It
went a lot faster after so much practice helped me to pick up handwriting
speed. Between what I wrote in my tablet, and writing letters, during the
rest of my time in prison I would guess I wrote a million words.

I suppose it was inevitable that as my word-base broadened, I could for   11
the first time pick up a book and read and now begin to understand what

the book was saying. Anyone who has read a great deal can imagine the new world that opened. Let me tell you something: from then until I left that prison, in every free moment I had, if I was not reading in the library I was reading on my bunk. You couldn't have gotten me out of books with a wedge. Between Mr. Muhammad's teachings, my correspondence, my visitors—usually Ella and Reginald—and my reading of books, months passed without my even thinking about being imprisoned. In fact, up to then, I never had been so truly free in my life.

The Norfolk Prison Colony's library was in the school building. A variety of classes was taught there by instructors who came from such places as Harvard and Boston universities. The weekly debates between inmate teams were also held in the school building. You would be astonished to know how worked up convict debaters and audiences would get over subjects like "Should Babies Be Fed Milk?" 12

Available on the prison library's shelves were books on just about every general subject. Much of the big private collection that Parkhurst had willed to the prison was still in crates and boxes in the back of the library—thousands of old books. Some of them looked ancient: covers faded, old-time parchment-looking binding. Parkhurst, I've mentioned, seemed to have been principally interested in history and religion. He had the money and the special interest to have a lot of books that you wouldn't have in general circulation. Any college library would have been lucky to get that collection. 13

As you can imagine, especially in a prison where there was heavy emphasis on rehabilitation, an inmate was smiled upon if he demonstrated an unusually intense interest in books. There was a sizable number of well-read inmates, especially the popular debaters. Some were said by many to be practically walking encyclopedias. They were almost celebrities. No university would ask any student to devour literature as I did when this new world opened to me, of being able to read and *understand*. 14

I read more in my room than in the library itself. An inmate who was known to read a lot could check out more than the permitted maximum number of books. I preferred reading in the total isolation of my own room. 15

When I had progressed to really serious reading, every night at about ten P.M. I would be outraged with the "lights out." It always seemed to catch me right in the middle of something engrossing. 16

Fortunately, right outside my door was a corridor light that cast a glow into my room. The glow was enough to read by, once my eyes adjusted to it. So when "lights out" came, I would sit on the floor where I could continue reading in that glow. 17

At one-hour intervals the night guards paced past every room. Each time I heard the approaching footsteps, I jumped into bed and feigned 18 sleep. And as soon as the guard passed, I got back out of bed onto the floor area of that light-glow, where I would read for another fifty-eight minutes—until the guard approached again. That went on until three or four every morning. Three or four hours of sleep a night was enough for me. Often in the years in the streets I had slept less than that.

• • •

Mr. Muhammad [a leader of the Black Muslims], to whom I was writing daily, had no idea of what a new world had opened up to me through my efforts to document his teachings in books.   19

When I discovered philosophy, I tried to touch all the landmarks of philosophical development. Gradually, I read most of the old philosophers, Occidental and Oriental. The Oriental philosophers were the ones I came to prefer; finally, my impression was that most Occidental philosophy had largely been borrowed from the Oriental thinkers. Socrates, for instance, traveled in Egypt. Some sources even say that Socrates was initiated into some of the Egyptian mysteries. Obviously Socrates got some of his wisdom among the East's wise men.   20

I have often reflected upon the new vistas that reading opened to me. I knew right there in prison that reading had changed forever the course of my life. As I see it today, the ability to read awoke inside me some long dormant craving to be mentally alive. I certainly wasn't seeking any degree, the way a college confers a status symbol upon its students. My home-made education gave me, with every additional book that I read, a little bit more sensitivity to the deafness, dumbness, and blindness that was afflicting the black race in America. Not long ago, an English writer telephoned me from London, asking questions. One was, "What's your alma mater?" I told him, "Books." You will never catch me with a free fifteen minutes in which I'm not studying something I feel might be able to help the black man.   21

• • •

But I'm digressing. I told the Englishman that my alma mater was books, a good library. Every time I catch a plane, I have with me a book that I want to read—and that's a lot of books these days. If I weren't out here every day battling the white man, I could spend the rest of my life reading, just satisfying my curiosity—because you can hardly mention anything I'm not curious about. I don't think anybody ever got more out of going to prison than I did. In fact, prison enabled me to study far more intensively than I would have if my life had gone differently and I had attended some college. I imagine that one of the biggest troubles with colleges is there are too many distractions, too much panty-raiding, fraternities, and boola-boola and all of that. Where else but in a prison   22 could I have attacked my ignorance by being able to study intensely sometimes as much as fifteen hours a day?

MUSINGS

In the first paragraph Malcolm X describes his ease of speaking "on the street" but his inability to write simple English. Do you have similar problems in transferring your ideas from speech to the written page?

Examine some of the differences between your spoken language and your written language. Tape an incident from your life and then try to transfer a portion into written language. Compare the spoken and written versions.

Paula Gunn Allen (1939–)

Paula Gunn Allen comes from a background of Laguna Pueblo and Sioux cultures mixed with Anglo-European, but it is her Native American background that deeply concerns her and shapes her writing. Her involvement in feminism drives her concern for the Native American woman's need to interact and draw from two dissimilar cultures—the Native American world of mysticism and spirits and the Anglo world in which she must live and function. Allen was born in Baghdad, Iraq, and attended university in England, earning a postgraduate degree in computer science from Cambridge University. She is currently a lecturer at the University of California at Berkeley and has written and edited a number of books with Native American themes. In Spider Woman's Granddaughters, *she collected essays from modern Native American women authors and blended them with old legends, such as the Pueblo's mother goddess of corn. Allen characterizes Native Americans as "something other than victims—mostly what we are is unrecognized." Most of her writings represent an effort to illuminate that recognition.*

The Sacred Hoop: Recovering the Feminine in American Indian Traditions, *a second collection of essays that explores the Native American woman's culture as it differs from the dominant American culture, was published in 1992. In the following selection from that book she states, "In no tribal definitions is she [the Indian woman] perceived in the same way as are women in western industrial and postindustrial cultures." She then delineates those differences.*

Where I Come from Is Like This

I

Modern American Indian women, like their non-Indian sisters, are deeply engaged in the struggle to redefine themselves. In their struggle they must reconcile traditional tribal definitions of women with industrial and postindustrial non-Indian definitions. Yet while these definitions seem to be more or less mutually exclusive, Indian women must somehow harmonize and integrate both in their own lives.

An American Indian woman is primarily defined by her tribal identity. In her eyes, her destiny is necessarily that of her people, and her sense of herself as a woman is first and foremost prescribed by her tribe. The definitions of woman's roles are as diverse as tribal cultures in the Americas. In some she is devalued, in others she wields considerable power. In some she

177

is a familial/clan adjunct, in some she is as close to autonomous as her economic circumstances and psychological traits permit. But in no tribal definitions is she perceived in the same way as are women in western industrial and postindustrial cultures.

In the west, few images of women form part of the cultural mythos, and these are largely sexually charged. Among Christians, the madonna is the female prototype, and she is portrayed as essentially passive: her contribution is simply that of birthing. Little else is attributed to her and she certainly possesses few of the characteristics that are attributed to mythic figures among Indian tribes. This image is countered (rather than balanced) by the witch-goddess/whore characteristics designed to reinforce cultural beliefs about women, as well as western adversarial and dualistic perceptions of reality. 3

The tribes see women variously, but they do not question the power of femininity. Sometimes they see women as fearful, sometimes peaceful, sometimes omnipotent and omniscient, but they never portray women as mindless, helpless, simple, or oppressed. And while the women in a given tribe, clan, or band may be all these things, the individual woman is provided with a variety of images of women from the interconnected supernatural, natural, and social worlds she lives in. 4

As a half-breed American Indian woman, I cast about in my mind for negative images of Indian women, and I find none that are directed to Indian women alone. The negative images I do have are of Indians in general and in fact are more often of males than of females. All these images come to me from non-Indian sources, and they are always balanced by a positive image. My ideas of womanhood, passed on largely by my mother and grandmothers, Laguna Pueblo women, are about practicality, strength, reasonableness, intelligence, wit, and competence. I also remember vividly the women who came to my father's store, the women who held me and sang to me, the women at Feast Day, at Grab Days, the women in the kitchen of my Cubero home, the women I grew up with; none of them appeared weak or helpless, none of them presented herself tentatively. I remember a certain reserve on those lovely brown faces; I remember the direct gaze of eyes framed by bright-colored shawls draped over their heads and cascading down their backs. I remember the clean cotton dresses and carefully pressed hand-embroidered aprons they always wore; I remember laughter and good food, especially the sweet bread and the oven bread they gave us. Nowhere in my mind is there a foolish woman, a dumb woman, a vain woman, or a plastic woman, though the Indian women I have known have shown a wide range of personal style and demeanor. 5

My memory includes the Navajo woman who was badly beaten by her Sioux husband; but I also remember that my grandmother abandoned her Sioux husband long ago. I recall the stories about the Laguna woman 6 beaten regularly by her husband in the presence of her children so that the children would not believe in the strength and power of femininity. And I remember the women who drank, who got into fights with other women and with the men, and who often won those battles. I have memories of tired women, partying women, stubborn women, sullen women, amicable women, selfish women, shy women, and aggressive women. Most of all I remember the women who laugh and scold and sit uncomplaining in the long sun on feast days and who cook wonderful food on wood stoves, in beehive mud ovens, and over open fires outdoors.

Among the images of women that come to me from various tribes as well as my own are White Buffalo Woman, who came to the Lakota long ago and brought them the religion of the Sacred Pipe which they still practice; Tinotzin the goddess who came to Juan Diego to remind him that she still walked the hills of her people and sent him with her message, her demand and her proof to the Catholic bishop in the city nearby. And from Laguna I take the images of Yellow Woman, Coyote Woman, Grandmother Spider (Spider Old Woman), who brought the light, who gave us weaving and medicine, who gave us life. Among the Keres she is known as Thought Woman who created us all and who keeps us in creation even now. I remember Iyatiku, Earth Woman, Corn Woman, who guides and counsels the people to peace and who welcomes us home when we cast off this coil of flesh as huskers cast off the leaves that wrap the corn. I remember Iyatiku's sister, Sun Woman, who held metals and cattle, pigs and sheep, highways and engines and so many things in her bundle, who went away to the east saying that one day she would return.

7

II

Since the coming of the Anglo-Europeans beginning in the fifteenth century, the fragile web of identity that long held tribal people secure has gradually been weakened and torn. But the oral tradition has prevented the complete destruction of the web, the ultimate disruption of tribal ways. The oral tradition is vital; it heals itself and the tribal web by adapting to the flow of the present while never relinquishing its connection to the past. Its adaptability has always been required, as many generations have experienced. Certainly the modern American Indian woman bears slight resemblance to her forebears—at least on superficial examination—but she is still a tribal woman in her deepest being. Her tribal sense of relationship to all that is continues to flourish. And though she is at times beset by her knowledge of the enormous gap between the life she lives and the life she was raised to live, and while she adapts her mind and being to the circumstances of her present life, she does so in tribal ways, mending

8

the tears in the web of being from which she takes her existence as she goes.

My mother told me stories all the time, though I often did not recog-   9
nize them as that. My mother told me stories about cooking and child-
bearing; she told me stories about menstruation and pregnancy; she told
me stories about gods and heroes, about fairies and elves, about goddesses
and spirits; she told me stories about the land and the sky, about cats and
dogs, about snakes and spiders; she told me stories about climbing trees
and exploring the mesas; she told me stories about going to dances and
getting married; she told me stories about dressing and undressing, about
sleeping and waking; she told me stories about herself, about her mother,
about her grandmother. She told me stories about grieving and laughing,
about thinking and doing; she told me stories about school and about
people; about darning and mending; she told me stories about turquoise
and about gold; she told me European stories and Laguna stories; she told
me Catholic stories and Presbyterian stories; she told me city stories and
country stories; she told me political stories and religious stories. She told
me stories about living and stories about dying. And in all of those stories
she told me who I was, who I was supposed to be, whom I came from, and
who would follow me. In this way she taught me the meaning of the
words she said, that all life is a circle and everything has a place within it.
That's what she said and what she showed me in the things she did and the
way she lives.

Of course, through my formal, white, Christian education, I discovered   10
that other people had stories of their own—about women, about Indians,
about fact, about reality—and I was amazed by a number of startling sup-
positions that others made about tribal customs and beliefs. According to
the un-Indian, non-Indian view, for instance, Indians barred menstruating
women from ceremonies and indeed segregated them from the rest of the
people, consigning them to some space specially designed for them. This
showed that Indians considered menstruating women unclean and not fit
to enjoy the company of decent (nonmenstruating) people, that is, men. I
was surprised and confused to hear this because my mother had taught me
that white people had strange attitudes toward menstruation: they
thought something was bad about it, that it meant you were sick, cursed,
sinful, and weak and that you had to be very careful during that time. She
taught me that menstruation was a normal occurrence, that I could go
swimming or hiking or whatever else I wanted to do during my period.
She actively scorned women who took to their beds, who were incapaci-
tated by cramps, who "got the blues."

As I struggled to reconcile these very contradictory interpretations of   11
American Indians' traditional beliefs concerning menstruation, I realized
that the menstrual taboos were about power, not about sin or filth. My

conclusion was later borne out by some tribes' own explanations, which, as you may well imagine, came as quite a relief to me.

The truth of the matter as many Indians see it is that women who are at the peak of their fecundity are believed to possess power that throws male power totally out of kilter. They emit such force that, in their presence, any male-owned or -dominated ritual or sacred object cannot do its usual task. For instance, the Lakota say that a menstruating woman anywhere near a yuwipi man, who is a special sort of psychic, spirit-empowered healer, for a day or so before he is to do his ceremony will effectively disempower him. Conversely, among many if not most tribes, important ceremonies cannot be held without the presence of women. Sometimes the ritual woman who empowers the ceremony must be unmarried and virginal so that the power she channels is unalloyed, unweakened by sexual arousal and penetration by a male. Other ceremonies require tumescent women, others the presence of mature women who have borne children, and still others depend for empowerment on postmenopausal women. Women may be segregated from the company of the whole band or village on certain occasions, but on certain occasions men are also segregated. In short, each ritual depends on a certain balance of power, and the positions of women within the phases of womanhood are used by tribal people to empower certain rites. This does not derive from a male-dominant view; it is not a ritual observance imposed on women by men. It derives from a tribal view of reality that distinguishes tribal people from feudal and industrial people.

Among the tribes, the occult power of women, inextricably bound to our hormonal life, is thought to be very great; many hold that we possess innately the blood-given power to kill—with a glance, with a step, or with a judicious mixing of menstrual blood into somebody's soup. Medicine women among the Pomo of California cannot practice until they are sufficiently mature; when they are immature, their power is diffuse and is likely to interfere with their practice until time and experience have it under control. So women of the tribes are not especially inclined to see themselves as poor helpless victims of male domination. Even in those tribes where something akin to male domination was present, women are perceived as powerful, socially, physically, and metaphysically. In times past, as in times present, women carried enormous burdens with aplomb. We were far indeed from the "weaker sex," the designation that white aristocratic sisters unhappily earned for us all.

I remember my mother moving furniture all over the house when she wanted it changed. She didn't wait for my father to come home and help—she just went ahead and moved the piano, a huge upright from the old days, the couch, the refrigerator. Nobody had told her she was too weak to do such things. In imitation of her, I would delight in loading trucks at my father's store with cases of pop or fifty-pound sacks of flour. Even when I was quite small I could do it, and it gave me a belief in my own physical strength that advancing middle age can't quite erase. My mother used to tell me about the Acoma Pueblo women she had seen as a child carrying huge ollas (water pots) on their heads as they wound their way up the tortuous stairwell carved into the face of the "Sky City" mesa, a feat I tried to imitate with books and tin buckets. ("Sky City" is the term used by the Chamber of Commerce for the mother village of Acoma, which is situated atop a high sandstone table mountain.) I was never very successful, but even the attempt reminded me that I was supposed to be strong and balanced to be a proper girl.

Of course, my mother's Laguna people are Keres Indian, reputed to be   15 the last extreme mother-right people on earth. So it is no wonder that I got notably nonwhite notions about the natural strength and prowess of women. Indeed, it is only when I am trying to get non-Indian approval, recognition, or acknowledgment that my "weak sister" emotional and intellectual ploys get the better of my tribal woman's good sense. At such times I forget that I just moved the piano or just wrote a competent paper or just completed a financial transaction satisfactorily or have supported myself and my children for most of my adult life.

Nor is my contradictory behavior atypical. Most Indian women I know   16 are in the same bicultural bind: we vacillate between being dependent and strong, self-reliant and powerless, strongly motivated and hopelessly insecure. We resolve the dilemma in various ways: some of us party all the time; some of us drink to excess; some of us travel and move around a lot; some of us land good jobs and then quit them; some of us engage in violent exchanges; some of us blow our brains out. We act in these destructive ways because we suffer from the societal conflicts caused by having to identify with two hopelessly opposed cultural definitions of women. Through this destructive dissonance we are unhappy prey to the self-disparagement common to, indeed demanded of, Indians living in the United States today. Our situation is caused by the exigencies of a history of invasion, conquest, and colonization whose searing marks are probably ineradicable. A popular bumper sticker on many Indian cars proclaims: "If You're Indian You're In," to which I always find myself adding under my breath, "Trouble."

MUSINGS

In explaining Native American attitudes toward women, Allen recognizes that oral culture "heals itself and the tribal web by adapting to the flow of the present while never relinquishing its connection to the past." Most families have stories that are repeated from generation to generation, which tell you about your family history and instruct your behavior. These are often stories that you have heard again and again, often from older members of your family.

Write about one of your family stories and explain what you learned from it. If you cannot think of one, ask your mother, father, or grandparents to tell you a story from their own childhood or one that was told to them by an older family member.

ARTHUR ASHE (1943–1993)

Arthur Ashe attained athletic stardom with his victory over Jimmy Connors at Wimbledon in 1975. After a heart attack in 1979 and quadruple-bypass surgery, he was forced to give up tennis and turned instead to writing; A Hard Road to Glory: A History of African American Athletes *was published in 1988. Tragically, Ashe contracted AIDS from a blood transfusion during the surgery and spent his last days working with Arnold Rampersad on his autobiography,* Days of Grace: A Memoir. *It was published in 1993 after his death. He was honored for his athletic ability, his writings, but most of all for the grace of his life. A eulogy in* Time *characterized him as a gentle man, "a paradigm of understated reason and elegance" and "a man of fire and grace."*

The following selection from his memoirs describes how he discovered that he had AIDS and his reaction to it. As a celebrity, he was reluctant to divulge his illness and only did so when a reporter uncovered the story.

The Beast in the Jungle

"Jeanne," I said. "Something is wrong with me."   1

It was a beautiful late-summer morning in 1988. I was standing in   2
front of her, in our suite at the Sagamore Resort on Lake George in upper
New York state. Camera, who was a year and a half old, was with us. We
had just come back from breakfast.

I had wanted to call home and monitor the messages on my telephone   3
answering machine. I raised my hand up to the telephone on the wall and
started dialing my number. Or rather, I tried to dial it. My fingers made an
attempt to respond to my will, but they struggled in vain to do what I
asked. I was trying to put my index finger on the buttons, but the finger
wasn't working very well. Perplexed, I looked at my hand and tried again.

"What is it, Arthur?" Jeanne asked.   4

"My fingers. I can't get them to work well."   5

"Maybe they are numb because you slept on them?"   6

"Yes," I said. "That must be it. But no, they aren't numb. I can feel   7
them, definitely. I just don't seem to be able to use them."

"I'll dial for you," Jeanne said. And she did, without giving a hint of alarm.   8

At this point, in fact, neither of us was alarmed. Mainly because we had   9
both been through some fairly harrowing times with doctors and illnesses,
an unresponsive finger did not seem like much to be concerned about.

A month or so before, I had gone to the Sagamore for an Aetna board   10
meeting. We on the board had been seeking some fresh approaches to certain problems, and decided that a change of scenery, away from the company headquarters in Hartford, might inspire us to think creatively. That
meeting, everyone agreed, had been a success. Clearly, the quality of the
resort and its superb location in the famous Finger Lakes region in upstate
New York had something to do with our results. A month later, when
Jeanne and I impulsively concluded that we needed to get away from our
Westchester County home in the village of Mount Kisco, north of New
York City, for two or three days, we thought at once of the Sagamore. We
would relax there, then return home in time for the start of the most im-
portant American tennis tournament of the year, the United States Open.
We needed to be rested, because the two-week tournament is typically a
happy madhouse.

Then we decided to invite Donald Dell and his wife, Carole, to come   11
along with us upstate. Donald and Carole, who were visiting from Po-
tomac, Maryland, where they live and where Donald's management firm,
ProServ, had its main offices, would also be going to the U.S. Open.

We were having a good time together, until this strange numbness in   12
my hand. I quickly dismissed the idea that what was happening to my fingers could have been caused by sleeping on my hand. Had I suffered a
small stroke? That was a distinct possibility. Should I leave the hotel early
and head home to my internist? We decided to stay. Frankly, I expected to
go to sleep that night and awake to find my fingers back to normal.

However, by the time we checked out of the Sagamore, my right hand   13
was hanging from the wrist, almost completely limp. Now I was somewhat alarmed. Nevertheless, when I telephoned my doctor, I did not suggest an emergency. Something seemed to be wrong with my hand; would
he look at it? He asked me to come in the next day, Friday, August 26.

In the morning, a television crew came to our house to interview   14
Jeanne and me for the "CBS This Morning" show with Harry Smith. In
those days, one feature of the show each Friday was a visit to someone's
home. Our house in Mount Kisco, built before the Civil War, was somewhat special. Thinking about my hand, Jeanne and I had considered for a
moment canceling the interview, but finally we decided against it. My appointment with the internist would come soon enough.

The television interview was pleasant in most respects but also some-   15
thing of an ordeal. No matter how hard I tried, I could not move a digit
up, down, or sideways. My right hand, now completely limp, literally
hung dead from my wrist. As I answered questions and talked about the
house, I tried to act as nonchalant as I could; I certainly told no one from
CBS that something was wrong. The truth is that I had to prop up my
right hand with my left. I still have no idea how I got through the inter-

view without anyone on the crew taking notice. I answered the questions with as much charm as I could muster, but my mind was elsewhere.

Around noon, I drove some eight minutes from our house to the offices of Dr. William Russell at the Mount Kisco Medical Group. I knew the way very well. The group offices were almost across the street from the Northern Westchester Hospital Center, where I served on the board of directors. I had confidence in Dr. Russell, an able internist whom we had consulted professionally in the past. He inspired confidence. Dr. Russell is the picture of the genial suburban family practitioner, someone almost out of Norman Rockwell's America of a bygone age, but with the latest medical and scientific technology and information close at hand. Mature in years and manner, he is gentle, attentive, reassuring. Whenever I consulted him, he would ask not only about me but about Jeanne and Camera; often he asked about them first, before inquiring about *my* health. I liked that. He didn't fumble for their names, but instead showed a genuine concern for their well-being. And he loved to play and watch tennis.   16

As I entered the office, I sensed such an unusual degree of excitement in the air that I wondered whether or not I was projecting my own nervousness onto the scene. As it turned out, Dr. Russell and his colleagues and staff in the medical group were on the verge of moving out of their old quarters into a new, sparkling facility across the street. But nothing interfered with the courtesy and orderliness of my reception, and I was soon ushered into Dr. Russell's office.   17

The sight of my hand, as limp as a flag on a still day, made him sit up. Listening to my complaints, he looked closely at the offending hand. He hefted it, pulled on my fingers, flopped it about.   18

"Have you been feeling dizzy at all?" he asked.   19

"No. Not at all."   20

"Shortness of breath? Any trouble breathing?"   21

"No. I feel fine."   22

"A fever of any kind?"   23

"No."   24

"Did anything strike your hand? Did you use it in some forceful way?"   25

"No. Nothing like that happened at all. It simply went dead."   26

"Well," Dr. Russell said, "I think there is only one way to go, and we have to do it right now. Something is interfering with the signals from your brain to the hand. The interference is almost certainly in the area of the brain, because I can't think of any other likely reason for your hand to stop working."   27

"What's next, then?"   28

"I am going to arrange for you to have a CAT scan of your brain right away. I don't want to alarm you unduly, but that's the main way to proceed right now. And I do mean right now."   29

The last time I heard a doctor speak to me with such a sense of urgency 30
was July 31, 1979, when Dr. Lee Wallace, playing tennis on a court near
my own, suspected that I was having a heart attack and insisted that I go
straightaway from the tennis court to New York Hospital.

Dr. Russell made a telephone call or two. When I went across the street 31
to the CT facility, the attendants were waiting for me. By this time I was
more nervous than when I arrived at Dr. Russell's. I had seen CAT-scan-
ning machines before; they look like a set of timpani drums turned upside
down. Keeping as still as I could, I waited while the machine's X-ray
mechanism did its business of photographing the brain at various angles.
The entire procedure took about twenty minutes.

When I joined Dr. Russell and a radiologist in an adjoining room, 32
there, up on the light box, were the CT images of my brain, very much
like smaller, more familiar X-ray pictures of my chest or my knee.

"Hmm," Dr. Russell said. At least, that's what I remember him saying, as 33
a look of genuine concern settled over his face. Stunned might be too
strong a term, but he was obviously taken aback. I looked quickly at him,
then looked again at the pictures. He was as professional as any doctor
could be, but I could tell that he did not at all like what he was seeing. Doctors are trained to be dispassionate, since they see sick people all the time.
However, trained or not, it is not always easy to react stoically to bad news.

I peered at the images, looking for clues to what had rattled him. I did 34
not think I knew what to look for. I had never seen CAT-scan images of
my brain before. Then I saw that the two hemispheres of my brain, which
should have been nearly identical, were not. The right side of the brain
was clear. The left side showed an irregularly round shape—a splotch. If
the rounded brain looked like the moon, then the splotch looked like one
of those arid lakes or seas on the moon. This splotch, I thought, looks exactly like the Sea of Rains. What was it doing on my brain?

As we sat and stared, I could feel Dr. Russell becoming more nervous, 35
more uncomfortable.

"What is that?" I asked, pointing at the splotch. 36

"Look," he said. He spoke slowly, choosing his words carefully. "I don't 37
want to steer you wrong. I'm not a neurologist or a neurosurgeon." The radiologist with us wasn't sure, either; we clearly needed some more opinions.

"Could you find someone at New York Hospital?" My heart surgeries 38
had both been at St. Luke's–Roosevelt Hospital on the Upper West Side in
Manhattan; but my cardiologist, Dr. Stephen Scheidt, was attached to
New York Hospital, on the Upper East Side.

"Of course." 39

The drive back home, although it took only eight minutes, was pretty 40
awful. Up until the moment of seeing the CAT scan, I had not felt extreme anxiety. What had triggered my anxiety now was not the CAT scan

itself but the jolting effect of the image on Dr. Russell. Obviously he thought that I had something serious to fear.

Was it a stroke? A small one now, but the precursor of a massive one? A massive stroke that might leave me unable to care for myself? Was it a tumor of the brain? Cancer of the brain—inoperable? Would I face months of extreme pain and then certain death? Or would an aneurysm snuff out my life in a split second, as it had snuffed out Grace Kelly's life as she drove her car with her daughter Stephanie in the beautiful hills of Monaco? 41

I knew a little about the brain from what I had learned in high school and in a course on physiological psychology I had taken at UCLA. Even the medical terms were somewhat familiar to me. Of course, while my knowledge of medicine was not negligible, most of it was limited to the subject of the heart. The brain was new territory. 42

In our kitchen, Jeanne listened to me explain what had happened. I talk about her now as my "co-patient," and she has been exactly that for a long time. 43

Around three-thirty that afternoon, carrying the CAT-scan images and trying to remain calm, I entered the office of Dr. John Caronna, a neurologist at New York Hospital. A woman, one of his colleagues, gave me a sort of rudimentary preliminary examination. 44

"Stand up, please," she instructed me. "Hold your arms out. Follow this object with your eyes." She needed to make sure what was functioning and what was not. My hand was definitely not functioning, but the rest of me seemed fine. 45

I watched as Dr. Caronna looked closely at the pictures of my brain. Thinking about it now, I realize that the splotch on the left side of my brain was by no means an entire mystery to him. He already had his preliminary diagnosis, or at least his informed suspicions. However, like Dr. Russell, he was cautious. 46

"Something is in there. We can see that. But what? I don't think we can know for certain without a biopsy." 47

"You mean a brain operation?" 48

"Yes," he replied. "We need to look at the tissue, examine it. I think we have to talk to a neurosurgeon. He can explain your options." 49

Now it was his turn to make telephone calls. Soon we were joined by a neurosurgeon, Dr. Russell Patterson, and Dr. Stephen Scheidt, my cardiologist. They looked at the images. They, too, were cautious. 50

"Mr. Ashe," Dr. Patterson assured me, "we don't have to do anything right away. Obviously something is going on, probably an infection of some sort. We can simply wait and see what happens next." 51

I laughed, a nervous laugh. Right, I thought to myself, we can wait, and watch the entire arm go dead. Then the rest of me. "What's the other option?" 52

"On the other hand, we could go in right now. As soon as possible. 53
That way, we would know exactly what we are dealing with. And we can
get as much of the infected tissue out as we can."

"Let's go in," I said. 54

I did not hesitate in making that decision. Nevertheless, the next day I 55
had an MRI at St. Agnes Diagnostic Center in White Plains, Westchester.
Then I sought a second opinion, based on the CAT scan and the MRI, at
Brunswick Hospital in Amityville, Long Island. The new experts told me
nothing different; all agreed that surgery was necessary.

This would be the fourth operation of my life. The first, in 1977, had 56
been comparatively minor, on my heel. The second had been major—my
quadruple-bypass in December 1979, after my heart attack the previous
July. The third had been my corrective double-bypass in June 1983. Now,
new ground: brain surgery.

My thoughts about the U.S. Open tournament vanished from my 57
mind. Although I had work to do there and columns to write for the
Washington *Post,* none of that mattered now; they would be put on hold.
On Wednesday, August 31, I checked into New York Hospital for a fresh
battery of tests, including a spinal tap and a blood test. On Friday, the results came back. Jeanne, Doug Stein, and Eddie Mandeville were with me
when I heard the bad news. In fact, they gave it to me. I was HIV-positive.

None of the physicians at the hospital had wanted the grim task of in- 58
forming me, so they passed the word to Eddie Mandeville, who had been
visiting me every day and, as a physician, had become entirely familiar
with my case. Eddie told Doug, who is also a doctor, and the two of them
waited for Jeanne to arrive that day at the hospital before letting her know.

"What does this mean about Jeanne?" I asked. She reached out quickly, 59
put her left arm around my shoulders, and squeezed my hand hard. "You
and me, babe," she said. "You and me." She herself had yet to be tested for
HIV.

We immediately traced the infection back to the two units of trans- 60
fused blood after my second heart-bypass operation, in 1983. The most
recent medical data had indicated that the HIV virus could stay dormant
for years after infecting one, then surface in the form of an opportunistic
infection. A brain operation would ascertain if I had such an infection.

On Thursday, September 8, Dr. Patterson performed the operation, 61
which lasted about forty-five minutes. Brain operations are delicate but
typically do not last long. When I regained consciousness after the operation, I felt far better than after my heart surgeries. Postoperative pain can
be quite substantial, and I was certainly groggy. But compared to the way
I felt after my second heart operation, I was fine. Although my head was
heavily bandaged, and I was receiving fluids intravenously, I felt very little
discomfort.

The first report I received was encouraging. I did not have a brain 62 tumor but rather an infection of some kind. The operation was a success, in that Dr. Patterson had removed all traces of the infection. Part of this matter was sent at once to the laboratory for a biopsy.

The following day, the results came back. Jeanne was with me in my hospital room when Dr. Patterson informed us that the infection was toxoplasmosis. When he gave us the news, I remember Jeanne taking my hand and squeezing it hard and long, as if she would never let it go, just as she had done when I heard the news of my HIV infection. Toxoplasmosis, which used to occur infrequently, had become notorious as one of the specific diseases that—in conjunction with the presence of HIV—marked the condition known as Acquired Immune Deficiency Syndrome, or AIDS. Not only was I HIV-positive; I had full-blown AIDS. 63

"Aha," I said; or so Jeanne tells me. 64

In facing past crises that amounted, like this one, to a *fait accompli*, my left-brain–dominated mind immediately summoned up two words to help me cope with the new reality: "That's that." The two findings of "HIV-positive" and "AIDS" were new facts of my life that I could not evade. There was nothing I could possibly do about either one except to treat them according to the most expert medical science available to me. Neither would go away, and I had to make the best of the situation. If that attitude and those feelings sound almost inhuman, at best stoical, I can respond only that this is my way of dealing with adversity. I wasn't frightened or nervous. The public hysteria over AIDS was probably then at its zenith, but I would not become hysterical. 65

At the hospital, in our moments alone, Jeanne and I wondered if God had chosen us to undergo publicly all these medical challenges. But there were perfectly sane and credible explanations for my medical condition. Heart disease is certainly hereditary, and both my parents had suffered from it. As for my AIDS, I was simply unlucky to have had a couple of units of transfused blood that may have been donated in 1983 by some gay or bisexual man, or some intravenous drug user who perhaps had needed the money badly. I will never know for sure, and this is not an issue I dwell on. 66

Pulling ourselves together after the shock, Jeanne and I talked about who should be told, and when. Of course, we were sure that half of the hospital staff already knew these results. And being a public figure made me further vulnerable; I knew that at some hospitals employees were secretly being paid by news organizations to provide them with morsels of gossip. But if the story could be kept out of the newspapers and magazines, and off of radio and television, then who should we tell? Almost certainly we would not tell my father; I did not think his heart could take news like that. We considered it an absolute blessing that Camera, only twenty-one months old, hardly needed to be told anything about my condition. Her need to know would come much later. 67

MUSINGS

Ashe chronicles his discovery of AIDS and his reaction to it. Because of his celebrity, he was reluctant to inform the media. Was he justified in withholding this information, first from his father and then from the public? Although former President Franklin Roosevelt carefully withheld the poor condition of his health during his third term, more recent presidents have been assiduous in informing the media.

The right to privacy is often not accorded to public figures; more and more, confidentiality is denied even to private citizens. Recount some event in your own life that you would have preferred to keep confidential, but that, because of circumstances, you were forced to disclose.

Richard Rodriguez (1944–)

Richard Rodriguez is a Mexican-American who was alienated from his own culture at a young age. Entering elementary school and knowing no English, he learned rapidly and later studied at prestigious universities. He earned his Bachelor of Arts from Stanford University and his Master's degree from Columbia University, and then studied Renaissance literature at London University. In spite of his minority status, or perhaps because of it, Rodriguez opposed affirmative action on the grounds that it "has primarily benefitted people who are no longer disadvantaged . . . as I no longer was at Stanford" while "ignoring the people who are truly disadvantaged." He maintained that he was "the beneficiary of truly disadvantaged Mexican-Americans. . . . I benefitted on their backs." He also opposed bilingual education, maintaining that "public language isn't just English or Spanish or any other formal language. It is the language of public society." Consequently, Rodriguez argued that everyone, whatever their ethnic background, needed to learn the public language. Both stands were highly unpopular at the time. He later modified his view, commenting that in becoming "an academic . . . a kind of anthropologist in the family kitchen," he had finally lost his ethnicity.

His first book, Hunger of Memory: The Education of Richard Rodriguez, *from which this selection is taken, was widely acclaimed by the critics, one of whom characterized it as "an honest and intelligent account of how education can alter a life." It also demonstrates the realities faced by a child growing up in a home where the private language, in this case Spanish, differs from the accepted public language, in this case English.*

A Public Language

1

I remember to start with that day in Sacramento—a California now nearly thirty years past—when I first entered a classroom, able to understand some fifty stray English words.   1

The third of four children, I had been preceded to a neighborhood Roman Catholic school by an older brother and sister. But neither of them had revealed very much about their classroom experiences. Each afternoon they returned, as they left in the morning, always together, speaking in Spanish as they climbed the five steps of the porch. And their mysterious   2 books, wrapped in shopping-bag paper, remained on the table next to the door, closed firmly behind them.

An accident of geography sent me to a school where all my classmates were white, many the children of doctors and lawyers and business executives. All my classmates certainly must have been uneasy on that first day of school—as most children are uneasy—to find themselves apart from their families in the first institution of their lives. But I was astonished. 3

The nun said, in a friendly but oddly impersonal voice, 'Boys and girls, this is Richard Rodriguez.' (I heard her sound out: *Rich-heard Road-ree-guess.*) It was the first time I had heard anyone name me in English. 'Richard,' the nun repeated more slowly, writing my name down in her black leather book. Quickly I turned to see my mother's face dissolve in a watery blur behind the pebbled glass door. 4

• • •

Many years later there is something called bilingual education—a scheme proposed in the late 1960s by Hispanic-American social activists, later endorsed by a congressional vote. It is a program that seeks to permit non-English-speaking children, many from lower-class homes, to use their family language as the language of school. (Such is the goal its supporters announce.) I hear them and am forced to say no: It is not possible for a child—any child—ever to use his family's language in school. Not to understand this is to misunderstand the public uses of schooling and to trivialize the nature of intimate life—a family's 'language.' 5

Memory teaches me what I know of these matters; the boy reminds the adult. I was a bilingual child, a certain kind—socially disadvantaged—the son of working-class parents, both Mexican immigrants. 6

In the early years of my boyhood, my parents coped very well in America. My father had steady work. My mother managed at home. They were nobody's victims. Optimism and ambition led them to a house (our home) many blocks from the Mexican south side of town. We lived among *gringos* and only a block from the biggest, whitest houses. It never occurred to my parents that they couldn't live wherever they chose. Nor was the Sacramento of the fifties bent on teaching them a contrary lesson. My mother and father were more annoyed than intimidated by those two or three neighbors who tried initially to make us unwelcome. ('Keep your brats away from my sidewalk!') But despite all they achieved, perhaps because they had so much to achieve, any deep feeling of ease, the confidence of 'belonging' in public was withheld from them both. They regarded the people at work, the faces in crowds, as very distant from us. They were the others, *los gringos*. The term was interchangeable in their speech with another, even more telling, *los americanos*. 7

I grew up in a house where the only regular guests were my relations.   8
For one day, enormous families of relatives would visit and there would be
so many people that the noise and the bodies would spill out to the back-
yard and front porch. Then, for weeks, no one came by. (It was usually a
salesman who rang the doorbell.) Our house stood apart. A gaudy yellow
in a row of white bungalows. We were the people with the noisy dog. The
people who raised pigeons and chickens. We were the foreigners on the
block. A few neighbors smiled and waved. We waved back. But no one in
the family knew the names of the old couple who lived next door; until I
was seven years old, I did not know the names of the kids who lived across
the street.

In public, my father and mother spoke a hesitant, accented, not always   9
grammatical English. And they would have to strain—their bodies
tense—to catch the sense of what was rapidly said by *los gringos*. At home
they spoke Spanish. The language of their Mexican past sounded in coun-
terpoint to the English of public society. The words would come quickly,
with ease. Conveyed through those sounds was the pleasing, soothing,
consoling reminder of being at home.

During those years when I was first conscious of hearing, my mother   10
and father addressed me only in Spanish; in Spanish I learned to reply. By
contrast, English *(inglés),* rarely heard in the house, was the language I
came to associate with *gringos.* I learned my first words of English over-
hearing my parents speak to strangers. At five years of age, I knew just
enough English for my mother to trust me on errands to stores one block
away. No more.

I was a listening child, careful to hear the very different sounds of Span-   11
ish and English. Wide-eyed with hearing, I'd listen to sounds more than
words. First, there were English *(gringo)* sounds. So many words were still
unknown that when the butcher or the lady at the drugstore said something to me, exotic polysyllabic sounds would bloom in the midst of their
sentences. Often, the speech of people in public seemed to me very loud,
booming with confidence. The man behind the counter would literally
ask, 'What can I do for you?' But by being so firm and so clear, the sound
of his voice said that he was a *gringo;* he belonged in public society.

I would also hear then the high nasal notes of middle-class American   12
speech. The air stirred with sound. Sometimes, even now, when I have
been traveling abroad for several weeks, I will hear what I heard as a boy.
In hotel lobbies or airports, in Turkey or Brazil, some Americans will pass,
and suddenly I will hear it again—the high sound of American voices. For
a few seconds I will hear it with pleasure, for it is now the sound of *my* society—a reminder of home. But inevitably—already on the flight headed
for home—the sound fades with repetition. I will be unable to hear it anymore.

When I was a boy, things were different. The accent of *los gringos* was   13
never pleasing nor was it hard to hear. Crowds at Safeway or at bus stops
would be noisy with sound. And I would be forced to edge away from the
chirping chatter above me.

I was unable to hear my own sounds, but I knew very well that I spoke   14
English poorly. My words could not stretch far enough to form complete
thoughts. And the words I did speak I didn't know well enough to make
into distinct sounds. (Listeners would usually lower their heads, better to
hear what I was trying to say.) But it was one thing for *me* to speak English
with difficulty. It was more troubling for me to hear my parents speak in
public: their high-whining vowels and guttural consonants; their sentences that got stuck with 'eh' and 'ah' sounds; the confused syntax; the
hesitant rhythm of sounds so different from the way *gringos* spoke. I'd notice, moreover, that my parents' voices were softer than those of *gringos*
we'd meet.

I am tempted now to say that none of this mattered. In adulthood I am   15
embarrassed by childhood fears. And, in a way, it didn't matter very much
that my parents could not speak English with ease. Their linguistic difficulties had no serious consequences. My mother and father made themselves understood at the county hospital clinic and at government offices.
And yet, in another way, it mattered very much—it was unsettling to hear
my parents struggle with English. Hearing them, I'd grow nervous, my
clutching trust in their protection and power weakened.

There were many times like the night at a brightly lit gasoline station (a   16
blaring white memory) when I stood uneasily, hearing my father. He was
talking to a teenaged attendant. I do not recall what they were saying, but
I cannot forget the sounds my father made as he spoke. At one point his
words slid together to form one word—sounds as confused as the threads
of blue and green oil in the puddle next to my shoes. His voice rushed
through what he had left to say. And, toward the end, reached falsetto
notes, appealing to his listener's understanding. I looked away to the lights
of passing automobiles. I tried not to hear anymore. But I heard only too
well the calm, easy tones in the attendant's reply. Shortly afterward, walking toward home with my father, I shivered when he put his hand on my
shoulder. The very first chance that I got, I evaded his grasp and ran on
ahead into the dark, skipping with feigned boyish exuberance.

But then there was Spanish. *Español:* my family's language. *Español:* the   17
language that seemed to me a private language. I'd hear strangers on the
radio and in the Mexican Catholic church across town speaking in Spanish, but I couldn't really believe that Spanish was a public language, like
English. Spanish speakers, rather, seemed related to me, for I sensed that
we shared—through our language—the experience of feeling apart from
los gringos. It was thus a ghetto Spanish that I heard and I spoke. Like

those whose lives are bound by a barrio, I was reminded by Spanish of my separateness from *los otros, los gringos* in power. But more intensely than for most barrio children—because I did not live in a barrio—Spanish seemed to me the language of home. (Most days it was only at home that I'd hear it.) It became the language of joyful return.

A family member would say something to me and I would feel myself specially recognized. My parents would say something to me and I would feel embraced by the sounds of their words. Those sounds said: *I am speaking with ease in Spanish. I am addressing you in words I never use with* los gringos. *I recognize you as someone special, close, like no one outside. You belong with us. In the family.*

(Ricardo.)

At the age of five, six, well past the time when most other children no longer easily notice the difference between sounds uttered at home and words spoken in public, I had a different experience. I lived in a world magically compounded of sounds. I remained a child longer than most; I lingered too long, poised at the edge of language—often frightened by the sounds of *los gringos,* delighted by the sounds of Spanish at home. I shared with my family a language that was startlingly different from that used in the great city around us.

For me there were none of the gradations between public and private society so normal to a maturing child. Outside the house was public society; inside the house was private. Just opening or closing the screen door behind me was an important experience. I'd rarely leave home all alone or without reluctance. Walking down the sidewalk, under the canopy of tall trees, I'd warily notice the—suddenly—silent neighborhood kids who stood warily watching me. Nervously, I'd arrive at the grocery store to hear there the sounds of the *gringo*—foreign to me—reminding me that in this world so big, I was a foreigner. But then I'd return. Walking back toward our house, climbing the steps from the sidewalk, when the front door was open in summer, I'd hear voices beyond the screen door talking in Spanish. For a second or two, I'd stay, linger there, listening. Smiling, I'd hear my mother call out, saying in Spanish (words): 'Is that you, Richard?' All the while her sounds would assure me: *You are home now; come closer; inside. With us.*

'*Sí,*' I'd reply.

Once more inside the house I would resume (assume) my place in the family. The sounds would dim, grow harder to hear. Once more at home, I would grow less aware of that fact. It required, however, no more than the blurt of the doorbell to alert me to listen to sounds all over again. The house would turn instantly still while my mother went to the door. I'd hear her hard English sounds. I'd wait to hear her voice return to soft-

18

19

20

21

22

23

sounding Spanish, which assured me, surely as did the clicking tongue of the lock on the door, that the stranger was gone.

Plainly, it is not healthy to hear such sounds so often. It is not healthy   24 to distinguish public words from private sounds so easily. I remained cloistered by sounds, timid and shy in public, too dependent on voices at home. And yet it needs to be emphasized: I was an extremely happy child at home. I remember many nights when my father would come back from work, and I'd hear him call out to my mother in Spanish, sounding relieved. In Spanish, he'd sound light and free notes he never could manage in English. Some nights I'd jump up just at hearing his voice. With *mis hermanos* I would come running into the room where he was with my mother. Our laughing (so deep was the pleasure!) became screaming. Like others who know the pain of public alienation, we transformed the knowledge of our public separateness and made it consoling—the reminder of intimacy. Excited, we joined our voices in a celebration of sounds. *We are speaking now the way we never speak out in public. We are alone—together,* voices sounded, surrounded to tell me. Some nights, no one seemed willing to loosen the hold sounds had on us. At dinner, we invented new words. (Ours sounded Spanish, but made sense only to us.) We pieced together new words by taking, say, an English verb and giving it Spanish endings. My mother's instructions at bedtime would be lacquered with mock-urgent tones. Or a word like *sí* would become, in several notes, able to convey added measures of feeling. Tongues explored the edges of words, especially the fat vowels. And we happily sounded that military drum roll, the twirling roar of the Spanish *r*. Family language: my family's sounds. The voices of my parents and sisters and brother. Their voices insisting: *You belong here. We are family members. Related. Special to one another. Listen!* Voices singing and sighing, rising, straining, then surging, teeming with pleasure that burst syllables into fragments of laughter. At times it seemed there was steady quiet only when, from another room, the rustling whispers of my parents faded and I moved closer to sleep.

2

Supporters of bilingual education today imply that students like me   25 miss a great deal by not being taught in their family's language. What they seem not to recognize is that, as a socially disadvantaged child, I considered Spanish to be a private language. What I needed to learn in school was that I had the right—and the obligation—to speak the public language of *los gringos*. The odd truth is that my first-grade classmates could have become bilingual, in the conventional sense of that word, more easily than I. Had they been taught (as upper-middle-class children are often taught early) a second language like Spanish or French, they could have regarded it simply as that: another public language. In my case such bilingualism could not have been so quickly achieved. What I did not believe was that I could speak a single public language.

Without question, it would have pleased me to hear my teachers address me in Spanish when I entered the classroom. I would have felt much less afraid. I would have trusted them and responded with ease. But I would have delayed—for how long postponed?—having to learn the language of public society. I would have evaded—and for how long could I have afforded to delay?—learning the great lesson of school, that I had a public identity.   26

Fortunately, my teachers were unsentimental about their responsibility. What they understood was that I needed to speak a public language. So their voices would search me out, asking me questions. Each time I'd hear them, I'd look up in surprise to see a nun's face frowning at me. I'd mumble, not really meaning to answer. The nun would persist, 'Richard, stand up. Don't look at the floor. Speak up. Speak to the entire class, not just to me!' But I couldn't believe that the English language was mine to use. (In part, I did not want to believe it.) I continued to mumble. I resisted the teacher's demands. (Did I somehow suspect that once I learned public language my pleasing family life would be changed?) Silent, waiting for the bell to sound, I remained dazed, diffident, afraid.   27

Because I wrongly imagined that English was intrinsically a public language and Spanish an intrinsically private one, I easily noted the difference between classroom language and the language of home. At school, words were directed to a general audience of listeners. ('Boys and girls.') Words were meaningfully ordered. And the point was not self-expression alone but to make oneself understood by many others. The teacher quizzed: 'Boys and girls, why do we use that word in this sentence? Could we think of a better word to use there? Would the sentence change its meaning if the words were differently arranged? And wasn't there a better way of saying much the same thing?' (I couldn't say. I wouldn't try to say.)   28

Three months. Five. Half a year passed. Unsmiling, ever watchful, my teachers noted my silence. They began to connect my behavior with the difficult progress my older sister and brother were making. Until one Saturday morning three nuns arrived at the house to talk to our parents. Stiffly, they sat on the blue living room sofa. From the doorway of another room, spying the visitors, I noted the incongruity—the clash of two worlds, the faces and voices of school intruding upon the familiar setting of home. I overheard one voice gently wondering, 'Do your children speak only Spanish at home, Mrs. Rodriguez?' While another voice added, 'That Richard especially seems so timid and shy.'   29

That Rich-heard! 30

With great tact the visitors continued, 'Is it possible for you and your 31
husband to encourage your children to practice their English when they
are home?' Of course, my parents complied. What would they not do for
their children's well-being? And how could they have questioned the
Church's authority which those women represented? In an instant, they
agreed to give up the language (the sounds) that had revealed and accen-
tuated our family's closeness. The moment after the visitors left, the
change was observed. '*Ahora,* speak to us *en inglés,*' my father and mother
united to tell us.

At first, it seemed a kind of game. After dinner each night, the family 32
gathered to practice 'our' English. (It was still then *inglés;* a language foreign to us, so we felt drawn as strangers to it.) Laughing, we would try to
define words we could not pronounce. We played with strange English
sounds, often overanglicizing our pronunciations. And we filled the smiling gaps of our sentences with familiar Spanish sounds. But that was
cheating, somebody shouted. Everyone laughed. In school, meanwhile,
like my brother and sister, I was required to attend a daily tutoring session.
I needed a full year of special attention. I also needed my teachers to keep
my attention from straying in class by calling out, *Rich-heard*—their English voices slowly prying loose my ties to my other name, its three notes,
Ri-car-do. Most of all I needed to hear my mother and father speak to me
in a moment of seriousness in broken—suddenly heartbreaking—English.
The scene was inevitable: One Saturday morning I entered the kitchen
where my parents were talking in Spanish, I did not realize that they were
talking in Spanish however until, at the moment they saw me, I heard
their voices change to speak English. Those *gringo* sounds they uttered
startled me. Pushed me away. In that moment of trivial misunderstanding
and profound insight, I felt my throat twisted by unsounded grief. I
turned quickly and left the room. But I had no place to escape to with
Spanish. (The spell was broken.) My brother and sisters were speaking
English in another part of the house.

Again and again in the days following, increasingly angry, I was obliged 33
to hear my mother and father: 'Speak to us *en inglés.*' *(Speak.)* Only then
did I determine to learn classroom English. Weeks after, it happened: One
day in school I raised my hand to volunteer an answer. I spoke out in a
loud voice. And I did not think it remarkable when the entire class understood. That day, I moved very far from the disadvantaged child I had been
only days earlier. The belief, the calming assurance that I belonged in public, had at last taken hold.

MUSINGS

Rodriguez describes through a number of incidents his "private language" as the "pleasing soothing reminder of being at home." With his parents' help he learned standard English, which allowed him to enter the public sphere but which eventually alienated him from his parents and his own ethnicity.

Rodriguez maintains that everyone has both a private and a public language, even in the case when both are the same. Do you feel that the language that you use at home is different from the one that you use in the classroom? Write a short paper analyzing your private language and how and why it is different. Using your own experience, argue in favor of or in opposition to learning a public language.

TIM O'BRIEN (1946–)

When Tim O'Brien graduated from Macalester College in 1968, he was immediately drafted, serving two years in the infantry in Vietnam. He wrote several novels about the Vietnam War, describing with fervor the people and their feelings. He asserted that his "passion as a human being and as a writer intersect in Vietnam, not in the physical stuff but in the issues of Vietnam—of courage, rectitude, enlightenment, holiness, trying to do the right thing in the world." O'Brien describes his attitude toward writing: "It's kind of a semantic game: lying versus truth-telling. . . . One does not invent merely for the sake of inventing. One does it for a particular purpose and that purpose always is to arrive at some kind of spiritual truth that one can't discover simply by recording the world as-it-is." O'Brien's Vietnam novels are, as one critic puts it, "a semi-fictionalized recounting of his own experiences." Many so-called autobiographies fall into the category of semi-fiction.

The following excerpt, from O'Brien's first book, If I Die in a Combat Zone, Box Me Up and Ship Me Home *(1973), is a series of anecdotes from his own experiences in Vietnam. Annie Gottlieb in her review called it "a beautiful, painful book, arousing pity and fear for the daily realities of modern disaster." In this selection O'Brien writes of his arrival in Vietnam as a private.*

Arrival in Vietnam

First there is some mist. Then, when the plane begins its descent, there 1 are pale gray mountains. The plane slides down, and the mountains darken and take on a sinister cragginess. You see the outlines of crevices, and you consider whether, of all the places opening up below, you might finally walk to that spot and die. In the far distance are green patches, the sea is below, a stretch of sand winds along the coast. Two hundred men draw their breath. No one looks at the others. You feel dread. But it is senseless to let it go too far, so you joke: there are only 365 days to go. The stewardess wishes you luck over the loudspeaker. At the door she gives out some kisses, mainly to the extroverts.

From Cam Ranh Bay another plane takes you to Chu Lai, a big base to 2 the south of Danang, headquarters for the Americal Division. You spend a week there, in a place called the Combat Center. It's a resortlike place, tucked in alongside the South China Sea, complete with sand and native girls and a miniature golf course and floor shows with every variety of the grinding female pelvis. There beside the sea you get your now-or-never training. You pitch hand grenades, practice walking through mine fields, learn to use a minesweeper. Mostly, though, you wonder about dying. You wonder how it feels, what it looks like inside you. Sometimes you stop, and your body tingles. You feel your blood and nerves working. At night you sit on the beach and watch fire fights off where the war is being fought. There are movies at night, and a place to buy beer. Carefully, you mark six days off your pocket calendar; you start a journal, vaguely hoping it will never be read.

Arriving in Vietnam as a foot soldier is akin to arriving at boot camp as   3
a recruit. Things are new, and you ascribe evil to the simplest physical objects around you: you see red in the sand, swarms of angels and avatars in the sky, pity in the eyes of the chaplain, concealed anger in the eyes of the girls who sell you Coke. You are not sure how to conduct yourself— whether to show fear, to live secretly with it, to show resignation or disgust. You wish it were all over. You begin the countdown. You take the inky, mildew smell of Vietnam into your lungs.

After a week at the Combat Center, a truck took six of us down High-   4
way One to a hill called LZ Gator.

A sergeant welcomed us, staring at us like he was buying meat, and he   5
explained that LZ Gator was headquarters for the Fourth Battalion, Twentieth Infantry, and that the place was our new home.

"I don't want you guys getting too used to Gator," he said. "You won't   6
be here long. You're gonna fill out some forms in a few minutes, then we'll get you all assigned to rifle companies, then you're going out to the boonies. Got it? Just like learning to swim. We just toss you in and let you hoof it and eat some C rations and get a little action under your belts. It's better that way than sitting around worrying about it.

"Okay, that's enough bullshit. Just don't get no illusions." He softened   7
his voice a trifle. "Of course, don't get too scared. We lose some men, sure, but it ain't near as bad as '66, believe me, I was in the Nam in '66, an' it was bad shit then, getting our butts kicked around. And this area—you guys lucked out a little, there's worse places in the Nam. We got mines, that's the big thing here, plenty of 'em. But this ain't the delta, we ain't got many NVA, so you're lucky. We got some mines and some local VC, that's it. Anyhow, enough bullshit, like I say, it ain't all that bad. Okay, we got some personnel cards here, so fill 'em out, and we'll chow you down."

Then the battalion Re-Up NCO came along. "I seen some action. I got   8
me two purple hearts, so listen up good. I'm not saying you're gonna get zapped out there. I made it. But you're gonna come motherfuckin' close, Jesus, you're gonna hear bullets tickling your asshole. And sure as I'm standing here, one or two of you men are gonna get your legs blown off. Or killed. One or two of you, it's gotta happen."

He paused and stared around like a salesman, from man to man, letting   9 it sink in. "I'm just telling you the facts of life, I'm not trying to scare shit out of you. But you better sure as hell be scared, it's gotta happen. One or two of you men, your ass is grass.

"So—what can you do about it? Well, like Sarge says, you can be care- 10 ful, you can watch for the mines and all that, and, who knows, you might come out looking like a rose. But careful guys get killed too. So what can you do about it then? Nothing. Except you can re-up."

The men looked at the ground and shuffled around grinning. "Sure, 11 sure—I know. Nobody likes to re-up [reenlist]. But just think about it a second. Just say you do it—you take your burst of three years, starting today; three more years of army life. Then what? Well, I'll tell you what, it'll save your ass, that's what, it'll save your ass. You re-up and I can get you a job in Chu Lai. I got jobs for mechanics, typists, clerks, damn near anything you want, I got it. So you get your nice, safe rear job. You get some on-the-job training, the works. You get a skill. You sleep in a bed. Hell, you laugh, but you sleep in the goddamn monsoons for two months on end, you try that sometime, and you won't be laughing. So. You lose a little time to Uncle Sam. Big deal. You save your ass. So, I got my desk in-side. If you come in and sign the papers—it'll take ten minutes—and I'll have you on the first truck going back to Chu Lai, no shit. Anybody game?" No one budged, and he shrugged and went down to the mess hall.

LZ Gator seemed a safe place to be. You could see pieces of the ocean 12 on clear days. A little village called Nuoc Man was at the foot of the hill, filled with pleasant, smiling people, places to have your laundry done, a whorehouse. Except when on perimeter guard at night, everyone went about the fire base with unloaded weapons. The atmosphere was dull and hot, but there were movies and floor shows and sheds-ful of beer.

I was assigned to Alpha Company. 13

"Shit, you poor sonofabitch," the mail clerk said, grinning. "Shit. How 14 many days you got left in Nam? 358, right? 357? Shit. You poor mother. I got twenty-three days left, twenty-three days, and I'm sorry but I'm gone! Gone! I'm so short I need a step ladder to hand out mail. What's your name?"

The mail clerk shook hands with me. "Well, at least you're a lucky 15 sonofabitch. Irish guys never get wasted, not in Alpha. Blacks and spics get wasted, but you micks make it every goddamn time. Hell, I'm black as the colonel's shoe polish, so you can bet your ass I'm not safe till that ol' free-dom bird lands me back in Seattle. Twenty-three days, you poor mother."

He took me to the first sergeant. The first sergeant said to forget all the 16 bullshit about going straight out to the field. He lounged in front of a fan, dressed in his underwear (dyed green, apparently to camouflage him from some incredibly sneaky VC), and he waved a beer at me. "Shit, O'Brien, take it easy. Alpha's a good square-shooting company, so don't sweat it.

Keep your nose clean and I'll just keep you here on Gator till the company comes back for a break. No sense sending you out there now, they're coming in to Gator day after tomorrow." He curled his toe around a cord and pulled the fan closer. "Go see a movie tonight, get a beer or something."

He assigned me to the third platoon and hollered at the supply sergeant to issue me some gear. The supply sergeant hollered back for him to go to hell, and they laughed, and I got a rifle and ammunition and a helmet, camouflage cover, poncho, poncho liner, back pack, clean clothes, and a box of cigarettes and candy. Then it got dark, and I watched Elvira Madigan and her friend romp through all the colors, get hungry, get desperate, and stupidly—so stupidly that you could only pity their need for common sense—end their lives. The guy, Elvira's lover, was a deserter. You had the impression he deserted for an ideal of love and butterflies, balmy days and the simple life, and that when he saw he couldn't have it, not even with blond and blue-eyed Elvira, he decided he could never have it. But, Jesus, to kill because of hunger, for fear to hold a menial job. Disgusted, I went off to an empty barracks and pushed some M-16 ammo and hand grenades off my cot and went to sleep. 17

In two days Alpha Company came to LZ Gator. They were dirty, loud, coarse, intent on getting drunk, happy, curt, and not interested in saying much to me. They drank through the afternoon and into the night. There was a fight that ended in more beer, they smoked some dope, they started sleeping or passed out around midnight. 18

At one or two in the morning—at first I thought I was dreaming, then I thought it was nothing serious—explosions popped somewhere outside the barracks. The first sergeant came through the barracks with a flashlight. "Jesus," he hollered. "Get the hell out of here! We're being hit! Wake up!" 19

I scrambled for a helmet for my head. For an armored vest. For my boots, for my rifle, for my ammo. 20

It was pitch dark. The explosions continued to pop; it seemed a long distance away. 21

I went outside. The base was lit up by flares, and the mortar pits were firing rounds out into the paddies. I hid behind a metal shed they kept the beer in. 22

No one else came out of the barracks. I waited, and finally one man ambled out, holding a beer. Then another man, holding a beer. 23

They sat on some sandbags in their underwear, drinking the beer and laughing, pointing out at the paddies and watching our mortar rounds land. 24

Two or three more men came out in five minutes; then the first sergeant started shouting. In another five minutes some of the men were finally outside, sitting on the sandbags. 25

Enemy rounds crashed in. The earth split. Most of Alpha Company   26
slept.

A lieutenant came by. He told the men to get their gear together, but no   27
one moved, and he walked away. Then some of the men spotted the flash
of an enemy mortar tube.

They set up a machine gun and fired out at it, over the heads of every-   28
one in the fire base.

In seconds the enemy tube flashed again. The wind whistled, and the   29
round dug into a road twenty feet from my beer shed. Shrapnel slammed
into the beer shed. I hugged the Bud and Black Label, panting, no thoughts.

The men hollered that Charlie was zeroing in on our machine gun, and   30
everyone scattered, and the next round slammed down even closer.

The lieutenant hurried back. He argued with a platoon sergeant, but   31
this time the lieutenant was firm. He ordered us to double-time out to the
perimeter. Muttering about how the company needed a rest and that this
had turned into one hell of a rest and that they'd rather be out in the
boonies, the men put on helmets and took up their rifles and followed the
lieutenant past the mess hall and out to the perimeter.

Three of the men refused and went into the barracks and went to sleep.   32

Out on the perimeter, there were two dead GI's. Fifty-caliber machine   33
guns fired out into the paddies, and the sky was filled with flares. Two or
three of our men, forgetting about the war, went off to chase parachutes
blowing around the bunkers. The chutes came from the flares, and they
made good souvenirs.

In the morning the first sergeant roused us out of bed, and we swept the   34
fire base for bodies. Eight dead VC were lying about. One was crouched
beside a roll of barbed wire, the top of his head resting on the ground like
he was ready to do a somersault. A squad of men was detailed to throw the
corpses into a truck. They wore gloves and didn't like the job, but they
joked. The rest of us walked into the rice paddy and followed a tracker dog
out toward the VC mortar positions. From there the dog took us into a
village, but there was nothing to see but some children and women. We
walked around until noon. Then the lieutenant turned us around, and we
were back at LZ Gator in time for chow.

"Those poor motherfuckin' dinks," the Kid said while we were filling   35
sandbags in the afternoon. "They should know better than to test Alpha
Company. They just know, they *ought* to know anyhow, it's like tryin' to
attack the Pentagon! Old Alpha comes in, an' there ain't a chance in hell
for 'em, they oughta know *that*, for Christ's sake. Eight to two, they lost
six more than we did." The Kid was only eighteen, but everyone said
to look out for him, he was the best damn shot in the battalion with an
M-79.

"Actually," the Kid said, "those two guys weren't even from Alpha. The two dead GI's. They were with Charlie Company or something, I don't know. Stupid dinks should know better." He flashed a buck-toothed smile and jerked his eyebrows up and down and winked. 36

Wolf said: "Look, FNG, I don't want to scare you—nobody's trying to scare you—but that stuff last night wasn't *shit!* Last night was a lark. Wait'll you see some really *bad* shit. That was a picnic last night. I almost slept through it." I wondered what an FNG was. No one told me until I asked. 37

"You bullshitter, Wolf. It's never any fun." The Kid heaved a shovelful of sand at Wolf's feet. "Except for me maybe. I'm charmed, nothing'll get me. Ol' Buddy Wolf's a good bullshitter, he'll bullshit you till you think he knows his ass from his elbow." 38

"Okay, FNG, don't listen to me, ask Buddy Barker. Buddy Barker, you tell him last night was a lark. Right? We got mortars and wire and bunkers and arty and, shit, what the hell else you want? You want a damn H bomb?" 39

"Good idea," Kid said. 40

But Buddy Barker agreed it had been a lark. He filled a sandbag and threw it onto a truck and sat down and read a comic. Buddy Wolf filled two more bags and sat down with Buddy Barker and called him a lazy bastard. While Kid and I filled more bags, Wolf and Barker read comics and played a game called "Name the Gang." Wolf named a rock song and Barker named the group who made it big. Wolf won 10 to 2. I asked the Kid how many Alpha men had been killed lately, and the Kid shrugged and said a couple. So I asked how many had been wounded, and without looking up, he said a few. I asked how bad the AO was, how soon you could land a rear job, if the platoon leader were gung-ho, if Kid had ever been wounded, and the Kid just grinned and gave flippant, smiling, say-nothing answers. He said it was best not to worry. 41

MUSINGS

The fear that O'Brien experiences runs through this chronicle, mounting with each exchange or event. Although he never says that he is afraid, his writing makes his fear so obvious that the reader can almost taste it. Note the irony in "the Kid's" final comment.

Recount a time when you experienced fear and make the reader aware of your feeling, not through stating it but by recounting the series of remarks or events that caused your fear.

BELL HOOKS (1955–)

Gloria Watkins took the pseudonym of bell hooks, the name of a woman who was not afraid of "talking back" and whom she adopted as her supporter and ally. A black feminist, hooks is one of the most provocative of today's writers. She writes about the oppression of black women from the days of slavery, when they suffered in a way quite different from male slaves, to the present day when they continue to suffer and endure as women. She contends that black and white feminists agree on some points but are divided on others, naming sexism, racism, and the class system as the three points of contention.

As a young woman, hooks attended Stanford University and is now a professor of Afro-American Studies and English at Yale University. She has written a number of books and essays on black women, feminism, and the civil rights movement, bringing penetrating and often controversial views to those subjects. A critic in Library Journal *commented: "Hooks continues to produce some of the most challenging, insightful, and provocative writing on race and gender in the United States today."*

In the following excerpt from her book, Talking Back: Thinking Feminist, Thinking Black, *hooks asserts that there is "'no calling' for talking girls, no legitimized rewarded speech." She claims that black women often talk to "ears that do not hear," and that they struggle to create a speech "that compels listeners, one that is heard." She maintains that "writing is a way to capture speech." Her career stands as proof of that assertion, as she is now widely heard and critically acclaimed.*

Talking Back

In the world of the southern black community I grew up in, "back talk" and "talking back" meant speaking as an equal to an authority figure. It meant daring to disagree and sometimes it just meant having an opinion. In the "old school," children were meant to be seen and not heard. My great-grandparents, grandparents, and parents were all from the old school. To make yourself heard if you were a child was to invite punishment, the back-hand lick, the slap across the face that would catch you unaware, or the feel of switches stinging your arms and legs.

To speak then when one was not spoken to was a courageous act—an act of risk and daring. And yet it was hard not to speak in warm rooms where heated discussions began at the crack of dawn, women's voices filling the air, giving orders, making threats, fussing. Black men may have excelled in the art of poetic preaching in the male-dominated church, but in

1

2

207

the church of the home, where the everyday rules of how to live and how to act were established, it was black women who preached. There, black women spoke in a language so rich, so poetic, that it felt to me like being shut off from life, smothered to death if one were not allowed to participate.

It was in that world of woman talk (the men were often silent, often absent) that was born in me the craving to speak, to have a voice, and not just any voice but one that could be identified as belonging to me. To make my voice, I had to speak, to hear myself talk—and talk I did—darting in and out of grown folks' conversations and dialogues, answering questions that were not directed at me, endlessly asking questions, making speeches. Needless to say, the punishments for these acts of speech seemed endless. They were intended to silence me—the child—and more particularly the girl child. Had I been a boy, they might have encouraged me to speak believing that I might someday be called to preach. There was no "calling" for talking girls, no legitimized rewarded speech. The punishments I received for "talking back" were intended to suppress all possibility that I would create my own speech. That speech was to be suppressed so that the "right speech of womanhood" would emerge.

Within feminist circles, silence is often seen as the sexist "right speech of womanhood"—the sign of woman's submission to patriarchal authority. This emphasis on woman's silence may be an accurate remembering of what has taken place in the households of women from WASP backgrounds in the United States, but in black communities (and diverse ethnic communities), women have not been silent. Their voices can be heard. Certainly for black women, our struggle has not been to emerge from silence into speech but to change the nature and direction of our speech, to make a speech that compels listeners, one that is heard.

Our speech, "the right speech of womanhood," was often the soliloquy, the talking into thin air, the talking to ears that do not hear you—the talk that is simply not listened to. Unlike the black male preacher whose speech was to be heard, who was to be listened to, whose words were to be remembered, the voices of black women—giving orders, making threats, fussing—could be tuned out, could become a kind of background music, audible but not acknowledged as significant speech. Dialogue—the sharing of speech and recognition—took place not between mother and child or mother and male authority figure but among black women. I can remember watching fascinated as our mother talked with her mother, sisters, and women friends. The intimacy and intensity of their speech—the satisfaction they received from talking to one another, the pleasure, the joy. It was in this world of woman speech, loud talk, angry words, women with tongues quick and sharp, tender sweet tongues, touching our world with their words, that I made speech my birthright—and the right to voice, to authorship, a privilege I would not be denied. It was in that world and because of it that I came to dream of writing, to write.

Writing was a way to capture speech, to hold onto it, keep it close. And so I wrote down bits and pieces of conversations, confessing in cheap diaries that soon fell apart from too much handling, expressing the intensity of my sorrow, the anguish of speech—for I was always saying the wrong thing, asking the wrong questions. I could not confine my speech to the necessary corners and concerns of life. I hid these writings under my bed, in pillow stuffings, among faded underwear. When my sisters found and read them they ridiculed and mocked me—poking fun. I felt violated, ashamed, as if the secret parts of my self had been exposed, brought into the open, and hung like newly clean laundry, out in the air for everyone to see. The fear of exposure, the fear that one's deepest emotions and innermost thoughts will be dismissed as mere nonsense, felt by so many young girls keeping diaries, holding and hiding speech, seems to me now one of the barriers that women have always needed and still need to destroy so that we are no longer pushed into secrecy or silence. 6

Despite my feelings of violation, of exposure, I continued to speak and write, choosing my hiding places well, learning to destroy work when no safe place could be found. I was never taught absolute silence, I was taught that it was important to speak but to talk a talk that was in itself a silence. Taught to speak and yet beware of the betrayal of too much heard speech, I experienced intense confusion and deep anxiety in my efforts to speak and write. Reciting poems at Sunday afternoon church service might be rewarded. Writing a poem (when one's time could be "better" spent sweeping, ironing, learning to cook) was luxurious activity, indulged in at the expense of others. Questioning authority, raising issues that were not deemed appropriate subjects brought pain, punishments—like telling mama I wanted to die before her because I could not live without her— that was crazy talk, crazy speech, the kind that would lead you to end up in a mental institution. "Little girl," I would be told, "if you don't stop all this crazy talk and crazy acting you are going to end up right out there at Western State." 7

Madness, not just physical abuse, was the punishment for too much talk if you were female. Yet even as this fear of madness haunted me, hanging over my writing like a monstrous shadow, I could not stop the words, making thought, writing speech. For this terrible madness which I feared, which I was sure was the destiny of daring women born to intense speech (after all, the authorities emphasized this point daily), was not as threatening as imposed silence, as suppressed speech. 8

Safety and sanity were to be sacrificed if I was to experience defiant speech. Though I risked them both, deep-seated fears and anxieties char- 9 acterized my childhood days. I would speak but I would not ride a bike, play hardball, or hold the gray kitten. Writing about the ways we are traumatized in our growing-up years, psychoanalyst Alice Miller makes the point in *For Your Own Good* that it is not clear why childhood wounds become for some folk an opportunity to grow, to move forward rather than backward in the process of self-realization. Certainly, when I reflect on the trials of my growing-up years, the many punishments, I can see now that in resistance I learned to be vigilant in the nourishment of my spirit, to be tough, to courageously protect that spirit from forces that would break it.

While punishing me, my parents often spoke about the necessity of breaking my spirit. Now when I ponder the silences, the voices that are not heard, the voices of those wounded and/or oppressed individuals who do not speak or write, I contemplate the acts of persecution, torture—the terrorism that breaks spirits, that makes creativity impossible. I write these words to bear witness to the primacy of resistance struggle in any situation of domination (even within family life); to the strength and power that emerges from sustained resistance and the profound conviction that these forces can be healing, can protect us from dehumanization and despair.

• • •

Recently, efforts by black women writers to call attention to our work serve to highlight both our presence and absence. Whenever I peruse women's bookstores, I am struck not by the rapidly growing body of feminist writing by black women, but by the paucity of available published material. Those of us who write and are published remain few in number. The context of silence is varied and multi-dimensional. Most obvious are the ways racism, sexism, and class exploitation act to suppress and silence. Less obvious are the inner struggles, the efforts made to gain the necessary confidence to write, to re-write, to fully develop craft and skill—and the extent to which such efforts fail.

Although I have wanted writing to be my life-work since childhood, it has been difficult for me to claim "writer" as part of that which identifies and shapes my everyday reality. Even after publishing books, I would often speak of wanting to be a writer as though these works did not exist. And though I would be told, "you are a writer," I was not yet ready to fully affirm this truth. Part of myself was still held captive by domineering forces of history, of familial life that had charted a map of silence, of right speech. I had not completely let go of the fear of saying the wrong thing, of being punished. Somewhere in the deep recesses of my mind. I believed I could avoid both responsibility and punishment if I did not declare myself a writer.

One of the many reasons I chose to write using the pseudonym bell hooks, a family name (mother to Sarah Oldham, grandmother to Rosa

Bell Oldham, great-grandmother to me), was to construct a writer-identity that would challenge and subdue all impulses leading me away from speech into silence. I was a young girl buying bubble gum at the corner store when I first really heard the full name bell hooks. I had just "talked back" to a grown person. Even now I can recall the surprised look, the mocking tones that informed me I must be kin to bell hooks—a sharp-tongued woman, a woman who spoke her mind, a woman who was not afraid to talk back. I claimed this legacy of defiance, of will, of courage, affirming my link to female ancestors who were bold and daring in their speech. Unlike my bold and daring mother and grandmother, who were not supportive of talking back, even though they were assertive and powerful in their speech, bell hooks as I discovered, claimed, and invented her was my ally, my support.

That initial act of talking back outside the home was empowering. It was the first of many acts of defiant speech that would make it possible for me to emerge as an independent thinker and writer. In retrospect, "talking back" became for me a rite of initiation, testing my courage, strengthening my commitment, preparing me for the days ahead—the days when writing, rejection notices, periods of silence, publication, ongoing development seem impossible but necessary. 14

Moving from silence into speech is for the oppressed, the colonized, the exploited, and those who stand and struggle side by side a gesture of defiance that heals, that makes new life and new growth possible. It is that act of speech, of "talking back," that is no mere gesture of empty words, that is the expression of our movement from object to subject—the liberated voice. 15

MUSINGS

In this selection hooks writes eloquently of "the right speech of womanhood" that was often "the soliloquy, the talking into thin air." This phenomenon of being ignored is true not only for women but for any outsiders in a situation—minorities, children, perhaps in some circumstances even students.

Have you experienced this feeling of not having been heard in some situation? Try to capture what was missed by addressing the same audience and presenting your ideas or opinions in writing.

4

BIOGRAPHY

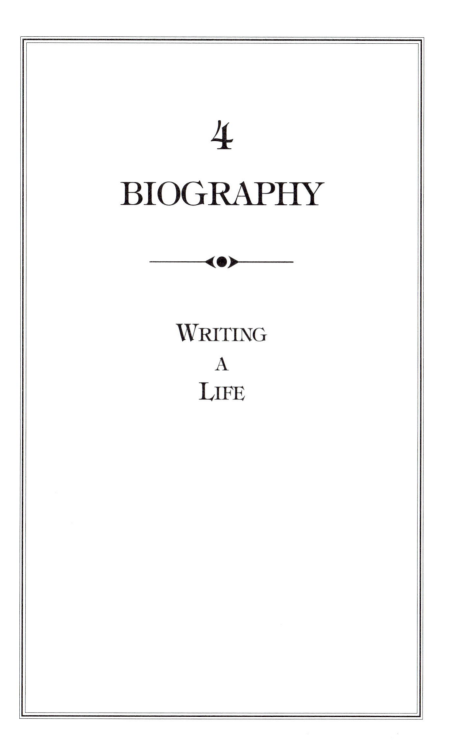

WRITING
A
LIFE

J ust like all other types of life writing, biographies are concerned with chronicling human lives. However, unlike the other forms discussed so far, biographers write about others rather than about themselves. As a consequence, the life being recorded is usually beyond the immediate experience of the author. Writing biography involves immersion not only in the experiences of another person, but also in that person's cultural context, possibly in another time or place. Biographies, like autobiographies, are usually written to a large, anonymous audience with readers of unknown gender, religion, ethnic background, and political affiliation.

Also like autobiographies, biographies are written for diverse purposes. A biographer may attempt to immortalize a famous subject or to rescue a less well-known one from obscurity. Maxine Hong Kingston resurrects her aunt from her watery grave by interweaving fact and fiction. Truman Capote, through his detailed accounting of the lives of two murderers, rescues them from the anonymity of the hangman's noose. Through the story of Dian Fossey, the ape Digit is as real and as lovable as the family pet; with her the reader mourns his death, but with the knowledge that he lives on in the pages of Fossey's own book as well as in those of her biography by Sy Montgomery, reprinted here.

While biographies immortalize their subjects, the biographers often remain little-known. Most readers know who Daniel Boone, Woody Allen, Leonard Bernstein, and Stevie Wonder are, but the names of their biographers, Faragher, Peyser, Lax, and Smith, would probably not ring a bell. A biographer often writes in order to correct or expand the views of a previous biography or biographies by choosing a different perspective. One biography might have covered the literary career of a writer; a second biography might chronicle the writer's personal life. Both biographers choose the same subject but emphasize different facets of their lives.

Biographies involve a great deal of research. The biographer must become intimately familiar with the time and place in which the subject lived. Letters must be read, sorted, and put into context. If other biographies of the subject exist, they must be read carefully and all leads followed. Diaries must be studied and interviews conducted with any living relatives and friends. These essential facts are only the beginning.

Biographers are the first to question the concept that their works are based only on "facts." The facts of someone's life could be listed on one page. What is important is the interpretation of the subject's life by the writer. In the introduction to her biography of Gloria Steinem, Carolyn Heilbrun asserts: "Biography is the imposition of the biographer's perception upon the life of the subject. There is no truth; there are, indeed, re-markably few facts." She adds that, although most biographers pretend to be objective, they often "fail to see their own biases."

As you begin writing biography, you need to question your own biases and recognize your perspective. Answers to the following questions will help you explore your subject, develop your ideas, and focus your writing:

- Why did you choose to write about your subject?
- What aspect of that person are you stressing?
- How do the incidents that you have selected reinforce that impression?
- Are letters and/or diaries available?
- With whom should you conduct interviews—relatives, professional colleagues?
- Who is your intended audience—family, friends, a professional or po-litical group, a largely unknown general public?

John Neihardt (1881–1973)

Black Elk Speaks, *actually an oral history, contains the words of Black Elk, a holy man of the Ogala Sioux, a Plains Indian tribe. His words were written down and edited by John Neihardt from the shorthand transcription made by Neihardt's daughter, who accompanied her father to the reservation. Neihardt had gained the confidence of Black Elk, who agreed to tell him of his vision and his people's dream.* Black Elk Speaks *(1932) was published with little notice, and it was only in the 1960s that interest in the spiritual values of Native Americans was renewed. The book continues to be read by those interested in learning more about the Plains Indians, as well as by Native Americans who look to it for spiritual strength and vindication of their heritage.*

The Battle of Wounded Knee, which took place on December 29, 1890, as narrated by Black Elk, was a tragic note in the conflicts between the U.S. government and Native Americans. In the decade before the battle the Sioux began following a holy man who promised through the performance of certain rituals an end to war, the return of their lands, and prosperity and lasting peace. U.S. marshalls, believing that Sitting Bull was the instigator of the movement, tried to arrest him and, when he resisted, killed him. His followers fled, pursued by the Seventh Cavalry, who finally corralled them into a camp near Wounded Knee Creek and ordered them to surrender their guns. A gunshot was inadvertently fired, and the army began shooting. Before the day was over they had massacred two hundred unarmed men, women, and children. Black Elk describes the grisly scene and concludes with great sadness, "A people's dream died there."

Black Elk: The Butchering at Wounded Knee

That evening before it happened, I went in to Pine Ridge and heard these things, and while I was there, soldiers started for where the Big Foots were. These made about five hundred soldiers that were there next morning. When I saw them starting I felt that something terrible was going to happen. That night I could hardly sleep at all. I walked around most of the night.

In the morning I went out after my horses, and while I was out I heard shooting off toward the east, and I knew from the sound that it must be wagon-guns (cannon) going off. The sounds went right through my body, and I felt that something terrible would happen.

When I reached camp with the horses, a man rode up to me and said: "Hey-hey-hey! The people that are coming are fired on! I know it!"

I saddled up my buckskin and put on my sacred shirt. It was one I had   4
made to be worn by no one but myself. It had a spotted eagle outstretched
on the back of it, and the daybreak star was on the left shoulder, because
when facing south that shoulder is toward the east. Across the breast, from
the left shoulder to the right hip, was the flaming rainbow, and there was
another rainbow around the neck, like a necklace, with a star at the bottom. At each shoulder, elbow, and wrist was an eagle feather; and over the
whole shirt were red streaks of lightning. You will see that this was from
my great vision, and you will know how it protected me that day.

I painted my face all red, and in my hair I put one eagle feather for the   5
One Above.

It did not take me long to get ready, for I could still hear the shooting   6
over there.

I started out alone on the old road that ran across the hills to Wounded   7
Knee. I had no gun. I carried only the sacred bow of the west that I had
seen in my great vision. I had gone only a little way when a band of young
men came galloping after me. The first two who came up were Loves War
and Iron Wasichu. I asked what they were going to do, and they said they
were just going to see where the shooting was. Then others were coming
up, and some older men.

We rode fast, and there were about twenty of us now. The shooting was   8
getting louder. A horseback from over there came galloping very fast toward us, and he said: "Hey-hey-hey! They have murdered them!" Then he
whipped his horse and rode away faster toward Pine Ridge.

In a little while we had come to the top of the ridge where, looking to   9
the east, you can see for the first time the monument and the burying
ground on the little hill where the church is. That is where the terrible
thing started. Just south of the burying ground on the little hill a deep dry
gulch runs about east and west, very crooked, and it rises westward to
nearly the top of the ridge where we were. It had no name, but the Wasichus sometimes call it Battle Creek now. We stopped on the ridge not far
from the head of the dry gulch. Wagon guns were still going off over there
on the little hill, and they were going off again where they hit along the
gulch. There was much shooting down yonder, and there were many cries,
and we could see cavalrymen scattered over the hills ahead of us. Cavalrymen were riding along the gulch and shooting into it, where the women
and children were running away and trying to hide in the gullies and the
stunted pines.

A little way ahead of us, just below the head of the dry gulch, there were   10
some women and children who were huddled under a clay bank, and
some cavalrymen were there pointing guns at them.

We stopped back behind the ridge, and I said to the others: "Take   11 courage. These are our relatives. We will try to get them back." Then we all sang a song which went like this:

A thunder being nation I am, I have said.
A thunder being nation I am, I have said.
You shall live.
You shall live.
You shall live.
You shall live.

Then I rode over the ridge and the others after me, and we were crying: "Take courage! It is time to fight!" The soldiers who were guarding our relatives shot at us and then ran away fast, and some more cavalrymen on the other side of the gulch did too. We got our relatives and sent them across the ridge to the northwest where they would be safe.   12

I had no gun, and when we were charging, I just held the sacred bow out in front of me with my right hand. The bullets did not hit us at all.   13

We found a little baby lying all alone near the head of the gulch. I could not pick her up just then, but I got her later and some of my people adopted her. I just wrapped her up tighter in a shawl that was around her and left her there. It was a safe place, and I had other work to do.   14

The soldiers had run eastward over the hills where there were some more soldiers, and they were off their horses and lying down. I told the others to stay back, and I charged upon them holding the sacred bow out toward them with my right hand. They all shot at me, and I could hear bullets all around me, but I ran my horse right close to them, and then swung around. Some soldiers across the gulch began shooting at me too, but I got back to the others and was not hurt at all.   15

By now many other Lakotas, who had heard the shooting, were coming up from Pine Ridge, and we all charged on the soldiers. They ran eastward toward where the trouble began. We followed down along the dry gulch, and what we saw was terrible. Dead and wounded women and children and little babies were scattered all along there where they had been trying to run away. The soldiers had followed along the gulch, as they ran, and murdered them in there. Sometimes they were in heaps because they had huddled together, and some were scattered all along. Sometimes bunches of them had been killed and torn to pieces where the wagon guns hit them. I saw a little baby trying to suck its mother, but she was bloody and dead.   16

There were two little boys at one place in this gulch. They had guns and they had been killing soldiers all by themselves. We could see the soldiers they had killed. The boys were all alone there, and they were not hurt. These were very brave little boys.   17

When we drove the soldiers back, they dug themselves in, and we were   18
not enough people to drive them out from there. In the evening they
marched off up Wounded Knee Creek, and then we saw all that they had
done there.

Men and women and children were heaped and scattered all over the   19
flat at the bottom of the little hill where the soldiers had their wagon-guns,
and westward up the dry gulch all the way to the high ridge, the dead
women and children and babies were scattered.

When I saw this I wished that I had died too, but I was not sorry for the   20
women and children. It was better for them to be happy in the other
world, and I wanted to be there too. But before I went there I wanted to
have revenge. I thought there might be a day, and we should have revenge.

After the soldiers marched away, I heard from my friend, Dog Chief,   21
how the trouble started, and he was right there by Yellow Bird when it
happened. This is the way it was:

In the morning the soldiers began to take all the guns away from the   22
Big Foots, who were camped in the flat below the little hill where the
monument and burying ground are now. The people had stacked most of
their guns, and even their knives, by the tepee where Big Foot was lying
sick. Soldiers were on the little hill and all around, and there were soldiers
across the dry gulch to the south and over east along Wounded Knee
Creek too. The people were nearly surrounded, and the wagon-guns were
pointing at them.

Some had not yet given up their guns, and so the soldiers were search-   23
ing all the tepees, throwing things around and poking into everything.
There was a man called Yellow Bird, and he and another man were standing in front of the tepee where Big Foot was lying sick. They had white
sheets around and over them, with eyeholes to look through, and they had
guns under these. An officer came to search them. He took the other man's
gun, and then started to take Yellow Bird's. But Yellow Bird would not let
go. He wrestled with the officer, and while they were wrestling, the gun
went off and killed the officer. Wasichus and some others have said he
meant to do this, but Dog Chief was standing right there, and he told me
it was not so. As soon as the gun went off, Dog Chief told me, an officer
shot and killed Big Foot who was lying sick inside the tepee.

Then suddenly nobody knew what was happening, except that the sol-   24
diers were all shooting and the wagon-guns began going off right in
among the people.

Many were shot down right there. The women and children ran into   25
the gulch and up west, dropping all the time, for the soldiers shot them as
they ran. There were only about a hundred warriors and there were nearly
five hundred soldiers. The warriors rushed to where they had piled their

guns and knives. They fought soldiers with only their hands until they got their guns.

Dog Chief saw Yellow Bird run into a tepee with his gun, and from there   26 he killed soldiers until the tepee caught fire. Then he died full of bullets.

It was a good winter day when all this happened. The sun was shining.   27 But after the soldiers marched away from their dirty work, a heavy snow began to fall. The wind came up in the night. There was a big blizzard, and it grew very cold. The snow drifted deep in the crooked gulch, and it was one long grave of butchered women and children and babies, who had never done any harm and were only trying to run away.

After the soldiers marched away, Red Crow and I started back toward   28 Pine Ridge together, and I took the little baby that I told you about. Red Crow had one too.

We were going back to Pine Ridge, because we thought there was peace   29 back home; but it was not so. While we were gone, there was a fight around the Agency, and our people had all gone away. They had gone away so fast that they left all the tepees standing.

It was nearly dark when we passed north of Pine Ridge where the hos-   30 pital is now, and some soldiers shot at us, but did not hit us. We rode into the camp, and it was all empty. We were very hungry because we had not eaten anything since early morning, so we peeped into the tepees until we saw where there was a pot with papa (dried meat) cooked in it. We sat down in there and began to eat. While we were doing this, the soldiers shot at the tepee, and a bullet struck right between Red Crow and me. It threw dust in the soup, but we kept right on eating until we had our fill. Then we took the babies and got on our horses and rode away. If that bullet had only killed me, then I could have died with papa in my mouth.

The people had fled down Clay Creek, and we followed their trail. It   31 was dark now, and late in the night we came to where they were camped without any tepees. They were just sitting by little fires, and the snow was beginning to blow. We rode in among them and I heard my mother's voice. She was singing a death song for me, because she felt sure I had died over there. She was so glad to see me that she cried and cried.

Women who had milk fed the little babies that Red Crow and I   32 brought with us.

I think nobody but the little children slept any that night. The snow   33 blew and we had no tepees.

When it was getting light, a war party went out and I went along; but   34 this time I took a gun with me. When I started out the day before to Wounded Knee, I took only my sacred bow, which was not made to shoot with; because I was a little in doubt about the Wanekia religion at that time, and I did not really want to kill anybody because of it.

But I did not feel like that any more. After what I had seen over there,   35
I wanted revenge; I wanted to kill.

We crossed White Clay Creek and followed it up, keeping on the west   36
side. Soon we could hear many guns going off. So we struck west, following a ridge to where the fight was. It was close to the Mission, and there
are many bullets in the Mission yet.

From this ridge we could see that the Lakotas were on both sides of the   37
creek and were shooting at soldiers who were coming down the creek. As
we looked down, we saw a little ravine, and across this was a big hill. We
crossed and rode up the hillside.

They were fighting right there, and a Lakota cried to me: "Black Elk,   38
this is the kind of a day in which to do something great!" I answered:
"How! [signifying assent]"

Then I got off my horse and rubbed earth on myself, to show the Pow-   39
ers that I was nothing without their help. Then I took my rifle, got on my
horse and galloped up to the top of the hill. Right below me the soldiers were
shooting, and my people called out to me not to go down there; that there
were some good shots among the soldiers and I should get killed for nothing.

But I remembered my great vision, the part where the geese of the   40
north appeared. I depended upon their power. Stretching out my arms
with my gun in the right hand, like a goose soaring when it flies low to
turn in a change of weather, I made the sound the geese make—br-r-r-p,
br-r-r-p, br-r-r-p; and, doing this, I charged. The soldiers saw, and began
shooting fast at me. I kept right on with my buckskin running, shot in
their faces when I was near, then swung wide and rode back up the hill.

All this time the bullets were buzzing around me and I was not   41
touched. I was not even afraid. It was like being in a dream about shooting. But just as I had reached the very top of the hill, suddenly it was like
waking up, and I was afraid. I dropped my arms and quit making the
goose cry. Just as I did this, I felt something strike my belt as though some
one had hit me there with the back of an ax. I nearly fell out of my saddle,
but I managed to hold on, and rode over the hill.

An old man by the name of Protector was there, and he ran up and held   42
me, for now I was falling off my horse. I will show you where the bullet
struck me sidewise across the belly here (showing a long deep scar on the
abdomen). My insides were coming out. Protector tore up a blanket in
strips and bound it around me so that my insides would stay in. By now I
was crazy to kill, and I said to Protector: "Help me on my horse! Let me go
over there. It is a good day to die, so I will go over there!" But Protector
said: "No, young nephew! You must not die to-day. That would be foolish.
Your people need you. There may be a better day to die." He lifted me into
my saddle and led my horse away down hill. Then I began to feel very sick.

By now it looked as though the soldiers would be wiped out, and the   43

Lakotas were fighting harder; but I heard that, after I left, the black Wa-sichu soldiers came, and the Lakotas had to retreat.

There were many of our children in the Mission, and the sisters and   44
priests were taking care of them. I heard there were sisters and priests right
in the battle helping wounded people and praying.

There was a man by the name of Little Soldier who took charge of me   45
and brought me to where our people were camped. While we were over at
the Mission Fight, they had fled to the O-ona-gazhee [sheltering place in
the Badlands] and were camped on top of it where the women and children would be safe from soldiers. Old Hollow Horn was there. He was a
very powerful bear medicine man, and he came over to heal my wound. In
three days I could walk, but I kept a piece of blanket tied around my belly.

It was now nearly the middle of the Moon of Frost in the Tepee (Janu-   46
ary). We heard that soldiers were on Smoky Earth River and were coming
to attack us in the O-ona-gazhee. They were near Black Feather's place. So
a party of about sixty of us started on the war-path to find them. My
mother tried to keep me at home, because, although I could walk and ride
a horse, my wound was not all healed yet. But I would not stay; for, after
what I had seen at Wounded Knee, I wanted a chance to kill soldiers.

We rode down Grass Creek to Smoky Earth, and crossed, riding down   47
stream. Soon from the top of a little hill we saw wagons and cavalry guarding them. The soldiers were making a corral of their wagons and getting
ready to fight. We got off our horses and went behind some hills to a little
knoll, where we crept up to look at the camp. Some soldiers were bringing
harnessed horses down to a little creek to water, and I said to the others:
"If you will stay here and shoot at the soldiers, I will charge over there and
get some good horses." They knew of my power, so they did this, and I
charged on my buckskin while the others kept shooting. I got seven of the
horses; but when I started back with these, all the soldiers saw me and
began shooting. They killed two of my horses, but I brought five back safe
and was not hit. When I was out of range, I caught up a fine baldfaced bay
and turned my buckskin loose. Then I drove the others back to our party.

By now more cavalry were coming up the river, a big bunch of them,   48
and there was some hard fighting for a while, because there were not
enough of us. We were fighting and retreating, and all at once I saw Red
Willow on foot running. He called to me: "Cousin, my horse is killed!" So
I caught up a soldier's horse that was dragging a rope and brought it to
Red Willow while the soldiers were shooting fast at me. Just then, for a little while, I was a wanekia [a "make-live" savior] myself. In this fight Long
Bear and another man, whose name I have forgotten, were badly
wounded; but we saved them and carried them along with us. The soldiers
did not follow us far into the Badlands, and when it was night we rode
back with our wounded to the O-ona-gazhee.

We wanted a much bigger war-party so that we could meet the soldiers   49
and get revenge. But this was hard, because the people were not all of the
same mind, and they were hungry and cold. We had a meeting there, and
were all ready to go out with more warriors, when Afraid-of-His-Horses
came over from Pine Ridge to make peace with Red Cloud, who was with
us there.

Our party wanted to go out and fight anyway, but Red Cloud made a   50
speech to us something like this: "Brothers, this is a very hard winter. The
women and children are starving and freezing. If this were summer, I
would say to keep on fighting to the end. But we cannot do this. We must
think of the women and children and that it is very bad for them. So we
must make peace, and I will see that nobody is hurt by the soldiers."

The people agreed to this, for it was true. So we broke camp next day   51
and went down from the O-ona-gazhee to Pine Ridge, and many, many
Lakotas were already there. Also, there were many, many soldiers. They
stood in two lines with their guns held in front of them as we went
through to where we camped.

And so it was all over.   52

I did not know then how much was ended. When I look back now   53
from this high hill of my old age, I can still see the butchered women and
children lying heaped and scattered all along the crooked gulch as plain as
when I saw them with eyes still young. And I can see that something else
died there in the bloody mud, and was buried in the blizzard. A people's
dream died there. It was a beautiful dream.

And I, to whom so great a vision was given in my youth,—you see me   54
now a pitiful old man who has done nothing, for the nation's hoop is broken and scattered. There is no center any longer, and the sacred tree is dead.

MUSINGS

In his introduction Neihardt speaks of the circumstances surrounding his
conversations with Black Elk and the difficulties of speaking with him:
"There were occasional brief intervals of rest when the old man, without
comments or apology, would lie down with his head on his arm and fall
asleep. . . . then awaken, evidently greatly refreshed, and continue."

Ask an older person—a member of your own family or a friend—to tell
you about some incident in his or her youth, such as the first day of
school, the first meeting with his or her spouse, or the first job. Have several possibilities in mind that would be of interest to both you and your
interviewee and that will call on his or her expertise and memory. Take
careful notes. Afterward, write the story from your notes as accurately as
you can.

The following selection is taken from Having Our Say, *a biography based on interviews by Amy Hill Hearth with the Delany sisters. Strictly speaking, the book falls into the category of oral history, but it is included here as books based on interviews are so carefully shaped by the interviewer's omissions, selections, and arrangements of material that they become in fact biographies. The sisters were well over 100 years old when the book, and the play based on the book, brought them fame. Asked how she felt about their sudden success, Bessie said, "Oooooh! I'm enjoying it."*

The Delany sisters had eight siblings, all of whom worked their way through college. At age 20, the sisters moved to New York to attend Columbia University. Bessie became a dentist and opened her practice in Harlem, while Sadie became the first domestic-science teacher in the city's public schools. Their father, a slave until he was seven, was the first elected black bishop of the Episcopal Church.

Although the sisters had a comparatively privileged childhood, they suffered the racial prejudice that every African-American endured. They speak of the "day that everything changed" in 1896 when the Jim Crow Laws, named for a minstrel show character, became entrenched in Southern society. African-Americans had long been segregated by custom, but these laws dictated separate facilities in schools, public transportation, and hospitals. The Delany sisters were children then, and in the following interview Sadie describes what Jim Crow meant to them. Legal segregation ended only with the Civil Rights Act of 1964.

The Delany Sisters: Jim Crow Laws

America has not ever been able to undo the mess created by those Jim Crow laws. 1

This is how we remember it: The reason they passed those Jim Crow laws is that powerful white people were getting more and more nervous with the way colored people, after the Civil War, were beginning to get their piece of the pie. Colored people were starting to accumulate some wealth, to vote, to make demands. At that time, many white people didn't think Negroes had souls. They thought we were just like animals. They wanted to believe that. 2

The pecking order was like this: White men were the most powerful, followed by white women. Colored people were absolutely below them 3 and if you think it was hard for colored men, honey, colored women were on the *bottom*. Yes, sir! Colored women took it from all angles!

You see, a lot of this Jim Crow mess was about sex, about keeping the races separate, so they wouldn't interbreed. Ironically, there were very few white people in those days, especially in the South, who did not have some nigger blood. All these white folks who thought they were above Negroes, well, many of them were not pure white! Some knew it, some didn't. But colored people could always pick them out. Papa used to joke that Negro blood must be superior, it must be strong stuff, 'cause it always showed up! You would see these beautiful white-skinned women with kinky hair, and honey, they got it from *somewhere*. This mixing was so common then that there was a saying among poor whites. They used to say, "Takes a little bit of nigger blood to bring out the beauty."

Some of this race mixing that was going on was left over from slavery days, because white men would often molest their slave women, and those women bore mulatto children. But a lot of this racial mixing, especially after slavery days, was just attraction between people, plain and simple, just like happened in our family, on Mama's side. You know, when people live in close proximity, they can't help but get attracted to each other. Also, a lot of white men turned to colored women for romance because they would get turned down by white women, sometimes even their wives. This was because sex in those days was dangerous, and women weren't so enthusiastic about it. Women died in childbirth; it was all risky business. And there were a lot of arranged marriages among the whites, with no love. So white women, who were more powerful than colored women, would sometimes refuse.

So, this Jim Crow mess was started to keep the races apart, and keep the Negroes down. Now, Mama and Papa knew these laws were coming, of course, but they didn't prepare us. I guess our parents could not find the words to explain it. They did not want to fill us with hatred. They did not want us to become bitter. They wanted us to be children and not carry the troubles of the world on our shoulders.

We encountered Jim Crow laws for the first time on a summer Sunday afternoon. We were about five and seven years old at the time. Mama and Papa used to take us to Pullen Park in Raleigh for picnics, and that particular day, the trolley driver told us to go to the back. We children objected loudly, because we always liked to sit in front, where the breeze would blow your hair. That had been part of the fun for us. But Mama and Papa just gently told us to hush and took us to the back without making a fuss.

When we got to Pullen Park, we found changes there, too. The spring where you got water now had a big wooden sign across the middle. On one side, the word "white" was painted, and on the other, the word "colored." Why, what in the world was all this about? We may have been little children but, honey, we got the message loud and clear. But when nobody was looking, Bessie took the dipper from the white side and drank from it.

On another day, soon afterward, a teacher from Saint Aug's took us to the drugstore for a limeade, which was something we had done hundreds of times. Well, this time, the man behind the counter said, "I can't wait on you." The teacher got very upset. She said, "I can see you not waiting on me, but surely you are not going to deny these young children?" And he said, "Sorry. It's the law." — 9

Funny thing is, the white man who owned that drugstore was married to a white lady, and had a colored family on the side. We know this for a fact, because his colored daughter was a friend of ours. She used to go over to the drugstore and he was real nice to her. This was all a big secret in the white community, but all of us colored folks knew all about it. It was kind of a joke, because you see, that was a very prominent white family. That fella even became the mayor of Raleigh. — 10

Jim Crow made it an even bigger stigma to be colored, and any hope of equality between the races came to a grinding halt. Papa used to say that real equality would come as Negroes became more educated and owned their own land. Negroes had to support each other, he used to say. — 11

So Papa would drag us all the way to Mr. Jones's store to buy groceries, since Mr. Jones was a Negro. It not only was inconvenient to shop at Mr. Jones's, it was more expensive. We used to complain about it, because we passed the A&P on the way. We would say, "Papa, why can't we just shop at the A&P?" And Papa would say, "Mr. Jones needs our money to live on, and the A&P does not. We are buying our economic freedom." So Papa put his money where his mouth was. Papa really had that good old American spirit. He believed in individuality, but at the same time, he was dedicated to the community. — 12

Now, lest you think Papa was some kind of a saint, well, he did have a weakness. He did slip into A&P now and then and buy that Eight O'-Clock Coffee, which he was very partial to. So you see, he wasn't perfect, but Lord, he did try! — 13

This race business does get under my skin. I have suffered a lot in my life because of it. If you asked me how I endured it, I would have to say it was because I had a good upbringing. My parents did not encourage me to be bitter. If they had, I'd have been so mean it would have killed my spirit a long, long time ago. — 14

As a child, every time I encountered prejudice—which was rubbed in your face, once segregation started under Jim Crow—I would feel it down to my core. I was not a crying child, except when it came to being treated badly because of my race, like when they wouldn't serve us at the drugstore counter. In those instances, I would go home and sit on my bed and weep and weep and weep, the tears streaming down my face. — 15

Now, Mama would come up and sit on the foot of my bed. She never 16
said a word. She knew what I was feeling. She just did not want to encourage my rage. So my Mama would just sit and look at me while I cried, and it comforted me. I knew that she understood, and that was the most soothing salve.

When I was a child, the words used to describe us most often were col- 17
ored, Negro, and nigger. I've also been called jiggerboo, pickaninny, coon—you name it, honey. Some of these words are worse than others, and how mean they are depends on who is saying them and why.

There was an attitude among some Negroes that to be lighter-skinned 18
was more desirable. There was a saying: "The blacker the berry, the sweeter the juice. But too much black and it ain't no use." If you were very dark-skinned you were looked down upon, even by other Negro people! I doubt that was true among Negro people back when we were in Africa. It's probably just a cultural thing that Negroes picked up from white people in America. We saw in our own family that people treated the lighter-skinned children better. But it was not something that was even *discussed* in our household. We were different shades, and it didn't make a bit of difference among us. It didn't matter if you were white, black, grizzly, or gray, you were *you.*

I don't use the word black very often to describe myself and my sister. 19
To us, black was a person who was, well, black, and honey, I mean *black as your shoe.* I'm not black, I'm brown! Actually, the best word to describe me, I think, is colored. I am a colored woman or a Negro woman. Either one is OK. People dislike those words now. Today they use this term *African American.* It wouldn't occur to me to use that. I prefer to think of myself as an American, that's all!

You see, I think I'm just as good as anyone. That's the way I was 20
brought up. I'll tell you a secret: I think I'm *better!* Ha! I remember being aware that colored people were supposed to feel inferior. I knew I was a smart little thing, a personality, an individual—a human being! I couldn't understand how people could look at me and not see that, because it sure was obvious to me.

It used to be that you would encounter white people who were very pa- 21
tronizing. In some ways, I disliked them the most. These were the type who thought we were all stupid. Little Negro children, in our day, had to put up with white folks rubbing their hands on your head for good luck. That's right. They thought that if they rubbed the head of a pickaninny, it would bring them luck, like a rabbit's foot, or something like that. So I'd try to keep my head out of reach of white folks, yes, sir.

You know, white people were always looking for good colored maids 22
and mammies. Why, sometimes white people would visit the campus and they would point to Sadie and me, and ask Mama if they could take one or

the other of us with them. Mama would bristle. "Those girls are my daughters, and they aren't going anywhere," she would say.

One time, as a girl, I was offered a job by a white lady to live at her 23
house and do some work for her. It was just off-campus, not far from home, and I thought, Hmmm, could make a little money. But Mama said, "It is completely out of the question!" I couldn't understand it then, but I do now. Mama did not want us to be maids for white people.

Nobody believes this, but it's true: Neither Sadie nor I ever worked for 24
white people in our entire lives! As a dentist, I had quite a few white patients, and Sadie worked for white principals in schools in New York City, but we never worked for white people in their homes. No, sir, not even once! That is one of the accomplishments in my life of which I am most proud, yes, sir! But there are colored people who say, "Well, how'd you make your money, then?" They simply can't believe it.

Mama and Papa tried to protect us, but the real world was out there, 25
and they couldn't shelter us forever. Papa had his newspapers, and he wouldn't let us see them, but we were nosy children, especially me. My grandpa, Mr. Miliam, used to say to Mama, "Nanny, every one of your children could have been detectives, especially Bessie." It was the truth!

It wasn't long before we learned the worst news imaginable: Colored 26
folks were being murdered. They were being lynched. We would hear the teachers talking among themselves about some poor Negro just walking down the side of the road, in the wrong place, at the wrong time. These rebby boys would just grab him and hang him from a tree, just for fun. It was like entertainment to those fellas.

Pretty much, these rebby boys left us alone at Saint Aug's. You'd think 27
they'd have gone after the uppity darkies at Saint Aug's who were getting an education, but I guess they knew that part of the school was a seminary. We got some protection just by being on the campus, within Raleigh.

But Papa still insisted that my brothers be home by dark and he taught 28
them how to keep out of trouble. You see, sometimes they'd lynch a colored man who objected to being called "uncle," things like that. If a white woman said a colored man had looked at her in a certain way, that was the end of him. The rebby boys would come in the middle of the night, and get him out of his bed and hang him up, in front of his wife and children. Sometimes they'd hang his whole family. Or he'd come home and find his woman hung, as punishment for something he supposedly had done. Why, there was one story I heard of a pregnant colored woman who was hung from her feet, and they slit her abdomen open and let the fetus fall out, and she and her unborn baby just died right there, like that.

Lord have mercy! I do not understand any of this. And it doesn't make 29
any more sense to me now than it did then. If it weren't for those kind

white missionaries at Saint Aug's, and my mother's white relatives who loved me, I would have hated all white people. Every last one.

Once in a while, God sends a good white person my way, even to this day. I think it's God's way of keeping me from becoming too mean. And when he sends a nice one to me, then I have to eat crow. And honey, crow is a tough old bird to eat, let me tell you.

30

MUSINGS

Sadie's language is simple and straightforward, but her ideas are thought-provoking. She raises a number of interesting issues in this interview. She talks about how her parents tried to protect her, "but the real world was out there and they couldn't shelter us forever." She speaks of the significance of the different skin shades and the names given to African-Americans, concluding that she prefers to think of herself "as an American, that's all."

Interview an older person who may have a different view from your own on one of the subjects suggested in Sadie's interview and then transfer it to paper. Feel free to edit by selecting, omitting, or rearranging material, making sure that the central idea and meanings are preserved.

TRUMAN CAPOTE (1924–1984)

Truman Capote's In Cold Blood *stands as a landmark in the histories of literature and journalism. In it he attempted a new kind of journalism, in what has come to be known as the new journalism or the nonfiction novel, by bringing "the art of the novelist together with the techniques of journalism." Journalists have always striven for factual representations, keeping themselves and personalities strictly separate from the facts. New journalism now recognizes that such separation is not always desirable and is in fact impossible.*

In writing In Cold Blood *Capote interspersed his own perspectives with the personalities of his characters. What resulted was an absorbing study of the many individuals involved. Published in 1966, it was a commercial and critical success. In it he chronicles in great detail the murder of a Kansas family, the subsequent events of the trial, and the final execution of the young perpetrators.*

The following selection begins with a quote from one of Capote's long interviews with Richard Hickock, one of the murderers, followed by a description of the events surrounding the hangings, told from the viewpoint of Alvin Dewey, one of the prosecutors in the case.

Richard Hickock: In Cold Blood

"Well, what's there to say about capital punishment? I'm not against it. Revenge is all it is, but what's wrong with revenge? It's very important. If I was kin to the Clutters, or any of the parties York and Latham dispensed with, I couldn't rest in peace till the ones responsible had taken that ride on the Big Swing. These people that write letters to the newspapers. There were two in a Topeka paper the other day—one from a minister. Saying, in effect, what is all this legal farce, why haven't those sonsabitches Smith and Hickock got it in the neck, how come those murdering sonsabitches are still eating up the taxpayers' money? Well, I can see their side. They're mad 'cause they're not getting what they want—revenge. And they're not going to get it if I can help it. I believe in hanging. Just so long as I'm not the one being hanged." 1

But then he was. 2

Another three years passed, and during those years two exceptionally skillful Kansas City lawyers, Joseph P. Jenkins and Robert Bingham, replaced Shultz, the latter having resigned from the case. Appointed by a Federal judge, and working without compensation (but motivated by a 3 hard-held opinion that the defendants had been the victims of a "nightmarishly unfair trial"), Jenkins and Bingham filed numerous appeals within the framework of the Federal court system, thereby avoiding three execution dates: October 25, 1962, August 8, 1963, and February 18, 1965. The attorneys contended that their clients had been unjustly convicted because legal counsel had not been appointed them until after they had confessed and had waived preliminary hearings; and because they were not competently represented at their trial, were convicted with the help of evidence seized without a search warrant (the shotgun and knife taken from the Hickock home), were not granted a change of venue even though the environs of the trial had been "saturated" with publicity prejudicial to the accused.

With these arguments, Jenkins and Bingham succeeded in carrying the   4
case three times to the United States Supreme Court—the Big Boy, as many litigating prisoners refer to it—but on each occasion the Court, which never comments on its decisions in such instances, denied the appeals by refusing to grant the writs of certiorari that would have entitled the appellants to a full hearing before the Court. In March, 1965, after Smith and Hickock had been confined in their Death Row cells almost two thousand days, the Kansas Supreme Court decreed that their lives must end between midnight and 2:00 A.M., Wednesday, April 14, 1965. Subsequently, a clemency appeal was presented to the newly elected Governor of Kansas, William Avery; but Avery, a rich farmer sensitive to public opinion, refused to intervene—a decision he felt to be in the "best interest of the people of Kansas." (Two months later, Avery also denied the clemency appeals of York and Latham, who were hanged on June 22, 1965.)

And so it happened that in the daylight hours of that Wednesday   5
morning, Alvin Dewey, breakfasting in the coffee shop of a Topeka hotel, read, on the first page of the Kansas City *Star,* a headline he had long awaited: DIE ON ROPE FOR BLOODY CRIME. The story, written by an Associated Press reporter, began: "Richard Eugene Hickock and Perry Edward Smith, partners in crime, died on the gallows at the state prison early today for one of the bloodiest murders in Kansas criminal annals. Hickock, 33 years old, died first, at 12:41 A.M.; Smith, 36, died at 1:19 . . ."

• • •

Dewey had watched them die, for he had been among the twenty-odd   6
witnesses invited to the ceremony. He had never attended an execution, and when on the midnight past he entered the cold warehouse, the scenery had surprised him: he had anticipated a setting of suitable dignity, not this bleakly lighted cavern cluttered with lumber and other debris. But the gallows itself, with its two pale nooses attached to a crossbeam, was

imposing enough; and so, in an unexpected style, was the hangman, who cast a long shadow from his perch on the platform at the top of the wooden instrument's thirteen steps. The hangman, an anonymous, leathery gentleman who had been imported from Missouri for the event, for which he was paid six hundred dollars, was attired in an aged double-breasted pin-striped suit overly commodious for the narrow figure inside it—the coat came nearly to his knees; and on his head he wore a cowboy hat which, when first bought, had perhaps been bright green, but was now a weathered, sweat-stained oddity.

Also, Dewey found the self-consciously casual conversation of his fellow witnesses, as they stood awaiting the start of what one witness termed "the festivities," disconcerting.   7

"What I heard was, they was gonna let them draw straws to see who   8
dropped first. Or flip a coin. But Smith says why not do it alphabetically. Guess 'cause S comes after H. Ha!"

"Read in the paper, afternoon paper, what they ordered for their last   9
meal? Ordered the same menu. Shrimp. French fries. Garlic bread. Ice cream and strawberries and whipped cream. Understand Smith didn't touch his much."

"That Hickock's got a sense of humor. They was telling me how, about   10
an hour ago, one of the guards says to him, 'This must be the longest night of your life.' And Hickock, he laughs and says, 'No. The shortest.'"

"Did you hear about Hickock's eyes? He left them to an eye doctor.   11
Soon as they cut him down, this doctor's gonna yank out his eyes and stick them in somebody else's head. Can't say I'd want to be that somebody. I'd feel peculiar with them eyes in my head."

"Christ! Is that *rain*? All the windows down! My new Chevy. Christ!"   12

The sudden rain rapped the high warehouse roof. The sound, not un-   13
like the rat-a-tat-tat of parade drums, heralded Hickock's arrival. Accompanied by six guards and a prayer-murmuring chaplain, he entered the death place handcuffed and wearing an ugly harness of leather straps that bound his arms to his torso. At the foot of the gallows the warden read to him the official order of execution, a two-page document; and as the warden read, Hickock's eyes, enfeebled by half a decade of cell shadows, roamed the little audience until, not seeing what he sought, he asked the nearest guard, in a whisper, if any member of the Clutter family was present. When he was told no, the prisoner seemed disappointed, as though he thought the protocol surrounding this ritual of vengeance was not being properly observed.

As is customary, the warden, having finished his recitation, asked the   14
condemned man whether he had any last statement to make. Hickock nodded. "I just want to say I hold no hard feelings. You people are sending me to a better world than this ever was"; then, as if to emphasize the point,

he shook hands with the four men mainly responsible for his capture and conviction, all of whom had requested permission to attend the executions: K.B.I. Agents Roy Church, Clarence Duntz, Harold Nye, and Dewey himself. "Nice to see you," Hickock said with his most charming smile; it was as if he were greeting guests at his own funeral.

The hangman coughed—impatiently lifted his cowboy hat and settled   15
it again, a gesture somehow reminiscent of a turkey buzzard huffing, then smoothing its neck feathers—and Hickock, nudged by an attendant, mounted the scaffold steps. "The Lord giveth, the Lord taketh away. Blessed is the name of the Lord," the chaplain intoned, as the rain sound accelerated, as the noose was fitted, and as a delicate black mask was tied round the prisoner's eyes. "May the Lord have mercy on your soul." The trap door opened, and Hickock hung for all to see a full twenty minutes before the prison doctor at last said, "I pronounce this man dead." A hearse, its blazing headlights beaded with rain, drove into the warehouse, and the body, placed on a litter and shrouded under a blanket, was carried to the hearse and out into the night.

Staring after it, Roy Church shook his head: "I never would have be-   16
lieved he had the guts. To take it like he did. I had him tagged a coward."

The man to whom he spoke, another detective, said, "Aw, Roy. The guy   17
was a punk. A mean bastard. He deserved it."

Church, with thoughtful eyes, continued to shake his head.   18

While waiting for the second execution, a reporter and a guard con-   19
versed. The reporter said, "This your first hanging?"

"I seen Lee Andrews."   20

"This here's my first."   21

"Yeah. How'd you like it?"   22

The reporter pursed his lips. "Nobody in our office wanted the assign-   23
ment. Me either. But it wasn't as bad as I thought it would be. Just like jumping off a diving board. Only with a rope around your neck."

"They don't feel nothing. Drop, snap, and that's it. They don't feel   24
nothing."

"Are you sure? I was standing right close. I could hear him gasping for   25
breath."

"Uh-huh, but he don't feel nothing. Wouldn't be humane if he did."   26

"Well. And I suppose they feed them a lot of pills. Sedatives."   27

"Hell, no. Against the rules. Here comes Smith."   28

"Gosh, I didn't know he was such a shrimp."   29

"Yeah, he's little. But so is a tarantula."   30

As he was brought into the warehouse, Smith recognized his old foe,   31
Dewey; he stopped chewing a hunk of Doublemint gum he had in his mouth, and grinned and winked at Dewey, jaunty and mischievous. But

after the warden asked if he had anything to say, his expression was sober. His sensitive eyes gazed gravely at the surrounding faces, swerved up to the shadowy hangman, then downward to his own manacled hands. He looked at his fingers, which were stained with ink and paint, for he'd spent his final three years on Death Row painting self-portraits and pictures of children, usually the children of inmates who supplied him with photographs of their seldom-seen progeny. "I think," he said, "it's a helluva thing to take a life in this manner. I don't believe in capital punishment, morally or legally. Maybe I had something to contribute, something—" His assurance faltered; shyness blurred his voice, lowered it to a just audible level. "It would be meaningless to apologize for what I did. Even inappropriate. But I do. I apologize."

Steps, noose, mask; but before the mask was adjusted, the prisoner spat   32
his chewing gum into the chaplain's outstretched palm. Dewey shut his eyes; he kept them shut until he heard the thudsnap that announces a rope-broken neck. Like the majority of American law-enforcement officials, Dewey is certain that capital punishment is a deterrent to violent crime, and he felt that if ever the penalty had been earned, the present instance was it. The preceding execution had not disturbed him, he had never had much use for Hickock, who seemed to him "a small-time chiseler who got out of his depth, empty and worthless." But Smith, though he was the true murderer, aroused another response, for Perry possessed a quality, the aura of an exiled animal, a creature walking wounded, that the detective could not disregard. He remembered his first meeting with Perry in the interrogation room at Police Headquarters in Las Vegas—the dwarfish boy-man seated in the metal chair, his small booted feet not quite brushing the floor. And when Dewey now opened his eyes, that is what he saw: the same childish feet, tilted, dangling.

Dewey had imagined that with the deaths of Smith and Hickock, he   33
would experience a sense of climax, release, of a design justly completed. Instead, he discovered himself recalling an incident of almost a year ago, a casual encounter in Valley View Cemetery, which, in retrospect, had somehow for him more or less ended the Clutter case.

The pioneers who founded Garden City were necessarily a Spartan peo-   34
ple, but when the time came to establish a formal cemetery, they were determined, despite arid soil and the troubles of transporting water, to create a rich contrast to the dusty streets, the austere plains. The result, which they named Valley View, is situated above the town on a plateau of modest altitude. Seen today, it is a dark island lapped by the undulating surf of surrounding wheat fields—a good refuge from a hot day, for there are many cool paths unbrokenly shaded by trees planted generations ago.

One afternoon the previous May, a month when the fields blaze with the   35 green-gold fire of half-grown wheat, Dewey had spent several hours at Valley View weeding his father's grave, an obligation he had too long neglected.

The graves of the Clutter family, four graves gathered under a single gray stone, lie in a far corner of the cemetery—beyond the trees, out in the sun, almost at the wheat field's bright edge. As Dewey approached them, he saw that another visitor was already there: a willowy girl with white-gloved hands, a smooth cap of dark-honey hair, and long, elegant legs. She smiled at him, and he wondered who she was. 36

"Have you forgotten me, Mr. Dewey? Susan Kidwell [childhood friend of Nancy Clutter]." 37

He laughed; she joined him. "Sue Kidwell. I'll be darned." He hadn't seen her since the trial; she had been a child then. "How are you? How's your mother?" 38

"Fine, thank you. She's still teaching music at the Holcomb School." 39

"Haven't been that way lately. Any changes?" 40

"Oh, there's some talk about paving the streets. But you know Holcomb. Actually, I don't spend much time there. This is my junior year at K.U.," she said, meaning the University of Kansas. "I'm just home for a few days." 41

"That's wonderful, Sue. What are you studying?" 42

"Everything. Art, mostly. I love it. I'm really happy." She glanced across the prairie. "Nancy and I planned to go to college together. We were going to be roommates. I think about it some times. Suddenly, when I'm very happy, I think of all the plans we made." 43

Dewey looked at the gray stone inscribed with four names, and the date of their death: November 15, 1959. "Do you come here often?" 44

"Once in a while. Gosh, the sun's strong." She covered her eyes with tinted glasses. . . . "Do you have the time? Oh," she cried, when he told her it was past four, "I've got to run! But it was nice to have seen you, Mr. Dewey." 45

"And nice to have seen you, Sue. Good luck," he called after her as she disappeared down the path, a pretty girl in a hurry, her smooth hair swinging, shining—just such a young woman as Nancy might have been. Then, starting home, he walked toward the trees, and under them, leaving behind him the big sky, the whisper of wind voices in the wind-bent wheat. 46

MUSINGS

Capote depicts a moving picture of the hangings of the two men, as well as the touching scene of the prosecutor at the graveyard where his father and the murdered family, the Clutters, are buried. Capote never tells the reader what Dewey's feelings are, but they come through quite clearly, particularly in the graveyard scene, by what he and other people say and do.

Think about an event that has moved you deeply but try to imagine how someone else might view it. Write an account of the incident from that person's viewpoint.

CAROLYN G. HEILBRUN (1926–)

The Education of a Woman: The Life of Gloria Steinem *is written by Carolyn Heilbrun, an emerita professor at Columbia University. Heilbrun is a biographer, feminist, and outstanding Victorian scholar who manages to write successful mysteries under a pseudonym.*

Gloria Steinem is a writer and political activist, a leader in the women's rights movement. After obtaining a degree from Smith College in 1956, Steinem studied in India at the Universities of Delhi and Calcutta. After the success of her article "I Was a Playboy Bunny," for which she worked undercover at a Playboy Club, she turned to journalism, publishing in a number of prestigious magazines. After producing a weekly column for New York Magazine, *she became involved in the feminist movement. Because of her journalism experience, Steinem was able to assist in the first issue of* Ms., *a magazine dealing with women's issues.*

Steinem remained committed to Ms. as it went on to become the voice of the feminist movement. Steinem serves as a role model for young women in the movement and maintains her belief that equality for women will result in equality and wholeness for men as well. Her writings include a number of essay collections and an insightful biography of Marilyn Monroe, for whom she felt great sympathy and understanding. She also wrote Revolution from Within: A Book of Self-Esteem, *in which she examined her own feelings about the feminist movement.*

The following chapter from Heilbrun's biography describes Steinem's determination to make her own decisions and take charge of her life.

Gloria Steinem:
The Transforming Interlude

At the end of the summer Steinem went to London, there to await her India visa. The visa did not come for three months, during which time Steinem worked illegally as a waitress at a coffee shop and spent a lonely Christmas. But a lonely Christmas was the least of it.

She had not been long in London when she discovered that she was pregnant. At the time she told no one, not even Jane Bird Nissen, the Smith classmate in whose home in Chelsea she was living. She did not tell Blair, who learned of the pregnancy only many years later. Certainly she did not tell her mother—with whom, in any case, she did not discuss her sex life—until sixteen years later, when she was about to sign her name to a list in *Ms.* magazine of those who declared they had had abortions. Desperate, but clearly intent on dealing with the matter alone, she even for a time, and uniquely in her life, contemplated suicide.

After falling in love with Chotzinoff, Steinem had gotten a diaphragm   3
in Northampton by telling the doctor she was going to be married. (Contraceptives were still difficult to acquire in Massachusetts, a state politically dominated by the Catholic Church.) When she broke the engagement, she discarded the diaphragm. She slept with Blair again, however, in the fall of that year, for reasons of long-standing sexual attraction.

In London she went to a G.P., Dr. John E. Sharpe, a man she has always   4
remembered with gratitude. She later discovered he was the Sitwells' doctor, but she had picked his name out of the telephone directory only because he was near the home of her hosts, the Nissens. Dr. Sharpe seemed quite old, at least to her at that time, and his office was one room filled with books, old carpets, and a gas grate you put pennies into. He was kind, and gave her a prescription to bring on her period if she was not pregnant, but of course she was.

After many terrifying weeks, Steinem met "a very egocentric and ag-   5
gressive American playwright at a party who, just in passing, was complaining about how many of the actresses in his play he had to get abortions for. That was how I learned it was possible in England with the written permission of two doctors saying something like this would be bad for one's health."

So she went back to Dr. Sharpe, who, after some hesitation, agreed to   6
be one of the two and reluctantly enlisted another doctor, a Harley Street woman surgeon, to perform the abortion. The surgeon was rather brusque and made it clear that she was participating only because of Dr. Sharpe. From this Steinem concluded that he was the one taking the risk, which increased her gratitude to him. The woman surgeon, whose name Steinem has forgotten, was memorable for her person, if not for her kindness. She wore a fashionable suit and smoked a cigarette in a long cigarette holder; not friendly, she said she hoped Steinem would use birth control in the future, especially in India. Nonetheless, she was good at her job, and Steinem, after a few days in bed taking pills for the bleeding, and telling her classmate she'd hurt her back, was fine. Dr. Sharpe, compassionate as the woman surgeon was not, asked of Steinem, as he signed the necessary paper, only that she never tell anyone and that she promise to do what she really wanted with her life. She promised that she would, and did not tell until after his death. The abortion, done at the last possible moment because of the difficulty in finding another doctor, cost Steinem almost half of the thousand dollars she had accumulated for her arrival in India.

Without question, the abortion, and the decision to take charge of her   7
own life and to speak of the matter to no one, indicated a newfound self-

sufficiency, a sense that her destiny could be in her own hands. It is tempting, in the light of her mother's Theosophy, to wonder at the apparent evidence of karma in providing Steinem not only with this, at that time, extremely unusual opportunity to travel throughout India and crystallize her emerging social convictions, but also with the chance to take upon herself total responsibility for her own actions. As she was later to observe, this was "the first time I stopped passively accepting whatever happened to me and took responsibility." It seems clear that this sharp need for responsibility and sense of commitment made even more significant the Indian adventure and its consequences. She would write, in a 1989 article for *Ms.*: "My own [abortion] had taken place in a time of such isolation, illegality, and fear that afterward, I did my best to just forget," but to deal with what must be dealt with and then to put it behind one are maneuvers indicative of maturity.

In January the visa came and she was off. At the time, of course, the decision to spend the greater part of a year in India had been a long and agonizing one, "all the time praying it wasn't a slow-boat-to-China, escape-type decision," as she wrote to David Shaber, a theater instructor from Smith who had become a friend. As it turned out, she would discover in India the political focus of her life; she would also learn that neither marriage nor the romantic plot was for her, although none of these discoveries would become palpable for some years.

Steinem set off across Europe, with a brief stop in Paris, a return visit to Geneva, and a hectic stop in Athens. On February 4, 1957, she stepped out of the plane in Bombay, as she put in a letter to Shaber. "all wool-clad and uncertain, to find sultry moonlight and staggering whiffs of jasmine and India." From that first whiff, she was entranced.

From Bombay she flew to New Delhi, where she joined Kayla Achter. They were enrolled in the University of Delhi for three months, during which time they became acclimated and agreed that they liked each other better occasionally than as constant companions; Steinem had already sensed that it would not be with other Westerners that she would discover India. On her own, she learned to wear a sari—"more a way of life than a dress"—and attended classes. From New Delhi she and Achter took one last shared trip to Mussoorie, a hill station in the Himalayas for two weeks of, as she put it in a letter to Shaber, "being still and just being." Then she went on alone to Calcutta.

By this time she was already struggling with a lack of money and the difficulty of dealing with what money she could earn in India. TWA, for example, for which she had written a travel brochure, paid her with a check, but she didn't have a checking account, and the check couldn't be paid over to any other person. And so it went. Except for news of India, money would continue to be the principal subject in letters to her family—how she earned it, how much they were sending, even the need to wash new clothes before sending them to India, because new clothes would be subject to tariff.

Steinem's preoccupation with money was due in the first place to the plain fact that she hadn't enough to get along on. She also indulged it in part to satisfy her mother, whose obsession with money began in a working-class family, intensified after her marriage to Leo, and only became greater with time. Money was scarce both at home and in India, and Steinem was constantly aware of the financial struggles of her family. It is certainly likely that the way of life Steinem adopted after she returned to the United States and went to work—a way exactly like her father's, without a regular nine-to-five job, a regular place of work, a budget, savings, or the payment of taxes—was an unconscious rejection of her mother's unabated if realistic anxiety about money.   12

To support herself, Steinem helped an Indian man design sandals for export, and she posed in a few advertisements for saris, toothpaste, shampoo, and cold cream, for which she was paid in rupees. She also wrote "The Thousand Indias" for the tourist bureau of the Indian government, which they later published as individual essays though never, as was originally proposed, as a book.   13

Steinem found it difficult to write her fellowship reports, however, because they were supposed to be for a Western audience about the "mysterious East," and she didn't find India mysterious; she felt oddly at home there. She had been warned by author Santha Rama Rau, whom she had visited in New York, to stay away from the Westernized parts of India, from the country clubs, café society, the well-to-do, the sophisticated those, in short, who took no part in the Indian life she sought—a warning that was hardly necessary. During her time in New Delhi she darkened her brown hair to go with the saris that young Indian women at the university would bring her to wear. Putting on the Bermuda shorts she had been given by her classmates at Smith (to wear instead of her cut-off jeans) had been like joining the enemy; putting on the saris was like joining friends. Since she had always identified with the least privileged, she found herself easily at home in India. By the 1980s, India seemed to have become a necessary stop on the itinerary of the diligent traveler, but that was far from true three decades earlier. In the 1950s there were few tourists interested in the non-Westernized parts of the country. For weeks at a time Steinem often saw no Westerners at all.   14

Steinem had, on arriving in India, "revirginated" herself, as she would later put it. Her practice of revirgination in India—that is, of allowing the assumption that she was a virgin—had to do both with the protection virginity offered and with the Toledo knowledge that once a woman "lost"   15 her virginity—or let it be known that her virginity was lost—she was ruined, or at least fair game. Steinem was not without a number of pursuing men, met and remet in India, but she consummated love affairs with none of them. ("Nick," a journalism student, one of the men in love with her, as his many letters testify, was, like Harish Kapur—also attracted to her sexually—conventional and would not sleep with a virgin.) Perhaps most important, however, was the conviction that, whether or not she felt that what she was experiencing was a kind of novitiate, sexual activity was not supposed to be part of a single woman's life in India.

After Calcutta, where she stayed about a month, Steinem set off south- [16] ward to Madras, having been told by Indians that this was the "real India." She made her third-class way by railroad through the South, savoring it all. Women were still taken care of in India, she wrote, meaning that women were given their own third-class car on the railroads, so that they could be safe from male attentions. During her trips in these cars, Steinem was repeatedly asked how many children she had, and when she said none, the immediate response would be: How do you manage it? Indira Gandhi reported the same experience to Steinem when they met years later. Asked how many children she had, Indira Gandhi would say "two," and poor women in similar railroad cars would ask her how she had limited herself to that number. Except for some handing down of traditional methods, women in India had little access to birth control, or could use it only if they could discover a method their husbands would be unaware of.

Steinem came finally to Gandhigram, where, as she had hoped, she met [17] up with a group of Gandhi's followers, who were preparing to walk through the Ramnad area to try to stop the caste riots, in which villages were burned and people killed because of caste tensions and the politicians who took advantage of them. The riots went largely unreported in the American papers; and news of them was also embargoed in India.

Gandhi had been campaigning, as Steinem reported in *Revolution from* [18] *Within,* for all castes "to be respected as one, all religions as one. He literally turned the hierarchy on its head, not by giving orders but by himself making the bottom rung his standard of living. He led by example."

Teams walked through the villages and invited people to come to meet- [19] ings and to make peace. There were too few women for the teams; women in the Hindu villages wouldn't come to meetings unless a woman was present, so at least one woman was needed with each team. That woman could also go into the women's quarters to invite them to the meeting. Steinem discovered an Indian from Delhi was as foreign in this area as a white person, so she was taken along.

Steinem had been told, upon joining the teams, that she could walk [20] many miles a day with a sari, a towel, a cup, and a comb. She found a freedom in having so few possessions, a freedom that would be for many years reflected in her style of living amid boxes and inadequate furnishings. Only with her inner revolution at fifty did this attitude change. But even then, she did not feel protective of her possessions, and would share them or give them away with ease.

And so in India she lived on what the villagers gave her, slept on mats in the women's quarters, washed in streams, and let her wet sari dry on her. The team set out, walking from five to eleven in the morning, sleeping through the midday heat, and then continuing from four to eleven at night. Each time they got to a village that had been burned and silenced, they held a meeting to say that people knew and cared about the village's plight, and to allow a place to talk about fears and discover facts instead of rumors, thus interrupting the chain of revenge. Steinem, as one of the speakers, developed a "sort of speech" on these subjects—speechifying was something she would not take up again for over ten years, and then with trepidation—that was simultaneously translated into a kind of Tamil. Then they would sing songs, and the team would be on its way again.   21

Women whose children had been tortured before their eyes brought Steinem rice and said they "had never thought anyone outside knew or cared." Steinem wrote this to David Shaber; it reads now as a prophecy of what she would be doing for most of the seventies and eighties, in grass-roots America. As she herself later phrased it, she remembered India as the first time in her life when she lived completely in the present, when neither the past nor the future impeded her enchantment with "now." "My sandals were tied on with thongs, I was bathed in streams and rubbed in coconut oil like an Indian girl, and I was hopelessly lost in caring for these people, those ageless, suffering, dignified people."   22

At last, her feet gave out. Blisters had become sores and the sores had become infected. When she reached a village with a doctor, he took one look, gave her penicillin, and told her to stay put. The others left her behind to stay with the doctor and his family, to sleep on clean straw and recover. She went back, finally, the way she had come, but this time by ox cart and bus, to Madurai. Then she traveled through the mountains to Trivandrum on the Malabar coast of Kerala, the only Indian state to vote the communists in, as well as the most literate, egalitarian, and matrilineal, though "entirely too beautiful to worry about politics, definitely Gauguin territory." She found she could live very well for fifty cents a day.   23

Thanks to assignments to write a brochure for a documentary film company and to do some travel pamphlets and newspaper supplements, she avoided carrying out an earlier decision to borrow money in order to get home. Some of these projects worked out; most did not. And she was past her first year in India.   24

Throughout the greater part of her Indian adventure Steinem was alone, in the sense of not having a constant or even intermittent Western   25 traveling companion. She found her way among people who, when she returned to the United States, would seem less strange to her than the segregated, bourgeois, consumer-oriented citizens of her own country. In India she had seen much of the huge subcontinent, met many people who would remain her friends, tried many jobs, had many adventures. As she reported in the Smith College *Sophian,* with that characteristic dullness apparently endemic to academic newspapers, "The longer I was in India, the more grateful I was for the first advantage of a small, personally administered fellowship such as mine: I was not confined for nine months of the year to one university in one part of a vast subcontinent. India, almost as much as Europe, is many countries in one, and I spent three or four months in several areas and several universities to get a realistic picture of the whole as well as to do research on my own project and special interests."

The truth was far more profound, indeed pivotal. As Steinem recog- 26
nized at the time of her sixtieth birthday, India was the event that marked "before" and "after" for her. And by the time she was sixty, she would find herself ready, as she had not been nearly forty years before, to report the radical advice, encapsulated in sayings she had learned from followers of Gandhi, and from the leader of her Gandhian team as it moved among the villagers:

> If you do something the people care about, the people will take care of you.
> If you want people to listen to you, you have to listen to them.
> If you hope people will change how they live, you have to know how they live.

She remembered another aphorism from that time: "If you want people 27
to see you, you have to sit down with them eye-to-eye."

MUSINGS

This selection demonstrates the events that changed Steinem's life, a period that she calls "the transforming interlude." Heilbrun concludes with several aphorisms that Steinem remembers from her sojourn in India.

Select one of those aphorisms and apply it to someone you know—a public figure, a member of your family, or a friend. Or, write about a transforming interlude or incident in the life of someone you know.

JOAN PEYSER (1931–)

Although conducting was his strongest talent, Leonard Bernstein was also a talented concert pianist and composer. He wrote three symphonies, two operas, and numerous scores for films and musicals, including West Side Story. *Later made into a movie, this light opera brought a new audience to his music. He was eager to bring serious music to people and wrote five books about the enjoyment of music, an idea that permeated all of his work. Best known as a conductor, he was the first American to head a major orchestra, the New York Philharmonic, for which he directed nearly a thousand concerts. During his tenure concert attendance more than doubled. One supporter commented that "No one before or since Bernstein has been so effective— artistically and commercially—in proselytizing and bringing alive serious music to a mass audience." At least 10 universities bestowed honorary degrees on him. In addition to several awards that he received for his books, he was granted the Lifetime Achievement Grammy Award and the Gold Medal from the American Academy of Arts and Letters in 1985.*

The following selection from his biography was written by Joan Peyser, a critically acclaimed biographer who served as editor of The Musical Quarterly *for seven years. It chronicles early influences on Bernstein, both good and bad.*

Leonard Bernstein:
Beginnings for a Musical Genius

One day in the mid-1950s, after Leonard Bernstein had conducted a 1 concert at Tanglewood, Sam Bernstein, his father, told a reporter, "Every genius had a handicap; Lenny had a father."

Sam Bernstein was wrong. He was no handicap. In fact he behaved in a 2 way that was conducive to his son's establishing his great career. Throughout history there have been musical geniuses who have felt harsh resistance from their fathers. Gentle support appears to induce indolence, while the father who insults, degrades, humiliates his son appears to stimulate the aggression necessary for the combat inherent in a life in the arts.

In the eighteenth century Handel had such a father; in the nineteenth 3 Schumann did. But in the twentieth, where rebellion has characterized so much of the tone of the art itself, the negative father is almost the rule. Varèse's father locked the piano, covered the instrument with a shroud, and threw away the key. Boulez had a father almost as intransigent. Encouraging his son to enter engineering, he put every possible obstacle in his musical path. Stravinsky's father, a bass singer, sent his son to law school. It was only after the elder Stravinsky died that Igor left law to study composition.

Sam Bernstein had even more reason than most to fight his son's choice of career. In 1908 at sixteen Sam had fled from his family in the Ukraine for a better life in the United States. At home he had known Jews as musicians only as *klezmers*. strolling players who performed for weddings and bar mitzvahs in exchange for a few kopecks, some food, or a night's lodging. Sam Bernstein refused to believe that he had gone through three weeks in the filthy steerage of a ship, hard work at the Fulton Fish Market in New York, menial chores in a Hartford, Connecticut, barbershop, and an aggressive career building a beauty supply business in Boston so that his firstborn son could spend his days playing piano "under a palm tree in some cocktail lounge."

Sam would often tell Leonard that it was all right if "you were a Koussevitzky, a Toscanini, a Rachmaninoff, but how many of these people are there around anyhow?" He did not have the slightest idea of the size of his son's talent. Well into the years of Leonard's success, he would ask his son's friends and colleagues, "Do you think he has something in him? Do you think this success can last?" Such an attitude is not unique. Stravinsky's mother chided her son for not "recognizing his betters, like Scriabin," and she did not hear *Le Sacre du Printemps,* one of the pathbreaking works of the century, until its twenty-fifth anniversary performance, a year before she died. Even then she told friends she did not expect to like it, that he did not write "her kind of music."

But every artist needs support from somewhere. Stravinsky's came from a cousin. Bernstein was more fortunate: He had the unqualified love of his sister, Shirley, and his mother, Jennie.

Jennie Bernstein had suffered the same kind of hard early life as Sam. She came to the United States at eight, and began to work full time in a factory at twelve. Jennie's mother, Pearl Resnick, wanted her daughter to marry Sam. He was smart, ambitious, religious, and had already shown a talent for making money. At first Jennie resisted his attentions. But she changed her mind when Sam was drafted during World War I and she thought he would have to fight in the war. When he returned home a few days later, discharged because of bad eyesight, she was so pleased to see him that she married him. They rented a small apartment in Mattapan, an economically depressed suburb of Boston.

Good marriages are rarely built on such moments. Sam and Jennie's was particularly bad. Visitors to their home in the 1930s remark on the constant fighting, the absence of mutual consideration, the joylessness between the couple. Because the tone of the marriage was angry from the start, Jennie left Sam to be with her mother in nearby Lawrence when it came time to give birth to their first child.

When the boy was born on August 25, 1918, Sam was still at home in Mattapan. Jennie's mother, a strong-willed woman, insisted he be named Louis, like her brother, for their father. Because Jennie and Sam preferred Leonard, that is what they called him. So the boy, during his first five years, did not know his legal name. When he first attended kindergarten, the teacher asked "Louis Bernstein" to stand up. Recalling the incident recently, Bernstein said he had looked around the room for a boy with the same last name as his. But the teacher kept pointing at him. When he returned home and asked his mother about what had happened, she admitted his real name was Louis. From then until he turned sixteen, when he applied for his first driver's license and changed his name legally, all of Bernstein's report cards and official documents bore the name "Louis."

On hearing this story from Bernstein, someone suggested that the early confusion surrounding his name may well account for a life that he himself has characterized as schizophrenic. He is, after all, known to be torn between composing and conducting, between art music and pop, between hetero- and homosexuality. Could these profound conflicts be traced to an identity crisis in his formative years?

This remark was delivered as something of a joke, but Bernstein appropriated the diagnosis. Weeks later, on his sixty-fifth birthday, which was being celebrated in his "hometown" of Lawrence, Massachusetts, he told a stadium audience of about twelve thousand people that his real name had been Louis, that he had always been called Lenny, and that the early confusion accounted for his schizophrenic ways.

Now in her eighties, Bernstein's mother speaks of him with adoration and pride: "Scratch any part of him and he oozes with talent. Where do you get a musician who could also write the Harvard lectures? In his apartment there are walls of books. He reads the Talmud, reads everything you can imagine. There are thousands of books on psychiatry alone.

"Leonard is a great musician. He is a Renaissance man. To write a book about him is like writing a book on Einstein."

Her son's birth provided Jennie with a ray of hope in the midst of her unhappiness with Sam. And her attentions to the infant Lenny increased when it became apparent that his health was frail. "From the beginning," his brother, Burton, writes, "he was special. Asthmatic, sensitive, intelligent, he left a deep impression on everyone, whether because of his chronic wheezing or because of his unmistakable precocity. Jennie knew she had an unusual child: 'When he was a sickly little boy and he'd turn blue from asthma, Sam and I were scared to death,' she has said. 'Every time he had an attack, we thought he was going to die. I would be up all night with steam kettles and hot towels, helping him to breathe. If Lenny so much as sneezed, we would turn pale with worry. . . . But sickly or not, Lenny was such a brilliant boy—always the leader of his gang, always the best in school.'"

Bernstein's own memories of his leadership days do not extend back to grammar school, which he remembers with some pain. He says he was not only thin and sickly but terrified of anti-Semitic neighborhood gangs. However, he recalls that he changed virtually overnight when an aunt in the process of a divorce, left an old upright piano in the Bernstein house. The aunt, Clara, was Sam's sister, a woman the older Bernstein could not abide. Throughout her life he called her "crazy Clara," and she became a favorite of the son, who claims her singing could shatter glass.

It was Leonard's discovery of the piano that he credits with transforming him from a frail nobody into a powerful human being, capable of conquering the world. Jennie says she was aware of her son's connection to music long before Aunt Clara's piano arrived: "When he was a little toddler creeping around on the floor and he heard music, he would stop on a dime and cry. We rented part of a summer house when he was almost two. We didn't have access to the living room but there was a piano in it and whenever someone played it, Lenny would press his ear to the wall.

"Lenny always had colds and had to stay inside. When he was about four or five he would play an imaginary piano on his windowsill. When he finally got a piano, he did what he now says he did: made love to it all the time."

There were other musical experiences as well, though hardly those of a Schoenberg or Stravinsky. In fact it is the absence of the kind of musical education and experience that every young European goes through and the plethora of idiosyncratic American ones that account for the freshness and vitality of Bernstein's music at its best.

By the late 1920s, the Bernsteins did own a phonograph but the only music Bernstein remembers coming from it was "Barney Google" and "Oh, by Jingo," the hit songs of the day. On his aunt's piano, he started to reconstruct the popular melodies in his head. "Blue Skies" was one of them. But he asked his parents for lessons and began to study with a neighbor's daughter, Frieda Karp, who charged a dollar a lesson. She gave him such beginning pieces as "On to Victory" and "The Mountain Belle." Bernstein says it was then he began to thrive, put on weight, and make friends with his schoolmates.

Leonard learned to read music quickly and before long was playing far better than Frieda Karp, who soon married and moved to California. At twelve, Leonard moved on to the New England Conservatory of Music, where he was assigned to Susan Williams, who charged three dollars an hour. That move enraged Sam. He interpreted it correctly: His son was serious about music.

MUSINGS

This excerpt relates the ways in which Bernstein's father discouraged him in his music but, on the other hand, emphasizes the support of his sister and his strong-willed mother. Although he suffered from ill health, Bernstein continued to read and study music. His mother is quoted throughout this excerpt and recalled that when Bernstein "finally got a piano, he did what he now says he did: made love to it all the time."

Notice how the frequent quotes, presumably from conversations with Bernstein's mother and Bernstein himself, enliven the writing. Try writing a biographical sketch based on interviews with your subject and his or her friends and associates, and use their quotes in your writing.

Maxine Hong Kingston (1940–)

"A blend of myth, legend, history and autobiography," is the way Maxine Hong Kingston creates "a genre of her own invention," writes Susan Currier in the Dictionary of Literary Biography, 1980. *Kingston's writings are generally classified as nonfiction, but critics recognize that her books are based on the "history and myth" passed on to her by her family and other Chinese-American "story-talkers" in the California community where she grew up.* The Woman Warrior, Memoirs of a Girlhood among Ghosts *(1976), from which the following selection is taken, won a number of awards. It demonstrates the often difficult blending and sometimes clashing of two widely divergent cultures with which a Chinese-American woman growing up in the United States must deal.* Washington Post *critic Henry Allen describes it as a "wild mix of myth, memory, history and a lucidity that verges on the eerie" as Kingston describes "their experiences as women, as Chinese coming to America and as Americans." Her mother dominates this book, and her father figures strongly in Kingston's subsequent* China Men, *which treated the bicultural problems of Chinese men living in North America and Hawaii.*

No Name Woman: My Aunt

Adultery is extravagance. Could people who hatch their own chicks and 1
eat the embryos and the heads for delicacies and boil the feet in vinegar for party food, leaving only the gravel, eating even the gizzard lining—could such people engender a prodigal aunt? To be a woman, to have a daughter in starvation time was a waste enough. My aunt could not have been the lone romantic who gave up everything for sex. Women in the old China did not choose. Some man had commanded her to lie with him and be his secret evil. I wonder whether he masked himself when he joined the raid on her family.

Perhaps she encountered him in the fields or on the mountain where 2
the daughters-in-law collected fuel. Or perhaps he first noticed her in the marketplace. He was not a stranger because the village housed no strangers. She had to have dealings with him other than sex. Perhaps he worked an adjoining field, or he sold the cloth for the dress she sewed and wore. His demand must have surprised, then terrified her. She obeyed him; she always did as she was told.

When the family found a young man in the next village to be her hus- 3 band, she stood tractably beside the best rooster, his proxy, and promised before they met that she would be his forever. She was lucky that he was her age and she would be the first wife, an advantage secure now. The night she first saw him, he had sex with her. Then he left for America. She had almost forgotten what he looked like. When she tried to envision him, she only saw the black and white face in the group photograph the men had taken before leaving.

The other man was not, after all, much different from her husband. They both gave orders: she followed. "If you tell your family, I'll beat you. I'll kill you. Be here again next week." No one talked sex, ever. And she might have separated the rapes from the rest of living if only she did not have to buy her oil from him or gather wood in the same forest. I want her fear to have lasted just as long as rape lasted so that the fear could have been contained. No drawn-out fear. But women at sex hazarded birth and hence lifetimes. The fear did not stop but permeated everywhere. She told the man, "I think I'm pregnant." He organized the raid against her.

On nights when my mother and father talked about their life back home, sometimes they mentioned an "outcast table" whose business they still seemed to be settling, their voices tight. In a commensal tradition, where food is precious, the powerful older people made wrongdoers eat alone. Instead of letting them start separate new lives like the Japanese, who could become samurais and geishas, the Chinese family, faces averted but eyes glowering sideways, hung on to the offenders and fed them leftovers. My aunt must have lived in the same house as my parents and eaten at an outcast table. My mother spoke about the raid as if she had seen it, when she and my aunt, a daughter-in-law to a different household, should not have been living together at all. Daughters-in-law lived with their husbands' parents, not their own; a synonym for marriage in Chinese is "taking a daughter-in-law." Her husband's parents could have sold her, mortgaged her, stoned her. But they had sent her back to her own mother and father, a mysterious act hinting at disgraces not told me. Perhaps they had thrown her out to deflect the avengers.

· · ·

If my aunt had betrayed the family at a time of large grain yields and peace, when many boys were born, and wings were being built on many houses, perhaps she might have escaped such severe punishment. But the men—hungry, greedy, tired of planting in dry soil, cuckolded—had been forced to leave the village in order to send food-money home. There were ghost plagues, bandit plagues, wars with the Japanese, floods. My Chinese brother and sister had died of an unknown sickness. Adultery, perhaps only a mistake during good times, became a crime when the village needed food.

The round moon cakes and round doorways, the round tables of grad-   7
uated size that fit one roundness inside another, round windows and rice
bowls—these talismans had lost their power to warn this family of the law:
a family must be whole, faithfully keeping the descent line by having sons
to feed the old and the dead who in turn look after the family. The villagers came to show my aunt and lover-in-hiding a broken house. The villagers were speeding up the circling of events because she was too
shortsighted to see that her infidelity had already harmed the village, that
waves of consequences would return unpredictably, sometimes in disguise,
as now, to hurt her. This roundness had to be made coin-sized so that she
would see its circumference: punish her at the birth of her baby. Awaken
her to the inexorable. People who refused fatalism because they could invent small resources insisted on culpability. Deny accidents and wrest fault
from the stars.

After the villagers left, their lanterns now scattering in various direc-   8
tions toward home, the family broke their silence and cursed her. "Aiaa,
we're going to die. Death is coming. Death is coming. Look what you've
done. You've killed us. Ghost! Dead Ghost! Ghost! You've never been
born." She ran out into the fields, far enough from the house so that she
could no longer hear their voices, and pressed herself against the earth, her
own land no more. When she felt the birth coming, she thought that she
had been hurt. Her body seized together. "They've hurt me too much,"
she thought. "This is gall, and it will kill me." With forehead and knees
against the earth, her body convulsed and then relaxed. She turned on her
back, lay on the ground. The black well of sky and stars went out and out
forever; her body and her complexity seemed to disappear. She was one of
the stars, a bright dot in blackness, without home, without a companion,
in eternal cold and silence. An agoraphobia rose in her, speeding higher
and higher, bigger and bigger; she would not be able to contain it; there
would be no end to fear.

Flayed, unprotected against space, she felt pain return, focusing her   9
body. This pain chilled her—a cold, steady kind of surface pain. Inside,
spasmodically, the other pain, the pain of the child, heated her. For hours
she lay on the ground, alternately body and space. Sometimes a vision of
normal comfort obliterated reality: she saw the family in the evening gam-
bling at the dinner table, the young people massaging their elder's backs.
She saw them congratulating one another, high joy on the mornings the
rice shoots came up. When these pictures burst, the stars drew yet further
apart. Black space opened.

She got to her feet to fight better and remembered that old-fashioned   10
women gave birth in their pigsties to fool the jealous, pain-dealing gods,
who do not snatch piglets. Before the next spasms could stop her, she ran
to the pigsty, each step a rushing out into emptiness. She climbed over the

fence and knelt in the dirt. It was good to have a fence enclosing her, a tribal person alone.

Laboring, this woman who had carried her child as a foreign growth   11
that sickened her every day, expelled it at last. She reached down to touch the hot, wet, moving mass, surely smaller than anything human, and could feel that it was human after all—fingers, toes, nails, nose. She pulled it up on to her belly, and it lay curled there, butt in the air, feet precisely tucked one under the other. She opened her loose shirt and buttoned the child inside. After resting, it squirmed and thrashed and she pushed it up to her breast. It turned its head this way and that until it found her nipple. There, it made little snuffling noises. She clenched her teeth at its preciousness, lovely as a young calf, a piglet, a little dog.

She may have gone to the pigsty as a last act of responsibility: she would   12
protect this child as she had protected its father. It would look after her soul, leaving supplies on her grave. But how would this tiny child without family find her grave when there would be no marker for her anywhere, neither in the earth nor the family hall? No one would give her a family hall name. She had taken the child with her into the wastes. At its birth the two of them had felt the same raw pain of separation, a wound that only the family pressing tight could close. A child with no descent line would not soften her life but only trail after her, ghostlike, begging her to give it purpose. At dawn the villagers on their way to the fields would stand around the fence and look.

Full of milk, the little ghost slept. When it awoke, she hardened her   13
breasts against the milk that crying loosens. Toward morning she picked up the baby and walked to the well.

Carrying the baby to the well shows loving. Otherwise abandon it.   14
Turn its face into the mud. Mothers who love their children take them along. It was probably a girl; there is some hope of forgiveness for boys.

"Don't tell anyone you had an aunt. Your father does not want to hear   15
her name. She has never been born." I have believed that sex was unspeakable and words so strong and fathers so frail that "aunt" would do my father mysterious harm. I have thought that my family, having settled among immigrants who had also been their neighbors in the ancestral land, needed to clean their name, and a wrong word would incite the kinspeople even here. But there is more to this silence: they want me to participate in her punishment. And I have.

In the twenty years since I heard this story I have not asked for details   16
nor said my aunt's name; I do not know it. People who comfort the dead can also chase after them to hurt them further—a reverse ancestor worship. The real punishment was not the raid swiftly inflicted by the villagers, but the family's deliberately forgetting her. Her betrayal so maddened them, they saw to it that she would suffer forever, even after

death. Always hungry, always needing, she would have to beg food from other ghosts, snatch and steal it from those whose living descendants give them gifts. She would have to fight the ghosts massed at crossroads for the buns a few thoughtful citizens leave to decoy her away from village and home so that the ancestral spirits could feast unharassed. At peace, they could act like gods, not ghosts, their descent lines providing them with paper suits and dresses, spirit money, paper houses, paper automobiles, chicken, meat, and rice into eternity—essences delivered up in smoke and flames, steam and incense rising from each rice bowl. In an attempt to make the Chinese care for people outside the family, Chairman Mao encourages us now to give our paper replicas to the spirits of outstanding soldiers and workers, no matter whose ancestors they may be. My aunt remains forever hungry. Goods are not distributed evenly among the dead.

My aunt haunts me—her ghost drawn to me because now, after fifty years of neglect, I alone devote pages of paper to her, though not origamied into houses and clothes. I do not think she always means me well. I am telling on her, and she was a spite suicide, drowning herself in the drinking water. The Chinese are always very frightened of the drowned one, whose weeping ghost, wet hair hanging and skin bloated, waits silently by the water to pull down a substitute.

17

MUSINGS

Kingston's family disowned her aunt and no one was allowed to mention her name: "The real punishment was not the raid swiftly inflicted by the villagers but the family's deliberately forgetting her." Kingston reverts to Chinese myth by asserting that her aunt would be "always hungry, always needing, she would have to beg food from other ghosts." Instead of the usual paper replicas and spirit money given to the dead, Kingston devotes "pages of paper to her," in an effort to expiate her own and her aunt's guilt.

Kingston blends history and myth in her account. Can you separate the two? Myth usually involves a traditional story with heroes and events that represent basic human truths. Write a story drawn from your culture or from your own family history, combining what you know to be fact and what you suspect to be myth.

ALICE WALKER (1944–)

This biographical sketch was written by Alice Walker as the foreword to Robert Hemenway's Zora Neale Hurston: A Literary Biography *(1977). Walker is a highly respected African-American writer; she is the author of eight novels, the most successful and well-known of which is* The Color Purple. *She won the Pulitzer Prize and the American Book Award for that novel in 1983 and has won other prizes, awards, and grants in recognition of her work. As an active worker in the feminist recovery movement—the rediscovery of women's writings—Walker was influential in the revival of interest in Hurston. Hurston, a folklorist and talented writer, died in poverty, ill and alone, separated from her friends and family.*

In this selection Walker describes Hurston's life and character, defending her against critics who faulted her for accepting grants from "'white folks'" by pointing out that Hurston fought poverty all her life and that "without money in a capitalist society, there is no such thing as independence." Walker is critical, however, of Hurston's autobiography, Dust Tracks on a Road, *faulting her for its "unctuousness" and for her "gratitude and kind words to people one knows she could not have respected." (See the selection from Hurston's autobiography that states her views earlier in this book.) Walker concludes with the justification for recovering Hurston's work: "A people do not throw their geniuses away."*

Zora Neale Hurston: Before Her Time

Zora was funny, irreverent (she was the first to call the Harlem Renaissance literati the "niggerati"), good-looking, and sexy. She once sold hot dogs in a Washington park just to record accurately how the black people who bought them talked. She would go anywhere she had to go—Harlem, Jamaica, Haiti, Bermuda—to find out anything she simply *had* to know. She loved to give parties. Loved to dance. Would wrap her head in scarves as black women in Africa, Haiti, and everywhere else have done for centuries. On the other hand, she loved to wear hats, tilted over one eye, and pants and boots. (I have a photograph of her in pants, boots, and broadbrim hat that was given to me by her brother Everette. She has her foot up on the running board of a car—presumably hers, and bright red—and looks racy.) She would light up a fag—which wasn't done by ladies then (and thank our saints, as a young woman she was never a lady) on the street.

1

Her critics disliked even the "rags" on her head. (They seemed curiously   2
incapable of telling the difference between an African-American queen
and Aunt Jemima.) They disliked her apparent sensuality: the way she
tended to marry or not marry men, but enjoyed them anyway, while never
missing a beat in her work. They hinted slyly that Zora was gay, or at least
bisexual—how else could they account for her drive?—though there is not
a shred of evidence that this was true. The accusation becomes humorous—and, of course, at all times irrelevant—when one considers that
what she *did* write about was some of the most healthily rendered heterosexual loving in our literature. In addition, she talked too much, got
things from white folks (Guggenheims, Rosenwalds, and footstools) much
too easily, was slovenly in her dress, and appeared maddeningly indifferent
to other people's opinions of her. With her easy laughter and her southern
drawl, her belief in doing cullud dancing *authentically,* Zora seemed—
among these genteel "New Negroes" of the Harlem Renaissance—*black.*
No wonder her presence was always a shock. Though almost everyone
agreed she was a delight, not everyone agreed such audacious black delight
was permissible, or, indeed, quite the proper image for the race.

Zora was before her time—in intellectual circles—in the lifestyle she   3
chose. By the sixties everyone understood that black women could wear
beautiful cloths on their beautiful heads and care about the authenticity of
things cullud *and* African. By the sixties it was no longer a crime to receive
financial assistance, in the form of grants and fellowships, for one's work.
(Interestingly, those writers who complained that Zora "got money from
white folks" were often themselves totally supported, down to the food
they ate—or, in Langston Hughes's case, *tried* to eat, after his white "god-
mother" discarded him—by white patrons.) By the sixties, nobody cared
that marriage didn't last forever. No one expected it to. And I do believe
that now, in the seventies, we do not expect (though we may wish and
pray) every black person who speaks to *always* speak *correctly* (since this is
impossible); or if we *do* expect it, we deserve all the silent leadership we are
likely to get.

During the early and middle years of her career Zora was a cultural rev-   4
olutionary simply because she was always herself. Her work, so vigorous
among the rather pallid productions of many of her contemporaries,
comes from the essence of black folklife. During her later years, for reasons
revealed for the first time in this monumental work (as so much is!), she
became frightened of the life she had always dared bravely before. Her
work, too, became reactionary, static, shockingly misguided and timid.
This is especially true of her last novel, *Seraph on the Suwanee,* which is not
even about black people, which is no crime, but *is* about white people who
are bores, which is.

A series of misfortunes battered Zora's spirit and health. And she was   5
broke.

Being broke made all the difference.   6

Without money of one's own in a capitalist society, there is no such   7
thing as independence. This is one of the clearest lessons of Zora's life, and
why I consider the telling of her life a "cautionary tale." We must learn
from it what we can.

Without money, an illness, even a simple one, can undermine the will.   8
Without money, getting into a hospital is problematic, and getting out
without money to pay for the treatment is nearly impossible. Without
money, one becomes dependent on other people who are likely to be—
even in their kindness—erratic in their support and despotic in their expectations of return. Zora was forced to rely, like Tennessee Williams's
Blanche, "on the kindness of strangers." Can anything be more dangerous,
if the strangers are forever in control? Zora, who worked so hard, was
never able to make a living from her work.

She did not complain about not having money. She was not the type.   9
(Several months ago I received a long letter from one of Zora's nieces, a
bright ten-year-old who explained to me that her aunt was so proud that
the only way the family could guess she was ill or without funds was by realizing they had no idea where she was. Therefore, none of the family attended either Zora's sickbed or her funeral.) Those of us who have had
"grants and fellowships from 'white folks'" know this aid is extended in
precisely the way welfare is extended in Mississippi. One is asked, *curtly,*
more often than not: How much do you need *just to survive?* Then one
is—if fortunate—given a third of that. What is amazing is that Zora, who
became a orphan at nine, a runaway at fourteen, a maid and manicurist
(because of necessity and not from love of the work) before she was
twenty, *with one dress,* managed to become Zora Neale Hurston, author
and anthropologist, at all.

For me, the most unfortunate thing Zora ever wrote is her autobiogra-   10
phy. After the first several chapters, it rings false. One begins to hear the
voice of someone whose life required the assistance of too many transitory
"friends." A Taoist proverb states that *to act sincerely with the insincere is
dangerous* (a mistake blacks as a group have tended to make in America).
And so we have Zora sincerely offering gratitude and kind words to people
one knows she could not have respected. But this unctuousness, so out of
character for Zora, is also a result of dependency, a sign of powerlessness,
her inability to pay back her debts with anything but words. They must
have been bitter ones for her. In her dependency, it should be remembered, Zora was not alone. For it is quite true that America does not support or honor us as human beings, let alone as blacks, women, or artists.

We have taken help where it was offered because we are committed to what we do and to the survival of our work. Zora was committed to the survival of her people's cultural heritage as well.

We are a people. A people do not throw their geniuses away. If they do, it is   11
our duty *as witnesses for the future* to collect them again for the sake of our
children. If necessary, bone by bone.

MUSINGS

Walker's biographical essay stresses Hurston's poverty and how it affected
her. Walker blames the falsity of Hurston's autobiography, *Dust Tracks on
the Road,* on her financial need and "her powerlessness, her inability to pay
back her debts with anything but words." Walker then makes the generalization that for all blacks, women, or artists, "America does not support or
honor us as human beings."

Write about an incident in which a lack of money constrained your activities. Try to move from that event to some generalization about the situation.

JOHN MACK FARAGHER (1945–)

*John Mack Faragher's 1992 biography of Daniel Boone (1734–1820) served to cor-
rect earlier versions, which were a mixture of myth, legend, and folklore and which
had brought notoriety and attention to the courageous frontiersman. Faragher carefully based his account on a thorough examination of letters, diaries, and legal records.*

*As a young man, Boone had been happily settled in the Yadkin River Valley, North
Carolina, with his wife, Rebecca Bryan, but the stories told to him by the teamster
John Finley about the Kentucky wilderness haunted him. Finally, Boone could no
longer resist the lure of the frontier. In 1769 Boone "opened the way to the far west by
blazing a trail through the Cumberland Gap." Although he at one time held large
tracts of land, he eventually lost them all through legal technicalities. He then left Kentucky, maintaining that it was getting far too crowded, as "he could hear the sound of
his neighbor's gun." With no money or land, Boone moved to the Upper Louisiana
Territory, now Missouri, and spent his remaining years in the home of his son and
near his large extended family.*

*The following excerpt relates the well-known story, preserved in paintings and
sculptures, of the kidnapping of his daughter and her two cousins by a group of Cherokees and Shawnees and the rescue carried out by Boone and his men. Early pioneers
considered Native Americans "savages" and feared them. Those pioneers failed to realize that they were infringing on what was historically and rightfully Native American
territory. Boone, on the other hand, had befriended the Indians and hunted and
tracked with them. Faragher bases his account on the firsthand reports of some of the
participants in the rescue and those of the girls who passed on their story to their descendants.*

Daniel Boone: The Rescue

On the afternoon of Sunday, July 14, 1776, Jemima Boone and Eliza-   1
beth and Frances Callaway, daughters of Richard Callaway, "tired of the
confinement of the fort," took a canoe out onto the Kentucky River.
Jemima had hurt her foot a few days before, and she wanted to soak it in
the cool river. She "was so fond of playing in the water," her cousin recalled, "her common name was Duck." The other girls went along to
gather flowers and wild grapes along the riverbank. Jemima and Fanny
were thirteen and fourteen, respectively, Betsy was sixteen and already engaged to marry Samuel Henderson, nephew of Richard Henderson.
Jemima would say later that her father had warned her to stay close to the

cabins and never to cross to the opposite shore. The Callaway girls teased her caution: "Perhaps she was more afraid of the yellow boys than she was of disobeying her father." Betsy guided the canoe through the eddies near the sycamore hollow, but suddenly it was caught up by the swift flow of the river. "Mother was an expert hand in managing a canoe," wrote Betsy's daughter, but "the current proved too strong" and the girls found themselves quickly carried downriver, toward the north bank.

A small war party of two Cherokees and three Shawnees, five men in all, were watching the settlement from the timber across the river. They had been in the area for a week or more and already had murdered an isolated farmer some miles away. Now they trailed the progress of the canoe downstream, and when the girls got within a few feet of the north shore, one of the warriors jumped into the river and grabbed the buffalo tug dangling from its bow. Little Fanny Callaway was sitting up front, and seeing the Indian dive in the water, she jumped up; but thinking he was a familiar Indian man who lived among the settlers at Boonesborough, she cried, "Law! Simon, how you scared me!" At almost the same instant she realized her mistake and laid into the warrior's head with the paddle. All three girls began to scream. "Grandmother said she screamed as loud as she could," wrote one of Jemima's descendants, "so her father would pursue them." But silently and swiftly the Indians drew the canoe to shore, where a warrior grabbed the hair of one of the girls, making signs with his knife that indicated clearly what would happen if they did not shut up. Then the Indians pulled them into the woods.

• • •

The alarm was raised by those who heard the girls' cries. One of Callaway's boys came running up to Reid and Floyd, screaming, "The savages have the girls." Within seconds men and women were shouting and running about the settlement. At the sound of the commotion, Boone jumped out of bed, snatched his pantaloons, and hopped into them as he ran along barefoot to the riverbank by the hollow, calling all the while for the men to join him. Samuel Henderson followed, sobbing in terror, his face half covered with shaving soap. Dick Callaway loaded his gun as he ran. Reaching the river, the men saw the canoe, swamped and useless on the opposite shore. Callaway, with his nephew Flanders Callaway, John Holder, the Harts, and a number of others, mounted horses and galloped for the ford of the river about a mile below. As the others stood helpless, twelve-year-old John Gass stripped, courageously dove into the swift-flowing current, and, while the men shouted encouragement, swam to the other shore. Righting the canoe, he paddled it back across. Boone, Floyd, Reid, Samuel Henderson, and William Bailey Smith jumped in and quickly recrossed. A number of men remained behind, to protect the settlement against a possible attack. About an hour of daylight remained as the rescuers ascended the steep bluff on the north side to the trail at the crest of the hill. There "Boone directed us to divide," said Reid, "in order to discover, as soon as possible, the course they had gone." With Floyd and Smith, he went upstream, while Boone and the others went down, where they soon met the horsemen. Here Boone once again counseled a division of forces. Believing that the Indians would be heading north with their captives for the towns in the Ohio country, he urged Callaway and the others to ride hard for the crossing of the Licking River in an attempt to cut them off.

• • •

After their capture, the crying and shrieking girls made every attempt 4
to slow the march of their captors, who pushed and pulled them northward through the woods. Jemima's injured foot caused her to fall, and she then made a point of tripping and sprawling at every opportunity, screaming in mock pain. When it grew dark the Indians made a cold camp and "held a little chat." Then, assembling the girls they "cut their clothes off to the knees, took off their shoes and stockings, and put on moccasins." The girls too had been clothed in their Sunday best, fancy little dresses, bonnets, and wooden-heeled shoes. This preparation was a sure sign that the Indians planned further travel. One of the men was a Cherokee named Scolacutta, known to Americans as Hanging Maw. He knew Boone and his family from their days on the Upper Yadkin or in Tennessee and could speak a little English. Recognizing Jemima by her long black hair, he asked if these were her sisters. Yes, she told him, believing that the Indians might think twice before harming Daniel Boone's daughters. "We have done pretty well for Old Boone this time," Hanging Maw laughed. That they were headed for the Shawnee towns in the Ohio country, he confirmed. The Indians all across the frontier were rising up against the Americans, he told her, and it would not be long before Boonesborough fell. Tying the girls together with rawhide tugs, the Indians retired with neither food nor water. While they slept, the girls strained uselessly at their cords. Jemima remembered a little penknife in her pocket and spent a frustrating night trying in vain to reach it.

The Indians were up before dawn and set a hard pace, refusing now to 5
be held back. When they could the girls broke brush, pulled up vines, anything to leave a track, and when discovered, the Indians threatened them with clubs or knives. There was no pause for rest or drink, and by afternoon they had put twenty-five miles between themselves and Boonesborough. Distraught and exhausted, the girls could hardly move another step, but they had not lost their ingenuity. When they finally paused to rest, one of the Indians went out to scout and came back with a haggard old horse

he had found abandoned in the wild. Harnessing it with a piece of tug, they tried to force the girls onto its back. These three had been practically reared on horseback, but in these circumstances they acted as if they had never before seen a horse. They kept falling off, and by pinching and kicking the poor animal got it to fight back, bucking and threatening with its teeth, which caused the Indians to "laugh and halloo," Jemima would recall later. It was her first indication that they were beginning to relax about being overtaken. She never wavered in her conviction that her father was on their trail, but these signs of Indian self-confidence were disheartening. Abandoning the horse, they pushed on several miles more before it grew dark. The Indians again went without fire, but they did draw water from a stream, and everyone drank; the girls, however, could not force themselves to eat the jerked buffalo tongue the Indians offered to share.

Boone and his men were perhaps ten miles behind the kidnappers at 6
the beginning of the second morning, but the trail was difficult to follow and they made little progress. After some miles, Boone stopped. This would never do, he declared, for the Indians "were making tracks faster than we were." From their general direction he now was certain that the captors were heading for the crossing of the Licking at the Upper Blue Licks, and, according to Reid, "paying no further attention to the trail, he now took a strait course through the woods, with increased speed, followed by the men in perfect silence." Breaking from the tracks made the men uncomfortable, but they could only rely on Boone's woodcraft. Later in the day they crossed the trail of the kidnappers once again, and, finding a sign left by the girls, their spirits revived and their confidence in Boone strengthened.

Both pursuer and pursued were pushing ahead at first light the third 7
day. The Indians forded Hinkston Creek, thirteen miles from the crossing of the Licking, in midmorning. Boone and his men crossed the same creek about an hour later. "Here Boone paused a moment," said Reid, "and remarked that from the course [the Indians] had travelled, he was confident that they had crossed the stream a short distance below." He shifted them northwest, "and strange to say, we had not gone down more than 200 yards before we struck the trail again." The Indians were traveling along a buffalo trace paralleling the Warrior's Path leading to the Upper Blue Licks. Boone set a jogging pace, which the men kept up for three-quarters of an hour. Now the rescuers began to encounter convincing evidence that they were closing in—muddied water at the crossing of a stream, a dead snake along the trail, and finally the carcass of a buffalo calf, recently butchered, blood still oozing from its hump. "The Indians would stop to cook at the first water," said Boone. Then at a branch now known as Bald Eagle Creek, just east of the present town of Sharpsburg, the trail disappeared. Boone divided the party, four men going in each direction. Their

aim, wrote Floyd, was "to get the prisoners without giving the Indians time to murder them." They proceeded without speaking, "no man to touch a trigger until he had received the sign from Boone." Reid had moved twenty or thirty yards downstream and, finding nothing, had turned around when he saw Billy Smith upstream "waving his hand for us to come on."

The Indians had grown confident. Their rear scout saw no evidence of   8 a party approaching from behind, and they were soon to cross the Licking, where they expected to link up with other war parties. They had paused to kill and butcher game and now had made camp, where they were roasting their meat on a spit. In a fine mood, one of them playfully pulled at Betsy's hair while she knelt at the fire warming herself, and she defiantly scooped up a load of hot coals with a piece of bark and dumped them on his moccasins. He hopped around in pain, much to the amusement of the other men, and Hanging Maw, admiring Betsy's spunk, called her "a fine young squaw."

As the spirits of the Indians rose, Betsy's fell. She had tried to buoy up   9 the two younger girls and had maintained her own courage by telling herself that her father would soon appear, but now, as the Indians enjoyed a laugh, she "gave herself up to dispair." Like her sister Fanny and Jemima, Betsy would remember in detail everything that happened during the next few moments. She collapsed on a log about ten steps from the fire, and the two others settled themselves at her feet, resting their heads on her lap. Betsy fell into a routine that must have been commonplace in the crowded conditions of the fort: "She unconsciously was opening their hair, lousing their heads, and shedding a torrent of tears." One or two Indians left the fire to gather fuel, one knelt tending the meat, and another reclined on the ground nearby. Off to the side the sentinel leaned his gun casually against a tree, walked back to the fire to light his pipe, and stood rummaging through his budget, looking for something.

Jemima heard a sound in the brush and saw the Indian at the fire sud-   10 denly look up, stare into the woods, then return to his work. The camp was in a small glen, and, glancing up along the ridge, she suddenly caught a glimpse of her father "creeping upon his breast like a snake." At a distance of a hundred yards their eyes met, and with the implicit language of father and daughter, he signed her to keep still. The other men were assembling on the ridge and were to fire down together, but in the excitement of seeing the camp below, one of them fired prematurely. Fanny had her eyes on the Indian at the campfire. Suddenly "she saw blood burst out of his breast before she heard the gun." He fell head first into the flames, then jumped up, holding his gut, and hobbled off into the brush. "That's Daddy!" Jemima cried. As Boone, Floyd, and another rescuer hurriedly got off their shots, Jemima and Fanny hit the ground, but Betsy leapt to her feet, and one of the Indians aimed his war club at her. "She sensibly felt it touch her head as it passed by," she would tell her children. Raising the war whoop, Boone and the others came charging down the slope while the Indians fled into the cane, as Floyd wrote, "almost naked, some without their mockisons, and no one of them so much as a knife or tomahawk." Betsy ran toward her rescuers. Dressed in the rough woolen matchcoat of one of the Indians, with her dress cut short and her legs exposed, her dark hair loose and disheveled, she was mistaken by one of the Americans for an Indian rushing to engage him, and he clubbed his gun, preparing to bash out her brains. "For God's sake," Boone bawled out, "don't kill her when we've travelled so far to save her."

Boone hollered at Betsy to get down, lest the Indians take to the trees and fire back, but their Indian captors had fled. The men rushed to the other girls and took them in their arms. They looked awful, their clothes torn to shreds, their legs scratched and bleeding, their eyes swollen from tears and lack of sleep. Boone took blankets from the packs and covered them. As the excitement of the moment began to subside, the man who had nearly made the fatal mistake collapsed in sobs. "Thank Almighty Providence, boys," said Boone, "for we have the girls safe. Let's all sit down by them now and have a hearty cry." As Jemima would remember it, "There was not a dry eye in the company." 11

MUSINGS

Faragher states in his introduction that "the record of Daniel Boone largely consists of the stories of humble American men and women, written out laboriously with blunt pencils on scraps of paper, or told aloud in backwoods cabins or around campfires and taken down verbatim by antiquarian collectors."

Write about someone either in the public sphere or in your own family about whom there are stories and legends. Try to reconstruct a faithful picture of the person by using these accounts, together with any public records, such as birth or marriage records and obituaries.

Sy Montgomery (1958–)

Sy Montgomery remarked to the editor of Contemporary Authors *that she writes "to illuminate the lives of nonhuman beings and our relationships with them." In her book* Walking with the Great Apes *(1991), she chronicles the work of three women, Jane Goodall, Dian Fossey, and Birute Galdikas, who scientifically researched the great apes under the guidance of noted anthropologist Louis B. Leakey. Leakey recognized the unique contribution of these women, in contrast with those of the male scientists who had conducted previous studies. The women painstakingly documented the animals' daily activities and familial relationships with feminine insight and sensitivity.*

Fossey, the subject of the following excerpt from Montgomery's book, began her work in what is now Zaire but was forced to flee because of a civil war. She escaped to Rwanda, where she set up camp between two extinct volcanoes and established the close relationship with Digit described here. She was fiercely protective of the apes, as they were increasingly threatened by poachers, nearby farmers, game wardens, and government officials. Fossey described her experiences in a carefully scientific but widely popular book, Gorillas in the Mist *(1983). In 1985 she was found in her camp, brutally hacked to death with a panga knife, a machete-like African weapon. The circumstances of her death remain a mystery.*

Dian Fossey: Among the Great Apes

By the end of her first three months in Rwanda, Dian was following   1
two gorilla groups regularly and observing another sporadically. She divided most of her time between Group 5's fifteen members, ranging on Visoke's southeastern slopes, and Group 4. Group 8, a family of nine, all adult, shared Visoke's western slopes with Group 4.

Dian still could not approach them. Gorilla families guard carefully   2
against intrusion. Each family has at least one member who serves as sentry, typically posted at the periphery of the group to watch for danger—a rival silverback or a human hunter. Gorilla groups seldom interact with other families, except when females transfer voluntarily out of their natal group to join the families of unrelated silverbacks or when rival silverbacks "raid" a neighboring family for females.

Adult gorillas will fight to the death defending their families. This is   3
why poachers who may be seeking only one infant for the zoo trade must often kill all the adults in the family to capture the baby. Once Dian

265

tracked one such poacher to his village; the man and his wives fled before her, leaving their small child behind.

At first Dian observed the animals from a distance, silently, hidden. Then slowly, over many months, she began to announce her presence. She imitated their contentment vocalizations, most often the *naoom, naoom, naoom,* a sound like belching or deeply clearing the throat. She crunched wild celery stalks. She crouched, eyes averted, scratching herself loud and long, as gorillas do. Eventually she could come close enough to them to smell the scent of their bodies and see the ridges inside the roofs of their mouths when they yawned; at times she came close enough to distinguish, without binoculars, the cuticles of their black, humanlike fingernails. 4

She visited them daily; she learned to tell by the contour pressed into the leaves which animal had slept in a particular night nest, made from leaves woven into a bathtub shape on the ground. She knew the sound of each individual voice belching contentment when they were feeding. But it was more than two years before she knew the touch of their skin. 5

Peanuts, a young adult male in Group 8, was the first mountain gorilla to touch his fingers to hers. Dian was lying on her back among the foliage, her right arm outstretched, palm up. Peanuts looked at her hand intently; then he stood, extended his hand, and touched her fingers for an instant. *National Geographic* photographer Bob Campbell snapped the shutter only a moment afterward: that the photo is blurry renders it dreamlike. The 250-pound gorilla's right hand still hangs in midair. Dian's eyes are open but unseeing, her lips parted, her left hand brought to her mouth, as if feeling for the lingering warmth of a kiss. 6

Peanuts pounded his chest with excitement and ran off to rejoin his group. Dian lingered after he left; she named the spot where they touched Fasi Ya Mkoni, "the Place of the Hands." With his touch, Peanuts opened his family to her; she became a part of the families she had observed so intimately for the past two years. Soon the gorillas would come forward and welcome her into their midst. 7

Digit was almost always the first member of Group 4 to greet her. "I received the impression that Digit really looked forward to the daily contacts," she wrote in the book. "If I was alone, he often invited play by flopping over on his back, waving stumpy legs in the air, and looking at me smilingly as if to say, 'How can you resist me?'" 8

At times she would be literally blanketed with gorillas, when a family would pull close around her like a black furry quilt. In one wonderful photo, Puck, a young female of Group 5, is reclining in back of Dian and, with the back of her left hand, touching Dian's cheek—the gesture of a mother caressing the cheek of a child. 9

Mothers let Dian hold their infants; silverbacks would groom her, parting her long dark hair with fingers thick as bananas, yet deft as a seam- 10 stress's touch. "I can't tell you how rewarding it is to be with them," Dian told a New York crowd gathered for a slide lecture in 1982. "Their trust, the cohesiveness, the tranquility . . ." Words failed her, and her hoarse, breathy voice broke. "It is really something."

Other field workers who joined Dian at Karisoke remember similar   11 moments. Photographer Bob Campbell recalls how Digit would try to groom his sleeves and pants and, finding nothing groomable, would pluck at the hairs of his wrist; most of the people who worked there have pictures of themselves with young gorillas on their heads or in their laps.

But with Dian it was different. Ian Redmond, who first came to   12 Karisoke in 1976, remembers one of the first times he accompanied Dian to observe Group 4. It was a reunion: Dian hadn't been out to visit the group for a while. "The animals filed past us, and each one paused and briefly looked into my face, just briefly. And then each one looked into Dian's eyes, at very close quarters, for half a minute or so. It seemed like each one was queuing up to stare into her face and remind themselves of her place with them. It was obvious they had a much deeper and stronger relationship with Dian than with any of the other workers."

In the early days Dian had the gorillas mostly to herself. It was in 1972   13 that Bob Campbell filmed what is arguably one of the most moving contacts between two species on record: Digit, though still a youngster, is huge. His head is more than twice the size of Dian's, his hands big enough to cover a dinner plate. He comes to her and with those enormous black hands gently takes her notebook, then her pen, and brings them to his flat, leathery nose. He gently puts them aside in the foliage and rolls over to snooze at Dian's side.

Once Dian spotted Group 4 on the opposite side of a steep ravine but   14 knew she was not strong enough to cross it. Uncle Bert, seeing her, led the entire group across the ravine to her. This time Digit was last in line. "Then," wrote Dian, "he finally came right to me and gently touched my hair. . . . I wish I could have given them all something in return."

At times like these, Dian wept with joy. Hers was the triumph of one   15 who has been chosen: wild gorillas would come to her.

• • •

But Digit was no pet. "Dian's relationship with the gorillas is really the   16 highest form of human-animal relationship," observed Ian Redmond. "With almost any other human-animal relationship, that involves feeding the animals or restraining the animals or putting them in an enclosure, or if you help an injured animal—you do something to the animal. Whereas Dian and the gorillas were on completely equal terms. It was nothing other than the desire to be together. And that's as pure as you can get."

When Digit was young, he and Dian played together like children. He 17 would strut toward her, playfully whacking foliage; she would tickle him; he would chuckle and climb on her head. Digit was fascinated by any object Dian had with her: once she brought a chocolate bar to eat for lunch and accidentally dropped it into the hollow stump of a tree where she was sitting next to Digit. Half in jest, she asked him to get it back for her. "And according to script," she wrote her Louisville friend, Betty Schwartzel, "Digit reached one long, hairy arm into the hole and retrieved the candy bar." But the chocolate didn't appeal to him. "After one sniff he literally threw it back into the hole. The so-called 'wild gorillas' are really very discriminating in their tastes!"

Dian's thermoses, notebooks, gloves, and cameras were all worthy of in- 18 vestigation. Digit would handle these objects gently and with great concentration. Sometimes he handed them back to her. Once Dian brought Digit a hand mirror. He immediately approached it, propped up on his forearms, and sniffed the glass. Digit pursed his lips, cocked his head, and then uttered a long sigh. He reached behind the mirror in search of the body connected to the face. Finding nothing, he stared at his reflection for five minutes before moving away.

Dian took many photos of all the gorillas, but Digit was her favorite 19 subject. When the Rwandan Office of Tourism asked Dian for a gorilla photo for a travel poster, the slide she selected was one of Digit. He is pictured holding a stick of wood he has been chewing, his shining eyes a mixture of innocence and inquiry. He looks directly into the camera, his lips parted and curved as if about to smile. "Come to meet him in Rwanda," exhorts the caption. When this poster began appearing in hotels, banks, and airports, "I could not help feeling that our privacy was on the verge of being invaded," Dian wrote.

Her relationship with Digit was one she did not intend to share. Hers 20 was the loyalty and possessiveness of a silverback: what she felt for the gorillas, and especially Digit, was exclusive, passionate, and dangerous.

No animal, Dian believed, was truly safe in Africa. Africans see most 21 animals as food, skins, money. "Dian had a compulsion to buy every animal she ever saw in Africa," remembers her friend Rosamond Carr, an American expatriate who lives in nearby Gisenyi, "to save it from torture." One day, Dian, driving in her Combi van, saw some children on the roadside, swinging a rabbit by the ears. She took it from them, brought it back to camp, and built a spacious hutch for it. Another time it would be a chicken: visiting villagers sometimes brought one to camp, intending, of course, that it be eaten. Dian would keep it as a pet.

Dian felt compelled to protect the vulnerable, the innocent. 22

• • •

Thereafter Dian's antipoaching tactics became more elaborate. She   23
learned from a friend in Ruhengeri that the trade in gorilla trophies was
flourishing; he had counted twenty-three gorilla heads for sale in that
town in one year. As loyal as a silverback, as wary as a sentry, Dian and her
staff patrolled the forest for snares and destroyed the gear poachers left behind in their temporary shelters.

Yet each day dawned to the barking of poachers' dogs. A field report she   24
submitted to the National Geographic Society in 1972 gave the results of
the most recent gorilla census: though her study groups were still safe, the
surrounding areas of the park's five volcanoes were literally under siege.
On Mount Muhavura census workers saw convoys of smugglers leaving
the park every forty-five minutes. Only thirteen gorillas were left on the
slopes of Muhavura. On neighboring Mount Gahinga no gorillas were
left. In the two previous years, census workers had found fresh remains of
slain silverbacks. And even the slopes of Dian's beloved Karisimbi, she
wrote, were covered with poachers' traps and scarred by heavily used cattle
trails; "poachers and their dogs were heard throughout the region."

It was that same year, 1972, that a maturing Digit assumed the role of   25
sentry of Group 4. In this role he usually stayed on the periphery of the
group to watch for danger; he would be the first to defend his family if
they were attacked. Once when Dian was walking behind her Rwandan
tracker, the dark form of a gorilla burst from the brush. The male stood
upright to his full height of five and a half feet; his jaw gaped open, exposing black gums and three-inch canines as he uttered two long, piercing
screams at the terrified tracker. Dian stepped into view, shoving the tracker
down behind her, and stared into the animal's face. They recognized each
other immediately. Digit dropped to all fours and ran back to his group.

Dian wrote that Digit's new role made him more serious. No longer   26
was he a youngster with the freedom to roll and wrestle with his playmate.
But Dian was still special to him. Once when Dian went out to visit the
group during a downpour, the young silverback emerged from the gloom
and stood erect before his crouching human friend. He pulled up a stalk of
wild celery—a favorite gorilla food that Digit had seen Dian munch on
many times—peeled it with his great hands, and dropped the stalk at her
feet like an offering. Then he turned and left.

• • •

One day, she ventured out along a trail as slippery as fresh buffalo dung   27
to find Group 4. By the time she found them, the rain was driving. They
were huddled against the downpour. She saw Digit sitting about thirty

feet apart from the group. She wanted to join him but resisted; she now feared that her early contact with him had made him too human-oriented, more vulnerable to poachers. She so settled among the soaking foliage several yards from the main group. She could barely make out the humped back forms in the heavy mist.

On sunny days there is no more beautiful place on earth than the Virungas; the sunlight makes the *Senecio* trees sparkle like fireworks in midexplosion; the gnarled old *Hagenias,* trailing lacy beards of gray-green lichen and epiphytic ferns, look like friendly wizards, and the leaves of palms seem like hands upraised in praise. But rain transforms the forest into a cold, gray hell. You stare out, tunnel-visioned, from the hood of a dripping raincape, at a wet landscape cloaked as if an evil enchantment. Each drop of rain sends a splintering chill into the flesh, and your muscles clench with cold; you can cut yourself badly on the razorlike cutty grass and not even feel it. Even the gorillas, with their thick black fur coats, look miserable and lonely in the rain. 28

Minutes after she arrived, Dian felt an arm around her shoulders. "I looked up into Digit's warm, gentle brown eyes," she wrote in *Gorillas in the Mist.* He gazed at her thoughtfully and patted her head, then sat by her side. As the rain faded to mist, she laid her head down in Digit's lap. 29

On January 1, 1978, Dian's head tracker returned to camp late in the day. He had not been able to find Group 4. But he had found blood along their trail. 30

Ian Redmond found Digit's body the next day. His head and hands had been hacked off. There were five spear wounds in his body. 31

Ian did not see Dian cry that day. She was almost supercontrolled, he remembers. No amount of keening, no incantation or prayer could release the pain of her loss. But years later she filled a page of her diary with a single word, written over and over: "Digit Digit Digit Digit . . ." 32

MUSINGS

Montgomery uses a number of sources to describe the close relationship between Fossey and Digit. She turns to several researchers who worked with Fossey and quotes Fossey's own book and letter to her sister.

Have you experienced a close relationship with an animal? If not, try to recall one from a movie or television show. Keep in mind that because animals are mute, they must express their feelings in other ways. Describe some of these ways, as Montgomery does, paying particular attention to their body movements, actions, eyes, and expressions.

GILES SMITH (1962–)

This selection from The New Yorker, *written by Giles Smith, profiles the American musician—singer, composer, and lyricist—Stevie Wonder. Born in 1950 as Steveland Judkins Morris, he was blind at birth but recognized as a precocious musician and dubbed "the little boy wonder," from which he derived his name. "Fingertips Part Two," written when he was only thirteen years old, was his first big hit. Since then Wonder has earned a number of gold records and won numerous Grammy Awards. His music is extremely innovative and incorporates elements from reggae, jazz, blues, and rock. Wonder widened his audience by performing the opening act to the Rolling Stones in 1972 and by a Carnegie Hall appearance the following year.*

The following selection describes how Wonder is always working, just as he is always late. He composes using a synthesizer hooked up to a computerized sequencer, which travels with him everywhere—to his hotel room or his dressing room. According to his assistants, Wonder appears to have music playing inside his head most of the time—in meetings, over meals, wherever or whenever. His ex-wife, who is still employed by him, said she understood that music was "really his No. 1 wife."

Stevie Wonder: Music Is His Life

Stevie Wonder, at forty-four, is revered as the composer of a thick catalogue of pop songs, many of them hits; as the blind former child prodigy who became an international star; as one of the most gifted and influential vocalists of his generation; as a pianist both fluid and intricately rhythmical; as a virtuoso harmonica player; as a pioneering record producer, who was among the first musicians to exploit synthesizer technology; and as a generous investor in a broad portfolio of humanitarian causes. Among his colleagues, though, he is known, above all, as a major lateness expert. Wonder's capacity for delay, procrastination, dilatoriness, and all things tardy has been honed to perfection over his three and a half decades in show business. Some years ago, thirty minutes before Wonder was due to perform in Seattle, he phoned his tour manager to let him know that he was just setting out from home in Los Angeles. If you have spent any time around Wonder, it is not difficult to imagine his tone as he imparted this news: sublimely untroubled, low, soft, with slightly hazed consonants— the same tone he uses to utter his favorite catchphrase these days, which is "I'm just chillin'."

In the face of boring, day-to-day stuff like time and place, Wonder has repeatedly shown himself capable of an indifference bordering on the heroic. In London in 1981, he arrived at his own lunchtime press conference a striking six hours after it started, by which point the press had eaten all the sandwiches and gone home. He is late with records, too. Deadlines proposed by his record company, Motown Records, frequently fail to capture his imagination. In the mid-seventies, as completion dates came and went for the album "Songs in the Key of Life," which was eventually released in 1976, employees at Motown took to wearing T-shirts with the logo "Stevie's Nearly Ready."

His . . . album, "Conversation Peace," is his first release in four years, but he's been working on it since 1987. . . . It's a strong record, contemporary in feeling, and vigorously sung—his most spirited album since "Hotter Than July," which came out fifteen years ago. Motown is hoping that the new record will put Wonder back in people's minds, and back onto the pop charts, where he has been only an intermittent presence in recent years. Jheryl Busby, the president of Motown, told me not long ago that he believed "Conversation Peace" would "reposition" Wonder. He immediately added that this was a word Wonder himself would hate.

• • •

Although his career since 1976 has had its points of brilliance, it has been characterized, too, by a tantalizing absence of momentum. It should be made clear, however, that his three-to-four-year patches of downtime bear no relation to the lavish sabbaticals that other rock stars award themselves periodically for the purpose of shopping for real estate or getting their blood changed. Just as Stevie Wonder is almost never not late, so he is almost never not working. In his case, the cliché "Music is his life" reads like a potentially slanderous understatement. The singer Syreeta Wright, who married Wonder in 1971 and divorced him a year and a half later, recalls, "He would wake up and go straight to the keyboard. I knew and understood that his passion was music. That was really his No. 1 wife."

Wonder, who has four children (Aisha, Keita, Mumtaz, and Kwame) from three subsequent relationships, has never remarried. But wherever he travels his No. 1 wife is by his side, in the form of a synthesizer that hooks up to a computerized sequencer capable of making and playing back detailed multitrack recordings. On tour, for instance, an assistant will rig up this hardware in Wonder's hotel room (the job takes about ten minutes); then, at the appropriate time, the assistant will pack it up, transport it to Wonder's dressing room, and set it up there; and at the end of the evening he will take it down again and put it back up in the hotel room. This is so that inspiration, which cannot be relied upon to call during office hours alone, can be seized, as Syreeta Wright puts it, "when the heavens send." I have seen Wonder turn in earnest to his computerized sketch pad of drumbeats and chord patterns and licks of partly formed melody at various times and in various places, none of them predictable: directly before shows, directly after shows, in the morning while he was having his hair braided, and, most memorably, in the middle of a conversation we were having in a hotel room in Paris in 1993.

Even in the brief periods when he is nowhere near a keyboard, Wonder frequently seems to be mulling over music—sitting or standing with his head thrown back and his upper body weaving from side to side, and fooling with scraps of tune in a soft falsetto, locked into some internal rhythm. At these moments, he is absolutely unreachable. In January, in Phoenix, Arizona, he attended a press conference concerning, among other things, his support for the American Express-sponsored Charge Against Hunger campaign. At the conclusion, Wonder posed, grinning, for photographs. Immediately after that, in the hotel elevator, he was quietly singing, toying with the line "I just caught you smiling"—raw experience transformed into art in a little under twenty seconds. Maybe this melody will show up on his next album. Maybe it will never appear. Maybe it will appear somewhere in the next decade.

· · ·

At Wonderland, the recording studio he owns on Western Avenue in Los Angeles, Wonder has been known to work for two and a half days without leaving the studio, while bleary-eyed engineers clocked in and out in shifts around him. The distinction between daytime and nighttime is not one that readily occurs to him, except as a lyrical trope. This indifference to the passage of time is frequently traced to his blindness. (Wonder was born prematurely, on May 13, 1950, and was probably blind at birth.) Most blind people manage to adjust themselves successfully to the clock by which the sighted world runs. Wonder is inclined to be a little looser, sleeping when he is tired, which may be in hours or half hours snatched in planes or limos. Or he may drop off during an interview for Italian television, as a Motown publicist told me he did in 1991. "Time is altogether another type of trip for him," Syreeta Wright says. She used to buy him watches but gave up after the third.

All of which must occasionally enrage the people who work for Wonder—those charged with shuffling his flights, rearranging his meetings, and generally scrapping and rebuilding and rescrapping and re-rebuilding his schedules. Chiefly, they appear to console themselves with the thought that Wonder's unreliability is both a consequence of and a testament to his genius, one of several signs that Stevie—or Steve, as those close to him call him—is not quite of this world.

MUSINGS

Wonder has peculiar work habits and an annoying practice of always being late. However, such behaviors are tolerated by reporters, his record company, and his friends, probably due to his genius and his financial success. Most of the people associated with him depend heavily on him in one way or another.

Do you know someone who has annoying habits that you tolerate? Write about this friend and her or his habits, and explain why you tolerate them.

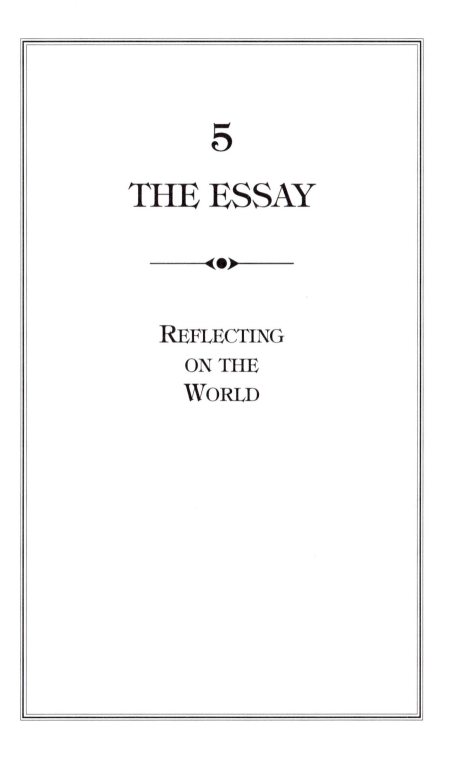

5

THE ESSAY

———◆———

REFLECTING
ON THE
WORLD

The term "essay," with origins in French and Latin, originally meant an attempt or trial. It was first used in connection with literature by Montaigne, a French writer of the sixteenth century, who called his *Essaies* attempts to record his experiences. Later in the same century the term was picked up by Francis Bacon, who entitled his religious meditations "Essays: Places of Persuasion and Dissuasion." Similarly, the modern essay is a record of significant experiences, in which the writer attempts to persuade the reader to a certain viewpoint. In the essays in this section, three elements are present: experience, meaning, and persuasion.

During bells hooks' childhood the ritual of hair straightening took place regularly on Saturday mornings. The author describes the general admiration for straight hair within her culture and the later visits to the beauty parlor, a place where African-American women could bond. She meditates on the wider meaning of this experience—the need for African-American women to celebrate their bodies, to find pleasure in "washing, combing, and caring" for their hair, and to participate in "a liberatory struggle that frees mind and heart." Looking back, she sees the years of hair straightening as a way of taking on the white supremacist culture. She persuades the reader to her view through the careful selection of details that make that experience so real and the meaning very clear.

Sometimes it is only one vividly told experience that inspires the search for meaning, as in Vidal's description of what he felt in going through the contents of Lincoln's pockets a century after the assassination, White's return to the lake, or Orwell's description of a hanging. It can also be based on a series of incidents, such as Selzer's experiences in Haiti, or Dillard's encounters with the Praying Mantis and the Polyphemus moth.

Usually the significance of the experience is explicitly stated; in the selections by hooks and Tan, the authors take their readers step by step from descriptions of the experiences to the establishment of their significance. Occasionally the meaning is only implied, or is stated with great subtlety. In "The Hanging," Orwell describes in great detail the damp weather, the impatience of the warden, the intrusion of the dog, the walk to the gallows, the hanging, and the reaction of the witnesses afterwards—their inappropriate jokes, their unseemly need to laugh, the need to have a drink. There is no need to state a message; in the wealth of small details that make the scene so real, the meaning is made all too clear.

The author's use of persuasion can also be either subtle or directly stated. In most of the essays included here the vivid writing and the tireless attention to detail lead readers through the experiences and ready them for the acceptance of the messages. Orwell describes the condemned prisoner as an ordinary human being, "a puny wisp of a man, with a shaven head and vague liquid eyes—and a moustache, much too big for his body." We follow in his steps as he wards off the dog and steps around the puddle, and we die a little bit when he is hanged. Such evocation of empathy is powerfully persuasive. Similarly, we share with Dillard the pitiful fate of the moth; the scene, as well as the unthinking human cruelty that caused it, remain fixed forever in our memory. Vidal persuades the reader to his view more directly by supporting his argument that Lincoln was a literary genius through a number of examples that act as proof.

The essay has always defied precise definition. Aldous Huxley called it "a literary device for saying almost everything about anything." The selections reprinted here are good examples of the numerous ways in which skilled writers use the essay to make a point. The analytical article strives to persuade by careful reasoning and by the establishment of objectivity. In contrast, the author is very much present in the essay, inviting the reader to share in the experience, offering recognition of the reader, and demanding a response.

In writing an essay, you can use the experience you have gained from your work in journals, letters, and autobiography. Like all life writing, an essay is the meeting place between the world as you have experienced it and the world as you recreate it in your writing. Lure your readers into that world by working bits of memory into vivid details. Demand recognition of the meaning of your experience through the use of powerful images. Invite your readers to respond to your position; by gaining an understanding of what an experience means to you, its significance to their own lives will become clear.

E. B. WHITE (1899–1945)

E. B. White was born and spent his life in the east; a reporter and free-lance writer, he worked for many years as a contributor to and editor of The New Yorker, *which was for so long associated with his name. He was a good friend and colleague of James Thurber and wrote an early book with him. Although a man of many talents, including poetry, he was best known as an essayist; his work is collected in a number of anthologies, including* The Second Tree from the Corner, An E. B. White Reader, *and* Essays of E. B. White. *In addition, he published two collections of the essays that had appeared in* The New Yorker *and in* Harper's. *White has often been called the essayist's essayist because his style was so admired by his colleagues. Joseph Wood Krutch, another well-known essayist, wrote in the* Saturday Review *that White is "generally concerned less with the Queen than with the little mouse under her chair." He received numerous awards, particularly for his children's books;* Charlotte's Web *has become a classic ranked by many critics alongside Lewis Carroll's* Alice in Wonderland.*

William Howarth commented that for White, "connecting small moments to big issues is a literary impulse." The following essay does just that. White describes the sights and sounds of the lake cottage where, as a child, he had spent summers with his own father, as well as an increasing sense of his own mortality caused by watching his son experience these same scenes. The essay combines the nostalgia and gentle melancholy that characterize so much of White's work.

Once More to the Lake

One summer, along about 1904, my father rented a camp on a lake in Maine and took us all there for the month of August. We all got ringworm from some kittens and had to rub Pond's Extract on our arms and legs night and morning, and my father rolled over in a canoe with all his clothes on; but outside of that the vacation was a success and from then on none of us ever thought there was any place in the world like that lake in Maine. We returned summer after summer—always on August 1st for one month. I have since become a salt-water man, but sometimes in summer there are days when the restlessness of the tides and the fearful cold of the sea water and the incessant wind that blows across the afternoon and into the evening make me wish for the placidity of a lake in the woods. A few weeks ago this feeling got so strong I bought myself a couple of bass hooks and a spinner and returned to the lake where we used to go, for a week's fishing and to revisit old haunts.

1

I took along my son, who had never had any fresh water up his nose   2
and who has seen lily pads only from train windows. On the journey over
to the like I began to wonder what it would be like. I wondered how time
would have marred this unique, this holy spot—the coves and streams, the
hills that the sun set behind, the camps and the paths behind the camps. I
was sure that the tarred road would have found it out and I wondered in
what other ways it would be desolated. It is strange how much you can remember about places like that once you allow your mind to return into
the grooves that lead back. You remember one thing, and that suddenly reminds you of another thing. I guess I remembered clearest of all the early
mornings, when the lake was cool and motionless, remembered how the
bedroom smelled of the lumber it was made of and of the wet woods
whose scent entered through the screen. The partitions in the camp were
thin and did not extend clear to the top of the rooms, and as I was always
the first up I would dress softly so as not to wake the others, and sneak out
into the sweet outdoors and start out in the canoe, keeping close along the
shore in the long shadows of the pines. I remembered being very careful
never to rub my paddle against the gunwale for fear of disturbing the still-
ness of the cathedral.

The lake had never been what you would call a wild lake. There were   3
cottages sprinkled around the shores, and it was in farming country although the shores of the lake were quite heavily wooded. Some of the cottages were owned by nearby farmers, and you would live at the shore and
eat your meals at the farmhouse. That's what our family did. But although
it wasn't wild, it was a fairly large and undisturbed lake and there were
places in it which, to a child at least, seemed infinitely remote and
primeval.

I was right about the tar: it led to within half a mile of the shore. But   4
when I got back there, with my boy, and we settled into a camp near a
farmhouse and into the kind of summertime I had known, I could tell
that it was going to be pretty much the same as it had been before—I
knew it, lying in bed the first morning, smelling the bedroom, and hearing
the boy sneak quietly out and go off along the shore in a boat. I began to
sustain the illusion that he was I, and therefore, by simple transposition,
that I was my father. This sensation persisted, kept cropping up all the
time we were there. It was not an entirely new feeling, but in this setting it
grew much stronger. I seemed to be living a dual existence. I would be in
the middle of some simple act, I would be picking up a bait box or laying
down a table fork, or I would be saying something, and suddenly it would
be not I but my father who was saying the words or making the gesture. It
gave me a creepy sensation.

We went fishing the first morning. I felt the same damp moss covering   5 the worms in the bait can, and saw the dragonfly alight on the tip of my rod as it hovered a few inches from the surface of the water. It was the arrival of this fly that convinced me beyond any doubt that everything was as it always had been, that the years were a mirage and there had been no years. The small waves were the same, chucking the rowboat under the chin as we fished at anchor, and the boat was the same boat, the same color green and the ribs broken in the same places, and under the floor-boards the same fresh-water leavings and debris—the dead hellgrammite, the wisps of moss, the rusty discarded fishhook, the dried blood from yesterday's catch. We stared silently at the tips of our rods, at the dragonflies that came and went. I lowered the tip of mine into the water, tentatively, pensively dislodging the fly, which darted two feet away, poised, darted two feet back, and came to rest again a little farther up the rod. There had been no years between the ducking of this dragonfly and the other one—the one that was part of memory. I looked at the boy, who was silently watching his fly, and it was my hands that held his rod, my eyes watching. I felt dizzy and didn't know which rod I was at the end of.

We caught two bass, hauling them in briskly as though they were mackerel, pulling them over the side of the boat in a businesslike manner without any landing net, and stunning them with a blow on the back of the head. When we got back for a swim before lunch, the lake was exactly where we had left it, the same number of inches from the dock, and there was only the merest suggestion of a breeze. This seemed an utterly enchanted sea, this lake you could leave to its own devices for a few hours and come back to, and find that it had not stirred, this constant and trust-worthy body of water. In the shallows, the dark, water-soaked sticks and twigs, smooth and old, were undulating in clusters on the bottom against the clean ribbed sand, and the track of the mussel was plain. A school of minnows swam by, each minnow with its small individual shadow, doubling the attendance, so clear and sharp in the sunlight. Some of the other campers were in swimming, along the shore, one of them with a cake of soap, and the water felt thin and clear and unsubstantial. Over the years there had been this person with the cake of soap, this cultist, and here he was. There had been no years.

Up to the farmhouse to dinner through the teeming, dusty field, the road under our sneakers was only a two-track road. The middle track was missing, the one with the marks of the hooves and splotches of dried, flaky manure. There had always been three tracks to choose from in choosing which track to walk in; now the choice was narrowed down to two. For a moment I missed terribly the middle alternative. But the way led past the tennis court, and something about the way it lay there in the sun reassured me; the tape had loosened along the backline, the alleys were green with plantains and other weeds, and the net (installed in June and removed in September) sagged in the dry noon, and the whole place steamed with midday heat and hunger and emptiness. There was a choice of pie for dessert, and one was blueberry and one was apple, and the waitresses were the same country girls, there having been no passage of time, only the illusion of it as in a dropped curtain—the waitresses were still fifteen; their hair had been washed, that was the only difference—they had been to the movies and seen the pretty girls with the clean hair.

Summertime, oh summertime, pattern of life indelible, the fade-proof lake, the woods unshatterable, the pasture with the sweetfern and the juniper forever and ever, summer without end; this was the background, and the life along the shore was the design, the cottages with their innocent and tranquil design, their tiny docks with the flagpole and the American flag floating against the white clouds in the blue sky, the little paths over the roots of the trees leading from camp to camp and the paths leading back to the outhouses and the can of lime for sprinkling, and at the souvenir counters at the store the miniature birch-bark canoes and the post cards that showed things looking a little better then they looked. This was the American family at play, escaping the city heat, wondering whether the newcomers in the camp at the head of the cove were "common" or "nice," wondering whether it was true that the people who drove up for Sunday dinner at the farmhouse were turned away because there wasn't enough chicken. 8

It seemed to me, as I kept remembering all this, that those times and those summers had been infinitely precious and worth saving. There had been jollity and peace and goodness. The arriving (at the beginning of August) had been so big a business in itself, at the railway station the farm wagon drawn up, the first smell of the pine-laden air, the first glimpse of the smiling farmer, and the great importance of the trunks and your father's enormous authority in such matters, and the feel of the wagon under you for the long ten-mile haul, and at the top of the last long hill catching the first view of the lake after eleven months of not seeing this cherished body of water. The shouts and cries of the other campers when they saw you, and the trunks to be unpacked, to give up their rich burden. (Arriving was less exciting nowadays, when you sneaked up in your car and parked it under a tree near the camp and took out the bags and in five minutes it was all over, no fuss, no loud wonderful fuss about trunks.) 9

Peace and goodness and jollity. The only thing that was wrong now, really, was the sound of the place, an unfamiliar nervous sound of the outboard motors. This was the note that jarred, the one thing that would sometimes break the illusion and set the years moving. In those other summertimes all motors were inboard; and when they were at a little distance, the noise they made was a sedative, an ingredient of summer sleep. 10

They were one-cylinder and two-cylinder engines, and some were make-and-break and some were jump-spark, but they all made a sleepy sound across the lake. The one-lungers throbbed and fluttered, and the twin-cylinder ones purred and purred, and that was a quiet sound too. But now the campers all had outboards. In the daytime, in the hot mornings, these motors made a petulant, irritable sound; at night, in the still evening when the afterglow lit the water, they whined about one's ears like mosquitoes. My boy loved our rented outboard, and his great desire was to achieve single-handed mastery over it, and authority, and he soon learned the trick of choking it a little (but not too much), and the adjustment of the needle valve. Watching him I would remember the things you could do with the old one-cylinder engine with the heavy flywheel, how you could have it eating out of your hand if you got really close to it spiritually. Motor boats in those days didn't have clutches, and you would make a landing by shutting off the motor at the proper time and coasting in with a dead rudder. But there was a way of reversing them, if you learned the trick, by cutting the switch and putting it on again exactly on the final dying revolution of the flywheel, so that it would kick back against compression and begin reversing. Approaching a dock in a strong following breeze, it was difficult to slow up sufficiently by the ordinary coasting method, and if a boy felt he had complete mastery over his motor, he was tempted to keep it running beyond its time and then reverse it a few feet from the dock. It took a cool nerve, because if you threw the switch a twentieth of a second too soon you could catch the flywheel when it still had speed enough to go up past center, and the boat would leap ahead, charging bull-fashion at the dock.

We had a good week at the camp. The bass were biting well and the sun shone endlessly, day after day. We would be tired at night and lie down in the accumulated heat of the little bedrooms after the long hot day and the breeze would stir almost imperceptibly outside and the smell of the swamp drift in through the rusty screens. Sleep would come easily and in the morning the red squirrel would be on the roof, tapping out his gay routine. I kept remembering everything, lying in bed in the mornings—the small steamboat that had a long rounded stern like the lip of a Ubangi, and how quietly she ran on the moonlight sails, when the older boys played their mandolins and the girls sang and we ate doughnuts dipped in sugar, and how sweet the music was on the water in the shining night, and what it had felt like to think about girls then. After breakfast we would go up to the store and the things were in the same place—the minnows in a bottle, the plugs and spinners disarranged and pawed over by the youngsters from the boys' camp, the Fig Newtons and the Beeman's gum. Outside, the road was tarred and cars stood in front of the store. Inside, all was just as it had always been, except there was more Coca-Cola and not so much Moxie and root beer and birch beer and sarsaparilla. We would walk out with a bottle of pop apiece and sometimes the pop would backfire up our noses and hurt. We explored the streams, quietly, where the turtles slid off the sunny logs and dug their way into the soft bottom; and we lay on the town wharf and fed worms to the tame bass. Everywhere we went I had trouble making out which was I, the one walking at my side, the one walking in my pants.

One afternoon while we were there at that lake a thunderstorm came up. It was like the revival of an old melodrama that I had seen long ago with childish awe. The second-act climax of the drama of the electrical disturbance over a lake in America had not changed in any important respect. This was the big scene, still the big scene. The whole thing was so familiar, the first feeling of oppression and heat and a general air around camp of not wanting to go very far away. In midafternoon (it was all the same) a curious darkening of the sky, and a lull in everything that had made life tick; and then the way the boats suddenly swung the other way at their moorings with the coming of a breeze out of the new quarter, and the premonitory rumble. Then the kettle drum, then the snare, then the bass drum and cymbals, then crackling light against the dark, and the gods grinning and licking their chops in the hills. Afterward the calm, the rain steadily rustling in the calm lake, the return of light and hope and spirits, and the campers running out in joy and relief to go swimming in the rain, their bright cries perpetuating the deathless joke about how they were getting simply drenched, and the children screaming with delight at the new sensation of bathing in the rain, and the joke about getting drenched linking the generations in a strong indestructible chain. And the comedian who waded in carrying an umbrella. 12

When the others went swimming my son said he was going in too. He pulled his dripping trunks from the line where they had hung all through the shower, and wrung them out. Languidly, and with no thought of going in, I watched him, his hard little body, skinny and bare, saw him wince slightly as he pulled up around his vitals the small, soggy, icy garment. As he buckled the swollen belt suddenly my groin felt the chill of death. 13

MUSINGS

In his vivid description of the scene of his childhood vacations, White develops the feeling that he has become his own father, and that "there had been no years" between his childhood and his manhood. He does notice differences, however, between arriving by farm wagon and coming by car, in the sounds of the motorboats on the lake, and in the kinds of soda sold at the store.

Recall a place that you visited as a child and describe it as it appeared at some later date. Note the things that have remained the same and those that have changed. Suggest ways that these differences affect you and ways in which you yourself may have changed.

GEORGE ORWELL (1903–1950)

Writing under the pseudonym George Orwell, Eric Blair was born in India in 1903, and, due to the period's lack of life-saving drugs, died tragically of tuberculosis at age forty-seven. His experiences at a boarding school in England were a lifelong source of bitterness. In "Such, Such Were the Joys" Orwell chronicles those years of suffering as a "middle-class student in a class-conscious society." This article provides the key to Orwell's later work, where he objects to England's hierarchical society and the misuse of power. In the early 1930s Orwell described himself as a "Tory Anarchist" and toward the end of his life as "a democratic Socialist."

"From an early age," Orwell wrote, "I knew that when I grew up I should be a writer." He spent most of his life in England working for the British Broadcasting Corporation and as literary editor for the London Tribune. *His first novels were not financially successful, and he struggled to make a living. His economic status changed markedly with the publication and wide success of* Animal Farm *(1945) and* Nineteen Eighty-Four *(1949). The former was inspired by his sight of a boy driving a horse along a narrow path and beating the animal whenever it tried to turn.* Animal Farm *is a fantasy of a barnyard revolt against their masters, paralleling humans' rebellion against their masters.* Nineteen Eighty-Four *describes a future society as "a boot stamping on a human face—forever." Orwell recognized that he wrote best when he had a political agenda.*

"A Hanging" is an early essay, written when Orwell was twenty-eight years old, which describes a hanging in careful and devastating detail—the cries of "Ram! Ram! Ram!" by the condemned man, the puddle that he carefully avoids, the dog: "He and we were a party of men walking together, seeing, hearing, feeling, understanding the same world; and in two minutes, with a sudden snap, one of us would be gone—one mind less, one world less."

A Hanging

It was in Burma, a sodden morning of the rains. A sickly light, like yellow tinfoil, was slanting over the high walls into the jail yard. We were waiting outside the condemned cells, a row of sheds fronted with double bars, like small animal cages. Each cell measured about ten feet by ten and was quite bare within except for a plank bed and a pot for drinking water. In some of them brown silent men were squatting at the inner bars, with their blankets draped round them. These were the condemned men, due to be hanged within the next week or two.

One prisoner had been brought out of his cell. He was a Hindu, a puny wisp of a man, with a shaven head and vague liquid eyes. He had a thick, sprouting moustache, absurdly too big for his body, rather like the moustache of a comic man on the films. Six tall Indian warders were guarding him and getting him ready for the gallows. Two of them stood by with rifles and fixed bayonets, while the others handcuffed him, passed a chain through his handcuffs and fixed it to their belts, and lashed his arms tight to his sides. They crowded very close about him, with their hands always on him in a careful, caressing grip, as though all the while feeling him to make sure he was there. It was like men handling a fish which is still alive and may jump back into the water. But he stood quite unresisting, yielding his arms limply to the ropes, as though he hardly noticed what was happening.

Eight o'clock struck and a bugle call, desolately thin in the wet air, floated from the distant barracks. The superintendent of the jail, who was standing apart from the rest of us, moodily prodding the gravel with his stick, raised his head at the sound. He was an army doctor, with a gray toothbrush moustache and a gruff voice. "For God's sake hurry up, Francis," he said irritably. "The man ought to have been dead by this time. Aren't you ready yet?"

Francis, the head jailer, a fat Dravidian in a white drill suit and gold spectacles waved his black hand. "Yes sir, yes sir," he bubbled. "All iss satisfactorily prepared. The hangman iss waiting. We shall proceed."

"Well, quick march, then. The prisoners can't get their breakfast till this job's over."

We set out for the gallows. Two warders marched on either side of the prisoner, with their rifles at the slope; two others marched close against him, gripping him by arm and shoulder, as though at once pushing and supporting him. The rest of us, magistrates and the like, followed behind. Suddenly, when we had gone ten yards, the procession stopped short without any order or warning. A dreadful thing had happened—a dog, come goodness knows whence, had appeared in the yard. It came bounding among us with a loud volley of barks, and leapt round us wagging its whole body, wild with glee at finding so many human beings together. It was a large woolly dog, half Airedale, half pariah. For a moment it pranced round us, and then, before anyone could stop it, it had made a dash for the prisoner and, jumping up, tried to lick his face. Everyone stood aghast, too taken aback even to grab at the dog.

"Who let that bloody brute in here?" said the superintendent angrily. "Catch it, someone!"

A warder, detached from the escort, charged clumsily after the dog, but it danced and gamboled just out of his reach, taking everything as part of the game. A young Eurasian jailer picked up a handful of gravel and tried to stone the dog away, but it dodged the stones and came after us again. Its yaps echoed from the jail walls. The prisoner, in the grasp of the two warders, looked on incuriously, as though this was another formality of the hanging. It was several minutes before someone managed to catch the dog. Then we put my handkerchief through its collar and moved off once more, with the dog still straining and whimpering.

It was about forty yards to the gallows. I watched the bare brown back   9
of the prisoner marching in front of me. He walked clumsily with his bound arms, but quite steadily, with that bobbing gait of the Indian who never straightens his knees. At each step his muscles slid neatly into place, the lock of hair on his scalp danced up and down, his feet printed themselves on the wet gravel. And once, in spite of the men who gripped him by each shoulder, he stepped slightly aside to avoid a puddle on the path.

It is curious, but till that moment I had never realized what it means to   10
destroy a healthy, conscious man. When I saw the prisoner step aside to avoid the puddle I saw the mystery, the unspeakable wrongness, of cutting a life short when it is in full tide. This man was not dying, he was alive just as we are alive. All the organs of his body were working—bowels digesting food, skin renewing itself, nails growing, tissues forming—all toiling away in solemn foolery. His nails would still be growing when he stood on the drop, when he was falling through the air with a tenth of a second to live. His eyes saw the yellow gravel and the gray walls, and his brain still re-membered, foresaw, reasoned—reasoned even about puddles. He and we were a party of men walking together, seeing, hearing, feeling, under-standing the same world; and in two minutes, with a sudden snap, one of us would be gone—one mind less, one world less.

The gallows stood in a small yard, separate from the main grounds of   11
the prison, and overgrown with tall prickly weeds. It was a brick erection like three sides of a shed, with planking on top, and above that two beams and a crossbar with the rope dangling. The hangman, a gray-haired con-vict in the white uniform of the prison, was waiting beside his machine. He greeted us with a servile crouch as we entered. At a word from Francis the two warders, gripping the prisoner more closely than ever, half led half pushed him to the gallows and helped him clumsily up the ladder. Then the hangman climbed up and fixed the rope round the prisoner's neck.

We stood waiting, five yards away. The warders had formed in a rough   12
circle around the gallows. And then, when the noose was fixed, the pris-oner began crying out to his god. It was a high, reiterated cry of "Ram! Ram! Ram! Ram!" not urgent and fearful like a prayer or cry for help, but steady, rhythmical, almost like the tolling of a bell. The dog answered the sound with a whine. The hangman, still standing on the gallows, pro-duced a small cotton bag like a flour bag and drew it down over the pris-

oner's face. But the sound, muffled by the cloth, still persisted, over and over again: "Ram! Ram! Ram! Ram! Ram!"

The hangman climbed down and stood ready, holding the lever. Minutes seemed to pass. The steady, muffled crying from the prisoner went on and on, "Ram! Ram! Ram!" never faltering for an instant. The superintendent, his head on his chest, was slowly poking the ground with his stick; perhaps he was counting the cries, allowing the prisoner a fixed number— fifty, perhaps, or a hundred. Everyone had changed color. The Indians had gone gray like bad coffee, and one or two of the bayonets were wavering. We looked at the lashed, hooded man on the drop, and listened to his cries—each cry another second of life; the same thought was in all our minds: oh, kill him quickly, get it over, stop that abominable noise!   13

Suddenly the superintendent made up his mind. Throwing up his head he made a swift motion with his stick. "Chalo!" he shouted almost fiercely.   14

There was a clanking noise, and then dead silence. The prisoner had vanished, and the rope was twisting on itself. I let go of the dog, and it galloped immediately to the back of the gallows; but when it got there, it stopped short, barked, and then retreated into a corner of the yard, where it stood along the weeds, looking timorously out at us. We went round the gallows to inspect the prisoner's body. He was dangling with his toes pointed straight downward, very slowly revolving, as dead as a stone.   15

The superintendent reached out with his stick and poked the bare brown body; it oscillated slightly. "*He's* all right," said the superintendent. He backed out from under the gallows, and blew out a deep breath. The moody look had gone out of his face quite suddenly. He glanced at his wrist watch. "Eight minutes past eight. Well, that's all for this morning, thank God."   16

The warders unfixed bayonets and marched away. The dog, sobered and conscious of having misbehaved itself, slipped after them. We walked out of the gallows yard, past the condemned cells with their waiting prisoners, into the big central yard of the prison. The convicts, under the command of warders armed with lathis, were already receiving their breakfast. They squatted in long rows, each man holding a tin pannikin, while two warders with buckets marched round ladling out rice; it seemed quite a homely, jolly scene, after the hanging. An enormous relief had come upon us now that the job was done. One felt an impulse to sing, to break into a run, to snigger. All at once everyone began chattering gaily.   17

The Eurasian boy walking beside me nodded toward the way we had come, with a knowing smile: "Do you know, sir, our friend [he meant the dead man] when he heard his appeal had been dismissed, he pissed on the floor of his cell. From fright. Kindly take one of my cigarettes, sir. Do you not admire my new silver case, sir? From the boxwalah, two rupes eight annas. Classy European style."   18

Several people laughed—at what, nobody seemed certain.   19

Francis was walking by the superintendent, talking garrulously: "Well,   20
sir, all hass passed off with the utmost satisfactoriness. It was all finished—
flick! like that. It iss not always so—oah, no! I have known cases where the
doctor wass obliged to go beneath the gallows and pull the prissoner's legs
to ensure decease. Most disagreeable!"

"Wriggling about, eh? That's bad," said the superintendent.   21

"Ach sir, it iss worse when they become refractory! One man, I recall,   22
clung to the bars of hiss cage when we went to take him out. You will
scarcely credit, sir, that it took six warders to dislodge him, three pulling at
each leg. We reasoned with him. 'My dear fellow,' we said, 'think of all the
pain and trouble you are causing to us!' But no, he would not listen! Ach,
he wass very troublesome!"

I found that I was laughing quite loudly. Everyone was laughing. Even   23
the superintendent grinned in a tolerate way. "You'd better all come out
and have a drink," he said quite genially. "I've got a bottle of whiskey in
the car. We could do with it."

We went through the big double gates of the prison into the road.   24
"Pulling at his legs!" exclaimed a Burmese magistrate suddenly, and burst
into a loud chuckling. We all began laughing again. At that moment Francis' anecdote seemed extraordinarily funny. We all had a drink together,
native and European alike, quite amicably. The dead man was a hundred
yards away.

MUSINGS

In this essay, Orwell makes an eloquent and persuasive case against capital
punishment by taking us step by step through a hanging. He first makes
us acutely aware of the basic human characteristics of the man with a detailed description: "He walked clumsily with his bound arms, but quite
steadily, with that bobbing gait of the Indian who never straightens his
knees. At each step his muscles slid neatly into place, the lock of hair on
his scalp danced up and down, his feet printed themselves on the wet
gravel. And once, in spite of the men who gripped him by each shoulder,
he stepped slightly aside to avoid a puddle on the path." He uses such details to make his attitude very apparent until the moment he describes
how he felt when he "realized what it means to destroy a healthy, conscious man." It is a powerfully persuasive essay without Orwell ever explicitly stating his purpose in writing it.

Write a detailed description of an event or incident that you watched or
participated in that you knew to be wrong. Describe the incident and
make your attitude clear by a careful selection of details without ever actually stating your position.

LOREN EISELEY (1907–1977)

Loren Eiseley, born in Lincoln, Nebraska, was a well-known anthropology scholar, a professor at the University of Lawrence, Oberlin College, and finally at the University of Pennsylvania, where he became department chair and provost. The recipient of over thirty-five honorary degrees, Eiseley was highly esteemed not only for his scientific work but also for his literary endeavors. He authored a number of scholarly publications and articles that combined scientific knowledge with insights into the human condition.

Written for a general readership, Eiseley's collections of essays earned him financial success and notoriety. Melvin Maddocks of Life magazine described Eiseley as a scientist "who can also write with poetic sensibility and with a fine sense of wonder and of reverence before the mysteries of life and nature." Another critic commented that Eiseley's "command of the language is that of a literary man. He is one of those transcendent imaginative thinkers who are not limited to one branch of science, nor to science itself. . . . He is a writer so good he can stop you dead in your tracks for a day or a week."

Eiseley's writings are often melancholy, like the following selection, which describes the homing instinct of all animals including human beings. He chronicles the homeless man sleeping in a waiting room, the mice burrowing in his flower pot, the displaced pigeons, and his search for the tree that he had planted with his father, only to find that it no longer existed and "bloomed on" only in his mind. The only way we can survive, Eiseley maintains, is "by fixing or transforming a bit of time into space or by securing a bit of space with its objects immortalized and made permanent in time."

The Brown Wasps

There is a corner in the waiting room of one of the great Eastern stations where women never sit. It is always in the shadow and overhung by rows of lockers. It is, however, always frequented—not so much by genuine travelers as by the dying. It is here that a certain element of the abandoned poor seeks a refuge out of the weather, clinging for a few hours longer to the city that has fathered them. In a precisely similar manner I have seen, on a sunny day in midwinter, a few old brown wasps creep slowly over an abandoned wasp nest in a thicket. Numbed and forgetful and frost-blackened, the hum of the spring hive still resounded faintly in their sodden tissues. Then the temperature would fall and they would drop away into the white oblivion of the snow. Here in the station it is in no way different save that the city is busy in its snows. But the old ones cling to their seats as through these were symbolic and could not be given up. Now and then they sleep, their gray old heads resting with painful awkwardness on the backs of the benches.

Also they are not at rest. For an hour they may sleep in the gasping exhaustion of the ill-nourished and aged who have to walk in the night. Then a policeman comes by on his round and nudges them upright. 2

"You can't sleep here," he growls. 3

A strange ritual then begins. An old man is difficult to waken. After a muttered conversation the policeman presses a coin into his hand and passes fiercely along the benches prodding and gesturing toward the door. In his wake, like birds rising and settling behind the passage of a farmer through a cornfield, the men totter up, move a few paces and subside once more upon the benches. 4

One man, after a slight, apologetic lurch, does not move at all. Tubercularly thin, he sleeps on steadily. The policeman does not look back. To him, too, this has become a ritual. He will not have to notice it again officially for another hour. 5

Once in a while one of the sleepers will not awake. Like the brown wasps, he will have had his wish to die in the great droning center of the hive rather than in some lonely room. It is not so bad here with the shuffle of footsteps and the knowledge that there are others who share the bad luck of the world. There are also the whistles and the sounds of everyone, everyone in the world, starting on journeys. Amidst so many journeys somebody is bound to come out all right. Somebody. 6

Maybe it was on a like thought that the brown wasps fell away from the old paper nest in the thicket. You hold till the last, even if it is only to a public seat in a railroad station. You want your place in the hive more than you want a room or a place where the aged can be eased gently out of the way. It is the place that matters, the place at the heart of things. It is life that you want, that bruises your gray old head with the hard chairs; a man has a right to his place. 7

But sometimes the place is lost in the years behind us. Or sometimes it is a thing of air, a kind of vaporous distortion above a heap of rubble. We cling to a time and place because without them man is lost, not only man but life. This is why the voices, real or unreal, which speak from the floating trumpets at spiritualist seances are so unnerving. They are voices out of nowhere whose only reality lies in their ability to stir the memory of a living person with some fragment of the past. Before the medium's cabinet both the dead and the living revolve endlessly about an episode, a place, an event that has already been engulfed by time. 8

This feeling runs deep in life; it brings stray cats running over endless miles, and birds homing from the ends of the earth. It is as though all living creatures, and particularly the more intelligent, can survive only by fix- 9 ing or transforming a bit of time into space or by securing a bit of space with its objects immortalized and made permanent in time. For example, I once saw, on a flower pot in my own living room, the efforts of a field mouse to build a remembered field. I have lived to see this episode repeated in a thousand guises, and since I have spent a large portion of my life in the shade of a nonexistent tree, I think I am entitled to speak for the field mouse.

One day as I cut across the field which at the time extended on one side   10
of our suburban shopping center, I found a giant slug feeding from a runnel of pink ice cream in an abandoned Dixie cup. I could see his eyes telescope and protrude in a kind of dim, uncertain ecstasy as his dark body bunched and elongated in the curve of the cup. Then, as I stood there at the edge of the concrete, contemplating the slug, I began to realize it was like standing on a shore where a different type of life creeps up and fumbles tentatively among the rocks and sea wrack. It knows its place and will only creep so far until something changes. Little by little as I stood there I began to see more of this shore that surrounds the place of man. I looked with sudden care and attention at things I had been running over thoughtlessly for years. I even waded out a short way into the grass and the wildrose thickets to see more. A huge black-belted bee went droning by and there were some indistinct scurryings in the underbrush.

Then I came to a sign which informed me that this field was to be the   11
site of a new Wanamaker suburban store. Thousands of obscure lives were about to perish, the spores of puffballs would go smoking off to new fields, and the bodies of little white-footed mice would be crunched under the inexorable wheels of the bulldozers. Life disappears or modifies its appearances so fast that everything takes on an aspect of illusion—a momentary fizzing and boiling with smoke rings, like pouring dissident chemicals into a retort. Here man was advancing, but in a few years his plaster and bricks would be disappearing once more into the insatiable maw of the clover. Being of an archaeological cast of mind, I thought of this fact with an obscure sense of satisfaction and waded back through the rose thickets to the concrete parking lot. As I did so, a mouse scurried ahead of me, frightened of my steps if not of that ominous Wanamaker sign. I saw him vanish in the general direction of my apartment house, his little body quivering with fear in the great open sun on the blazing concrete. Blinded and confused, he was running straight away from his field. In another week scores would follow him.

I forgot the episode then and went home to the quiet of my living   12
room. It was not until a week later, letting myself into the apartment, that I realized I had a visitor. I am fond of plants and had several ferns standing on the floor in pots to avoid the noon glare by the south window.

As I snapped on the light and glanced carelessly around the room, I saw   13 a little heap of earth on the carpet and a scrabble of pebbles that had been kicked merrily over the edge of one of the flower pots. To my astonishment I discovered a full-fledged burrow delving downward among the fern roots. I waited silently. The creature who had made the burrow did not appear. I remembered the wild field then, and the flight of the mice. No house mouse, no *Mus domesticus,* had kicked up this little heap of earth or sought refuge under a fern root in a flower pot. I thought of the desperate little creature I had seen fleeing from the wild-rose thicket. Through intricacies of pipes and attics, he, or one of his fellows, had climbed to this high green solitary room. I could visualize what had occurred. He had an image in his head, a world of seed pods and quiet, of green sheltering leaves in the dim light among the weed stems. It was the only world he knew and it was gone.

Somehow in his flight he had found his way to this room with drawn 14 shades where no one would come till nightfall. And here he had smelled garden leaves and run quickly up the flower pot to dabble his paws in common earth. He had even struggled half the afternoon to carry his burrow deeper and had failed. I examined the hole, but no whiskered twitching face appeared. He was gone. I gathered up the earth and refilled the burrow. I did not expect to find traces of him again.

Yet for three nights thereafter I came home to the darkened room and 15 my ferns to find the dirt kicked gaily about the rug and the burrow reopened, though I was never able to catch the field mouse within it. I dropped a little food about the mouth of the burrow, but it was never touched. I looked under beds or sat reading with one ear cocked for rustlings in the ferns. It was all in vain; I never saw him. Probably he ended in a trap in some other tenant's room.

But before he disappeared I had come to look hopefully for his evening 16 burrow. About my ferns there had begun to linger the insubstantial vapor of an autumn field, the distilled essence, as it were, of a mouse brain in exile from its home. It was a small dream, like our dreams, carried a long and weary journey along pipes and through spider webs, past holes over which loomed the shadows of waiting cats, and finally, desperately, into this room where he had played in the shuttered daylight for an hour among the green ferns on the floor. Every day these invisible dreams pass us on the street, or rise from beneath our feet, or look out upon us from beneath a bush.

Some years ago the old elevated railway in Philadelphia was torn down 17 and replaced by a subway system. This ancient El with its barnlike stations containing nut-vending machines and scattered food scraps had, for generations, been the favorite feeding ground of flocks of pigeons, generally one flock to a station along the route of the El. Hundreds of pigeons were dependent upon the system. They flapped in and out of its stanchions and steel work or gathered in watchful little audiences about the feet of anyone who rattled the peanut-vending machines. They even watched people who jingled change in their hands, and prospected for food under the feet of the crowds who gathered between trains. Probably very few among the waiting people who tossed a crumb to an eager pigeon realized that this El was like a food-bearing river, and that the life which haunted its banks was dependent upon the running of the trains with their human freight.

I saw the river stop. 18

The time came when the underground tubes were ready; the traffic was 19 transferred to a realm unreachable by pigeons. It was like a great river subsiding suddenly into desert sands. For a day, for two days, pigeons continued to circle over the El or stand close to the red vending machines. They were patient birds, and surely this great river which had flowed through the lives of unnumbered generations were merely suffering from some momentary drought.

They listened for the familiar vibrations that had always heralded an 20 approaching train; they flapped hopefully about the head of an occasional workman walking along the steel runways. They passed from one empty station to another, all the while growing hungrier. Finally they flew away.

I thought I had seen the last of them about the El, but there was a re- 21 vival and it provided a curious instance of the memory of living things for a way of life or a locality that has long been cherished. Some weeks after the El was abandoned workmen began to tear it down. I went to work every morning by one particular station, and the time came when the demolition crews reached this spot. Acetylene torches showered passersby with sparks, pneumatic drills hammered at the base of the structure, and a blind man who, like the pigeons, had clung with his cup to a stairway leading to the change booth, was forced to give up his place.

It was then, strangely, momentarily, one morning that I witnessed the 22 return of a little band of the familiar pigeons. I even recognized one or two members of the flock that had lived around this particular station before they were dispersed into the streets. They flew bravely in and out among the sparks and the hammers and the shouting workmen. They had returned—and they had returned because the hubbub of the wreckers had convinced them that the river was about to flow once more. For several hours they flapped in and out through the empty windows, nodding their heads and watching the fall of girders with attentive little eyes. By the following morning the station was reduced to some burned-off stanchions in the street. My bird friends had gone. It was plain, however, that they retained a memory for an insubstantial structure now compounded of air and time. Even the blind man clung to it. Someone had provided him with a chair, and he sat at the same corner staring sightlessly at an invisible stairway where, so far as he was concerned, the crowds were still ascending to the trains.

I have said my life has been passed in the shade of a nonexistent tree, so 23
that such sights do not offend me. Prematurely I am one of the brown wasps and I often sit with them in the great droning hive of the station, dreaming sometimes of a certain tree. It was planted sixty years ago by a boy with a bucket and a toy spade in a little Nebraska town. That boy was myself. It was a cottonwood sapling and the boy remembered it because of some words spoken by his father and because everyone died or moved away who was supposed to wait and grow old under its shade. The boy was passed from hand to hand, but the tree for some intangible reason had taken root in his mind. It was under its branches that he sheltered; it was from this tree that his memories, which are my memories, led away into the world.

After sixty years the mood of the brown wasps grows heavier upon one. 24
During a long inward struggle I thought it would do me good to go and look upon that actual tree. I found a rational excuse in which to clothe this madness. I purchased a ticket and at the end of two thousand miles I walked another mile to an address that was still the same. The house had not been altered.

I came close to the white picket fence and reluctantly, with great effort, 25
looked down the long vista of the yard. There was nothing there to see. For sixty years that cottonwood had been growing in my mind. Season by season its seeds had been floating farther on the hot prairie winds. We had planted it lovingly there, my father and I, because he had a great hunger for soil and live things growing, and because none of these things had long been ours to protect. We had planted the little sapling and watered it faithfully, and I remembered that I had run out with my small bucket to drench its roots the day we moved away. And all the years since it had been growing in my mind, a huge tree that somehow stood for my father and the love I bore him. I took a grasp on the picket fence and forced myself to look again.

A boy with the hard bird eye of youth pedaled a tricycle slowly up be- 26
side me.

"What'cha lookin' at?" he asked curiously. 27

"A tree," I said. 28

"What for?" he said. 29

"It isn't there," I said, to myself mostly, and began to walk away at a 30
pace just slow enough not to seem to be running.

"What isn't there?" the boy asked. I didn't answer. It was obvious I was 31
attached by a thread to a thing that had never been there, or certainly not for long. Something that had to be held in the air, or sustained in the

mind, because it was part of my orientation in the universe and I could not survive without it. There was more than an animal's attachment to a place. There was something else, the attachment of the spirit to a grouping of events in time; it was part of our morality.

So I had come home at last, driven by a memory in the brain as surely 32 as the field mouse who had delved long ago into my flower pot or the pigeons flying forever amidst the rattle of nut-vending machines. These, the burrow under the greenery in my living room and the red-bellied bowls of peanuts now hovering in midair in the minds of pigeons, were all part of an elusive world that existed nowhere and yet everywhere. I looked once at the real world about me while the persistent boy pedaled at my heels.

It was without meaning, though my feet took a remembered path. In 33 sixty years the house and street had rotted out of my mind. But the tree, the tree that no longer was, that had perished in its first season, bloomed on in my individual mind, unblemished as my father's words. "We'll plant a tree here, son, and we're not going to move any more. And when you're an old, old man you can sit under it and think how we planted it here, you and me, together."

I began to outpace the boy on the tricycle. 34

"Do you live here, Mister?" he shouted after me suspiciously. I took a 35 firm grasp on airy nothing—to be precise, on the bole of a great tree. "I do," I said. I spoke for myself, one field mouse, and several pigeons. We were all out of touch but somehow permanent. It was the world that had changed.

MUSINGS

Eiseley describes the homing instinct common to all animals from a human perspective—the preservation of a place nurtured by memory, preserved over time.

Can you think of such a place that you revisit in your mind? What significance does it have for you? Describe why.

GORE VIDAL (1925–)

Gore Vidal is an energetic and talented essayist, novelist, and playwright. In his life-time he has written approximately twenty-three novels, at least a dozen original tele-plays and a number of television adaptations, screenplays, stageplays, and essays. At nineteen years of age Vidal published his first novel, Williwaw, *which describes an Arctic squall (called a williwaw) and its effects. He subsequently wrote almost a novel a year, with some time off for his venture into television and films. One of the most well-known literary figures of the twentieth century, Vidal has been a frequent and witty talk-show guest and ran twice for political office. Vidal was greatly influenced by his grandfather, Oklahoma Senator Thomas P. Gore, and at a young age developed an enduring passion for politics and the machinations of government. Vidal once stated that "I do nothing but think about my country. . . . The United States is my theme and all that dwell in it," and commented "The only thing I've ever really wanted in my life was to be President." His political interests informed much of his writing, and his historical novels always connect in some way with the present political scene.*

In 1984 Vidal's historical novel Lincoln *was published. Called "a masterpiece" by Stephen Rubin in the* Chicago Tribune Book World, *the critic continues: "The intel-ligence, the wit, the humor, the outrageousness are omnipresent." Critics seem to agree, nevertheless, that his novel* Myra Breckinridge, *which takes place in modern America, is his masterpiece.*

In the following essay Vidal begins with his reaction after examining the items that Lincoln had in his pocket the night of his assassination. After describing a life mask made of Lincoln while he was still alive, Vidal then speculates about Lincoln's speech-making ability and writing, calling him "a literary genius who was called upon to live, rather than merely write, a high tragedy."

Lincoln Up Close

Once, at the Library of Congress in Washington, I was shown the con-tents of Lincoln's pockets on the night that he was shot at Ford's Theater. There was a Confederate bank note, perhaps acquired during the presi-dent's recent excursion to the fallen capital, Richmond; a pocket knife; a couple of newspaper cuttings (good notices for his administration); and two pairs of spectacles. It was eerie to hold in one's hand what looked to be the same spectacles that he wore as he was photographed reading the Sec-ond Inaugural Address, the month before his murder. One of the wire "legs" of the spectacles had broken off and someone, presumably Lincoln himself, had clumsily repaired it with a piece of darning wool. I tried on the glasses: he was indeed farsighted, and what must have been to him the clearly printed lines "let us strive on to finish the work we are in; to bind up the nation's wounds" was to my myopic eyes a gray quartzlike blur.

Next I was shown the Bible which the president had kissed as he swore his second oath to preserve, protect, and defend the Constitution of the United States; the oath that he often used, in lieu of less spiritual argument, to justify the war that he had fought to preserve the Union. The Bible is small and beautifully bound. To the consternation of the custodian, I opened the book. The pages were as bright and clear as the day they were printed; in fact, they stuck together in such a way as to suggest that no one had ever even riffled them. Obviously the book had been sent for at the last moment; then given away, to become a treasured relic.

Although Lincoln belonged to no Christian church, he did speak of the "Almighty" more and more often as the war progressed. During the congressional election of 1846, Lincoln had been charged with "infidelity" to Christianity. At the time, he made a rather lawyerly response. To placate those who insist that presidents must be devout monotheists (preferably Christian and Protestant), Lincoln allowed that he himself could never support "a man for office, whom I knew to be an open enemy of, and scoffer at, religion." The key word, of course, is "open." As usual, Lincoln does not lie—something that the Jesuits maintain no wise man does—but he shifts the argument to his own advantage and gets himself off the atheistical hook much as Thomas Jefferson had done almost a century earlier.

Last, I was shown a life mask, made shortly before the murder. The hair on the head has been tightly covered over, the whiskers greased. When the sculptor Saint-Gaudens first saw it, he thought it was a *death* mask, so worn and remote is the face. I was most startled by the smallness of the head. In photographs, with hair and beard, the head had seemed in correct proportion to Lincoln's great height. But this vulpine little face seems strangely vulnerable. The cheeks are sunken in. The nose is sharper than in the photographs, and the lines about the wide thin mouth are deep. With eyes shut, he looks to be a small man, in rehearsal for his death.

Those who knew Lincoln always thought it a pity that there was never a photograph of him truly smiling. A non-user of tobacco, he had splendid teeth for that era, and he liked to laugh, and when he did, Philip Hone noted, the tip of his nose moved like a tapir's.

Gertrude Stein used to say that U. S. Grant had the finest American prose style. The general was certainly among our best writers, but he lacked music (Gertrude lacked it too, but she did have rhythm). Lincoln deployed the plain style as masterfully as Grant; and he does have music. In fact, there is now little argument that Lincoln is one of the great masters of prose in our language, and the only surprising aspect of so demonstrable a fact is that there are those who still affect surprise. Partly this is due to the Education Mafia that has taken over what little culture the United States has, and partly to the sort of cranks who maintain that since Shakespeare had little Latin and less Greek and did not keep company with kings, he could never have written so brilliantly of kings and courts, and so not he but some great lord wrote the plays in his name.

For all practical purposes, Lincoln had no formal education. But he studied law, which meant not only reading Blackstone (according to Jeremy Bentham, a writer "cold, reserved and wary, exhibiting a frigid pride") but brooding over words in themselves and in combination. In those days, most good lawyers, like good generals, wrote good prose; if they were not precisely understood, a case or a battle might be lost.   7

William Herndon was Lincoln's law partner in Springfield, Illinois, from 1844 to February 18, 1861, when Lincoln went to Washington to be inaugurated president. Herndon is the principal source for Lincoln's pre-presidential life. He is a constant embarrassment to Lincoln scholars because they must rely on him, yet since Lincoln is the national deity, they must omit a great deal of Herndon's testimony about Lincoln. For one thing, Lincoln was something of a manic-depressive, to use current jargon. In fact, there was a time when, according to Herndon, Lincoln was "*as 'crazy as a loon' in this city in 1841.*" Since this sort of detail does not suit the history departments, it is usually omitted or glossed over, or poor Herndon is accused of telling lies.   8

The Lincoln of the hagiographers is forever serene and noble, in defeat as well as in victory. With perfect hindsight, they maintain that it was immediately apparent that the Lincoln–Douglas contest had opened wide the gates of political opportunity for Lincoln. Actually, after Lincoln's defeat by Douglas for the U.S. Senate, he was pretty loonlike for a time; and he thought that the gates of political opportunity had slammed shut for him. Lincoln's friend Henry C. Whitney, in a letter to Herndon, wrote: 9

> I shall never forget the day—January 6, 1859—I went to your office and found Lincoln there alone. He appeared to be somewhat dejected—in fact I never saw a man so depressed. I tried to rally his drooping spirits . . . but with ill success. He was simply steeped in gloom. For a time he was silent . . . blurting out as he sank down: "Well, whatever happens I expect everyone to desert me now, but Billy Herndon."

• • •

Despite the busyness of the Lincoln priests, the rest of us can still discern the real Lincoln by entering his mind through what he wrote, a se-   10 ductive business, by and large, particularly when he shows us unexpected views of the familiar. Incidentally, to read Lincoln's letters in holograph is revelatory; the writing changes dramatically with his mood. In the eloquent, thought-out letters to mourners for the dead, he writes a clear firm hand. When the governor of Massachusetts, John A. Andrew, in the summer of 1862 wrote that he could not send troops because his paymasters were incapable of "quick work," Lincoln replied, "Please say to these gentlemen that if they do not work quickly I will make quick work of them. In the name of all that is reasonable, how long does it take to pay a couple of regiments?" The words tumble from Lincoln's pen in uneven rows upon the page, and one senses not only his fury but his terror that the city of Washington might soon fall to the rebels.

Since 1920 no American president has written his state speeches; lately, 11 many of our presidents seem to experience some difficulty in reading aloud what others have written for them to say. But until Woodrow Wilson suffered a stroke, it was assumed that the chief task of the first magistrate was to report to the American people, in their Congress assembled, upon the state of the union. The president was elected not only to execute the laws but to communicate to the people his vision of the prospect before us. As a reporter to the people, Lincoln surpassed all presidents. Even in his youthful letters and speeches, he is already himself. The prose is austere and sharp; there are few adjectives and adverbs; and then, suddenly, sparks of humor.

> Fellow Citizens—It will be but a very few words that I shall undertake to say. I was born in Kentucky, raised in Indiana and lived in Illinois. And now I am here, where it is my business to care equally for the good people of all the States. . . . There are but few views or aspects of this great war upon which I have not said or written something whereby my own opinions might be known. But there is one—the recent attempts of our erring brethren, as they are sometimes called—to employ the negro to fight for them. I have neither written nor made a speech on that subject, because that was their business, not mine; and if I had a wish upon the subject I had not the power to introduce it, or make it effective. The great question with them was, whether the negro, being put into the army, would fight for them. I do not know, and therefore cannot decide. They ought to know better than we. I have in my lifetime heard many arguments why the negroes ought to be slaves; but if they fight for those who would keep them in slavery it will be a better argument than any I have yet heard. He who will fight for that ought to be a slave. They have concluded at last to take one out of four of the slaves, and put them in the army; and that one out of the four who will fight to keep the others in slavery ought to be a slave himself

unless he is killed in a fight. While I have often said that all men ought to be free, yet I would allow those colored persons to be slaves who want to be; and next to them those white persons who argue in favor of making other people slaves. I am in favor of giving an opportunity to such white men to try it on for themselves.

Also, as a lawyer on circuit, Lincoln was something of a stand-up co-median, able to keep an audience laughing for hours as he appeared to im-provise his stories; actually, he claimed no originality as "I am a re-tailer." 12

Lincoln did not depend very much on others for help when it came to the writing of the great papers. Secretary of State William Seward gave him a line or two for the coda of the First Inaugural Address, while the poetry of Shake-speare and the prose of the King James version of the Bible were so much in Lincoln's blood that he occasionally slipped into iambic pentameter. 13

The Annual Message to Congress, December 1, 1862, has echoes of Shakespeare's *Julius Caesar* and *Macbeth* (ominously, Lincoln's favorite play): 14

> We can not escape history. We of this Congress and this administration will be remembered in spite of ourselves. No personal significance, or insignifi-cance, can spare one or another of us. The fiery trial through which we pass will light us down, in honor or dishonor, to the latest generation.

A few years earlier, at Brown University, Lincoln's young secretary, John Hay, wrote a valedictory poem. Of his class's common memories, "Our hearts shall bear them safe through life's commotion / Their fading gleam shall light us to our graves." But of course, Macbeth had said long before Hay, "And all our yesterdays have lighted fools / The way to dusty death."

Of Lincoln's contemporaries, William Herndon had given us the best close-up view of the man that he had shared an office with for seventeen years. "He was the most continuous and severest thinker in America. He read but little and that for an end. Politics were his Heaven, and his Hades metaphysics." As for the notion that Lincoln was a gentle, humble, holy man, even John Hay felt obliged to note that "no great man was ever mod-est. It was [Lincoln's] intellectual arrogance and unconscious assumption of superiority that men like Chase and Sumner could never forgive." Along with so much ambition and secretiveness of nature, Lincoln also had an impish sense of humor; he liked to read aloud comic writers like Petroleum V. Nasby, and he told comic stories to divert, if not others, him-self from the ongoing tragedy at whose center he was. 15

What was it like to be in the audience when Lincoln made a speech? What did he really look like? What did he sound like? To the first question 16 we have the photographs; but they are motionless. He was six feet four, "more or less stoop-shouldered," wrote Herndon. "He was very tall, thin, and gaunt. . . . When he first began speaking, he was shrill, squeaking, piping, unpleasant; his general look, his form, his pose, the color of flesh, wrinkled and dry, his sensitiveness, and his momentary diffidence, everything seemed to be against him." Then, "he gently and gradually warmed up . . . voice became harmonious, melodious, musical, if you please, with face somewhat aglow. . . . Lincoln's gray eyes would flash fire when speaking against slavery or spoke volumes of hope and love when speaking of liberty, justice and the progress of mankind."

Of Lincoln's politics, Herndon wrote, he "was a conscientious conserv-   17
ative; he believed in Law and Order. See his speech before Springfield Lyceum in 1838." This speech is indeed a key to Lincoln's character, for it is here that he speaks of the nature of ambition and how, in a republic that was already founded, a tyrant might be tempted to reorder the state in his own image. At the end Lincoln himself did just that. There is a kind of terrible Miltonian majesty in his address to the doubtless puzzled young men of the Springfield Lyceum. In effect, their twenty-nine-year-old contemporary was saying that for the ambitious man, it is better to reign in hell than serve in heaven.

In the end, whether or not Lincoln's personal ambition undid him and   18
the nation is immaterial. He took a divided house and jammed it back together. He was always a pro-Union man. As for slavery, he was averse, rather than adverse, to the institution but no Abolitionist. Lincoln's eulogy on Henry Clay (July 6, 1852) is to the point. Of Clay, Lincoln wrote,

> As a politician or statesman, no one was so habitually careful to avoid all sectional ground. Whatever he did, he did for the whole country. . . . Feeling as he did, and as the truth surely is, that the world's best hope depended on the continued union of the States, he was ever jealous of, and watchful for, whatever might have the slightest tendency to separate them.

He supports Clay's policy of colonizing the blacks elsewhere; today any mention of Lincoln's partiality for this scheme amuses black historians and makes many of the white ones deal economically with the truth.

Eight years later, the eulogist, now the president, promptly made war   19
on those states that had chosen to depart the Union on the same high moral ground that Lincoln himself had so eloquently stated at the time of the Mexican War in 1848: "Any people anywhere, being inclined and having the power, have the right to rise up, and shake off the existing government, and form a new one that suits them better." Lawyer Lincoln would probably have said, rather bleakly, that the key phrase here was "and having the power." The Confederacy did not have the power; six hundred

thousand men died in the next four years; and the Confederacy was smashed and Lincoln was murdered.

In a sense, we have had three republics. The first, a loose confederation of former British colonies, lasted from 1776 to 1789, when the first Congress under the Constitution met. The second republic ended April 9, 1865, with the South's surrender. In due course Lincoln's third republic was transformed (inevitably?) into the national security state where we have been locked up for forty years. A fourth republic might be nice.

In any event, for better or worse, we still live in the divided house that Lincoln cobbled together for us, and it is always useful to get to know through his writing not the god of the establishment-priests but a literary genius who was called upon to live, rather than merely to write, a high tragedy. I can think of no one in literary or political history quite like this essential American writer.

MUSINGS

In this essay, Vidal begins with a description of his feelings as one day at the Library of Congress he was allowed to view the articles that were in Lincoln's pockets on the night he was assassinated. He expands on this experience by drawing on the research he had done for his historical novel on Lincoln, quoting from various speeches and letters to support his contention that Lincoln was not only a figure in a high tragedy, the Civil War, but also a literary genius.

Select an artist that you admire—a writer, a musician, a singer, or a painter. Start your essay with your first encounter with the artist's work and follow your reasons for admiring his or her work with supportive evidence from the body of work.

RICHARD SELZER (1928–)

Richard Selzer, a practicing surgeon, uses his own medical experience as a basis for his essays and short stories, relentlessly drawing the reader into the operating room to face the realities of life and death, to share the surgeon's successes and heartbreaking failures. Elizabeth Peer states in Newsweek *that "by dwelling on the mechanics of death, [Selzer] celebrates life." Others, however, have criticized the graphic and sometimes gory details of his writing; Christopher Lehmann-Haupt writes that "There may be some beauty in the way Dr. Selzer writes about these encounters with sickness and death, but to me the art of them seems gratuitous. It is quite enough that such things happen."*

In 1974 Selzer wrote a volume of short stories Rituals of Surgery, *but it was his collection of essays* Mortal Lessons *(1977) that earned him the attention of the critics as well as a wide readership. A second volume of essays,* Confessions of a Knife *(1979), was followed by a group of essays and fiction,* Letters to a Young Doctor *(1982), based on his experiences as a young doctor. In one essay Selzer recounts a plastic surgeon's operation on a young girl to correct a cleft lip, which ends in tragedy when she dies under anesthesia. He awakens the next day to discover that during the night the surgeon has performed surgery on the corpse and corrected the girl's lip.*

The following essay chronicles Selzer's encounter with prostitutes in Port-au-Prince, Haiti, and his later visit to an AIDS clinic, where he has been invited by a local doctor who explains the voodoo ritual that requires a man to perform anal sodomy on another man in order to attain the status of houngan. *Selzer later discusses the situation with the hotel keeper, whose only concern is tourism and who blames the media for ruining travel to Haiti because of the fear of AIDS. Selzer leaves Haiti knowing that the epidemic will continue because of the lassitude and inertia of the people: "Perhaps one day," he concludes, "the plague will be rendered in poetry, music, painting but not now. Not now."*

A Mask on the Face of Death

It is ten o'clock at night as we drive up to the Copacabana, a dilapidated   1
brothel on the rue Dessalines in the red-light district of Port-au-Prince. My guide is a young Haitian, Jean-Bernard. Ten years before, J-B tells me, at the age of fourteen, "like every good Haitian boy" he had been brought here by his older cousins for his *rite de passage*. From the car to the entrance, we are accosted by a half dozen men and women for sex. We enter, go down a long hall that breaks upon a cavernous room with a stone floor.

The cubicles of the prostitutes, I am told, are in an attached wing of the building. Save for a red-purple glow from small lights on the walls, the place is unlit. Dark shapes float by, each with a blindingly white stripe of teeth. Latin music is blaring. We take seats at the table farthest from the door. Just outside, there is the rhythmic lapping of the Caribbean Sea. About twenty men are seated at the tables or lean against the walls. Brightly dressed women, singly or in twos or threes, stroll about, now and then exchanging banter with the men. It's as though we have been deposited in act two of Bizet's *Carmen*. If this place isn't Lillas Pastia's tavern, what is it?

Within minutes, three light-skinned young women arrive at our table. 2
They are very beautiful and young and lively. Let them be Carmen, Mercedes and Frasquita.

"I want the old one," says Frasquita, ruffling my hair. The women 3
laugh uproariously.

"Don't bother looking any further," says Mercedes. "We are the pretti- 4
est ones."

"We only want to talk," I tell her. 5

"Aaah, aaah," she crows. "*Massissi.* You are *massissi.*" It is the contemp- 6
tuous Creole term for homosexual. If we want only to talk, we must be gay. Mercedes and Carmen are slender, each weighing one hundred pounds or less. Frasquita is tall and hefty. They are dressed for work: red taffeta, purple chiffon and black sequins. Among them a thousand gold bracelets and earrings multiply every speck of light. Their bare shoulders are like animated lamps gleaming in the shadowy room. Since there is as yet no business, the women agree to sit with us. J-B orders beer and cigarettes. We pay each woman $10.

"Where are you from?" I begin. 7

"We are Dominican." 8

"Do you miss your country?" 9

"Oh, yes, we do." Six eyes go muzzy with longing. "Our country is the 10
most beautiful in the world. No country is like the Dominican. And it doesn't stink like this one."

"Then why don't you work there? Why come to Haiti?" 11

"Santo Domingo has too many whores. All beautiful, like us. All light- 12
skinned. The Haitian men like to sleep with light women."

"Why is that?" 13

"Because always, the whites have all the power and the money. The 14
black men can imagine they do, too, when they have us in bed."

Eleven o'clock. I looked around the room that is still sparsely peopled 15
with men.

"It isn't getting any busier," I say. Frasquita glances over her shoulder. 16
Her eyes drill the darkness.

"It is still early," she says.   17

"Could it be that the men are afraid of getting sick?" Frasquita is of-   18
fended.

"Sick! They do not get sick from us. We are healthy, strong. Every week   19
we go for a checkup. Besides, we know how to tell if we are getting sick."

"I mean sick with AIDS." The word sets off a hurricane of taffeta, chif-   20
fon and gold jewelry. They are all gesticulation and fury. It is Carmen who
speaks.

"AIDS!" Her lips curl about the syllable. "There is no such thing: It is a   21
false disease invented by the American government to take advantage of
the poor countries. The American President hates poor people, so now he
makes up AIDS to take away the little we have." The others nod vehemently.

"*Mira, mon cher.* Look, my dear," Carmen continues. "One day the po-   22
lice came here. Believe me, they are worse than the *tonton macoutes* with
their submachine guns. They rounded up one hundred and five of us and
they took our blood. That was a year ago. None of us have died, you see?
We are all still here. *Mira,* we sleep with all the men and we are not sick."

"But aren't there some of you who have lost weight and have diarrhea?"   23

"One or two, maybe. But they don't eat. That is why they are weak."   24

"Only the men die," says Mercedes. "They stop eating, so they die. It is   25
hard to kill a woman."

"Do you eat well?"   26

"Oh, yes, don't worry, we do. We eat like poor people, but we eat."   27
There is a sudden scream from Frasquita. She points to a large rat that has
emerged from beneath our table.

"My God!" she exclaims. "It is big like a pig." They burst into laugher.   28
For a moment the women fall silent. There is only the restlessness of their
many bracelets. I give them each another $10.

"Are many of the men here bisexual?"   29

"Too many. They do it for money. Afterward, they come to us." Car-   30
men lights a cigarette and looks down at the small lace handkerchief she
has been folding and unfolding with immense precision on the table. All
at once she turns it over as though it were the ace of spades.

"*Mira, blanc . . .* look, white man," she says in a voice suddenly full of   31
foreboding. Her skin too seems to darken to coincide with the tone of her
voice.

"*Mira,* soon many Dominican women will die in Haiti!"   32

"Die of what?"   33

She shrugs. "It is what they do to us."   34

"Carmen," I say, "if you knew that you had AIDS, that your blood was   35
bad, would you still sleep with men?" Abruptly, she throws back her head
and laughs. It is the same laughter with which Frasquita had greeted the
rat at our feet. She stands and the others follow.

"*Méchant!* You wicked man," she says. Then, with terrible solemnity,   36
"You don't know anything."

"But you are killing the Haitian men," I say.   37

"As for that," she says, "everyone is killing everyone else." All at once, I   38
want to know everything about these three—their childhood, their
dreams, what they do in the afternoon, what they eat for lunch.

"Don't leave," I say. "Stay a little more." Again, I reach for my wallet.   39
But they are gone, taking all the light in the room with them—Mercedes
and Carmen to sit at another table where three men have been waiting.
Frasquita is strolling about the room. Now and then, as if captured by the
music, she breaks into a few dance steps, snapping her fingers, singing to
herself.

Midnight. And the Copacabana is filling up. Now it is like any other   40
seedy nightclub where men and women go hunting. We get up to leave. In
the center a couple are dancing a *méringue.* He is the most graceful dancer
I have ever watched; she, the most voluptuous. Together they seem to be
riding the back of the music as it gallops to a precisely sexual beat. Closer
up, I see that the man is short of breath, sweating. All at once, he collapses
into a chair. The woman bends over him, coaxing, teasing, but he is
through. A young man with a long polished stick blocks my way.

"I come with you?" he asks. "Very good time. You say yes? Ten dollars?   41
Five?"

I have been invited by Dr. Jean William Pape to attend the AIDS clinic   42
of which he is the director. Nothing from the outside of the low white-
washed structure would suggest it as a medical facility. Inside, it is divided
into many small cubicles and a labyrinth of corridors. At nine A.M. the
hallways are already full of emaciated silent men and women, some sitting
on the few benches, the rest leaning against the walls. The only sounds are
subdued moans of discomfort interspersed with coughs. How they eat us
with their eyes as we pass.

The room where Pape and I work is perhaps ten feet by ten. It contains   43
a desk, two chairs and a narrow wooden table that is covered with a sheet
that will not be changed during the day. The patients are called in one at a
time, asked how they feel and whether there is any change in their symp-
toms, then examined on the table. If the patient is new to the clinic, he or
she is questioned about sexual activities.

A twenty-seven-year-old man whose given name is Miracle enters. He is   44
wobbly, panting, like a groggy boxer who has let down his arms and is
waiting for the last punch. He is neatly dressed and wears, despite the
heat, a heavy woolen cap. When he removes it, I see that his hair is thin,
dull reddish and straight. It is one of the signs of AIDS in Haiti, Pape tells
me. The man's skin is covered with a dry itchy rash. Throughout the inter-

view and examination he scratches himself slowly, absentmindedly. The rash is called prurigo. It is another symptom of AIDS in Haiti. This man has had diarrhea for six months. The laboratory reports that the diarrhea is due to an organism called cryptosporidium, for which there is no treatment. The telltale rattling of the tuberculous moisture in his chest is audible without a stethoscope. He is like a leaky cistern that bubbles and froths. And, clearly, exhausted.

"Where do you live?" I ask. 45

"Kenscoff." A village in the hills above Port-au-Prince. 46

"How did you come here today?" 47

"I came on the *tap-tap*." It is the name given to the small buses that 48
swarm the city, each one extravagantly decorated with religious slogans, icons, flowers, animals, all painted in psychedelic colors. I have never seen a *tap-tap* that was not covered with passengers as well, riding outside and hanging on. The vehicles are little masterpieces of contagion, if not of AIDS then of the multitude of germs which Haitian flesh is heir to. Miracle is given a prescription for a supply of Sera, which is something like Gatorade, and told to return in a month.

"Mangé kou bêf," says the doctor in farewell. "Eat like an ox." What can 49
he mean? The man has no food or money to buy any. Even had he food, he has not the appetite to eat or the ability to retain it. To each departing patient the doctor will say the same words— *"Mangé kou bêf."* I see that it is his way of offering a hopeful goodbye.

"Will he live until his next appointment?" I ask. 50

"No." Miracle leaves to catch the *tap-tap* for Kenscoff. 51

Next is a woman of twenty-six who enters holding her right hand to her 52
forehead in a kind of permanent salute. In fact, she is shielding her eye from view. This is her third visit to the clinic. I see that she is still quite well nourished.

"Now, you'll see something beautiful, tremendous," the doctor says. 53
Once seated upon the table, she is told to lower her hand. When she does, I see that her right eye and its eyelid are replaced by a huge fungating ulcerated tumor, a side product of her AIDS. As she turns her head, the cluster of lymph glands in her neck to which the tumor has spread is thrown into relief. Two years ago she received a blood transfusion at a time when the country's main blood bank was grossly contaminated with AIDS. It has since been closed down. The only blood available in Haiti is a small supply procured from the Red Cross.

"Can you give me medicine?" the woman wails. 54

"No." 55

"Can you cut it away?" 56

"No." 57

"Is there radiation therapy?" I ask. 58

"No."

"Chemotherapy?" The doctor looks at me in what some might call weary amusement. I see that there is nothing to do. She has come here because there is nowhere else to go.

"What will she do?"

"Tomorrow or the next day or the day after that she will climb up into the mountains to seek relief from the *houngan,* the voodoo priest, just as her slave ancestors did two hundred years ago."

Then comes a frail man in his thirties, with a strangely spiritualized face, like a child's. Pus runs from one ear onto his cheek, where it has dried and caked. He has trouble remembering, he tells us. In fact, he seems confused. It is from toxoplasmosis of the brain, an effect of his AIDS. This man is bisexual. Two years ago he engaged in oral sex with foreign men for money. As I palpate the swollen glands of his neck, a mosquito flies between our faces. I swat at it, miss. Just before coming to Haiti I had read that the AIDS virus had been isolated from a certain mosquito. The doctor senses my thought.

"Not to worry," he says. "So far as we know there has never been a case transmitted by insects."

"Yes," I say. "I see."

And so it goes until the last, the thirty-sixth AIDS patient has been seen. At the end of the day I am invited to wash my hands before leaving. I go down a long hall to a sink. I turn on the faucets but there is no water.

"But what about *you?*" I ask the doctor. "You are at great personal risk here—the tuberculosis, the other infections, no water to wash . . ." He shrugs, smiles faintly and lifts his hands palm upward.

We are driving up a serpiginous steep road into the barren mountains above Port-au-Prince. Even in the bright sunshine the countryside has the bloodless color of exhaustion and indifference. Our destination is the Baptist Mission Hospital, where many cases of AIDS have been reported. Along the road there are slow straggles of schoolchildren in blue uniforms who stretch out their hands as we pass and call out, "Give me something." Already a crowd of outpatients has gathered at the entrance to the mission compound. A tour of the premises reveals that in contrast to the aridity outside the gates, this is an enclave of productivity, lush with fruit trees and poinsettia.

The hospital is clean and smells of creosote. Of the forty beds, less than a third are occupied. In one male ward of twelve beds, there are two patients. The chief physician tells us that last year he saw ten cases of AIDS each week. Lately the number has decreased to four or five.

"Why is that?" we want to know.

"Because we do not admit them to the hospital, so they have learned not to come here."

"Why don't you admit them?"   72

"Because we would have nothing but AIDS here then. So we send them   73
away."

"But I see that you have very few patients in bed."   74

"That is also true."   75

"Where do the AIDS patients go?"   76

"Some go to the clinic in Port-au-Prince or the general hospital in the   77
city. Others go home to die or to the voodoo priest."

"Do the people with AIDS know what they have before they come here?"   78

"Oh, yes, they know very well, and they know there is nothing to be   79
done for them."

Outside, the crowd of people is dispersing toward the gate. The clinic   80
has been canceled for the day. No one knows why. We are conducted to
the office of the reigning American pastor. He is a tall, handsome Mid-
westerner with an ecclesiastical smile.

"It is voodoo that is the devil here." He warms to his subject. "It is a de-   81
monic religion, a cancer on Haiti. Voodoo is worse than AIDS. And it is
one of the reasons for the epidemic. Did you know that in order for a man
to become a *houngan* he must perform anal sodomy on another man? No,
of course you didn't. And it doesn't stop there. The *houngans* tell the men
that in order to appease the spirits they too must do the same thing. So
you have ritualized homosexuality. That's what is spreading the AIDS."
The pastor tells us of a nun who witnessed two acts of sodomy in a provincial hospital where she came upon a man sexually assaulting a houseboy
and another man mounting a male patient in his bed.

"Fornication," he says. "It is Sodom and Gomorrah all over again, so   82
what can you expect from these people?" Outside his office we are shown
a cage of terrified, cowering monkeys to whom he coos affectionately. It is
clear that he loves them. At the car, we shake hands.

"By the way," the pastor says, "what is your religion? Perhaps I am a   83
kinsman?"

"While I am in Haiti," I tell him, "it will be voodoo or it will be noth- 84
ing at all."

Abruptly, the smile breaks. It is as though a crack had suddenly ap-   85
peared in the face of an idol.

From the mission we go to the general hospital. In the heart of Port-au-   86
Prince, it is the exact antithesis of the immaculate facility we have just
left—filthy, crowded, hectic and staffed entirely by young interns and res-
idents. Though it is associated with a medical school, I do not see any
members of the faculty. We are shown around by Jocelyne, a young intern
in a scrub suit. Each bed in three large wards is occupied. On the floor
about the beds, hunkered in the posture of the innocent poor, are family

members of the patients. In the corridor that constitutes the emergency room, someone lies on a stretcher receiving an intravenous infusion. She is hardly more than a cadaver.

"Where are the doctors in charge?" I ask Jocelyne. She looks at me questioningly.

"We are in charge."

"I mean your teachers, the faculty."

"They do not come here."

"What is wrong with that woman?"

"She has had diarrhea for three months. Now she is dehydrated." I ask the woman to open her mouth. Her throat is covered with the white plaques of thrush, a fungus infection associated with AIDS.

"How many AIDS patients do you see here?"

"Three or four a day. We send them home. Sometimes the families abandon them, then we must admit them to the hospital. Every day, then, a relative comes to see if the patient has died. They want to take the body. That is important to them. But they know very well that AIDS is contagious and they are afraid to keep them at home. Even so, once or twice a week the truck comes to take away the bodies. Many are children. They are buried in mass graves."

"Where do the wealthy patients go?"

"There is a private hospital called Canapé Vert. Or else they go to Miami. Most of them, rich and poor, do not go to the hospital. Most are never diagnosed."

"How do you know these people have AIDS?"

"We don't know sometimes. The blood test is inaccurate. There are many false positives and false negatives. Fifteen percent of those with the disease have negative blood tests. We go by their infections—tuberculosis, diarrhea, fungi, herpes, skin rashes. It is not hard to tell."

"Do they know what they have?"

"Yes. They understand at once and they are prepared to die."

"Do the patients know how AIDS is transmitted?"

"They know, but they do not like to talk about it. It is taboo. Their memories do not seem to reach back to the true origins of their disaster. It is understandable, is it not?"

"Whatever you write, don't hurt us any more than we have already been hurt." It is a young Haitian journalist with whom I am drinking a rum punch. He means that any further linkage of AIDS and Haiti in the media would complete the economic destruction of the country. The damage was done early in the epidemic when the Centers for Disease Control in Atlanta added Haitians to the three other high-risk groups—hemophiliacs, intravenous drug users and homosexual and bisexual men. In fact,

Haitians are no more susceptible to AIDS than anyone else. Although the CDC removed Haitians from special scrutiny in 1985, the lucrative tourism on which so much of the country's economy was based was crippled. Along with tourism went much of the foreign business investment. Worst of all was the injury to the national pride. Suddenly Haiti was indicted as the source of AIDS in the western hemisphere.

What caused the misunderstanding was the discovery of a large number   104 of Haitian men living in Miami with AIDS antibodies in their blood. They denied absolutely they were homosexuals. But the CDC investigators did not know that homosexuality is the strongest taboo in Haiti and that no man would ever admit to it. Bisexuality, however, is not uncommon. Many married men and heterosexually oriented males will occasionally seek out other men for sex. Further, many, if not most, Haitian men visit female prostitutes from time to time. It is not difficult to see that once the virus was set loose in Haiti, the spread would be swift through both genders.

Exactly how the virus of AIDS arrived is not known. Could it have   105 been brought home by the Cuban soldiers stationed in Angola and thence to Haiti, about fifty miles away? Could it have been passed on by the thousands of Haitians living in exile in Zaire, who later returned home or immigrated to the United States? Could it have come from the American and Canadian homosexual tourists, and, yes, even some U.S. diplomats who have traveled to the island to have sex with impoverished Haitian men all too willing to sell themselves to feed their families? Throughout the international gay community Haiti was known as a good place to go for sex.

On a private tip from an official at the Ministry of Tourism, J-B and I   106 drive to a town some fifty miles from Port-au-Prince. The hotel is owned by two Frenchmen who are out of the country, one of the staff tells us. He is a man of about thirty and clearly he is desperately ill. Tottering, short of breath, he shows us about the empty hotel. The furnishings are opulent and extreme—tiger skins on the wall, a live leopard in the garden, a bedroom containing a giant bathtub with gold faucets. Is it the heat of the day or the heat of my imagination that makes these walls echo with the painful cries of pederasty?

The hotel where we are staying is in Pétionville, the fashionable suburb   107 of Port-au-Prince. It is the height of the season but there are no tourists, only a dozen or so French and American businessmen. The swimming pool is used once or twice a day by a single person. Otherwise, the water remains undisturbed until dusk, when the fruit bats come down to drink in midswoop. The hotel keeper is an American. He is eager to set me straight on Haiti.

"What did and should attract foreign investment is a combination of reliable weather, an honest and friendly populace, low wages and multilingual managers."

"What spoiled it?"

"Political instability and a bad American press about AIDS." He pauses, then adds: "To which I hope you won't be contributing."

"What about just telling the truth?" I suggest.

"Look," he says, "there is no more danger of catching AIDS in Haiti than in New York or Santo Domingo. It is not where you are but what you do that counts." Agreeing, I ask if he had any idea that much of the tourism in Haiti during the past few decades was based on sex.

"No idea whatsoever. It was only recently that we discovered that that was the case."

"How is it that you hoteliers, restaurant owners and the Ministry of Tourism did not know what *tout* Haiti knew?"

"Look. All I know is that this is a middle-class, family-oriented hotel. We don't allow guests to bring women, or for that matter men, into their rooms. If they did, we'd ask them to leave immediately."

At five A.M. the next day the telephone rings in my room. A Creole-accented male voice.

"Is the lady still with you, sir?"

"There is no lady here."

"In your room, sir, the lady I allowed to go up with a package?"

"There is no lady here, I tell you."

At seven A.M. I stop at the front desk. The clerk is a young man.

"Was it you who called my room at five o'clock?"

"Sorry," he says with a smile. "It was a mistake, sir. I meant to ring the room next door to yours." Still smiling, he holds up his shushing finger.

Next to Dr. Pape, director of the AIDS clinic, Bernard Liautaud, a dermatologist, is the most knowledgeable Haitian physician on the subject of the epidemic. Together, the two men have published a dozen articles on AIDS in international medical journals. In our meeting they present me with statistics:

- There are more than one thousand documented cases of AIDS in Haiti, and as many as one hundred thousand carriers of the virus.
- Eighty-seven percent of AIDS is now transmitted heterosexually. While it is true that the virus was introduced via the bisexual community, that route has decreased to 10 percent or less.
- Sixty percent of the wives or husbands of AIDS patients tested positive for the antibody.

- Fifty percent of the prostitutes tested in the Port-au-Prince area are infected.
- Eighty percent of the men with AIDS have had contact with prostitutes.
- The projected number of active cases in four years is ten thousand. (Since my last visit, the Haitian Medical Association broke its silence on the epidemic by warning that one million of the country's six million people could be carriers by 1992.)

The two doctors have more to tell. "The crossing over of the plague   125
from the homosexual to the heterosexual community will follow in the
United States within two years. This, despite the hesitation to say so by
those who fear to sow panic among your population. In Haiti, because bisexuality is more common, there was an early crossover into the general
population. The trend, inevitably, is the same in the two countries."

"What is there to do, then?"   126

"Only education, just as in America. But here the Haitians reject the   127
use of condoms. Only the men who are too sick to have sex are celibate."

"What is to be the end of it?"   128

"When enough heterosexuals of the middle and upper classes die, per-   129
haps there will be the panic necessary for the people to change their sexual
lifestyles."

This evening I leave Haiti. For two weeks I have fastened myself to this 130
lovely fragile land like an ear pressed to the ground. It is a country to break
a traveler's heart. It occurs to me that I have not seen a single jogger. Such
a public expenditure of energy while everywhere else strength is ebbing—
it would be obscene. In my final hours, I go to the Cathédral of Sainte
Trinité, the inner walls of which are covered with murals by Haiti's most
renowned artists. Here are all the familiar Bible stories depicted in naîveté
and piety, and all in such an exuberance of color as to tax the capacity of
the retina to receive it, as though all the vitality of Haiti had been turned
to paint and brushed upon these walls. How to explain its efflorescence at
a time when all else is lassitude and inertia? Perhaps one day the plague
will be rendered in poetry, music, painting, but not now. Not now.

MUSINGS

This essay simply records Selzer's days in Haiti, "this lovely fragile
land . . . a country to break a traveler's heart." He seldom strays from re-
porting the tragic facts of the spread of the AIDS virus as he learns of it
through his visit to a brothel, his work in a clinic, an incident in his own

hotel, and a discovery of a few statistics. He tells the story through description of actions and inaction, and recording conversations. It is not until his closing paragraph that he openly laments the tragic results of the disease by comparing the apathy about AIDS with the wonderful paintings on the walls of the Cathedral.

Use description of a single incident or a series of incidents to get an idea across. Select the incident or incidents carefully and include only those details that will reinforce and support your main idea.

JOAN DIDION (1934–)

*Joan Didion is a native Californian who graduated from the University of California
at Berkeley, where in 1976 she was appointed Visiting Regents Lecturer in English.
The author of at least four novels, she is probably best known for her carefully styled
and highly personal essays. Didion revises and reworks her writing to select just the
right details and the best possible sequence. In all of her writings she draws on her own
experience and moves from there to universal human truths.*

In the following essay, first published in The Saturday Evening Post *in 1967,
Didion describes her visit to her childhood home, going over the details of looking
through her youthful belongings, driving to the ranch with her father, visiting the family graveyard, making the mandatory visit to her elderly aunts, overseeing her daughter's birthday party, and dreading her husband's phone call, which would break the
continuity of her nostalgic return. She thinks that probably her age group "was born
into the last generation to carry the burden of 'home'." Among her birthday gifts to her
daughter, Didion says that she would like to promise her "that she will grow up with a
sense of her cousins and of rivers and of her great-grandmother's teacups . . . would like
to give her* home *for her birthday." However, she concludes regretfully that "we live
differently now and I can promise her nothing like that."*

On Going Home

I am home for my daughter's first birthday. By "home" I do not mean   1
the house in Los Angeles where my husband and I and the baby live, but
the place where my family is, in the Central Valley of California. It is a
vital although troublesome distinction. My husband likes my family but is
uneasy in their house, because once there I fall into their ways, which are
difficult, oblique, deliberately inarticulate, not my husband's ways. We live
in dusty houses ("D-U-S-T," he once wrote with his finger on surfaces all
over the house, but no one noticed it) filled with mementos quite without
value to him (what could the Canton dessert plates mean to him? how
could he have known about the assay scales, why should he care if he did
know?), and we appear to talk exclusively about people we know who have
been committed to mental hospitals, about people we know who have
been booked on drunk-driving charges, and about property, particularly
about property, land, price per acre and C-2 zoning and assessments and
freeway access. My brother does not understand my husband's inability
to perceive the advantage in the rather common real-estate transaction

317

known as "sale-leaseback," and my husband in turn does not understand why so many of the people he hears about in my father's house have recently been committed to mental hospitals or booked on drunk-driving charges. Nor does he understand that when we talk about sale-leasebacks and right-of-way condemnations we are talking in code about things we like best, the yellow fields and the cottonwoods and the rivers rising and falling and the mountain roads closing when the heavy snow comes in. We miss each other's points, have another drink and regard the fire. My brother refers to my husband, in his presence, as "Joan's husband." Marriage is the classic betrayal.

Or perhaps it is not any more. Sometimes I think that those of us who are now in our thirties were born into the last generation to carry the burden of "home," to find in family life the source of all tension and drama. I had by all objective accounts a "normal" and a "happy" family situation, and yet I was almost thirty years old before I could talk to my family on the telephone without crying after I had hung up. We did not fight. Nothing was wrong. And yet some nameless anxiety colored the emotional charges between me and the place that I came from. The question of whether or not you could go home again was a very real part of the sentimental and largely literary baggage with which we left home in the fifties; I suspect that it is irrelevant to the children born of the fragmentation after World War II. A few weeks ago in a San Francisco bar I saw a pretty young girl on crystal take off her clothes and dance for the cash prize in an "amateur-topless" contest. There was no particular sense of moment about this, none of the effect of romantic degradation, of "dark journey," for which my generation strived so assiduously. What sense could that girl possibly make of, say *Long Day's Journey into Night?* Who is beside the point?

That I am trapped in this particular irrelevancy is never more apparent to me than when I am home. Paralyzed by the neurotic lassitude engendered by meeting one's past at every turn, around every corner, inside every cupboard, I go aimlessly from room to room. I decide to meet it head-on and clean out a drawer, and I spread the contents on the bed. A bathing suit I wore the summer I was seventeen. A letter of rejection from *The Nation,* an aerial photograph of the site for a shopping center my father did not build in 1954. Three teacups hand-painted with cabbage roses and signed "E.M.," my grandmother's initials. There is no final solution for letters of rejection from *The Nation* and teacups hand-painted in 1900. Nor is there any answer to snapshots of one's grandfather as a young man on skis, surveying around Donner Pass in the year 1910. I smooth out the snapshot and look into his face, and do and do not see my own. I close the drawer, and have another cup of coffee with my mother. We get along very well, veterans of a guerrilla war we never understood.

Days pass. I see no one. I come to dread my husband's evening call, not only because he is full of news of what by now seems to me our remote life in Los Angeles, people he has seen, letters which require attention, but because he asks what I have been doing, suggests uneasily that I get out, drive to San Francisco or Berkeley. Instead I drive across the river to a family graveyard. It has been vandalized since my last visit and the monuments are broken, overturned in the dry grass. Because I once saw a rattlesnake in the grass I stay in the car and listen to a country-and-Western station. Later I drive with my father to a ranch he has in the foothills. The man who runs his cattle on it asks us to the roundup, a week from Sunday, and although I know that I will be in Los Angeles I say, in the oblique way my family talks, that I will come. Once home I mention the broken monuments in the graveyard. My mother shrugs.

4

I go to visit my great-aunts. A few of them think now that I am my cousin, or their daughter who died young. We recall an anecdote about a relative last seen in 1948, and they ask if I still like living in New York City. I have lived in Los Angeles for three years, but I say that I do. The baby is offered a horehound drop, and I am slipped a dollar bill "to buy a treat." Questions trail off, answers are abandoned, the baby plays with the dust motes in a shaft of afternoon sun.

5

It is time for the baby's birthday party: a white cake, strawberry-marshmallow ice cream, a bottle of champagne saved from another party. In the evening, after she has gone to sleep, I kneel beside the crib and touch her face, where it pressed against the slats, with mine. She is an open and trusting child, unprepared for and unaccustomed to the ambushes of family life, and perhaps it is just as well that I can offer her little of that life. I would like to give her more. I would like to promise her that she will grow up with a sense of her cousins and of rivers and of her great-grandmother's teacups, would like to pledge her a picnic on a river with fried chicken and her hair uncombed, would like to give her *home* for her birthday, but we live differently now and I can promise her nothing like that. I give her a xylophone and a sundress from Maderia, and promise to tell her a funny story.

6

MUSINGS

Didion goes to her family home for her daughter's birthday and reminisces about her youth as she visits familiar spots, makes the obligatory calls on older relatives, and repeats once more the well-known rituals of her own childhood. She maintains that her generation probably will be the last to carry the "burden" of home; curiously, she would like to give her young daughter "home" for her birthday.

Describe a place that you think of as "home." It might be the home of your parents or your grandparents, or even the home of a friend. In your mind, is it a "burden" or a place that you like to remember? Select details that support your particular point of view.

ANNIE DILLARD (1945–)

Annie Dillard, a much admired contemporary writer, graduated with a Master's degree from Hollins College and now lives in Middletown, Connecticut, where she teaches as a distinguished visiting professor and writer-in-residence at Wesleyan University. Her first publication was a collection of poems, but it was her first book, Pilgrim at Tinker's Creek, *that earned her the Pulitzer Prize for Nonfiction, met with popular and critical acclaim, and established her as an important writer.* Holy the Firm *(1978) was a mystical examination of faith in an often cruel world and was inspired by the pain endured by a neighbor child recovering from severe burns. Dillard also wrote a book recalling her own childhood,* An American Childhood, *and in 1989 published* The Writing Life, *in which she examines her own writing process. In 1992 she ventured into a new genre with* The Living, *a historical novel of the Pacific Northwest. Wendy Law-Yone, a critic for the* Washington Post, *describes Dillard's style "as a mystic's wonder at the physical world expressed in beautiful, near biblical prose." Dillard constantly combines religion with nature in examining the world around her and finds in that scrutiny a mystical truth. She struggles constantly with a world where she sees wonder and beauty juxtaposed with cruelty.*

In the following selection, taken from Pilgrim at Tinker's Creek, *Dillard plays on the dichotomies of life and death, beauty and ugliness, goodness and cruelty. She carefully collects the praying mantis cases in order to study them and hangs them near some protected bushes to save them from the destruction of the neighbor's tractor. She examines the cruelty of the mating scene, which she describes in ugly detail, and concludes with the horrible picture of the Polyphemus moth struggling to emerge from its cocoon inside the confines of the mason jar. Later, Dillard relates the heartbreaking scene of the mortally wounded moth, "crawling down the driveway, crawling down the driveway hunched, crawling down the driveway on six furred feet, forever," as it remains forever etched in her memory.*

The Fixed

I have just learned to see praying mantis egg cases. Suddenly I see them 1
everywhere; a tan oval of light catches my eye, or I notice a blob of thickness in a patch of slender weeds. As I write I can see the one I tied to the
mock orange hedge outside my study window. It is over an inch long and
shaped like a bell, or like the northern hemisphere of an egg cut through
its equator. The full length of one of its long sides is affixed to a twig; the
side that catches the light is perfectly flat. It has a dead straw, deadweed

color, and a curious brittle texture, hard as varnish, but pitted minutely, like frozen foam. I carried it home this afternoon, holding it carefully by the twig, along with several others—they were light as air. I dropped one without missing it until I got home and made a count.

Within the week I've seen thirty or so of these egg cases in a rose-grown field on Tinker Mountain, and another thirty in weeds along Carvin's Creek. One was on a twig of tiny dogwood on the mud lawn of a newly built house. I think the mail-order houses sell them to gardeners at a dollar apiece. It beats spraying, because each case contains between one hundred twenty-five to three hundred fifty eggs. If the eggs survive ants, woodpeckers, and mice—and most do—then you get the fun of seeing the new mantises hatch, and the smug feeling of knowing, all summer long, that they're out there in your garden devouring gruesome numbers of fellow insects all nice and organically. When a mantis has crunched up the last shred of its victim, it cleans its smooth green face like a cat.

In late summer I often see a winged adult stalking the insects that swarm about my porch light. Its body is a clear, warm green; its naked, triangular head can revolve uncannily, so that I often see one twist its head to gaze at me as it were over its shoulder. When it strikes, it jerks so suddenly and with such a fearful clatter of raised wings, that even a hardened entomologist like J. Henri Fabre confessed to being startled witless every time.

Adult mantises eat more or less everything that breathes and is small enough to capture. They eat honeybees and butterflies, including monarch butterflies. People have actually seen them seize and devour garter snakes, mice, and even *hummingbirds*. Newly hatched mantises, on the other hand, eat small creatures like aphids and each other. When I was in elementary school, one of the teachers brought in a mantis egg case in a Mason jar. I watched the newly hatched mantises emerge and shed their skins; they were spidery and translucent, all over joints. They trailed from the egg case to the base of the Mason jar in a living bridge that looked like Arabic calligraphy, some baffling text from the Koran inscribed down the air by a fine hand. Over a period of several hours, during which time the teacher never summoned the nerve or the sense to release them, they ate each other until only two were left. Tiny legs were still kicking from the mouths of both. The two survivors grappled and sawed in the Mason jar; finally both died of injuries. I felt as though I myself should swallow the corpses, shutting my eyes and washing them down like jagged pills, so all that life wouldn't be lost.

When mantises hatch in the wild, however, they straggle about prettily, dodging ants, till all are lost in the grass. So it was in hopes of seeing an eventual hatch that I pocketed my jackknife this afternoon before I set out to walk. Now that I can see the egg cases, I'm embarrassed to realize how many I must have missed all along. I walked east through the Adams' woods to the cornfield, cutting three undamaged egg cases I found at the edge of the field. It was a clear, picturesque day, a February day without clouds, without emotion or spirit, like a beautiful woman with an empty face. In my fingers I carried the thorny stems from which the egg cases hung like roses; I switched the bouquet from hand to hand, warming the free hand in a pocket. Passing the house again, deciding not to fetch gloves, I walked north to the hill by the place where the steers come to drink from Tinker Creek. There in the weeds on the hill I found another eight egg cases. I was stunned—I cross this hill several times a week, and I always look for egg cases here, because it was here that I had once seen a mantis laying her eggs.

It was several years ago that I witnessed this extraordinary procedure, but I remember, and confess, an inescapable feeling that I was watching something not real and present, but a horrible nature movie, a "secrets-of-nature" short, beautifully photographed in full color, that I had to sit through unable to look anywhere else but at the dimly lighted EXIT signs along the walls, and that behind the scenes some amateur moviemaker was congratulating himself on having stumbled across this little wonder, or even on having contrived so natural a setting, as though the whole scene had been shot very carefully in a terrarium in someone's greenhouse.

6

I was ambling across this hill that day when I noticed a speck of pure white. The hill is eroded; the slope is a rutted wreck of red clay broken by grassy hillocks and low wild roses whose roots clasp a pittance of topsoil. I leaned to examine the white thing and saw a mass of bubbles like spittle. Then I saw something dark like an engorged leech rummaging over the spittle, and then I saw the praying mantis.

7

She was upside-down, clinging to a horizontal stem of wild rose by her feet which pointed to heaven. Her head was deep in dried grass. Her abdomen was swollen like a smashed finger; it tapered to a fleshy tip out of which bubbled a wet, whipped froth. I couldn't believe my eyes. I lay on the hill this way and that, my knees in thorns and my cheeks in clay, trying to see as well as I could. I poked near the female's head with a grass; she was clearly undisturbed, so I settled my nose an inch from that pulsing abdomen. It puffed like a concertina, it throbbed like a bellows; it roved, pumping, over the glistening, clabbered surface of the egg case testing and patting, thrusting and smoothing. It seemed to act so independently that I forgot the panting brown stick at the other end. The bubble creature seemed to have two eyes, a frantic little brain, and two busy, soft hands. It looked like a hideous, harried mother slicking up a fat daughter for a beauty pageant, touching her up, slobbering over her, patting and hemming and brushing and stroking.

8

The male was nowhere in sight. The female had probably eaten him.

9

Fabre says that, at least in captivity, the female will mate with and devour up to seven males, whether she has laid her egg cases or not. The mating rites of mantises are well known: a chemical produced in the heat of the male insect says, in effect, "No, don't go near her, you fool, she'll eat you alive." At the same time a chemical in his abdomen says, "Yes, by all means, now and forever yes."

While the male is making up what passes for his mind, the female tips the balance in her favor by eating his head. He mounts her. Fabre describes the mating, which sometimes lasts six hours, as follows: "The male, absorbed in the performance of his vital functions, holds the female in a tight embrace. But the wretch has no head; he has no neck; he has hardly a body. The other, with her muzzle turned over her shoulder continues very placidly to gnaw what remains of the gentle swain. And, all the time, that masculine stump, holding on firmly, goes on with the business! . . . I have seen it done with my own eyes and have not yet recovered from my astonishment."   10

I watched the egg-laying for over an hour. When I returned the next day, the mantis was gone. The white foam had hardened and browned to a dirty suds; then, and on subsequent days, I had trouble pinpointing the case, which was only an inch or so off the ground. I checked on it every week all winter long. In the spring the ants discovered it; every week I saw dozens of ants scrambling over the sides, unable to chew a way in. Later in the spring I climbed the hill every day, hoping to catch the hatch. The leaves of the trees had long since unfolded, the butterflies were out, and the robins' first broods were fledged; still the egg case hung silent and full on the stem. I read that I should wait for June, but still I visited the case every day. One morning at the beginning of June everything was gone. I couldn't find the lower thorn in the clump of three to which the egg case was fixed. I couldn't find the clump of three. Tracks ridged the clay, and I saw the lopped stems: somehow my neighbor had contrived to run a tractor-mower over that steep clay hill on which there grew nothing to mow but a few stubby thorns.   11

So. Today from this same hill I cut another three undamaged cases and carried them home with the others by their twigs. I also collected a suspiciously light cynthia moth cocoon. My fingers were stiff and red with cold, and my nose ran. I had forgotten the Law of the Wild, which is, "Carry Kleenex." At home I tied the twigs with their egg cases to various sunny bushes and trees in the yard. They're easy to find because I used white string; at any rate, I'm unlikely to mow my own trees. I hope the woodpeckers that come to the feeder don't find them, but I don't see how they'd get a purchase on them if they did.   12

Night is rising in the valley; the creek has been extinguished for an hour, and now only the naked tips of trees fire tapers into the sky like trails of sparks. The scene that was in the back of my brain all afternoon, ob-   13 scurely, is beginning to rise from night's lagoon. It really has nothing to do with praying mantises. But this afternoon I threw tiny string lashings and hitches with frozen hands, gingerly, fearing to touch the egg cases even for a minute because I remembered the Polyphemus moth.

I have no intention of inflicting all my childhood memories on anyone. Far less do I want to excoriate my old teachers who, in their bungling, unforgettable way, exposed me to the natural world, a world covered in chitin, where implacable realities hold sway. The Polyphemus moth never made it to the past; it crawls in that crowded, pellucid pool at the lip of the great waterfall. It is as present as this blue desk and brazen lamp, as this blackened window before me in which I can no longer see even the white string that binds the egg case to the hedge, but only my own pale astonished face. 14

Once, when I was ten or eleven years old, my friend Judy brought in a Polyphemus moth cocoon. It was January; there were doily snowflakes taped to the schoolroom panes. The teacher kept the cocoon in her desk all morning and brought it out when we were getting restless before recess. In a book we found what the adult moth would look like; it would be beautiful. With a wingspread of up to six inches, the Polyphemus is one of the few huge American silk moths, much larger than, say, a giant or tiger swallowtail butterfly. The moth's enormous wings are velveted in a rich, warm brown, and edged in bands of blue and pink delicate as a watercolor wash. A startling "eyespot," immense, and deep blue melding to an almost translucent yellow, luxuriates in the center of each hind wing. The effect is one of a masculine splendor foreign to the butterflies, a fragility unfurled to strength. The Polyphemus moth in the picture looked like a mighty wraith, a beating essence of the hardwood forest, alien-skinned and brown, with spread, blind eyes. This was the giant moth packed in the faded cocoon. We closed the book and turned to the cocoon. It was an oak leaf sewn into a plump oval bundle; Judy had found it loose in a pile of frozen leaves. 15

We passed the cocoon around; it was heavy. As we held it in our hands, the creature within warmed and squirmed. We were delighted, and wrapped it tighter in our fists. The pupa began to jerk violently, in heart-stopping knocks. Who's there? I can still feel those thumps, urgent through a muffling of spun silk and leaf, urgent through the swaddling of many years, against the curve of my palm. We kept passing it around. When it came to me again it was hot as a bun; it jumped half out of my hand. The teacher intervened. She put it, still heaving and banging, in the ubiquitous Mason jar. 16

It was coming. There was no stopping it now, January or not. One end of the cocoon dampened and gradually frayed in a furious battle. The whole cocoon twisted and slapped around in the bottom of the jar. The 17 teacher fades, the classmates fade, I fade: I don't remember anything but that thing's struggle to be a moth or die trying. It emerged at last, a sodden crumple. It was a male; his long antennae were thickly plumed, as wide as his fat abdomen. His body was very thick, over an inch long, and deeply furred. A gray, furlike plush covered his head; a long, tan furlike hair hung from his wide thorax over his brown-furred, segmented abdomen. His multijointed legs, pale and powerful, were shaggy as a bear's. He stood still, but he breathed.

He couldn't spread his wings. There was no room. The chemical that coated his wings like varnish, stiffening them permanently, dried, and hardened his wings as they were. He was a monster in a Mason jar. Those huge wings stuck on his back in a torture of random pleats and folds, wrinkled as a dirty tissue, rigid as leather. They made a single nightmare clump still wracked with useless, frantic convulsions. 18

The next thing I remember, it was recess. The school was in Shadyside, a busy residential part of Pittsburgh. Everyone was playing dodgeball in the fenced playground or racing around the concrete schoolyard by the swings. Next to the playground a long delivery drive sloped downhill to the sidewalk and street. Someone—it must have been the teacher—had let the moth out. I was standing in the driveway, alone, stock-still, but shivering. Someone had given the Polyphemus moth his freedom, and he was walking away. 19

He heaved himself down the asphalt driveway by infinite degrees, unwavering. His hideous crumpled wings lay glued and rucked on his back, perfectly still now, like a collapsed tent. The bell rang twice; I had to go. The moth was receding down the driveway, dragging on. I went; I ran inside. The Polyphemus moth is still crawling down the driveway, crawling down the driveway hunched, crawling down the driveway on six furred feet, forever. 20

MUSINGS

Dillard juxtaposes the beauty of seeing the praying mantises hatch in the mason jar with the horror of watching them eat each other, and the thrill of watching the Polyphemus moth emerge from its cocoon with her memories of it battering itself inside the mason jar and later dragging its beaten and crippled body down the driveway. In both instances human interference with the natural process proved to be disastrous.

Select a natural phenomenon in which human intervention has altered the normal course of events, such as the effect of confinement on a family pet or how the construction of concrete parking lots affects the environment.

BELL HOOKS (1952–)

A strong advocate of black feminism, bell hooks is a professor at Yale University and the author of a number of books published by South End Press. She discusses her differences with white feminists in her first book, Ain't I a Woman: Black Women and Feminism *(1981), and resumes this theme in* Feminist Theory: From Margin to Center *(1984). A number of hooks' other works explore her other ideas, such as destroying the U.S. hierarchical system, set up by the white male patriarchy and supported by white women; as a black woman, hooks sees herself at the bottom of the power structure. These works include* Talking Back *(see the selection in the Autobiography section of this book);* Yearning: Race, Gender, and Cultural Politics *(1990), in which hooks broadens her cultural criticism, using contemporary critical theories; and* Breaking Bread: Insurgent Black Intellectual Life *(1992), which is a dialogue with Cornel West, a social critic. In this book and in* Black Looks: Race and Representation *(1993), hooks continues the theme of how "black womanhood, feminism, the civil rights movement and critical theory—cooperate and clash in the world at large and within herself." Readers and reviewers have criticized the Marxism that runs through all of her works.*

In the following essay, which appeared in Z Magazine, *hooks recalls her childhood and the Saturday morning ritual of hair straightening. In looking back she sees it as representing "an imitation of the dominant white group's appearance" and associates it with "internalized racism, self-hatred and/or low self-esteem." She describes her liberation from straightening her hair and her subsequent pleasure in washing, combing, and accepting it just as it is. She equates this freedom with the larger issues of "celebrating our bodies" and participating in a "liberatory struggle."*

Straightening Our Hair

On Saturday mornings we would gather in the kitchen to get our hair fixed, that is straightened. Smells of burning grease and hair, mingled with the scent of our freshly washed bodies, with collard greens cooking on the stove, with fried fish. We did not go to the hairdresser. Mama fixed our hair. Six daughters—there was no way we could have afforded hairdressers. In those days, this process of straightening black women's hair with a hot comb (invented by Madame C. J. Waler) was not connected in my mind with the effort to look white, to live out standards of beauty set by white supremacy. It was connected solely with rites of initiation into womanhood. To arrive at that point where one's hair could be straightened was to move from being perceived as child (whose hair could be neatly combed and braided) to being almost a woman. It was this moment of transition my sisters and I longed for.

Hair pressing was a ritual of black women's culture—of intimacy. It was an exclusive moment when black women (even those who did not know one another well) might meet at home or in the beauty parlor to talk with one another, to listen to the talk. It was as important a world as that of the male barber shop—mysterious, secret. It was a world where the images constructed as barriers between one's self and the world were briefly let go, before they were made again. It was a moment of creativity, a moment of change.

I wanted this change even though I had been told all my life that I was one of the "lucky" ones because I had been born with "good hair"—hair that was fine, almost straight—not good enough but still good. Hair that had no nappy edges, no "kitchen," that area close to the neck that the hot comb could not reach. This "good hair" meant nothing to me when it stood as a barrier to my entering this secret black woman world. I was overjoyed when mama finally agreed that I could join the Saturday ritual, no longer looking on but patiently waiting my turn. I have written of this ritual: "For each of us getting our hair pressed is an important ritual. It is not a sign of our longing to be white. There are no white people in our intimate world. It is a sign of our desire to be women. It is a gesture that says we are approaching womanhood . . . Before we reach the appropriate age we wear braids, plaits that are symbols of our innocence, our youth, our childhood. Then, we are comforted by the parting hands that comb and braid, comforted by the intimacy and bliss. There is a deeper intimacy in the kitchen on Saturdays when hair is pressed, when fish is fried, when sodas are passed around, when soul music drifts over the talk. It is a time without men. It is a time when we work as women to meet each other's needs, to make each other feel good inside, a time of laughter and outrageous talk."

Since the world we lived in was racially segregated, it was easy to overlook the relationship between white supremacy and our obsession with hair. Even though black women with straight hair were perceived to be more beautiful than those with thick, frizzy hair, it was not overtly related to a notion that white women were a more appealing female group or that their straight hair set a beauty standard black women were struggling to live out. While this was probably the ideological framework from which the process of straightening black women's hair emerged, it was expanded so that it became a real space of black woman bonding through ritualized, shared experience. The beauty parlor was a space of consciousness raising, a space where black women shared life stories—hardship, trials, gossip; a place where one could be comforted and one's spirit renewed. It was for some women a place of rest where one did not need to meet the demands of children or men. It was the one hour some folk would spend "off their feet," a soothing, restful time of meditation and silence. These positive empowering implications of the ritual of hair pressing mediate but do not change negative implications. They exist alongside all that is negative.

Within white supremacist capitalist patriarchy, the social and political 5 context in which the custom of black folks straightening our hair emerges, it represents an imitation of the dominant white group's appearance and often indicates internalized racism, self-hatred, and/or low self-esteem. During the 1960s black people who actively worked to critique, challenge, and change white racism pointed to the way in which black people's obsession with straight hair reflected a colonized mentality. It was at this time that the natural hairdo, the "afro," became fashionable as a sign of cultural resistance to racist oppression and as a celebration of blackness. Naturals were equated with political militancy. Many young black folks found just how much political value was placed on straightened hair as a sign of respectability and conformity to societal expectations when they ceased to straighten their hair. When black liberation struggles did not lead to revolutionary change in society the focus on the political relationship between appearance and complicity with white racism ceased and folks who had once sported afros began to straighten their hair.

In keeping with the move to suppress black consciousness and efforts to 6 be self-defining, white corporations began to acknowledge black people and most especially black women as potential consumers of products they could provide, including hair-care products. Permanents specially designed for black women eliminated the need for hair pressing and the hot comb. They not only cost more but they also took much of the economy and profit out of black communities, out of the pockets of black women who had previously reaped the material benefits (see Manning Marable's *How Capitalism Underdeveloped Black America,* South End Press). Gone was the context of ritual, of black woman bonding. Seated under noisy hair dryers black women lost a space for dialogue, for creative talk.

Stripped of the positive binding rituals that traditionally surrounded 7 the experience, black women straightening our hair seemed more and more to be exclusively a signifier of white supremacist oppression and exploitation. It was clearly a process that was about black women changing their appearance to imitate white people's looks. This need to look as much like white people as possible, to look safe, is related to a desire to succeed in the white world. Before desegregation black people could worry less about what white folks thought about their hair. In a discussion with black women about beauty at Spelman College, students talked about the importance of wearing straight hair when seeking jobs. They were convinced and probably rightly so that their chances of finding good jobs would be enhanced if they had straight hair. When asked to elaborate they focused on the connection between radical politics and natural hairdos, whether natural or braided. One woman wearing a short natural told of purchasing a straight wig for her job search. No one in the discussion felt black women were free to wear our hair in natural styles without reflecting on the possible negative consequences. Often older black adults, especially parents, respond quite negatively to natural hairdos. I shared with the group that when I arrived home with my hair in braids shortly after accepting my job at Yale my parents told me I looked disgusting.

Despite many changes in racial politics, black women continue to obsess about their hair, and straightening hair continues to be serious business. It continues to tap into the insecurity black women feel about our value in this white supremacist society. Talking with groups of women at various college campuses and with black women in our communities there seems to be general consensus that our obsession with hair in general reflects continued struggles with self-esteem and self-actualization. We talk about the extent to which black women perceive our hair as the enemy, as a problem we must solve, a territory we must conquer. Above all it is a part of our black female body that must be controlled. Most of us were not raised in environments where we learned to regard our hair as sensual or beautiful in an unprocessed state. Many of us talk about situations where white people ask to touch our hair when it is unprocessed then show surprise that the texture is soft or feels good. In the eyes of many white folks and other non-black folks, the natural afro looks like steel wool or a helmet. Responses to natural hairstyles worn by black women usually reveal the extent to which our natural hair is perceived in white supremacist culture as not only ugly but frightening. We also internalize that fear. The extent to which we are comfortable with our hair usually reflects on our overall feelings about our bodies. In our black women's support group, *Sisters of the Yam,* we talk about the ways we don't like our bodies, especially our hair. I suggested to the group that we regard our hair as though it is not part of our body but something quite separate—again a territory to be controlled. To me it was important for us to link this need to control with sexuality, with sexual repression. Curious about what black women who had hot-combed or had permanents felt about the relationship between straightened hair and sexual practice I asked whether people worried about their hairdo, whether they feared partners touching their hair. Straightened hair has always seemed to me to call attention to the desire for hair to stay in place. Not surprisingly many black women responded that they felt uncomfortable if too much attention was focused on their hair, if it seemed to be too messy. Those of us who have liberated our hair and let it go in whatever direction it seems fit often receive negative comments.

8

Looking at photographs of myself and my sisters when we had straightened hair in high school I noticed how much older we looked than when our hair was not processed. It is ironic that we live in a culture that places so much emphasis on women looking young, yet black women are encouraged to change our hair in ways that make us appear older. This past semester we read Toni Morrison's *The Bluest Eye* in a black women's fiction class. I ask students to write autobiographical statements which reflect their thoughts about the connection between race and physical beauty. A vast majority of black women wrote about their hair. When I asked individual women outside class why they continued to straighten their hair, many asserted that naturals don't look good on them, or that they required too much work. Emily, a favorite student with very short hair, always straightened it and I would tease and challenge her. She explained to me convincingly that a natural hairdo would look horrible with her face, that she did not have the appropriate forehead or bone structure. Later she shared that during spring break she had gone to the beauty parlor to have her perm and as she sat there waiting, thinking about class reading and discussion, it came to her that she was really frightened that no one else would think she was attractive if she did not straighten her hair. She acknowledged that this fear was rooted in feelings of low self-esteem. She decided to make a change. Her new look surprised her because it was so appealing. We talked afterwards about her earlier denial and justification for wearing straightened hair. We talked about the way it hurts to realize connection between racist oppression and the arguments we use to convince ourselves and others that we are not beautiful or acceptable as we are.

In numerous discussions with black women about hair one of the strongest factors that prevent black women from wearing unprocessed hairstyles is the fear of losing other people's approval and regard. Heterosexual black women talked about the extent to which black men respond more favorably to women with straight or straightened hair. Lesbian women point to the fact that many of them do not straighten their hair, raising the question of whether or not this gesture is fundamentally linked to heterosexism and a longing for male approval. I recall visiting a woman friend and her black male companion in New York years ago and having an intense discussion about hair. He took it upon himself to share with me that I could be a fine sister if I would do something about my hair (secretly I thought mama must have hired him). What I remember is his shock when I calmly and happily asserted that I like the touch and feel of unprocessed hair.

When students read about race and physical beauty, several black women describe periods of childhood when they were overcome with longing for straight hair as it was so associated with desirability, with being

9

10

11

loved. Few women had received affirmation from family, friends, or lovers when choosing not to straighten their hair and we have many stories to tell about advice we receive from everyone, including total strangers, urging to understand how much more attractive we would be if we would fix (straighten) our hair. When I interviewed for my job at Yale, white female advisers who had never before commented on my hair encouraged me not to wear braids or a large natural to the interview. Although they did not say straighten your hair, they were suggesting that I change my hairstyle so that it would most resemble theirs, so that it would indicate a certain conformity. I wore braids and no one seemed to notice. When I was offered the job I did not ask if it mattered whether or not I wore braids. I tell this story to my students so that they will know by this one experience that we do not always need to surrender our power to be self-defining to succeed in an endeavor. Yet I have found the issue of hairstyle comes up again and again with students when I give lectures. At one conference on black women and leadership I walked into a packed auditorium, my hair unprocessed wild and all over the place. The vast majority of black women seated there had straightened hair. Many of them looked at me with hostile contemptuous stares. I felt as though I was being judged on the spot as someone out on the fringe, an undesirable. Such judgments are made particularly about black women in the United States who choose to wear dreadlocks. They are seen and rightly so as the total antithesis of straightening one's hair, as a political statement. Often black women express contempt for those of us who choose this look.

Ironically, just as the natural unprocessed hair of black women is the 12
subject of disregard and disdain we are witnessing return of the long dyed, blonde look. In their writing my black women students described wearing yellow mops on their heads as children to pretend they had long blonde hair. Recently black women singers who are working to appeal to white audiences, to be seen as crossovers, use hair implanting and hair weaving to have long straight hair. There seems to be a definite connection between a black female entertainer's popularity with white audiences and the degree to which she works to appear white, or to embody aspects of white style. Tina Turner and Aretha Franklin were trend setters; both dyed their hair blonde. In everyday life we see more and more black women using chemicals to be blonde. At one of my talks focusing on the social construction of black female identity within a sexist and racist society, a black woman came to me at the end of the discussion and shared that her seven-year-old daughter was obsessed with blonde hair, so much so that she had made a wig to imitate long blonde curls. This mother wanted to know what she was doing wrong in her parenting. She asserted that their home was a place where blackness was affirmed and celebrated. Yet she had not

considered that her processed straightened hair was a message to her daughter that black women are not acceptable unless we alter our appearance or hair texture. Recently I talked with one of my younger sisters about her hair. She uses bright colored dyes, various shades of red. Her skin is very dark. She has a broad nose and short hair. For her these choices of straightened dyed hair were directly related to feelings of low self-esteem. She does not like her features and feels that the hairstyle transforms her. My perception was that her choice of red straightened hair actually called attention to the features she was trying to mask. When she commented that this look receives more attention and compliments, I suggested that the positive feedback might be a direct response to her own projection of a higher level of self-satisfaction. Folk may be responding to that and not her altered looks. We talked about the messages she is sending her dark-skinned daughters—that they will be most attractive if they straighten their hair.

A number of black women have argued that straightened hair is not necessarily a signifier of low self-esteem. They argue that it is a survival strategy; it is easier to function in this society with straightened hair. There are fewer hassles. Or as some folk stated, straightened hair is easier to manage, takes less time. When I responded to this argument in our discussion at Spelman by suggesting that perhaps the unwillingness to spend time on ourselves, caring for our bodies, is also a reflection of a sense that this is not important or that we do not deserve such care. In this group and others, black women talked about being raised in households where spending too much time on appearance was ridiculed or considered vanity. Irrespective of the way individual black women choose to do their hair, it is evident that the extent to which we suffer from racist and sexist oppression and exploitation affects the degree to which we feel capable of both self-love and asserting an autonomous presence that is acceptable and pleasing to ourselves. Individual preferences (whether rooted in self-hate or not) cannot negate the reality that our collective obsession with straightening black hair reflects the psychology of oppression and the impact of racist colonization. Together racism and sexism daily reinforce to all black females via the media, advertising, etc. that we will not be considered beautiful or desirable if we do not change ourselves, especially our hair. We cannot resist this socialization if we deny that white supremacy informs our efforts to construct self and identity. 13

Without organized struggles like the ones that happened in the 1960s and early 1970s, individual black women must struggle alone to acquire the critical consciousness that would enable us to examine issues of race and beauty, our personal choices, from a political standpoint. There are times when I think of straightening my hair just to change my style, just for fun. Then I remind myself that even though such a gesture could be simply play- 14 ful on my part, an individual expression of desire, I know that such a gesture would carry other implications beyond my control. The reality is: straightened hair is linked historically and currently to a system of racial domination that impresses upon black people, and especially black women, that we are not acceptable as we are, that we are not beautiful. To make such a gesture as an expression of individual freedom and choice would make me complicit with a politic of domination that hurts us. It is easy to surrender this freedom. It is more important that black women resist racism and sexism in every way; that every aspect of our self-representation be a fierce resistance, a radical celebration of our care and respect for ourselves.

Even though I have not had straightened hair for a long time, this did not mean that I am able to really enjoy or appreciate my hair in its natural state. For years I still considered it a problem. (It wasn't naturally nappy enough to make a decent interesting afro. It was too thin.) These complaints expressed my continued dissatisfaction. True liberation of my hair came when I stopped trying to control it in any state and just accepted it as it is. It has been only in recent years that I have ceased to worry about what other people would say about my hair. It has been only in recent years that I could feel consistent pleasure washing, combing, and caring for my hair. These feelings remind me of the pleasure and comfort I felt as a child sitting between my mother's legs feeling the warmth of her body and being as she combed and braided my hair. In a culture of domination, one that is essentially anti-intimacy, we must struggle daily to remain in touch with ourselves and our bodies, with one another. Especially black women and men, as it is our bodies that have been so often devalued, burdened, wounded in alienated labor. Celebrating our bodies, we participate in a liberatory struggle that frees mind and heart.

15

MUSINGS

Starting from a simple description of the childhood Saturday morning ritual of hair straightening, hooks moves on to the concept of hair within the black culture and continuing attempts to imitate the hair of the dominate white culture. When hooks was growing up straight hair was seen as a sign of beauty within the African-American culture; she continues to expand her topic by equating this with the larger issue of accepting and celebrating a body that has historically been "devalued, burdened and wounded."

Describe an incident in your life and connect it with a larger issue that adds deeper significance to the original experience.

Amy Tan (1952–)

*Amy Tan was born in Oakland, California, the daughter of Chinese parents. From 1983 to 1987 she worked as a technical writer; putting in almost ninety hours a week on the job, Tan realized that she had become a workaholic. Seeking help for her problem, she became discouraged when her counselor kept going to sleep while she was talking. Tan then turned to writing as therapy. Having been told by one of her employers that writing was not her strong point, she defiantly turned to fiction and wrote two highly successful novels—*The Joy Luck Club *(1989) and* The Kitchen God's Wife *(1991). In both books she explores the problems of Chinese-Americans and especially the ambivalence of women born in the United States with parents born in China.*

In an interview after the publication of her first novel, Tan admitted that, although she had once denied her ethnicity, writing The Joy Luck Club *made her realize how very Chinese she was, and "how much had stayed with me that I had tried to deny." Both novels were highly praised by critics.*

In the following essay, which first appeared in the Threepenny Review, *Tan explores her "Mother Tongue," which she confesses was at one time a great source of embarrassment to her. She now realizes, though, that her mother's language revealed "her intent, her passion, her imagery, the rhythms of her speech and the nature of her thoughts." Tan also speaks of envisioning her mother as her reader and her mother's final accolade about her writing: "So easy to read."*

Mother Tongue

1   I am not a scholar of English or literature. I cannot give you much more than personal opinions on the English language and its variations in this country or others.

2   I am a writer. And by that definition, I am someone who has always loved language. I am fascinated by language in daily life. I spend a great deal of my time thinking about the power of language—the way it can evoke an emotion, a visual image, a complex idea, or a simple truth. Language is the tool of my trade. And I use them all—all the Englishes I grew up with.

3   Recently, I was made keenly aware of the different Englishes I do use. I was giving a talk to a large group of people, the same talk I had already given to half a dozen other groups. The nature of the talk was about my writing, my life, and my book, *The Joy Luck Club.* The talk was going along well enough, until I remembered one major difference that made

the whole talk sound wrong. My mother was in the room. And it was perhaps the first time she had heard me give a lengthy speech, using the kind of English I have never used with her. I was saying things like, "The intersection of memory upon imagination" and "There is an aspect of my fiction that relates to thus-and-thus"—a speech filled with carefully wrought grammatical phrases, burdened, it suddenly seemed to me, with nominalized forms, past perfect tenses, conditional phrases, all the forms of standard English that I had learned in school and through books, the forms of English I did not use at home with my mother.

Just last week, I was walking down the street with my mother, and I again found myself conscious of the English I was using, and the English I do use with her. We were talking about the price of new and used furniture and I heard myself saying this: "Not waste money that way." My husband was with us as well, and he didn't notice any switch in my English. And then I realized why. It's because over the twenty years we've been together I've often used that same kind of English with him, and sometimes he even uses it with me. It has become our language of intimacy, a different sort of English that relates to family talk, the language I grew up with. 4

So you'll have some idea of what this family talk I heard sounds like, I'll quote what my mother said during a recent conversation which I videotaped and then transcribed. During this conversation, my mother was talking about a political gangster in Shanghai who had the same last name as her family's, Du, and how the gangster in his early years wanted to be adopted by her family, which was rich by comparison. Later, the gangster became more powerful, far richer than my mother's family, and one day showed up at my mother's wedding to pay his respects. Here's what she said in part: 5

"Du Yusong having business like fruit stand. Like off the street kind. He is Du like Du Zong—but not Tsung-ming Island people. The local people call putong, the river east side, he belong to that side local people. That man want to ask Du Zong father take him in like become own family. Du Zong father wasn't look down on him, but didn't take seriously, until that man big like become a mafia. Now important person very hard to inviting him. Chinese way, came only to show respect, don't stay for dinner. Respect for making big celebration, he shows up. Mean gives lots of respect. Chinese custom. Chinese social life that way. If too important won't have to stay too long. He come to my wedding. I didn't see, I heard it. I gone to boy's side, they have YMCA dinner. Chinese age I was nineteen." 6

You should know that my mother's expressive command of English belies how much she actually understands. She reads the *Forbes* report, listens to *Wall Street Week,* converses daily with her stockbroker, reads all of Shirley MacLaine's books with ease—all kinds of things I can't begin to understand. Yet some of my friends tell me they understand 50 percent of 7 what my mother says. Some say they understand 80 to 90 percent. Some say they understand none of it, as if she were speaking pure Chinese. But to me, my mother's English is perfectly clear, perfectly natural. It's my mother tongue. Her language, as I hear it, is vivid, direct, full of observation and imagery. That was the language that helped shape the way I saw things, expressed things, made sense of the world.

Lately, I've been giving more thought to the kind of English my mother 8
speaks. Like others, I have described it to people as "broken" or "fractured" English. But I wince when I say that. It has always bothered me that I can think of no way to describe it other than "broken," as if it were damaged and needed to be fixed, as if it lacked a certain wholeness and soundness. I've heard other terms used, "limited English," for example. But they seem just as bad, as if everything is limited, including people's perceptions of the limited English speaker.

I know this for a fact, because when I was growing up, my mother's 9
"limited" English limited *my* perception of her. I was ashamed of her English. I believed that her English reflected the quality of what she had to say. That is, because she expressed them imperfectly her thoughts were imperfect. And I had plenty of empirical evidence to support me: the fact that people in department stores, at banks, and at restaurants did not take her seriously, did not give her good service, pretended not to understand her, or even acted as if they did not hear her.

My mother has long realized the limitations of her English as well. 10
When I was fifteen, she used to have me call people on the phone to pretend I was she. In this guise, I was forced to ask for information or even to complain and yell at people who had been rude to her. One time it was a call to her stockbroker in New York. She had cashed out her small portfolio and it just so happened we were going to go to New York the next week, our very first trip outside California. I had to get on the phone and say in an adolescent voice that was not very convincing, "This is Mrs. Tan."

And my mother was standing in the back whispering loudly, "Why he 11
don't send me check, already two weeks late. So mad he lie to me, losing me money."

And then I said in perfect English, "Yes, I'm getting rather concerned. 12
You had agreed to send the check two weeks ago, but it hasn't arrived."

Then she began to talk more loudly. "What he want, I come to New 13
York tell him front of his boss, you cheating me?" And I was trying to calm her down, make her be quiet, while telling the stockbroker, "I can't tolerate any more excuses. If I don't receive the check immediately, I am going to speak to your manager when I'm in New York next week." And sure enough, the following week there we were in front of this astonished stockbroker, and I was sitting there red-faced and quiet and my

mother, the real Mrs. Tan, was shouting at his boss in her impeccable broken English.

We used a similar routine just five days ago, for a situation that was far 14 less humorous. My mother had gone to the hospital for an appointment, to find out about a benign brain tumor a CAT scan had revealed a month ago. She said she had spoken very good English, her best English, no mistakes. Still, she said, the hospital did not apologize when they said they had lost the CAT scan and she had come for nothing. She said they did not seem to have any sympathy when she told them she was anxious to know the exact diagnosis, since her husband and son had both died of brain tumors. She said they would not give her any more information until the next time and she would have to make another appointment for that. So she said she would not leave until the doctor called her daughter. She wouldn't budge. And when the doctor finally called her daughter, me, who spoke in perfect English—lo and behold—we had assurances the CAT scan would be found, promises that a conference call on Monday would be held, and apologies for any suffering my mother had gone through for a most regrettable mistake.

I think my mother's English almost had an effect on limiting my possi- 15 bilities in life as well. Sociologists and linguists probably will tell you that a person's developing language skills are more influenced by peers. But I do think that the language spoken in the family, especially in immigrant families which are more insular, plays a large role in shaping the language of the child. And I believe that it affected my results on achievement tests, IQ tests, and the SAT. While my English skills were never judged as poor, compared to math, English could not be considered my strong suit. In grade school I did moderately well, getting perhaps B's, sometimes B-pluses, in English and scoring perhaps in the sixtieth or seventieth percentile on achievement tests. But those scores were not good enough to override the opinion that my true abilities lay in math and science, because in those areas I achieved A's and scored in the ninetieth percentile or higher.

This was understandable. Math is precise; there is only one correct an- 16 swer. Whereas, for me at least, the answers on English tests were always a judgment call, a matter of opinion and personal experience. Those tests were constructed around items like fill-in-the-blank sentence completion, such as, "Even though Tom was _____, Mary thought he was _____ ." And the correct answer always seemed to be the most bland combinations of thoughts, for example, "Even though Tom was shy, Mary thought he was charming," with the grammatical structure "even though" limiting the correct answer to some sort of semantic opposites, so you wouldn't get answers like, "Even though Tom was foolish, Mary thought he was ridiculous." Well, according to my mother, there were very few limitations as to what Tom could have been and what Mary might have thought of him. So I never did well on tests like that.

The same was true with word analogies, pairs of words in which you were supposed to find some sort of logical, semantic relationship—for example, "*Sunset* is to *nightfall* as _____ is to _____ ." And here you would be presented with a list of four possible pairs, one of which showed the same kind of relationship: *red* is to *stoplight, bus* is to *arrival, chills* is to *fever, yawn* is to *boring.* Well, I could never think that way. I knew what the tests were asking, but I could not block out of my mind the images already created by the first pair, "*sunset* is to *nightfall*"—and I would see a burst of colors against a darkening sky, the moon rising, the lowering of a curtain of stars. And all the other pairs of words—red, bus, stoplight, boring—just threw up a mass of confusing images, making it impossible for me to sort out something as logical as saying: "A sunset precedes nightfall" is the same as "a chill precedes a fever." The only way I would have gotten that answer right would have been to imagine an associative situation, for example, my being disobedient and staying out past sunset, catching a chill at night, which turns into feverish pneumonia as punishment, which indeed did happen to me.

I have been thinking about all this lately, about my mother's English, about achievement tests. Because lately I've been asked, as a writer, why there are not more Asian Americans represented in American literature. Why are there few Asian Americans enrolled in creative writing programs? Why do so many Chinese students go into engineering? Well, these are broad sociological questions I can't begin to answer. But I have noticed in surveys—in fact, just last week—that Asian students, as a whole, always do significantly better on math achievement tests than in English. And this makes me think that there are other Asian-American students whose English spoken in the home might also be described as "broken" or "limited." And perhaps they also have teachers who are steering them away from writing and into math and science, which is what happened to me.

Fortunately, I happen to be rebellious in nature and enjoy the challenge of disproving assumptions made about me. I became an English major my first year in college, after being enrolled as pre-med. I started writing nonfiction as a freelancer the week after I was told by my former boss that writing was my worst skill and I should hone my talents toward account management.

But it wasn't until 1985 that I finally began to write fiction. And at first I wrote using what I thought to be wittily crafted sentences, sentences that would finally prove I had mastery over the English language. Here's an example from the first draft of a story that later made its way into *The Joy*

Luck Club, but without this line: "That was my mental quandary in its nascent state." A terrible line, which I can barely pronounce.

Fortunately, for reasons I won't get into today, I later decided I should 21 envision a reader for the stories I would write. And the reader I decided upon was my mother, because these were stories about mothers. So with this reader in mind—and in fact she did read my early drafts—I began to write stories using all the Englishes I grew up with: the English I spoke to my mother, which for lack of a better term might be described as "simple"; the English she used with me, which for lack of a better term might be described as "broken"; my translation of her Chinese, which could certainly be described as "watered down"; and what I imagined to be her translation of her Chinese if she could speak in perfect English, her internal language, and for that I sought to preserve the essence, but neither an English nor a Chinese structure. I wanted to capture what language ability tests can never reveal: her intent, her passion, her imagery, the rhythms of her speech and the nature of her thoughts.

Apart from what any critic had to say about my writing, I knew I had 22 succeeded where it counted when my mother finished reading my book and gave me her verdict: "So easy to read."

MUSINGS

This essay chronicles Tan's thinking process as she works through her feelings about her mother's use of English and her own writing. Starting with an incident that made her realize the marked differences between her school English and the language she used with her mother, she carefully analyzes her mother's expressive use of English. It is this form of English, often characterized as broken, that she holds responsible for the Asian-American preference for careers in math and science; she contends that they have been steered away from literature and the arts by teachers who perceived their language as "limited." In writing her book, Tan visualizes a particular reader, her mother, and attempts to reproduce "her intent, her passion, her imagery, the rhythms of her speech."

Think of some conclusion that you have reached or some idea that you have had on a controversial issue. Write an essay that carried the reader through your thinking process to your final conclusion.

CREDITS

341

INDEX OF AUTHORS AND TITLES